Users and Abusers of Psychiatry

Users and Abusers of Psychiatry is a radically different, critical account of day-to-day practice in psychiatric settings. Using real-life examples and her own experience as a clinical psychologist, Lucy Johnstone argues that the traditional way of treating mental distress can often exacerbate people's original difficulties, leaving them powerless and re-traumatised.

She draws on a range of evidence to present a very different understanding of psychiatric breakdown than that found in standard medical textbooks, and to suggest new ways forward.

The extended introduction to this Classic Edition brings the book up to date by revisiting its themes and tracing the changes in mental health practice over the last three decades. The book's accessibility and clarity have ensured that it remains a classic in a growing field, and it is as relevant today as when it was first published.

Users and Abusers of Psychiatry is a challenging but ultimately inspiring read for all who are involved in mental health – whether as professionals, students, service users, relatives or interested lay people.

Dr Lucy Johnstone is a Consultant Clinical Psychologist and worked in Adult Mental Health for many years. She has written and lectured widely on critical perspectives in mental health theory and practice. She is a lead author of 'The Power Threat Meaning Framework', an ambitious and influential project outlining a conceptual alternative to psychiatric diagnosis.

Routledge Mental Health Classic Editions

The Routledge Mental Health Classic Editions series celebrates Routledge's commitment to excellence within the field of mental health. These books are recognized as timeless classics covering a range of important issues and continue to be recommended as key reading for professionals and students in the area. With a new introduction that explores what has changed since the books were first published, and why these books are as relevant now as ever, the series presents key ideas to a new generation.

Rhythms of Recovery
Trauma, Nature, and the Body (Classic Edition)
By Leslie E. Korn

Grief and Bereavement in Contemporary Society
Bridging Research and Practice (Classic Edition)
By Robert A. Neimeyer, Darcy L. Harris, Howard R. Winokuer, and Gordon F. Thornton

Do Funerals Matter?
The Purposes and Practices of Death Rituals in Global Perspective (Classic Edition)
By William G. Hoy

Users and Abusers of Psychiatry
A Critical Look at Psychiatric Practice (Classic Edition)
Lucy Johnstone

For more information about this series, please visit: https://www.routledge.com/Routledge-Mental-Health-Classic-Editions/book-series/RMHCE

Users and Abusers of Psychiatry

A Critical Look at Psychiatric Practice

Classic Edition

Lucy Johnstone

Routledge
Taylor & Francis Group

LONDON AND NEW YORK

Classic edition published 2022
by Routledge
2 Park Square, Milton Park, Abingdon, Oxon, OX14 4RN

and by Routledge
605 Third Avenue, New York, NY 10158

Routledge is an imprint of the Taylor & Francis Group, an informa business

© 2022 Lucy Johnstone

The right of Lucy Johnstone to be identified as authors
of this work has been asserted by her in accordance with
sections 77 and 78 of the Copyright, Designs and Patents
Act 1988.

First edition published 1989
Second edition published by Routledge 2000

British Library Cataloguing-in-Publication Data
A catalogue record for this book is available from the
British Library

Library of Congress Cataloging-in-Publication Data
A catalog record for this book has been requested

DOI: 10.4324/9781003095958

ISBN: 978-0-367-55982-3 (hbk)
ISBN: 978-0-367-55981-6 (pbk)
ISBN: 978-1-003-09595-8 (ebk)

Typeset in Galliard
by Apex CoVantage, LLC

In memory of Roy and Mary McKay

Contents

Introduction to the Classic Edition

I wrote the first edition of *Users and Abusers of Psychiatry* (1989) in my twenties, spanning my first and second posts as a clinical psychologist. The substantially revised second edition appeared in 2000. This introduction to the 'Classic' edition, written from the other end of my career, traces the book's themes and the changes in mental health practice since my first, longhand effort over thirty years ago. It may make sense to read the book first, and return to this update afterwards.

The introduction is a powerful illustration of one of the paradoxes of the field of psychiatry; everything changes, and yet everything remains the same. Since 1989, there have been new theories, evidence, movements, practices and critiques, some of which I will now describe. At the same time, the basic principles of medical model psychiatry remain intact; modified in some ways, but repackaged rather than abandoned, and still dominating the field, despite increasing challenges on all fronts. This means that much of the original book remains relevant. As I wrote in 1989, and would still write today: 'The time is long overdue for a new metaphor, a new way of understanding mental distress, and the overthrow of the whole medical model tradition'.[1] However, I do have a sense, previously absent, that the end of the medical paradigm of distress is in sight. I will elaborate on this by bringing the book up to date with reference to my and others' writing since 2000.

Growing trends

It is encouraging to see an expansion of the critiques and alternatives described in the first two editions of *Users and Abusers*. New and damning assessments of diagnostic practice have emerged, including 'Cracked', psychotherapist James Davies' devastating report based on interviews with members of the Diagnostic and Statistical Manual of Disorders (DSM) committees,[2] and psychiatrist Sami Timimi's various books placing the massive rise in labels for children and young people in a socio-economic and cultural context.[3] An accessible British Psychological Society report arguing that 'Hearing voices or feeling paranoid are common experiences which can often be a reaction to trauma, abuse or deprivation. Calling them symptoms of mental illness, psychosis or schizophrenia is only one way of thinking about them, with advantages and disadvantages'[4] has been translated into four languages. There is even a standard psychology textbook, *Psychology, Mental Health and Distress*,[5] which is not structured by diagnostic categories and is co-authored with service users.

Most significantly of all, the publication of the fifth edition of the DSM in 2013 saw some of the strongest concerns about diagnosis being raised by establishment figures including the chair of the DSM-III committee, Professor Robert Spitzer, and the DSM-IV committee, Professor Allen Frances. In fact Frances openly admitted 'There is no reason to believe that DSM 5 is safe or scientifically sound'.[6] At the same time my own professional body, the Division of Clinical Psychology, issued a formal statement calling for 'a paradigm shift in relation to the experiences that these diagnoses refer to, towards a conceptual system that is no longer based on a "disease" model'.[7]

It is important to note that influential clinicians like Frances are not against diagnosis as such; in fact, millions of dollars are being invested – or wasted, depending on your perspective – in developing new classification systems from scratch. In the meantime, as a *New Scientist* editorial put it in 2014:

> Just over a year ago, the world's largest mental health research organisation signalled its intent to tear up 60 years of psychiatry and start again . . . Almost everyone agrees that the old system is no longer fit for purpose and that patients deserve better. Delivering something better, however, is going to be a long, slow process.[8]

However, very few patients are told that the labels ascribed to or imposed on them are not in any scientific sense accurate or 'true'. In this period of uncertainty and upheaval, it is my strong belief that

> If the authors of the diagnostic manuals are admitting that psychiatric diagnoses are not supported by evidence, then no one should be forced to accept them. If many mental health workers are openly

questioning diagnosis and saying we need a different and better system, then service users and carers should be allowed to do so too.[9]

This is a quote from my 2014 book *A Straight Talking Introduction to Psychiatric Diagnosis* (second edition due in 2022), which presents the arguments in an accessible form so that people can make an informed choice about whether they wish to define themselves and their problems in diagnostic terms.

So, although psychiatric diagnosis remains a highly contentious topic, the issues are out there – to question it may not be popular in all quarters, but nor is it met with blank incomprehension. One response is an outbreak of goalpost-shifting. 'Schizophrenia', once seen as the 'prototypical psychiatric disease'[10] is being quietly replaced by the friendlier-sounding but even less reliable category of 'psychosis'. Many voice-hearers who would once have been – or were – diagnosed as 'schizophrenic' are now, thanks to the infinite flexibility of psychiatric labels, said to have 'borderline personality disorder' – not a diagnosis I had ever come across in 2000, but now the basis of a flourishing industry, with its own experts, therapies, conferences and treatment paths. Meanwhile, the medicalisation of distress is making huge inroads into the lives of children and young people, vast numbers of whom are now labelled with 'ADHD' and 'Autistic spectrum disorder'. Nowadays we no longer wait for a clinician to diagnose us – a combination of anti stigma campaigns, celebrity confessions and the internet encourages us all to self-diagnose.

We are also seeing various ingenious modifications to the official position on diagnosis. Densely worded academic articles argue that a properly nuanced understanding of the philosophy of psychiatry shows that 'diagnosis' doesn't necessarily imply medical illness or biological dysfunction. Instead of continuing the search for definitive biomarkers or tests, there is a switch to redefining the notions of disease/disorder themselves, such that it is sufficient for someone to be suffering in some way in order to be 'ill' and qualify for a psychiatric label.[11]

On these grounds, we might as well subsume every area of our lives under the umbrella of psychiatry – in fact, we seem to be well on the way to doing that – although it is not clear why doctors, nurses, hospitals and so on would be essential in such an all-inclusive definition of its territory. This reframe might also be puzzling to those who have been diagnosed; as I phrased it in a recent debate:

> I have yet to hear any real life service user say, 'Although the doctor told me I have schizophrenia I'm not too worried, because "illness"

is really being used as a metaphor for suffering in this case and it doesn't exclude personal meaning.' I am sure readers are aware that the consequences of being diagnosed—such as being sectioned, forcibly injected, and so on—are not just metaphorical.[12]

This pseudo-intellectual wriggling simply won't work. The debate has been opened up, the gaping holes in diagnostic validity have been exposed, and the genie will not be put back in the bottle.

The crumbling of the classification system, which is the essential foundation of all psychiatric theory and practice, has been accompanied by the collapse of many of psychiatry's core claims.[13] The 'chemical imbalance' theory of 'mental illness', promoted without evidence since the 1980s by a coalition of drug companies and medical prescribers, is still accepted as fact by the general public, although the Royal College of Psychiatrists, in a less than generous admission that service users have been actively misled for decades, now admits that 'the original idea that antidepressants "correct a chemical imbalance in the brain" is an over-simplification' – or to put it more bluntly, it is plain wrong.[14] A senior US psychiatrist, Dr Pies, actually claims that 'the "chemical imbalance theory" was never a real theory, nor was it widely propounded by responsible practitioners in the field of psychiatry'.[15] The real origins of what must therefore qualify as a mass outbreak of delusional thinking are not made clear by Dr Pies, and we still await the public health campaign that is surely needed so that these false beliefs can be corrected.

In a similar vein, much-heralded discoveries of genetic and other causes of mental distress have come to nothing, even though the claims have been watered down to vanishing point. No longer are we searching for the 'gene for schizophrenia'; rather, we are told that hundreds of interacting genetic variants may collectively make a tiny contribution to 'mental disorder' – as indeed they do to any and every form of human experience and behaviour, both 'normal' and 'abnormal'. So far, the clinical relevance of these findings is precisely nil.[16] In a breathtaking statement as he departed for a more promising job with Google, which will attempt to identify the digital markers of 'mental illness', Dr Thomas Insel, former head of the prestigious National Institute of Mental Health in the US, admitted:

I spent 13 years at NIMH really pushing on the neuroscience and genetics of mental disorders, and when I look back on that I realize that, while I think I succeeded at getting lots of really cool papers published by cool scientists at fairly large costs – I think

$20 billion – I don't think we moved the needle in reducing suicide, reducing hospitalizations, improving recovery for the tens of millions of people who have mental illness.[17]

New critiques of psychiatric drugs and ECT have also emerged. Psychiatrist Joanna Moncrieff, while acknowledging that these drugs have uses, has exploded the myth that they 'treat illnesses' in any meaningful sense. Rather, her 'drug-centred model' suggests that they have a range of general effects on people's mental states, which may or may not be experienced positively, but which have considerable costs in both the short term and the long term.[18] Clinical psychologist John Read and his colleagues have mounted a long and ultimately successful campaign, against considerable opposition, to persuade the Royal College of Psychiatrists, the National Institute of Health and Care Excellence (NICE), and Public Health England to recognise the risk of severe withdrawal effects from 'anti depressants'.[19] In America, science journalist Robert Whitaker published 'Anatomy of an Epidemic', a ground-breaking investigation into the strong evidence that all psychiatric drugs increase, rather than reduce or cure, disability over the long term.[20]

In this mixed picture, we can celebrate the fact that since 2000, and certainly since 1989, critique of the core aspects of medical model psychiatry has entered the mainstream, driven by a loose coalition of professionals from all backgrounds (including psychiatrists from the Critical Psychiatry Network[21] and nurses from the Critical Mental Health Nurses network[22]) along with service users/survivors/carers. The pros and cons of biomedical practice are extensively and not always politely discussed on social media, which despite its drawbacks, does allow for more open and democratic challenges from those who have been harmed by the mental health system. Social media also enables the dissemination of information beyond official sources, and has allowed new and influential networks to form. The 'A disorder for everyone!' movement, initiated by psychotherapist Jo Watson, has taken its challenging and inspiring workshops on alternatives to the diagnostic approach around the UK and, thanks to the internet, across the world.[23] Online platforms like Mad in America, which now has affiliates in nine countries including the UK, offer an accessible forum for blogs, debates, webinars, reports on new initiatives, and collaboration in fighting for new ways forward.[24]

In this more open climate, the Hearing Voices Movement, offering an alternative perspective on voice-hearing and other unusual sensory experiences, has grown from a fringe organisation in 2000 into a thriving network of peer-led groups in 29 countries.[25] No longer is it taboo for clinicians to ask people about their voices; in fact, this is a core part of the much-promoted development Cognitive Behavioural Therapy for Psychosis. Eleanor Longden's TED talk describing how she dropped her label of 'schizophrenia' through making peace with her voices, has been viewed over 5 million times.[26] The survivor movement has flourished in numerous areas such as peer support, research, campaigning, training and advocacy.[27] There is no single service user view, but representation of their voices in organisations and official documents is expected, although sometimes tokenistic.

The general public, fed by standard national media narratives about the need for 'more mental health services' to 'treat' what are invariably described as 'mental illnesses', is still largely unaware of either critiques or alternatives. But even here, alongside celebrity 'Me and my bipolar disorder'-type accounts, there are journalists like Johann Hari challenging the accepted truths by drawing on both personal and professional experiences, and showing that healing comes through human connection, meaningful lives and fair societies, not simply drugs and labels.[28]

New developments

From my current perspective, it seems odd that explicit mention of formulation-based practice is almost completely absent from both editions of *Users and Abusers*, although the general principle – that distress can be understood in the light of people's relational and social contexts and the sense they have made of them – runs through all the case histories. (Chapter 1 of *Users and Abusers* essentially offers a formulation, or narrative-based understanding, of the life of Elaine, the 'depressed housewife', as an alternative to the many diagnoses that were applied to her.) Much of my subsequent career has been spent on developing, practising, training in, writing about and researching into psychological formulation, sometimes defined as a hypothesis or 'best guess' about the reasons for someone's distress.[29]

A formulation is a written summary which integrates the professional's clinical and research knowledge with the service user's expertise in their own life. It is an evolving, collaboratively constructed narrative which is not just based on problems and difficulties, or the things that are supposedly wrong with you, but on talents and strengths in surviving difficult life situations, both past and present. Formulation has found a firm foothold in adult, older adult, child and intellectual disability services, mainly practised by psychologists but increasingly seen as a core skill for other professions as well. In its team version, a whole team is facilitated to develop a shared, non-medical understanding of someone's difficulties,[30] a process that has been described as 'a powerful way of shifting team cultures'.[31]

Another notable omission from *Users and Abusers* is Judith Herman's 1992 book, *Trauma and Recovery*,[32] and the large body of work it inspired, known as the trauma-informed approach. 'Trauma' here is understood in its wider sense, which includes emotional and physical abuse and neglect, domestic violence, bullying and many other adversities. The trauma-informed approach is based on a synthesis of findings from trauma studies, attachment theory and neuroscience, and integrates the causal roles of the mind, the body, relationships and the social world.[33] It demonstrates beyond doubt that psychosocial adversities, particularly in early life, increase the risk of all kinds of mental distress, and also of negative physical health, employment, educational and social outcomes.

These findings will come as no surprise to anyone who has worked in the mental health system, but as well as confirming this common sense view, the approach has generated plausible accounts of the causal pathways involved, and effective strategies for supporting people to move forward in their lives. Evidence from neuroscience shows that our minds and bodies have creative ways of coping with emotionally overwhelming events and situations. We may go into an automatic fight/flight/freeze response to protect us from danger. We may cut off from feelings and memories which are too much to bear at the time, in a process called dissociation. From a trauma-informed perspective, what the biomedical model calls 'symptoms' are not signs of illnesses to be treated but survival strategies. All of these responses were essential at the time of the traumatic situation but may become problematic in their own right if they persist once the threat has gone. The message of the trauma-informed approach is: 'You have survived very difficult circumstances in the best way you could at the time. These strategies are no longer needed or useful and, with the right kind of support, you can learn to leave them behind.' Originating in the US, the trauma-informed approach is now endorsed in many Department of Health documents, and has a particularly high profile in Scotland, where there are ambitious plans to ensure all staff have trauma-informed training.

There are now a number of other innovative approaches embodying the popular survivor slogan 'Instead of asking what's wrong with me, ask what has happened to me'. To mention just a few, Open Dialogue, a family and social network-centred intervention for people at risk of diagnosis with 'psychosis', has spread from its origins in Western Lapland

and there are now several UK projects.[34] The Leeds Survivor Led Crisis Service (LSLCS) was set up in 1999 by a group of mental health service users who wanted a place of sanctuary not based on a diagnostic, medical approach to mental health crisis, and its impressive results have been replicated in other cities.[35] 'Psychologists for Social Change', along with community psychology in general, have forcefully made the link between adverse social and economic policies and environments, and their emotional impact on both the individual and society as a whole.[36] Trauma-informed approaches increasingly recognise that structural inequality, in the form of poverty, deprivation, racial discrimination and so on, provides the context within which relationship traumas flourish. Although a great deal remains to be done, there are more Black and minority ethnic services and advocacy projects, and there is more awareness of the impact of racism and the need for both psychiatry and psychology to decolonise their curricula and their practices.[37]

In summary, we now have something unimaginable twenty years ago – credible alternatives to both diagnosis itself and to the medical model it supports, and successful examples of practical applications of these ideas. Trauma-informed, formulation-based practice has been endorsed at the highest levels. Thus, former MP Sir Norman Lamb was co-chair with peer specialist Sue Sibbald of a 'Consensus Statement for People with a Diagnosis of Personality Disorder', signed by most of the leading UK mental health professions and organisations, which concluded: 'We would like to abandon the term "personality disorder" entirely . . . A trauma-informed, formulation driven, whole system approach to care is necessary'.[38] Perhaps most important is the support from the United Nations Special Rapporteur, psychiatrist Dainius Puras, in his 2017 report[39] stating that:

> many of the concepts supporting the biomedical model in mental health have failed to be confirmed by further research. Diagnostic tools, such as the ICD and the DSM, continue to expand the parameters of individual diagnosis, often without a solid scientific basis.
>
> . . . the field of mental health continues to be over-medicalized and the reductionist biomedical model, with support from psychiatry and the pharmaceutical industry, dominates clinical practice, policy, research agendas, medical education and investment in mental health around the world . . . We have been sold a myth that the best solutions for addressing mental health challenges are medications and other biomedical interventions.

Among his recommendations were:

- The urgent need for a shift in approach should prioritize policy innovation at the population level, targeting social determinants and abandon the predominant medical model that seeks to cure individuals by targeting 'disorders'.
- The crisis in mental health should be managed not as a crisis of individual conditions, but as a crisis of social obstacles which hinders individual rights. Mental health policies should address the 'power imbalance' rather than 'chemical imbalance'.

As a newly qualified professional in 1989, I often felt very alone in my views. For some years now, I have felt part of a large, informal network of friends and allies, who encourage, inspire and support each other. But the battle is far from over. Before we get too excited, it is sadly true that Chapter 9 (2000) 'Resistance in the system' is still relevant – if anything, more so.

Resistance and backlash

The more effective the challenge, the bigger the backlash. Hardest to detect is the process I described as functioning to 'disarm critics by assimilating aspects of different approaches without actually changing the basic medical standpoint'.[40] As one survivor put it:

> Co-optation is a process by which a dominant group attempts to absorb or neutralise a weaker opposition that it believes poses a threat to its continued power. Co-optation can take a variety of forms. Dominant groups may adopt the language of marginalised groups and alter definitions of words over time, until terms like 'empowerment' and 'peer' become empty buzzwords or mean the opposite of what they once meant. The dominant group may selectively embrace part of the less powerful group's agenda and then water down these ideas so they become non-threatening and ineffective.[41]

The high profile 'Recovery Movement' is one example. Originating in service user descriptions of their journeys through 'a transformative process in which the old self is gradually let go and a new sense of self emerges',[42] it is now a central plank of UK mental health policy. Although some excellent work happens in the new 'Recovery Colleges', there is also suspicion that the concept has been grafted onto, rather than replacing, traditional medical approaches, along with a message that it is now the personal responsibility of the individual to 'recover' in socially approved ways.

There have been attempts to assimilate all the progressive developments I have described so far. Take formulation as an example. The Division of Clinical Psychology (DCP) Good Practice Guidelines for Psychological Formulation clearly position it as an alternative to psychiatric diagnosis; one of the criteria states that formulation 'Is not premised on a functional psychiatric diagnosis (e.g. schizophrenia, personality disorder)'.[43] This is in contrast to the Royal College of Psychiatrists (RCP) guidelines which require trainee psychiatrists to 'demonstrate the ability to construct formulations of patients' problems that include appropriate differential diagnoses'.[44] As two senior psychiatrists phrased it in an editorial in the *British Journal of Psychiatry* titled 'Psychiatric diagnosis: impersonal, imperfect and important':[45]

> The key is to produce a formulation that goes beyond a simple list of facts and that complements the diagnosis by including information about important clinical variables that have relevance for the management plan. We should continue to make diagnoses complemented by formulations in which a range of additional factors are brought together that are relevant to management and prognosis.

It will be obvious that the RCP version of a formulation, which might be rendered as 'Psychosis/bipolar disorder triggered by stress at work', is very different from the DCP one, which might appear as 'Hearing voices as a reaction to experiences of sexual abuse'. The first simply fleshes out a diagnosis with a few details, along the lines of the so-called 'biopsychosocial model', thus giving a limited acknowledgement of psychological factors while relegating them to the status of 'trigger' of an underlying 'disorder'. The second, if sensitive exploration of the person's life story shows it to be accurate, makes a diagnosis redundant. Once you have a reasonably complete hypothesis or formulation about the reasons for someone's difficulties, you don't need a competing one that says 'It's also because you have schizophrenia/a personality disorder/clinical depression'. But the psychiatric formulation has the strategic advantage of filling in some of the embarrassing gaps left by a diagnosis, and thus extending the shelf life of these unscientific and stigmatising labels. It is no accident that formulation – usually of the 'psychiatric' kind – is finding new favour in documents and services.

I could give many other examples. *Users and Abusers* described Dr Dennis Scott's radical approach to crisis work, in which conversations with families replaced the usual admit-and-diagnose procedures, allowing for underlying issues to be revealed rather than sealed off behind a label applied to the identified patient. Every psychiatric hospital now has its own crisis team, but I have rarely heard a good word about them. Without a coherent philosophy except to reduce admission rates, they frequently offer little more than dismissal if the person in distress fails to display sufficiently severe 'symptoms' to qualify for a grossly over-stretched service, or a brief, medically oriented stay on an overcrowded ward if they do. A recent TV documentary, featuring crisis team staff based in what is now the Dennis Scott Unit, suggested that little of his legacy has survived.

Mental health services have fragmented into numerous components – Community Mental Health teams, Assertive Outreach teams, Early Intervention teams, Crisis teams and so on, which in England are overlaid by clusters, or pathways, of particular problems in order to facilitate Payment by Results calculations. This combination of a medical model with a managerial, target-driven model and a business model on top of that, has been disastrous. The absolutely crucial ingredient of successful support, as Scott emphasised, is consistency of personnel and of the understanding of the problem. All this is lost when teams are set up to play a game of 'Pass the parcel' between many overlapping and competing parts of the service.

In another illustration of the process of co-option and assimilation, DSM 5 has recognised the influence of trauma studies by adding a new chapter on 'Trauma and stressor-related disorders', which is described as 'unique within DSM-5 for requiring the identification of a triggering external event'.[46] This chapter joins the DSM and ICD one on 'Dissociative Disorders' – dissociation being a key mechanism in trauma-informed approaches – which are also framed as responses to adverse psychosocial events. From one perspective this, along with the possibility of diagnosing 'Complex Trauma' in ICD 11, could be seen as an advance; from another, it is simply a case of subsuming an ever-widening range of human experiences into a 'disorder' model. The newly identified phenomenon of 'climate trauma'[47] – sometimes called climate distress, eco fear or eco trauma – has yet to appear in DSM or ICD, and I hope it never will. We do not want to see our responses to the most profound threat we have ever faced reduced to a personal deficit.

In *Users and Abusers* I noted the 'predictable cycles of opinion' in which new psychiatric drug 'treatments' pass from accidental discovery to glowing descriptions of safe and effective action in a range of previously problematic conditions, to reluctant acknowledgement of drawbacks, to tacit admission that the drug is 'either useless, of very limited use, or even positively harmful', at which point 'the treatment is abandoned and the whole cycle starts again with something else'.[48] There have been a number of iterations of this process since then. As described above, 'anti depressants' seem to be next in line for a catastrophic fall from grace, as evidence mounts that their clinical benefits are barely detectable while their harms may be permanent. Despite similar evidence about so-called 'anti psychotics', their re-branding from the more accurate term 'major tranquillisers, as they were still known in 2000, appears to have bought them a little more time. However, we are poised to embrace a new miracle drug, esketamine, derived from the addictive street drug ketamine, and recently licensed for 'treatment-resistant depression' in the USA, the UK and Europe. This is despite the lack of rationale or solid evidence of benefit, and the real possibility of harms, including bladder damage, cognitive dysfunction, and unexpected death.[49]

Back in 1989, I wrote 'Although this book has on the whole advocated psychotherapy as an alternative to physical treatments, it is important to remember that the former can be just as powerful a way of enforcing social norms as the latter'.[50] The roll-out of a narrow version of cognitive behaviour therapy across the country, under the multi-million-pound Improved Access to Psychological Therapy project, perfectly illustrates this. Nowadays, many of the clients I described would not get near an actual mental health team. They would instead be directed by their GP towards a set number of manualised, diagnostically based sessions, as part of a project set up by economist Lord Richard Layard with the explicit aim of covering its costs by getting people back into work, however poorly paid and stressful that work might be.[51] Individualised approaches to psychosocial problems – or what we might call 'medical model psychology' – have not been any more successful than those based on psychiatric drugs, which is perhaps not surprising given that the model seems designed to minimise the relationship factors that are known to be the healing ingredients in any therapy. In fact, recovery rates appear to be, if anything, lower than would be expected through natural remission. Meanwhile, IAPT counsellors themselves – who are invariably conscientious and hard-working – are buckling under the pressure of this assembly-line, target-driven model of care.[52]

It gets worse. A most unwelcome newcomer is the Movement for Global Mental Health (MGMH), launched in 2008 on the basis of a series of articles in *The Lancet* and supported by the World Health Organisation.[53] It aims to 'scale up' services in low-income and middle-income countries where there is said to be a 'treatment gap' depriving the majority of people of Western psychiatric interventions for their 'mental disorders'. Although there have been positive examples of support and collaboration, the main exports are psychiatric labels, psychiatric drugs and narrow versions of CBT. A number of authors have noted the irony of this development at the very time when the conspicuous lack of success in improving outcomes in the West is causing increased controversy. Psychologist David Ingleby, whom I cited in 2000, points out that 'Western psychiatry can certainly provide low- and middle-income countries with instructive examples – but they are mainly examples of what not to do'.[54] As critical psychiatrist Dr Derek Summerfield writes:

> Psychiatric universalism risks being imperialistic, reminding us of the colonial era when it was pressed upon indigenous people that there were different kinds of knowledge and that theirs was second rate. We need to challenge the relentless self-aggrandisement of the Western mental health industry, forever claiming that yet more funding is required to tackle 'massive" unmet mental health needs. This is an industry out of control, risking hubris and arguably deserving it.[55]

The MGMH is itself an illustration of a new narrative in which we are encouraged to believe, by everyone from anti stigma campaigners to members of the Royal Family, that 'we all have mental health'. Both the power and the contradictions of this regrettable, if well-intended, perspective have been highlighted by the COVID-19 epidemic. As I put it in an article in the *British Journal of Psychiatry Bulletin*:[56]

> The COVID-19 pandemic is one of a series of interlinked global emergencies that will affect everyone on the planet. But it is important to challenge the idea that, as numerous headlines are telling us, we are now facing a 'pandemic of mental health disorders' . . . if ever there was an example of our reactions being appropriate in the circumstances, this is it. It has never been more obvious that the thoughts, feelings and behaviours we call 'mental illness' are defined in relation to social norms. Suddenly, being too scared to leave the house for fear of contracting a fatal disease, and spending most of the day washing our hands and wiping down doorknobs, are not signs of 'OCD' but of a responsible citizen. Arguably, the

'abnormal' people are now the four in ten of us whose anxiety levels have not increased. Who can say how we ought to be feeling at such a time?

. . . How and why is the 'mental health pandemic' narrative being promoted when it is contradicted by the evidence and the reality on the ground? Part of the answer may lie in the high-profile public health campaigns in schools, the media and so on, which urge us all to 'talk about mental health' – this mysterious, indefinable but apparently fragile state of mind – more or less constantly. We are encouraged to use the ubiquitous term 'mental health' as a synonym for 'how we all feel' in relation to any state of mind short of complete contentment. We then become legitimate targets for mass professional and technical monitoring and intervention, focused not on the real-life situations that evoke our reactions, but on the newly defined 'mental health problems' themselves. Moreover, while it is still generally believed that only a minority of us is 'mentally ill', the new discourse reminds us that 'we all have mental health'. This apparently innocuous, indeed nonsensical, phrase draws us all into the realm of surveillance and potential 'treatment'.

If we allow psychiatric diagnoses to individualise and depoliticise our responses, we will simply revert to a way of life that, even before COVID-19, was leading many people to self-harm, despair and suicide. Instead, we need the courage to stay connected with our feelings, and the feelings of those around us, not file them away in boxes marked 'anxiety disorders and depression'. People who have lost their jobs are likely to feel desperate, but we don't have to describe this as 'clinical depression' and prescribe drugs for it. Those with backgrounds of severe trauma may find that their worst memories are being triggered, but we don't have to describe this as a relapse of their 'borderline personality disorder'. The economic recession that will follow the pandemic may lead to as many suicides as austerity measures did, but we don't have to say that 'mental illness' caused these deaths . . ..

Not a single new research study is needed to confirm that being poor, jobless, isolated, ill and bereaved makes people unhappy, or to work out the appropriate remedies . . . The COVID-19 pandemic is an opportunity to implement what we already know about universal human needs for social contact, financial security and sufficient material resources, protection from trauma, abuse and neglect, especially in early years, decent healthcare, and a sense of purpose and belonging. As an editorial in The Lancet puts it, COVID-19 is 'overturning core values, norms, and rules that sit at the heart of long-standing market-oriented political agendas' and presenting us with the need for 're-making the social contract'.

The more we can challenge the 'mental health' narrative, the clearer our current dilemmas and future directions will become. It is not a pandemic of 'mental health' problems that we need to fear, but a pandemic of 'mental health' thinking.

I have quoted this at some length because the morals apply far beyond responses to the pandemic that is raging as I write. Rates of psychiatric diagnoses are soaring across the Westernised world. A recent survey from New Zealand found that nearly *nine out of ten* people will meet the criteria for at least one 'mental illness' by the age of 45.[57] The figure is creeping slowly but surely towards ten in ten, if it isn't already there. At this point, paradoxically, we will all become 'mentally well', because 'mental illness' is defined in relation to deviations from the norm; when everyone is 'mentally ill', no one is 'mentally ill'. It would be nice to think that before we reach that point, we might, as societies, be prepared to look a little deeper into the reasons why the Westernised way of life seems to be driving the majority of its citizens mad.

Despite the new freedom of speech offered by social media, any critic of the psychiatric status quo is likely to be subjected to backlash ranging from personal insults to formal complaints and loss of employment, and I am no exception. No longer are responses confined to the relatively civilised arenas of conferences, book reviews and 'Letters to the Editor'. Invited to explain and debate my views in an academic journal,[58] I summarised the Twitter responses thus:

> My @PsychTimes interview has been described by professionals as dangerous, flaky, incoherent, misguided, brainless, Jurassic, strawman, harmful, reductionist, anti-psychiatry drivel which ignores the evidence and arises from guild war and prescription envy; I am an awful, hostile, egotistical, vicious, arrogant, bullying, Trump-like dinosaur and anti-vaxxer who has never worked in mental health, can't tolerate dissent, denigrates colleagues, doesn't believe in COVID, and should never have had a platform. But not a single opposer has addressed the actual arguments.[59]

As a seasoned professional, I am relatively well protected, but it is shocking to see service users themselves – including those who describe themselves as part of the #PrescribedHarm community – being treated equally badly.

Both editions of *Users and Abusers* ended by citing Thomas Kuhn's work on the evolution of scientific ideas, noting that abandoning a core set of assumptions, such as the medical model of distress, is always strongly resisted. Even in the face of severe and prolonged anomalies, Kuhn argues, defenders of the status quo

> do not renounce the paradigm that has led them into crisis. They do that, that is, treat anomalies as counter instances . . . They will devise numerous articulations and ad hoc modifications of their theory in order to eliminate any apparent conflict.[60]

Whether or not this explains the picture I have painted, I remain convinced that 'The time is long overdue for a new metaphor, a new way of understanding mental distress, and the overthrow of the whole medical model tradition'.[61]

This brings us on to a description of the Power Threat Meaning Framework.

The Power Threat Meaning Framework

In many ways, the Power Threat Meaning Framework (PTMF) represents the culmination of the collective life work of its main authors, and their shared clinical, research and lived experience expertise. I first met the other lead author, Mary Boyle, after the publication of *Users and Abusers* in 1989, a year before she published her classic text *Schizophrenia: A Scientific Delusion?* Contributing authors and psychologists John Cromby, Dave Harper, Peter Kinderman, Dave Pilgrim, John Read, and survivors Jacqui Dillon and Eleanor Longden, are all longstanding critics of the medical model, and we have known each other for many years. Over an intense and at times very challenging five-year period, we together outlined the conceptual principles of a replacement for the diagnostic model of distress.[62]

Launched in January 2018 and funded by the BPS Division of Clinical Psychology, the PTMF has already attracted a great deal of interest within and beyond services, and from service user groups, training courses, voluntary organisations, researchers and campaigners. It will shortly be available in five other languages, and there have been invited presentations across the UK and in many other countries, including Australia and New Zealand. This suggests a wide appetite for change. The documents, resources and good practice examples can be accessed here: www.bps.org.uk/power-threat-meaning-framework and this book offers a brief, practical introduction to the PTMF in practice: www.pccs-books.co.uk/products/a-straight-talking-introduction-to-the-power-threat-meaning-framework-an-alternative-to-psychiatric-diagnosis.

Like other developments discussed above, the PTMF is a continuation of the core themes of *Users and Abusers of Psychiatry*. In 1989 and again in 2000 I identified the need to move away from not just biomedical models and their various modifications, but the positivist approach in general – in other words 'the particular way of thinking that underlies nearly all scientific research and enquiry' adopted from the natural sciences,[63] which underpins much of psychology as well as psychiatry. The PTMF attempts this task by returning to the philosophical roots of this largely Western set of assumptions. It places formulation and trauma-informed practice within a much wider context of psychological, therapeutic, sociological, and political perspectives and approaches. It uses the term 'narrative' to include not just formulation but any kind of meaning-making, whether inside or outside services, including art, music, poetry, community myths, rituals and ceremonies. It also places a strong emphasis on the socio-economic policies and contexts within which adverse events and circumstances arise, and on the largely unquestioned standards and ideals of Western industrialised societies, which encourage us to feel shame and guilt if we are unable to live up to them. All of this can lead to distress, even if we have not experienced any of the commonly recognised 'traumas', as we struggle to find a sense of self-worth, meaning, identity and connection with others. Thus, the PTMF applies not just to people who have been diagnosed but to all of us. It offers tools for anyone to challenge a diagnostic narrative and construct an alternative one, whether or not they are in contact with services, and with or without professional support.

A central focus of the PTMF is on how power in all its guises, both positive and negative, operates in our lives. It highlights the links between distress and social factors such as poverty, discrimination, social exclusion and inequality, along with relational adversities such as abuse, neglect and violence. The role of ideological power – that is, the power to support certain interests through the language we use, the assumptions and social norms we uphold and the meanings we create – is less often recognised. However, ideological power is central to all other kinds of power. From a PTMF perspective, imposing a psychiatric label on someone is a very good example of the operation of this kind of power.

The PTMF integrates a great deal of existing evidence, including lived experience, about the impact of various forms of power in people's lives, the kinds of threat that misuses of power pose to us, and the ways we as human beings have learned to respond to threat. In traditional mental health practice, these threat responses are sometimes called 'symptoms'.

The main aspects of the PTMF are summarised in this expanded version of the survivor slogan, 'Instead of asking what's wrong with me, ask what has happened to me'.

- 'What has happened to you?' (How is **power** operating in your life?)
- 'How did it affect you?' (What kind of **threats** does this pose?)
- 'What sense did you make of it?' (What is the **meaning** of these situations and experiences to you?)
- 'What did you have to do to survive?' (What kinds of **threat response** are you using?)

In addition, two further questions help us to think about what skills and resources individuals, families or social groups might have, and how we might pull all these ideas and responses together into a personal narrative or story:

- 'What are your strengths?' (What access to **power resources** do you have?)
- 'What is your story?' (How does all this fit together?)

The core questions can be used to help people to create more hopeful narratives or stories about their lives and the difficulties they may be have faced or are still facing, instead of seeing themselves as blameworthy, weak, flawed or 'mentally ill'. These personal narratives can be seen as variations on larger, meaning-based patterns of distress which offer a more appropriate foundation for understanding and alleviating emotional suffering than hypothesised patterns of biological dysfunction like those found in general medicine. We have described them as 'Patterns of embodied, meaning-based threat responses to the negative operation of power'.

In addition, the PTMF offers a new way of thinking about culturally specific perspectives on the experiences called 'mental health problems'. If patterns of distress are fundamentally shaped by meaning, we should not be surprised to find that experiences and expressions of distress may be very different around the globe and in some minority groups in the

UK. The DSM response to this puzzling (from a medical viewpoint) fact is to try to translate such phenomena back into the diagnostic model, as the Movement for Global Mental Health does. The PTMF, on the other hand, encourages respect for the many creative and non-medical ways of understanding distress around the world, and the varied forms of narrative and healing practices that may be used, as explored in these blogs.[64]

The PTMF is an overarching framework, not a model as such. It is intended to support, not replace, existing creative examples of non-medical approaches such as those already described under 'Growing Trends' and 'New Developments' in the hope that they ultimately become standard practice. The PTMF also suggests new ways forward, which restore the links between threats and threat responses, or in other words, personal/family/community distress and social inequality and injustice. In this way, the PTMF takes us beyond the individual and shows that we are all part of a wider struggle for a fairer society.

It is my hope that this brief overview will not just bring *Users and Abusers of Psychiatry* up to date, but will also inspire others to contribute to the fraught, chaotic, exhausting, but vital and exhilarating struggle for new ways to understand and heal emotional distress.

Acknowledgements

My thanks to Helen Cottee, Tom Donald, Celia Kitzinger, Ron Lacey, Viv Lindow, Alan Moore, Joan Neil, Dr Lawrence Ratna, Dr Dennis Scott, Lilly Stuart, Andy Treacher, David Winter; to my faithful panel of lay readers: Graham and Ann Johnstone, Roy and Mary McKay, Stephen and Jessica Pidgeon, James Johnstone and Carole Cerasi; and to all the people whose stories appear in this book.

For the second edition: additional thanks to Tony Fraher, Liz Frost, Amanda Hall, Neil Harris, Linda Hart, Sue Kemsley, Joanne Lee, Margaret Miners and John Waite.

And with very special thanks to the most important people in my life, David Miners, Alissa and Alex, for their patience, love and understanding during this long ordeal.

Permissions

The author would like to thank the following for permission to quote extracts from their work:

From RELOCATING MADNESS by Peter Barham and Robert Hayward, paperback edition first published by Free Association Books Ltd, 57 Warren Street, London W1P 5PA © Peter Barham and Robert Hayward 1995.

From *Aliens and Alienists: Ethnic minorities and psychiatry* 3rd editon by R. Littlewood and M. Lipsedge published by Routledge, 1997.

From *Phone at Nine just to Say You're Alive* by Linda Hart published by Douglas Elliot Press, 1995, with permission from Pan/Macmillan.

From 'Psychiatry: are we all allowed to disagree?' by Lucy Johnstone first published in *Clinical Psychology Forum* 56 (1993).

From *Recovery from Schizophrenia: Psychiatry and political economy* by Richard Warner published by Routledge, 1985.

From *Not Made of Wood: A psychiatrist discovers his own profession* by Jan Foudraine published by Quartet Books, 1974.

From 'Stress and coping in mental health nursing: a sociopolitical analysis' by J. Handy in J. Carson, L. Fagin and S. Ritter (eds) *Stress in Mental Health Nursing* published by Chapman and Hall, 1995.

From the audiotape accompanying Module 2 of *Mental Health and Distress: Perspectives and Practice*, G. Gifford and J. Read (1997). With permission from the Open University.

Every attempt has been made to trace copyright holders and obtain permissions. Any omissions brought to our attention will be remedied in future editions.

Glossary

A *psychiatrist* has a medical training and is able to prescribe drugs. Psychiatrists are at the head of the traditional psychiatric team.

A *clinical psychologist* is not medically trained, but has a degree in psychology followed by a post-graduate training course.

Psychotherapist or *counsellor* are general terms for anyone of whatever profession who practises psychotherapy or counselling: the process of helping someone to understand and overcome their problems by talking through them in regular sessions.

More detailed descriptions of the various professions can be found in Chapter 6.

There is no single satisfactory word to refer to those people who are on the receiving end of psychiatric treatment. I have generally used the term 'patient' when describing people who are in hospital or medical settings, and 'service user' elsewhere.

Names and identifying details of the people whose stories appear in this book have been changed.

Chapter 1

The story of a depressed housewife

This is the story of Elaine Jones, who is typical of very many women who break down and are taken into psychiatric hospitals.

ELAINE'S STORY

Elaine is 46, married with four children. Her husband is a van driver for a local firm, where she worked as a cleaner before her marriage. She is warm, outgoing and intelligent, and cares very deeply for her family. Generally she seems to cope well with her life, which since her marriage has consisted mainly of looking after her husband and children.

However, six months after the birth of her last child fifteen years ago, she suffered the first of many recurring episodes of depression, which have often been so severe that she has tried to kill herself. She has had over twenty admissions to psychiatric hospitals, varying in length from a few days to several months. Her treatment has consisted mainly of medication; she has been prescribed twenty different drugs, and has been taking at least one of them ever since her first breakdown. She has also had ECT (electro-convulsive therapy). While in the occupational therapy department, she has followed programmes of cooking and sewing, pottery and art. None of this has prevented her from breaking down again, sometimes only weeks or months after being discharged.

On Elaine's twenty-second admission, a new member of the psychiatric team, hearing that she had had a very unhappy child-hood, suggested that she might benefit from a different treatment

DOI: 10.4324/9781003095958-1

approach. This new team member was prepared to offer Elaine psychotherapy sessions to try and understand the background to and reasons for her depression. The consultant, who had had a lot of contact with Elaine over the past ten years, was not keen on this idea. He was inclined to believe that Elaine was not so much depressed as seeking an escape from chores at home, and pointed out that a few weeks after admission she usually appeared looking perfectly cheerful and asking to be discharged. However, he eventually agreed to the new plan.

Elaine, too, had mixed feelings about starting psychotherapy. She knew very little about it, and in any case she and her family had been told by her doctors that her depression was due to a recurrent illness. She found the idea of looking too closely at her feelings rather frightening. Nevertheless, she wanted to try anything that might help.

In the first session, Elaine started to reveal the depression behind the brave face that she felt compelled to put on for the world. Ever since childhood she had been known as the 'strong one', and she felt tremendously guilty about not being able to be strong for her family all the time. Although the battle had often been horrific, she had forced herself to carry on through many bouts of depression without coming into hospital. Sometimes she had vomited because of the strain of preparing herself for family gatherings; but not wanting to let people down, she somehow got through them without her social façade cracking. At other times, however, she reached the point where even washing a plate seemed like climbing a mountain, and she collapsed and retreated to bed in an extremity of exhaustion, guilt and despair.

Elaine also described how hurt she was that others did not understand how she felt. Her brother slammed down the telephone one night when for once she rang for help. Tears came to her eyes as she recalled the incident. But she expressed nothing but gratitude to the hospital for taking her in so often. The consultant insisted on discharging her once after a three-month stay when she had not improved at all, and although she had thought she would not be able to stand it, she had struggled through in the end. At the time she had thought him harsh, but looking back she was grateful for his firmness.

In that initial session, Elaine also revealed for the first time the incident that precipitated her first breakdown. She had been feeling very low after the birth of her third child, when some homeless relatives and their children arrived on the doorstep. She and her husband had felt obliged to take them in, and most of the burden of looking after two families in a medium-sized council house had fallen on Elaine's shoulders. The visiting husband started drinking heavily, and the whole family departed after six months without a word of thanks. Elaine broke down shortly afterwards.

In twice-weekly meetings over the next four months, Elaine and her therapist continued to trace the roots of her depression. A theme that emerged very strongly was the resentment and anger behind Elaine's guilt and depression. She had helped to set up a situation in which it was somehow always she who did the giving while getting no acknowledgement from anyone else. For example, in the build-up to the present admission, her stepmother had invited an extra six relatives for Christmas lunch at Elaine's house. Since it had always been Elaine's task to cook the meal, she had felt unable to refuse or ask for extra help. Her Christmas had been a nightmare of shopping, cooking and organising. Elaine's life was filled with similar incidents. Her sons expected dinner to be ready as soon as they came in, although sometimes they arrived hours late and offered no apologies. Her father and stepmother were offended if she did not visit them, and yet often they neglected to visit her when she was in hospital. Even on her weekend leaves from hospital she rushed around doing household chores while the rest of the family had a lie-in. She described tearfully how it was always she who went forward to kiss her children and parents at visiting time and ask them how they were. 'Why can't it be the other way round for once?' she cried.

The irony was that Elaine's 'brave face' was too effective. Patients mistook her for a nurse and implied that she didn't need to be in hospital, while her sister said openly that she was just looking for an escape from her responsibilities. Elaine feared that the hospital staff thought the same, though they denied it to her face. Elaine had set a trap for herself; she felt she had no right to protest or be dissatisfied. So she struggled on, putting on a façade which others were deceived by, and then felt angry and hurt about being so badly misunderstood, as well as guilty at not being able to cope. She tried to suppress these feelings too, and so the vicious circle continued.

Elaine and her therapist started looking into her childhood for the origins of this pattern. The accumulation of hurts, resentments and losses went back many years. Elaine was nine when her mother died. Shortly afterwards, Elaine's father remarried and two further children were born. Elaine and the two boys from the first marriage were shunned; but although still a child herself, Elaine had to bring up her younger brothers. She was kept back from school to do the housework and despatched to relatives to help out, while her half-sisters had every attention and comfort. Elaine, known as the 'strong one', was expected to cope with all this without acknowledgement, support or affection: and as a young child she had little option but to comply. It was very painful for Elaine to recall these events from her past. At one point she cried out in anguish, 'Why did they do it to me? I needed love too! Why did they have everything and I had nothing?' and she wept bitterly. But as the hurts were gradually released, she experienced the sensation of a hard lump in her chest slowly dissolving.

Elaine and her therapist discussed the ways in which she was continuing her childhood role of serving others, bottling up her feelings, having to be 'strong' and not having anything for herself. On the one hand, she seemed to spend her life apologising and fighting for the right to exist. On the other, a part of her was starting to say more strongly, as she put it, 'I'm me, I'm an individual – I'm not just a cook and wife and mother! I've got to have some life of my own!'

Slowly, Elaine started to make changes in her life. She resolved that this time she would not discharge herself from hospital long before she was fully recovered, telling the doctors untruthfully that she was fine because she felt so guilty at taking up their time and neglecting her home. She allowed herself to let down the brave front a little, and asked the staff for help and support when she was at her worst. She was firmer with people who questioned her need to be in hospital, whether they were staff, patients or family. Her therapist arranged a different occupational therapy programme that included some enjoyable and relaxing activities.

The major changes had to take place within her family. There were some successes. On weekend leave, instead of cleaning out the kitchen cupboards, she started to go on outings with her husband. She summoned up the courage to tell her brother how much his actions had hurt her. Although he was not very receptive, she found an unexpected ally in her sister-in-law. In fact, they discovered that they were both fed up with various aspects of Elaine's parents' behaviour, and decided to visit them less often, even if there were complaints and 'bad atmospheres'.

However, Elaine was still very fragile, and often despaired of the possibility of changing entrenched patterns of behaviour in her own home. Her two daughters, who uncomplainingly took on the role of cleaning and caring for the men of the family during Elaine's admissions, had never given much trouble, but they, like Elaine, found it hard to break the habit of running around after everyone else. Her two sons resisted change very fiercely. Elaine asked for her husband's support in challenging the long-standing tradition that they contributed none of their earnings for food, keep or laundry, and a furious row broke out. For once Elaine held her ground, only to be told by her sons that she was 'hysterical', 'crazy', and needed 'another spell in the loony bin'. Most hurtfully of all, her husband changed sides and accused her of stirring up trouble and being too hard on young lads who deserved a bit of fun. Still fragile and unsure of herself, Elaine was driven close to despair by such incidents. She felt it was desperately unfair that, while everyone else was allowed to get angry and have their say, she was labelled as 'crazy' when she spoke up for once instead of trying to soothe everyone else, and the whole family ranged themselves against her. Yet she now realised very clearly that her only hope of staying out of hospital was to bring about changes at home. Both options seemed so bleak that she sometimes contemplated running away and leaving the family, but they were her whole life and she felt she could never do it.

Elaine tried to explain some of this to her husband. He had coped valiantly with the children during her many admissions and had refused to put them into care, and she deeply appreciated how much he had had to bear over the years. At the same time the changes in her were beginning to highlight severe difficulties in their relationship. She knew him well enough to sense that he was feeling very low himself, yet he refused to confide in her, his GP or anyone else. Nor would he come up to the hospital for a joint session, saying, 'The next thing, they'll put *me* in there too!' When they made time to sit down quietly and talk, he would try to understand what she was going through; but in family crises he was as likely to shout at her as to support her. He frequently exploded in violent rages. Elaine told her therapist, 'Sometimes I think *he* should be here talking to you, instead of me.'

Over the following weeks, Elaine needed a great deal of support, which she gained both from her therapist and from a small therapy group of other patients. Slowly, she increased in strength and confidence. Indeed, she said, 'If I'd had this sort of help fifteen years ago, I might not have needed to be on pills all this time.' But she couldn't afford to look back with regrets because she knew the struggle to bring about changes in her family would continue for many months and need all her courage and determination. After a longer stay than most, she reached the point of being genuinely ready for discharge. She intended this admission to be her last one. Time will tell whether she succeeds.

Elaine's story is a clear illustration of many of the themes with which this book will be concerned. It can be understood and examined on various levels.

THE PSYCHOTHERAPEUTIC ANGLE

Let us look at Elaine's episodes of depression from a psychological point of view. Her psychotherapy gives us a way of understanding her depression as part of her whole person, of all of her past and present experiences and relationships, rather than just as an unpleasant recurring illness.

Clearly, Elaine was severely emotionally (and to some extent materially) deprived from a very young age. Not only did she miss out on the love, care and attention that all children need, she was also expected to provide it for others – her younger brothers and relatives. She was bearing adult responsibilities without getting the emotional nourishment that she needed for herself. Her parents seem to have justified this treatment by designating her as the 'strong one' who could cope with anything. Elaine learned to accept this view, which effectively stopped her from complaining or questioning the set-up. She too believed that she should be able to cope. In any case, she had very little choice in the matter.

Since the capacity to meet other people's needs depends on having your own needs met in the first place, someone in Elaine's position is in constant danger of becoming emotionally overdrawn, as it were, and of not having the resources to cope with others' demands. Moreover, someone like Elaine is particularly likely to get into the situation where others are making a lot of demands, since the role of looking after others is one they have been trained in from childhood. As Elaine herself came to realise through her therapy, she had contributed to setting up a repetition of her childhood circumstances, and still felt she had no right to protest about it.

Obviously a lifestyle based on such fragile foundations cannot continue indefinitely. There comes a point where so much more is being given out than taken in that the whole system breaks down. Sometimes the event that is the 'last straw' seems fairly trivial. Since the family, psychiatric staff, and indeed the woman herself have usually subscribed to the myth of her as strong and capable, the sort of person who helps *others* with their problems, they are often at a loss to understand why a relatively minor incident precipitates such a severe reaction. They are unlikely to appreciate that, from a psychological point of view, the breakdown can be understood as a cry for rest, care and the replenishment of depleted resources, and as a desperate protest against an intolerable lifestyle.

The significance of the precipitating event for Elaine's first breakdown now becomes clearer. After the birth of her last child, she was fragile and vulnerable. At the same time, she was required to meet the needs of others – her baby and her existing family – and to push her own needs into the background. It was a repetition of her childhood predicament. For many women, made vulnerable by similar backgrounds, childbirth on its own is enough to trigger what is usually described as 'post-natal depression', but often has its roots much further back. For Elaine, however, the problem was compounded by a whole extra set of demands from the relatives who came to stay. There was just too much weight on the wrong side of the fragile balancing act, and Elaine tipped over from 'strong one' to 'sick one'.

Real recovery from depression, as opposed to merely managing and containing it with medication, involved change on a whole-person level. Elaine had to find a way of completing the many unfinished events from her past that still haunted her. Much of this work was done in the therapy sessions, where she was able to release the hurt and anger she had been carrying around for so many years. By shouting, weeping and grieving,

Elaine was able to work through and come to an acceptance of her past, and to liberate the energy that had been bound up in keeping all this pain inside. At the same time, she needed to fill her emptiness with support, understanding and care from her individual and group sessions. Her feelings had to be recognised and validated, not labelled and dismissed. Finally she could turn to the task of redefining herself and her life.

Elaine's therapy also showed that her depression had to be understood, not just as part of a whole person, but as part of a whole system. She was involved in a network of relationships which included her husband, parents, children, brothers and sisters, friends, patients and hospital staff, and many of the interactions between these people were actually helping to maintain her depression. For most of her fifteen-year career as a psychiatric patient, this system was stable, if uncomfortable: various people continued to hurt and use her; Elaine continued to allow herself to be hurt and used; and the psychiatrists continued to admit her to hospital at regular intervals to administer the same treatment as before. Through her therapy, Elaine was made aware of this pattern and the way in which she had, in her own words, 'made a rod for my own back'. As she started to change her contribution to the pattern – for example, refusing to do her sons' laundry – other members of the system found that their roles were being challenged too. If, in certain instances, she was not willing to be the servant, they were no longer so clearly the masters. Change was forced upon them too.

When someone like Elaine starts off this process of change, two things characteristically occur. First, it becomes less clear who really is the 'patient'. Elaine and her family had long accepted the doctors' definition of her as the 'sick one' in the family. However, as she began to make sense of her depression and climb out of the passive, suffering 'sick role' to become more active and assertive, the problems in the rest of the family started to come into focus. Her husband, in particular, seemed to be or to become quite depressed himself. It began to look as if it had been part of Elaine's function to 'carry' the depression for both partners in the relationship. While she was the 'sick one', he could continue the familiar but limited role of strong, silent head of the family. As she changed and demanded more understanding and emotional support from him, it became apparent that he was completely unable to deal with his own or other people's feelings other than by blocking them off. Other members of the family had their difficulties too – the daughters tending to follow their mother's lead, and the sons to follow their father. In fact, it could be said that in some ways Elaine's depression had served the function of camouflaging the problems of the whole family.

The second characteristic occurrence is that there is strong resistance to change from other members of the system, who find themselves being challenged in very uncomfortable ways. Elaine's sons didn't want to do their own laundry; her husband was scared of acknowledging his own feelings; her brother was reluctant to admit he had been hurtful. Although they would doubtless all have said they would do anything to cure the 'illness' which had brought the whole family such unhappiness, a view of her difficulties which included a critical look at their own contributions was not so welcome. In fact, their reaction was to try and push Elaine back into the 'sick role' by labelling her new and assertive behaviour as 'hysterical' and 'crazy'. Thus their own investment in keeping her sick was revealed.

For Elaine, too, it was tempting to fall back into this familiar role, to keep quiet and struggle on as before, paying the price of needing future hospital admissions. Some people who become psychiatric patients actually prefer to stay in the sick role, with the compensating benefit of avoiding painful conflict. Many others stay in the role that psychiatrists and other staff assign to them because they do not get the help they need to break out of it. Either way, a false solution, a kind of unhappy compromise, is reached. No one is especially happy but, on the other hand, everyone can avoid facing certain painful issues. In such cases, the unresolved problem tends to be passed on, to reappear in future generations. This can be seen in Elaine's case. Elaine's daughters had learned to take over her role, stepping in to do the cooking, shopping and cleaning for the whole family, including their grown-up brothers. Possibly they too had unfulfilled emotional needs because of their mother's depression and absences during their upbringing. Their compliant behaviour allowed the men of the family to act selfishly and ignore other people's rights and feelings. All the children were thus set up to repeat the pattern in their own families: the men prepared to exploit, and the women to allow themselves to be exploited. In this way, the sins of the fathers (and mothers) are visited upon the sons (and daughters).

THE MEDICAL ANGLE

Let us now look at the part played by the hospital and its staff in Elaine's story.

In fifteen years and twenty-two admissions to two different hospitals, Elaine had come into contact with more than twenty psychiatrists, including three consultants, and a large number of nurses, occupational therapists and other staff. Some of the psychiatrists saw her simply as an unfortunate victim of a recurrent illness which caused her to become depressed. Most of the others would have agreed, if asked, that childhood experiences and family relationships play a part in depression; but with little or no training in psychotherapy, they did not have the skills to work out how this might apply to Elaine. In this they were no wiser than Elaine herself, who hadn't realised how her upbringing was still affecting her and blamed herself for everything, and who initially presented a picture of a happy family where only she was at fault. With a long list of other patients to be seen, it was easier for the psychiatrists to fall back on something they did know about: medical-style treatment consisting of diagnosis, hospitalisation and medication, all of which carried the implication that Elaine was suffering from some kind of mental illness. In Elaine's notes, the words 'depressive neurosis' or 'endogenous depression' appeared in the space left for diagnosis. Although details of Elaine's childhood were dutifully recorded by each of the many doctors who admitted her, no one was able to make sense of it in relation to her breakdowns; nor were the interactions between Elaine and her extended family investigated or discussed. In other words, Elaine's depression was treated, whether deliberately or in default of any alternative, not as part of a *whole person* and a *whole system*, but as an isolated phenomenon. Elaine and her family accepted the professional view that frequent admissions and permanent medication were the best hope of keeping it under control.

In fifteen years of pill-taking, Elaine had been prescribed the following drugs:

Stelazine	Tofranil
Largactil	Nardil
Melleril	Nomifensine
Procyclidine	Tranxene
Amitriptyline	Valium
Prothiaden	Mogadon
Tryptizol	Priadel
Tryptophan	Dothiepin

She also had ECT (electro-convulsive therapy or electric shock treatment) during which an electric current is passed through the brain, simulating an epileptic fit.

Elaine also received treatment on what might be called a behavioural level, that is, focusing quite simply on the activities, or behaviours, that she was unable to carry out. Here the equation seemed to be:

Problem: She says she can't cope with the household chores.
Solution: Make her do the household chores.

Hence she was assigned to cooking and household management programmes in occupational therapy, as well as art, pottery and discussion groups.

Clearly, Elaine's physical treatment was not particularly successful. Her doctors might have argued that she would have been even worse off without medication, which at least kept her going for a time, although Elaine herself said she was nearly always aware of depression lurking in the background. But there seems to have been general resignation to the fact that she would need to come into hospital regularly, and to be supported with medication – supervised in fortnightly or monthly outpatient appointments – in between. Since 1991 patients have had the right, except in some limited circumstances, to read their medical notes. However, since no one may quote from them without the permission of the health authority, some fictional examples based on typical real-life extracts will serve to illustrate how the 'medical model' approach works in practice.

In cases such as Elaine's, the accumulation of notes and letters tends to follow a predictable sequence. There will be a pile of memos from psychiatrist to GP monitoring progress and making minor adjustments to medication following the fifteen-minute appointment, along the lines of:

Dear Michael, re: Mrs Elaine Jones, I saw this patient of yours today in my outpatient clinic. Her depression is improved and she is doing rather well on Dothiepin 150 mgs nocte. I have suggested she reduces the Tranxene to 15 mgs daily. I will see her again in two weeks' time.

After some months or years of ringing the changes in this way, with no substantial alteration in the patient's condition, a slight note of desperation may creep in, although the remedy is still to prescribe more of the same treatment rather than to revise the treatment approach itself. One might then see:

Dear Michael, I saw Mrs Elaine Jones who is still complaining of severe depression, with associated early morning wakening, lethargy, and loss of appetite. Although I appreciate she has not done very well on tricyclics, I thought it might be worth starting her on Tofranil, possibly combined with ECT and/or admission at a later date if her condition seems to warrant it.

Or there may be a bald statement about recent stresses, without any suggestion that it might be useful or relevant to discuss the meaning and implications of these with the patient: 'Her son has recently left home to start a college course, and her elderly mother is ill. I will be seeing her again on . . . ' At this stage, there may be some grasping of straws, at the possibility that another physical cause will be found so that she can be put right, perhaps: 'She seems to be worse pre-menstrually, and I wonder if it would be worth referring her to Dr Smith for possible hormonal therapy.' Even a psychological hypothesis may be put forward, usually to be dismissed: 'One suspects that her marriage plays some part in her depression, but I am doubtful about the likelihood of change in that area.' A male psychiatrist's identification with the husband who also has to deal with this awkward woman may be revealed by such phrases as: 'Mr Jones has put up with his wife's outbursts with remarkably good humour over the years.'

Finally, a note of persecution creeps in. The patient has obstinately refused to get better, and someone who started off five years ago as 'this pleasant lady' may end up as 'this difficult woman' or worse.

If we look at the effect of the medical model approach on Elaine's depression, we can see that one result of ignoring the whole-person, whole-system approach is to deny that her feelings and reactions have any validity. It is not that she has reason to be depressed, or exhausted, or tearful – these are merely 'symptoms' of her 'illness'. This effectively traps her in her situation. She does not strive for change, because important professionals who know about these matters have defined her problem in such a way that she is prevented from realising that change is necessary. Her part is to comply obediently with the treatment that they prescribe. Indeed, the underlying message of giving pills to a patient is: 'Let *me* diagnose and treat this problem for you. Follow my instructions and you will be better.' This may be very appropriate for earache or 'flu, but for someone like Elaine it is not only not helpful, it is actually harmful. The final irony is that she even thanks the hospital for their treatment, and feels especially grateful to the consultant who discharged her, protesting, despairing, and unhelped, back to the very situation that was contributing to her problems in the first place.

As we have seen, the illness model also reinforces the family's natural tendency to exempt themselves from playing any part in Elaine's depression. Their need to see the entire problem as located in Elaine and her 'illness' is legitimised.

To summarise, Elaine's treatment not only failed to address the wider issues at stake, but actually ensured that they would not be addressed. It not only failed to help Elaine, it actually perpetuated her difficulties. Indeed, one could go further and say that the medical model approach not only perpetuates, but actually creates the difficulties it purports to solve because, as we have seen, Elaine's children are set up to carry the problem down the generations.

Elaine's story is all too common among people having psychiatric treatment. This is not to say that Elaine would have suffered the same fate everywhere. The standards of psychiatric practice vary, and there are some excellent wards, community centres and teams which offer a very good service to those in need. Nevertheless, the fact that the combined efforts of more than twenty psychiatrists and many other staff over fifteen years failed even to start to help Elaine make sense of her depression indicates that she was not just the victim of an unfortunate oversight. Nor is such treatment found only in the more backward asylums; most of Elaine's admissions were to a modern psychiatric unit in a district general hospital. She had in fact received fairly standard psychiatric care as practised in the majority of hospitals in this country. If this is so, how and why does it happen?

Part of the answer lies in the training that doctors, nurses and other psychiatric staff receive. Contrary to popular belief, most of these professionals are *not* primarily trained to understand people and their problems. Doctors are mainly trained to diagnose and prescribe, nurses to manage wards, occupational therapists to run activity and discussion groups, and so on. If they do have additional skills in counselling or psychotherapy, these will probably have been gained on courses taken voluntarily after training or picked up on the job.

Another factor is that even the best efforts are compromised by working within the psychiatric system. Some of Elaine's nurses spent hours talking with her and some of her doctors would doubtless have learned to understand her much better had they not been obliged to move on every six months to fulfil their training requirements, or had they had more time and supervision. However, the overall policy towards a patient tends to sabotage whatever more constructive work may be carried out, unofficially, by staff lower down the hierarchy. By the time someone gets to be a 'known depressive', usually about their second or third admission, the chances of them getting treatment different from before become fairly remote – partly because success would challenge the correctness of the original decisions. As we saw, Elaine's consultant was reluctant for her to have psychotherapy, even though his efforts had not met with notable success. So, while individual members of staff may be trying their best to understand the patient as a person in a difficult position, their efforts will be undermined by the overall message that she or he is 'ill'.

Finally, the 'illness' model enables the psychiatric staff themselves, like Elaine's family, to avoid facing and sharing the enormous amount of pain that Elaine and others like her are carrying around inside them. They can distance themselves from their own hurts, fears and frustrations which might otherwise be stirred up. They do not have to confront the difficult questions that Elaine's anguish might raise about their own attitudes, families, beliefs, roles, and the society in which these things take place.

THE 'SEX ROLE' ANGLE

Let us look at Elaine's depression from yet another perspective, that of sex role expectations.

Elaine, like most people who are diagnosed as suffering from depression, is a woman.[1] One way of viewing her problems, and those of many of her fellow-patients, is that she was caught in the contradictions of the traditional female role.

Part of Elaine's dilemma was that she was expected to give without receiving enough in return, leading to a build-up of need and resentment. Believing that she ought to be able to cope with this, she blamed all her failures on herself, without questioning the role that had been thrust upon her. This was not just Elaine's particular misfortune, although she had had an especially rigorous training in it. Despite changing roles in recent years, women in general, especially older women and those from working-class backgrounds, are expected to spend their lives giving to others – their husbands, children and extended families. They are often defined not as individuals, but in relation to others – wife, mother. Even outside the family, the jobs that involve most in terms of giving, and return least in salary and status, are still held mainly by women – nurses, cleaners, primary school teachers, secretaries, childminders. When Elaine cried out, 'I'm not just a wife and mother, I'm me! I'm an individual! I've got to have some life of my own!' she was speaking not just for herself, but for her whole sex. The women who break down and come into psychiatric hospitals tend to be those who have adopted the traditional woman's role most completely.[2]

Behind every woman trapped in her sex role, there is a man trapped in his. The partner who presents to the psychiatric hospital is often the woman, since women in trouble characteristically become unable to *act* but are overwhelmed by their *feelings*. Men, on the other hand, who are generally less in touch with their *feelings*, but are freer to *act* in the world, are more likely to deal with distress by such means as drinking, violence and delinquency, and ultimately to end up in prisons rather than psychiatric hospitals. They may also manifest distress in physical illnesses. While Elaine followed the woman's pattern, her husband was prone to violent outbursts. As Elaine progressed, his inability to deal with his feelings in any other way became very apparent. His male conditioning did not equip him to deal with years of strain or to meet his wife on an emotional level. He was trapped too.

Again, the hospital served to reinforce rather than to challenge these complementary roles. As far as Elaine's husband was concerned, no attempt was made to allow for his feelings over fifteen difficult years, to encourage him to express them or to see his wife's desperation as anything more than the symptom of an illness. His part in the treatment was limited to meeting the doctors from time to time to discuss what was going to be done to his wife next.

As for Elaine, the hospital's message was quite clear. She was supposed to be able to cope with all her domestic duties without protesting. Indeed, successful treatment was defined in terms of her being able to return home and uncomplainingly continue the same activities. Obediently following this regime on the advice of experts, Elaine felt she had no one but herself to blame when she did not get better, and yet more guilt was added to her despair. In this too she was following the pattern of the rest of her sex, who characteristically blame themselves, their inadequacy, their weakness, their stupidity, their weight and their appearance, rather than question the obligation to meet these standards in the first place.

Hospital staff, like Elaine's family, often resist healthy assertiveness in a person who is taking steps towards real recovery. Someone who sits miserably but quietly in a corner, taking their medication regularly, is easier to deal with than someone who is prepared to disagree, protest and complain. Staff may show their resistance in the same way as Elaine's family did – by pushing her back into the 'sick role'. Patients are likely to acquire labels like 'aggressive' and 'paranoid' if their behaviour becomes too challenging.

What might be called the 'depressed housewife' syndrome, with variations, makes up the everyday bread-and-butter work of psychiatry. The unlucky ones will be getting exactly the same treatment as Elaine.

If traditional psychiatry fails these women so badly, as I believe it does, then it does little better with other categories of patient – people who have acquired the labels of schizophrenia, obsessional-compulsive disorder, manic-depression, anorexia, and so on. A recent survey found that 40 per cent of psychiatric in-patients had previously been admitted within the same year; 13 per cent had had another admission within the previous six weeks.[3] For a substantial proportion, this will be the start of a pattern lasting twenty or thirty years. Such a situation would be unacceptable in any other branch of medicine. Yet a psychiatric admission costs £50,000 per person per year, and overall treatment costs of psychiatric disorders run at an estimated £4.2 billion a year.[4] Why are such enormous sums expended on methods that are not only ineffective, but damaging? I have indicated some of the reasons why this state of affairs continues. A fuller answer takes us on to the rest of the book.

Chapter 2

The Rescue Game

There are many misconceptions about people who receive a psychiatric diagnosis. Surveys show that although people believe that they deserve sympathy and the best possible treatment, a significant and apparently growing minority also believe that they are potentially violent and dangerous, and may pose a risk to others in the community.[1] An international study found that 'schizophrenia' was ranked fourth of forty diseases in terms of stigma, after rabies, alcoholism and drug addiction.[2] This damaging and inaccurate picture is reinforced by the media, where even quality newspapers frequently run headlines such as 'Schizophrenic raped three' and 'Schizophrenic killer given probation',[3] which would rightly be condemned as racist if they contained the phrase 'black man' instead. In fact, black people, and particularly black men, may be doubly demonised: articles on homicides by psychiatric patients are often illustrated by pictures of black men, although four out of five perpetrators of these crimes are white.[4] Such reports are never balanced by less dramatic, but much more representative, announcements such as 'Psychiatric patient settles peacefully into the community'.

The Glasgow Media Group analysed media items dealing with mental health issues and found that the theme of violence to others accounted for 66 per cent of all coverage in the sample month. Sympathetic stories, in contrast, made up only 18 per cent of the items. In exploring the impact of these messages, they found that two-thirds of their audience sample believed that mental illness was associated with violence, and most gave the media as the source of this belief. Worryingly, such beliefs sometimes prevailed even when contradicted by personal experience of those diagnosed as mentally ill. The researchers concluded that 'the media can play a significant role . . . in fuelling beliefs which contribute to the stigmatisation of mental illness'.[5]

DOI: 10.4324/9781003095958-2

Campaigning groups such as the Schizophrenia Media Agency[6] have been formed to counteract this kind of press coverage. But what is the real risk of being murdered in a 'frenzied attack' by a 'mad axeman' released from the local asylum? There were 699 homicides in 1995, of which 32, or 4.6 per cent, were carried out by mentally disturbed suspects.[7] The risk per year of being murdered (by anyone) is one in 100,000.[8] Given that only a very small percentage of murders are carried out by those with a psychiatric diagnosis, the risk of being killed by someone with a mental health problem has been estimated at only one in 2,000,000 (compared, for example, to a risk of one in 25,000 of dying in an accident at home[9]). Nearly all these homicides are of family members;[10] although horrific for all those involved, this is not consistent with the picture of widespread random attacks on total strangers. Contrary to alarmist reports, there is no evidence of an increase in such incidents since the introduction of community care, despite the fact that the rate of homicides in general has risen; in fact there has been a small decline.[11] While tragic events do occasionally happen, and are rightly investigated so that lessons can be learned from them, there is no justification for stigmatising a whole group of people, or for condemning the policy of community care on these grounds.

Far less attention is paid to two important ways in which a diagnosis of mental illness clearly does have links with violence. One is the risk of suicide, which has been estimated to be up to sixteen times the rate in the general population.[12] The other is that the very people most often seen as *perpetrators* of violence are in fact more likely to be *victims* – previously in their lives, they are disproportionately likely to have suffered physical and sexual abuse.[13] And in their present daily lives, nearly half can expect to be publicly harassed, attacked or abused (for example, having local gangs spit at them and call them 'nutter', or finding dog faeces pushed through their letterboxes) simply because they have a diagnosis of mental illness.[14]

The vast majority of people using psychiatric services, then, are ordinary men and women who are temporarily overwhelmed by a complex mixture of emotional and social problems. On making contact with the psychiatric services, they are given a diagnosis in accordance with standard medical practice. The main division is into psychotics (people who are out of touch with reality, or in a layperson's terms 'mad') versus neurotics. Under the first heading come diagnoses such as schizophrenia, manic depression and paranoia. Under the second heading would come agoraphobia, obsessive-compulsive disorder, most cases of depression and anxiety, and many others. In order to get a clearer picture of what actually goes on in psychiatry, I propose to look at groups of patients, not according to their diagnosis, but according to how they use the services and how the services characteristically respond:

1   There is a group of people who are asking for help with problems that are really relationship and family issues. Elaine Jones is an obvious example.

2   There are people who ask for help with problems which, while still involving those around them, are not primarily to do with current partners or family relationships. An example might be someone who has been bereaved, or who is a victim of rape or sexual abuse, or who has had an accumulation of stressful life events.

3   There are other people who, usually for lack of alternative options or more appropriate forms of help, opt for the career of psychiatric patient as the only escape from painful situations in their lives.

4   There are those who use the hospital or out-patient services mainly to meet social or economic needs, perhaps because they are lonely and isolated or have no suitable place to live. Hospitals may also be used for what is often called 'time out', or respite. For example, an exhausted mother might come in for a break, or a disturbed adolescent might be admitted for a week mainly to relieve his parents. However, pressure on beds means that such admissions are far less frequent than they used to be.

5   There is a group of people who are suffering from conditions of definite physical origin, such as senile dementia, Huntingdon's Chorea and severe head injury.

6   Finally, there are more extreme examples of the first category, where family relationships are so intense and entangled that one person in the system breaks down very severely.

Obviously these divisions are very rough, and many people will cut across several of them. There are typical diagnoses for some of the categories – 'schizophrenia' is often the choice for the sixth group – but by using these categories rather than medical diagnoses as a guide, I hope to show what the psychiatric services actually do in response to people's overt or covert requests. The people who fall into categories 3–6 will be discussed in subsequent chapters. Meanwhile, we shall look at the first group.

PEOPLE WHO ARE ASKING FOR HELP WITH PROBLEMS THAT ARE REALLY RELATIONSHIP OR FAMILY ISSUES

The 'depressed housewife' is the classic example of this type. She may be middle or working class, and may be treated as an in- or out-patient, producing many variations on the same theme. Let us look briefly at another depressed housewife fifteen years after her first breakdown.

Susan's story

Susan Smith is 58, a frail, timid, anxious-looking woman. She has been in and out of hospital for many years. Her admissions have usually been precipitated by complaints from her husband, Bill, that she is not keeping up with the household chores. He makes an out-patient appointment for her and brings her along, complaining forcefully about this and various other 'symptoms', such as her irrational fear that he is about to have an affair. She looks nervous and tearful, agrees she is depressed, and is admitted and medicated.

After many years of this treatment, a discussion in the team meeting led to a different attempt to help. In accordance with current practice, the team had been trying to avoid admission by assigning Susan a community psychiatric nurse to visit her and offer her support at home. This had not worked. At the most recent out-patient appointment, Bill angrily insisted that his wife needed to be kept in hospital for the rest of her life. However, the nurses commented that as soon as she arrived on the ward, Susan brightened up, settled in extremely happily, and showed no signs of depression. The clear indication was that the problems lay in the marital situation rather than simply in an 'illness' suffered by Susan. A member of the team agreed to see the couple, not, this time, to pass a medical judgement on the wife, but to find out more about the marital relationship.

There were two sessions, both dominated by Bill. This large, well-built man loudly accused his thin, timorous wife of under-feeding him, of neglecting the housework and of having an irrational fear of his being unfaithful. He talked down to the therapist and demanded to know what she was going to do to improve the situation. The therapist, feeling rather overpowered, tried to point out that change would have to come from them both, and that Susan might have her point of view too. But Susan, who sat in tremulous silence throughout these outbursts, could not take advantage of this invitation to voice her opinions. She seemed to have been completely cowed by years of submission and the therapist found out that she was fighting Susan's battle for her rather than helping her fight it for herself. Meanwhile Bill frustrated all attempts to get him to listen to his wife by interrupting and loudly insisting that he had always tried every possible way to help. The therapist was only able to claim the limited success of blocking his demand that Susan should once again be admitted to hospital. The opportunity to work on the relationship problems seemed to have passed many years ago.

Here again we see how medicalising a relationship problem heavily reinforced the unhealthy aspects of the marriage – the husband's bullying dominance, which was the counterpart to his wife's cowering submission. If the problem had been seen in a whole-person, whole-system way right back when it started, it might have been possible to do some constructive work with the couple. Alternatively, if the hospital had refused to get involved at all, the resulting crisis might have forced change to occur. But by taking an unhappy middle line, defusing each periodic crisis by admitting Susan without actually taking any steps to deal with the underlying problems, the hospital played a crucial role in helping to maintain this destructive relationship exactly as it was. It was the necessary third player in this unhappy game.

Again, the values of the traditional woman's role were accepted without question. The husband's complaints were accepted at face value, although it emerged in the sessions that one reason for Susan's so-called irrational fear of his being unfaithful was his continual threat to be exactly that if she did not pull herself together. Indeed, the therapist strongly suspected that he was already having affairs, and that his demands for his wife's hospitalisation coincided with times when it would be convenient to have her out of the way. However, by the time a more community-based, psychotherapeutic approach was available, the situation was too entrenched for change.

Not very long ago, Susan might have become one of the long-stay patients whose world is bounded by the grounds of a large Victorian asylum, where years of case notes slowly accumulate in the files. In today's world, community teams who inherit such cases are likely to be involved in a long, demoralising struggle with the legacy of the earlier medical approach. And because community teams still incorporate many elements of the medical model – for example, the use of diagnoses and medication – the overriding messages are still likely to be the 'illness' ones that are keeping the situation so stuck. From a nursing point of view, this can be extemely frustrating, as one researcher observed:

> In contrast to the ward, where the nurses had collective responsibility for dealing with a group of patients within a ward environment dominated by the ethos of organic psychiatry . . . the community nurses were heavily committed to the idea of establishing a personal relationship with their patients and helping to resolve their problems through individual psychological counselling . . . [However], the social role of the mental health system in modern society ensured that the contradictions and stresses which often led the ward nurses to withdraw from patient contact were recreated within the community setting . . . The community nurses' failure to perceive the underlying continuities within the structure of the mental health system could cause them to respond to changes in their work with initial enthusiasm followed by growing disillusionment.[15]

THE RESCUE GAME

There are two predominant models or ways of viewing mental distress in psychiatry, one official and one unofficial. The first is the medical model, and second might be called the 'pull-yourself-together' approach. They combine very destructively to take away responsibility from the identified patient, and then to blame them for their helplessness. We saw with Elaine and Susan how the medical view initially encouraged them and their relatives to see them as helpless victims of an illness unconnected to the rest of their lives, which meant that the psychiatric services had to step in and take responsibility for them. Logically, when this fails to help, as it inevitably does, the conclusion should be either that the illness is more severe or complex than had at first appeared, or that something else is going on. In general hospitals, patients do not get blamed for suffering from incurable illnesses or being misdiagnosed. In psychiatric hospitals, however, the suspicion that psychological and/or social problems are involved tends to manifest itself in a gradual switch from pitying to blaming the patient. The same process can happen outside the hospital as well, with clients who are seen by the community mental health team. They turn from 'mad' to 'bad' and come to acquire one of the many diagnostic labels reserved for people whom the staff do not know how to help: hysterical, attention-seeking, manipulative, immature, inadequate, aggressive, histrionic. At this point, the person may be abruptly discharged. They are then in a much worse state than before: they have been encouraged to hand over control and responsibility to the psychiatric services and to look to them for a solution, and have then been blamed for the service's failure to provide one. What they *are* left with is the original problem plus confusion, a sense of failure, possible dependence on medication, and a psychiatric label.

The process can be illustrated by a concept from the school of therapy called Transactional Analysis. Transactional Analysis analyses many of the interactions between people as games with predictable outcomes, in which set roles are adopted by the participants. One common example is the Rescue Game, in which the two players take turns to adopt the three main roles of Rescuer, Persecutor and Victim (see Figure 2.1).

'Rescuing' occurs when one person needs help and another person tries to help them. The Rescuer, however, fundamentally believes that people cannot really be helped, and cannot help themselves either. The corresponding position of the Victim (or patient) is: 'I'm helpless and hopeless – try and help me.' The Rescuer responds to this challenge by stepping in and taking over the responsibility for the Victim. Rescuing does not work and the Rescuer soon begins to feel angry with the Victim for being so helpless and hopeless and switches to Persecuting or punishing ('This manipulative patient . . . '). Or the Rescuer may end up being Persecuted by the Victim, who gets angry at being treated as less

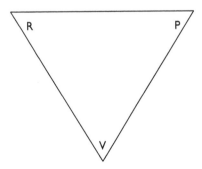

Figure 2.1 The drama triangle
Source: Adapted from S.B. Karpman, 'Script drama analysis', *Transactional Analysis Bulletin* 7 (26) (1968), 39–43

than equal, and may get his or her own back by making awkward demands, taking up staff time, and so on. Or, like Elaine, the patient may Rescue the staff by pretending to be better. (Rescuing was, of course, a lifelong pattern for Elaine.) The theory says that each player will occupy every position in the game at some time.

What the three positions have in common is that none of them can be a basis for relating to others as equals. You are either all-powerful or helpless. Some careers – nursing, medicine, the helping professions in general – are particularly suited to those who wish to play a lifelong game of Rescue. The medical profession, with its emphasis on power, status and specialised knowledge, provides an excellent basis for Rescuing if that is what a person wants to do.

In her research on stress in mental health nursing, Jocelyn Handy describes very clearly how nurses can get caught up in the contradictions of the system and, lacking a wider analysis of the situation, end up blaming the patients:

> The patient . . . was an ex-school teacher in her early thirties who had been diagnosed as manic-depressive and was being treated within an organic model involving the long-term administration of lithium salts. The patient definitely exhibited quite severe mood swings . . . Whilst these symptoms may have had an organic basis, the nurse's comments indicate that the patient's behaviour also seemed to be influenced by a number of social factors which were not being dealt with because her problem was officially conceptualised in biological terms. In this instance, the main precipitant of a severe mood swing seemed to be a serious row with her boyfriend which had involved him threatening to leave her. The patient's hospitalisation had always reconciled the couple and provided them with a needed respite in which to re-negotiate their relationship. However . . . the long-term effect of this was that the hospital had become involved in their relationship as a third party which simultaneously bound the couple together and made their relationship more unstable by ensuring that both partners could relinquish responsibility for their acts and blame the patient's illness for the problems in their relationship . . . The nurse's description of this patient indicates that she experienced some confusion and frustration about this case. While she was obviously aware of the effect of the patient's personal relationship on her behaviour, she did not seem to consider the effects of the more general mental health context beyond claiming that the patient always 'played the sick role' to manipulate an admission. This statement then

seemed to strike the nurse as too extreme and she immediately qualified it by affirming in another part of her diary that the patient had 'genuine mood swings' which were stabilised through lithium. The nurse's attempts to explain the patient's behaviour thus oscillated rapidly between an individually-oriented psychological model in which the patient took full responsibility for her actions and a medical model in which the patient had no responsibility . . . She later commented to me, rather bitterly, that the patient 'was never satisfied until she's proved she's ill by making you give her an injection' . . . The nurse's descriptions of her interactions with other patients illustrated the same problems and indicated that the paradoxes of the mental health system coloured most of her relationships with them.[16]

In psychiatry, the switch from Rescuer to Persecutor, from 'this patient is mad' to 'this patient is bad' is seen all the time. Some people present themselves as Victims at first assessment. Some are pushed into the Victim role by the process of medicalising their problems and gradually become more helpless and dependent on the psychiatric system, which in turn gradually becomes more Persecutory as harsher remedies are tried out.

This is not to say that Rescuing is always inappropriate. In emergencies – after an overdose, perhaps, or in the relatively rare instances where someone's mental state puts their own or other people's safety at risk – it may be necessary for someone else to take total responsibility for a short while. But in the long term any successful attempt to help people to change needs to be based on a treatment contract drawn up by both parties as equal and responsible agents. This flies in the face of all the usual assumptions about the capabilities of those who are called mentally ill. There will be further discussion of this issue later (pp. 59–61). Meanwhile, we can illustrate many of the themes we have been discussing by looking at how the psychiatric system characteristically intervenes in particular situations.

PEOPLE WHO ASK FOR HELP WITH PROBLEMS WHICH, WHILE STILL INVOLVING THOSE AROUND THEM, ARE NOT PRIMARILY TO DO WITH CURRENT RELATIONSHIP OR FAMILY ISSUES

Linda Hart's moving and compelling account of nine months in a psychiatric hospital, originally written as a diary, won the MIND book of the year award in 1995.[17] I quote extracts from it below.

Linda's early life was extremely difficult. Her biological father was married to her mother's mother, who looked after her while her mother went out to work. Linda was the youngest of six children and brought up in poverty. Her father was violent and a heavy drinker, but he did show Linda special affection, which made her siblings angry and envious. She received little attention or warmth from anyone else. When she was three, Linda found her father dead in the lavatory.

As an adult, married with two sons, Linda became, in her words: 'some kind of Wonderwoman', working full-time, running and renovating a large house, and taking an active part in her local community. Perhaps inevitably, she broke down and was diagnosed as 'schizophrenic' although she believed that she was actually suffering from severe depression. After many years of admissions, her marriage ended. She was working part-time for Social Services in a mental health project when familiar feelings began to recur:

> Gradually, high spirits and extravagant behaviour tipped over the line. I started getting up at 4 a.m. and couldn't relax during the evenings . . . That Wednesday evening . . . things began to turn. I was sitting in the kitchen and smelled the maggots in the rotting flesh in my stomach. I could hear my father's voice abusing me, saying I was nothing but a heap of shit and I deserved to die.

Her consultant psychiatrist visited:

> I didn't want to go into hospital but Graham [the consultant] said he was going to call for an ambulance and if I didn't go voluntarily then he would get my G.P. and I would be sectioned [that is, admitted against her will] . . . Walking the short distance from my gate to the ambulance made me feel very humiliated and I dared not look around to see if I was being watched by anyone.

On the ward, Linda battled with overwhelming feelings of despair and anguish. Some of the staff were very caring; others were less so:

> Last night was very difficult. I could see holograms on the chairs and floor. I spoke to Peter the nurse who tried to help me in my distress. I told him I felt very unsafe. It's as if I have a black stone inside me which continues to cause me despair and torture and has not really shifted an inch.

In her distress, relationships with the staff assumed enormous importance, and stirred up very powerful feelings:

> Yesterday . . . I became extremely distraught. It centred around the way Laura was treating me. She didn't actually do anything but her manner was very distant, curt and abrupt. At lunchtime I became overwhelmed by the feeling that everyone on the ward, staff and patients, thoroughly hated me . . . My father jumped on the bandwagon and told me everyone hated the sight of me and they were all fed up because I wasn't better. I feel very much in need of love and care but find it difficult to accept because I also feel unworthy. I have a degree of charm which people fall for but what they don't know is that I'm full of shit and maggots and putrid flesh. Someone take care of me, I'm very young . . .

Although she needed the ward, many aspects of institutional life were hard to bear:

> Here on the ward the room for smoking in is really grotty. It's yellow from nicotine; the chairs all collapse under us; the TV changes channels by itself and has to be hit on frequent occasions; the carpet and coffee table are dirty and there's an extractor fan which makes a terrible droning noise . . . Things are always running out, like Flora and marmalade, butter, jam and toilet paper and tea bags and sugar and tissues.

The petty restrictions added to her feeling of powerlessness as a psychiatric patient:

> They employ catering staff to stand by the bowls of cereal to make sure you don't take two Weetabix . . . I asked [a nurse] if I could have my medication early so I could go to bed. He tried to argue

that I had to wait till ten because it's better not to do it in dribs and drabs. I said it has taken longer for him to argue than it would have been to hand out the pills. Then I got really angry and said it was humiliating for me at the age of 47 years to have to beg to go for a walk and to ask if I can go to bed.

She was also on very large doses of medication, which produced severe side-effects:

If I sit in a car seat or in an armchair my back muscles go into spasm and I arch my back. This is very uncomfortable and means I can't relax in an easy chair and sitting in a car for long periods is most uncomfortable. Then my stomach is very distended. It sticks right out and starts from under my breasts and goes right down so that I look eight months pregnant. I'm lactating [another effect of the drugs], so my breasts are enlarged. I have electrical sensations in my limbs, which make me jerk and twitch. My nasal passages are blocked so I breathe through my mouth, which gawps and makes me look like an idiot. My head feels fuzzy and I'm distanced from people and find sustained conversation a strain. My toes spread and in sandals this looks weird. I'm constipated, tired and very unhappy with my lot. [Her consultant decided to increase her medication yet again.] Afterwards I slumped into a deep depression. I saw Laura and couldn't make much sense of what she was saying because I was emotionally overladen. I felt a terrible fear about the medication but when I saw her later I realised that the fear was a projection. I felt unsafe myself and converted that into being afraid of the staff and to thinking they were trying to kill me with drugs.

In deep despair at her inability to escape her father's voice, Linda made a very serious suicide attempt and was found only just in time. Afterwards various nurses came to see her:

Christine came to special me [that is, to keep her under close observation]. She looked hostile. She said I was selfish, had betrayed her and when I cried she said she had no compassion whatsoever for me . . . Chris, the ward manager, kept away for several days and when he did come in he looked serious and said he had felt angry with me. Laura was also serious and said she felt very upset. I was kept in isolation in the room, only using the loo and the shower en suite. The nurses had each other in their teams, I had nothing. Only my nightie. Jack, who had more to lose than anyone, did not accuse me. He was forgiving and kind and gentle . . . I felt beaten, hated, abused . . . I did try to argue that because I was on a Section 3 [that is, detained on hospital against her will], legally I was not responsible for my actions. They told me over and over again that I couldn't go home and leave the ward because I wasn't considered responsible; but when it came to the hanging, suddenly I was considered responsible . . . I was taking instructions from my father. I had no resources left in my battle against him.

Linda was temporarily transferred to a locked ward, supposedly a safer environment for her. Here, there was little attempt to provide anything more than physical security. Linda felt rejected, terrified and punished:

I started wandering around the ward crying and terribly distressed. The nurse, Bridget, said I had to sit down and talk. I thought to myself I would never talk to a single soul again. How could I trust anyone? Eventually they made me take extra medication, but that didn't have any effect. Then Margaret came and held my hand. That was what I needed.

Very gradually, over a period of months, Linda started to emerge from her despair. She started to make sense of some of her experiences:

The emotions I've experienced [over some incidents on the ward], which are to do with doing something wrong and not being forgiven, have a deeper origin, I think . . . On reflection, I think it has to do with rejection, because when you are rejected by significant people you do feel you have done something wrong, or at least, you are unlovable and to blame. I can remember two occasions of significant rejection. One was my father dying and two was when Gordon [her ex-husband] told me he was leaving me to set up home with Ann. I think the first occasion was very traumatic and I've never really faced it. To find my father dead; to never get him back again; the finality; the panic and fear; to feel responsible for it; to feel guilty and to blame; and he never forgave me for finding him dead on the toilet with his dentures falling on the floor . . . I have never mourned his death, which is why he's still alive. I need to lay him to rest, but can I let him go? Isn't a tormentor better than a void? I wish there was somebody here to hold my hand.

Linda was eventually discharged and was successful in arguing for community-based help; she would be supported at home, and would have weekly visits from Laura, her nurse from the ward, for counselling sessions to explore the meaning of her 'symptoms' and experiences, and in particular the unresolved relationship with her dead father. Although there is a long way to go, she feels she is finally getting the kind of help she needs.

Linda's story is a further illustration of the themes we have been discussing so far. Although it might seem intuitively obvious that Linda had good *reasons* for breaking down, the medical approach on which her treatment was based saw her distress as an *illness*, which turns her experiences of feeling maggots in her stomach, hearing her father's voice and so on into *symptoms*. On this model, discussing the *meaning* of these experiences is as irrelevant as analysing the speech of someone who is delirious. Indeed, the traditional teaching has been that to do so is actually harmful to the patient; Linda's consultant advised her at one point not to look too deeply into herself. The main aim of her treatment, then, is to *suppress* rather than *understand* her 'symptoms'.

The commonest way to try and eliminate symptoms is by prescribing drugs. In more extreme cases, more extreme steps are taken. On a previous admission, Linda had been given ECT (electro-convulsive therapy); contrary to popular belief, ECT is still used throughout Britain on about 11,000 people a year. The flaw in all these interventions is the assumption that removing or relieving the 'symptom' is the same as solving the problem. Since this is not the case, repeated rounds of medication and/ or ECT are usually necessary. Moreover, because real healing has not taken place, people may be unable to break their dependence on whatever is keeping them going – drugs, hospital admissions or ECT – and may become increasingly reliant on props that are steadily undermining their power to direct and control their own lives.

The Rescue Game is clearly at work in Linda's account. She was initially Rescued, or taken into hospital under the threat of compulsory admission, a decision that may well have been necessary at the time. However, the staff were very reluctant to allow her to step out of the patient/Victim role and play an equal part in decisions about her care. This, and the numerous petty restrictions of life on the ward, reinforced her sense of fear and powerlessness. Ironically, as Linda herself tried to point out, it was at her time of greatest need and despair that she was finally seen as 'responsible' and in fact blameworthy, as the staff Persecuted her for being desperate enough to try to kill herself. Such reactions are not unusual; one authority on suicide noted that in the build-up towards such acts: 'ward staff became critical of [the patients'] behaviour, which was construed as provocative, unreasonable, or over-dependent . . . Such alienation appears to have been malignant, in the sense that it gathered momentum inexorably and was associated with a fatal outcome.'[18]

Cruel and damaging as such responses are, they too have to be seen in context. In a setting based upon a medical rather than a psychotherapeutic model, little allowance is made for the feelings of the staff, who are left to struggle largely unsupported with the sometimes overwhelming impact of others' distress. And, as we discussed earlier in the chapter, staff too tend to be caught in the paradoxes of the mental health system: 'the dynamics of the psychiatric system are not those of "oppressors and oppressed" but of an institution manifestly failing to meet the human needs of both those it exists to help and those who labour within it'.[19] Damaging and Persecutory responses are the inevitable result.

Another inevitable consequence is that in ignoring the meaning of people's experiences, and failing to see them as part of a whole person and a whole system, the psychiatric services end up recreating the conflicts that lie behind their breakdowns. Coldness from the staff, who were caught up in their own reactions to Linda's distress, reinforced all her feelings of unworthiness and made her father's voice more abusive. Banished to a locked ward after her suicide attempt, Linda felt as lonely, rejected and punished as she had as a child. All aspects of someone's behaviour on the ward, or of their relationship to a community worker, can give vital clues to their difficulties, and can, if understood correctly, provide a unique opportunity for learning and growth. With insufficient training and support in psychotherapeutic approaches, staff all too often ignore or encourage compliant and passive behaviour, and Persecute anger or dissent.

What was also overlooked was the meaning that physical treatments had for Linda. Not only were the side-effects extremely unpleasant, adding considerably to her distress, but the fear of being persuaded or compelled to take larger and larger doses increased her distrust and fed into her beliefs about her father. Of course, medication can be very unpleasant in general medicine – chemotherapy for cancer, for example – and this isn't necessarily a reason not to prescribe it. Applying the same model in psychiatry, Linda's doctors presumably believed that the imposition of extremely powerful chemical compounds was justified by the urgent need to treat her underlying 'illness'. However, the analogy is false; Linda was looking for help, not with a physical state, but a mental one, and medication at these levels was actually making her mental state worse.

A psychotherapeutic understanding of Linda's difficulties would perhaps see the 'maggots' in her stomach as a vivid metaphor for her self-hatred, and her father's voice as expressing her guilt and confusion about his death. With the help of a counsellor, Linda has built on these insights. She believes that his loss, and the circumstances of his death, were simply too much for a three-year-old to bear. She also suspects that, abusive as he was, a bad father was better than no father at all in her hostile family, and that at some level she has been unable to let him go. Although she still hears his voice, she now feels more in control and less of a victim of these terrifying experiences.[20]

Unfortunately, although community-based teams can often offer talking treatments alongside other interventions, there tends to be little time or support for such work in hospital. This has been even more true in recent years, when the closure of beds has meant that only the most disturbed are admitted to hospital and there is constant pressure to discharge them as quickly as possible. In the words of a recent report, people who are admitted to psychiatric wards enter a 'care vacuum' where, instead of an individualised appproach, they are offered 'the same service, facilities and environment, regardless of their circumstances or needs, with only minor differences in therapeutic interventions'. In summary, 'hospital care is a non-therapeutic intervention' which may actually increase distress in the long term.[21] Even if psychotherapy is offered, it may actually be necessary to undo the effects of medical treatment before the original problem can be tackled; for example, Elaine and her family's view of her depression, and the way the family relationships were organised around these beliefs.

We can summarise the principles of two major models of understanding mental distress, the medical and the psychotherapeutic, as follows:

Medical	Psychotherapeutic
Deals with the 'illness'	Deals with the person
Problem is within the individual	Problem seen in relationship/ cultural context.
Looks at 'symptoms'	Looks at meanings
Need to categorise, relate findings to theory	Need to understand, form a relationship
Aims to return patient to previous state	Sees opportunity for learning and growth
Staff feelings marginalised/ ignored	Staff feelings acknowledged and supported, as central to the work.

Of course, in any enlightened medical setting there will be attempts to support the staff, form good relationships with the patients and see people in their wider context. However, this will be *in addition to* the real treatment – the operation, the medication regime and so on – and is perfectly appropriate for most physical illnesses. In a psychotherapeutic setting, where emotional distress is the focus, *the relationships are the treatment*. The healing comes not from medication (although it may help someone to cope), but from other human beings. Linda's story illustrates the point. In her greatest distress, she wanted to be offered, not pills, but a hand to hold. She was searching, not for the correct diagnosis, but for a way to understand her experiences. She is working towards healing, not with the aid of drugs – in fact, she is weaning herself off them – but with the help of a trusting relationship within which she can come to terms with her past.

Most contemporary psychiatrists would see themselves as using an 'eclectic' approach – that is, they draw from a number of different models, including psychotherapeutic ones, as appropriate to the situation. However, the above summary, and the stories we have heard so far, make it clear that medical and psychotherapeutic models are fundamentally incompatible. They start from opposing assumptions, give contradictory messages to patients and staff, and have different aims. It would be more accurate to describe the so-called eclectic model as unintegrated, in terms of its poorly thought-out philosophy and inconsistent application. An American psychiatrist describes his observations during training:

> I listened carefully to staff psychiatrists who made discontinuous switches back and forth between the two dominant paradigms [models] in discussion of a single case, within the same spoken paragraph, and I realised that psychiatry does not have a coherent, unified model or doctrine. In one instance, a psychiatrist was discussing a young man with schizophrenia from a biomedical . . . point of view. Suddenly, he lurched into a discussion of projection as the underlying mechanism for some of the man's symptoms; then after a couple of sentences, he as suddenly returned to his biomedical mode and vocabulary.[22]

This kind of confusion can be observed on a daily basis in psychiatry. For example, a young man is referred to the psychiatric team after the death of his father, and counselling is recommended to help him through his grief. However, as soon as he becomes tearful and low – a necessary part of coming to terms with his loss, from a psychotherapeutic view – he is prescribed anti-depressants, which suppress his feelings again. Community mental health teams have moved away from the hospital site, but since the medical way of thinking still runs in parallel with psychotherapeutic models, the same kind of muddle still follows. Clients who have suffered major traumas may be assessed as having a 'depressive illness' rather than an understandable emotional response, and be offered medication in parallel with counselling. Survivors of sexual abuse may find that therapy is only offered at the cost of acquiring a psychiatric label.

In my experience, the switch from psychotherapeutic to medical language has very little to do with the patient and his/her problems. It tends to occur when mental health professionals, and psychiatrists in particular, reach the limits of their own ability to see someone's distress in psychological terms and to bear the feelings that this stirs up. Since most professionals only have a very basic training in counselling, if any at all (see Chapter 7), these limits are reached fairly rapidly. Medical and/or Persecutory interventions are the rule for patients who are more distressed than the staff can bear, as Linda discovered. As one woman put it, 'I feel that, essentially, when a doctor prescribes a pill for me, it's to put *him* out of *my* misery.'[23]

The split in the treatment approaches can come to reflect the split in the patient: 'Can I bear to get in touch with my feelings, or shall I try and push them away?' Unless this split in the treatment is resolved, there is no chance of resolving it within the patient. He or she will simply become trapped in the mixed messages from the staff, who are themselves trapped in the mixed messages of the system they work in.

We have now seen numerous examples of the ways in which the main model of mental distress, on which psychiatry as a branch of medicine is based, that is the medical/illness model, undermines and opposes the psychotherapeutic one, often with disastrous results for patients and staff. However, the split is not just between different models of intervention. There is also a fundamental split between the way service users generally see their problems and the way their difficulties are seen by psychiatrists. When asked what made them break down, service users typically give this kind of response:

> I was depressed and upset following the death of my mother. We had a difficult relationship and I never felt wanted by her. While she was alive I felt she never loved me. After her death there was no chance to put that right. Also earlier abuse by a family member affected me and the relationship I had with my husband as a result.

Long periods of unemployment. Society in general saying that there was plenty of work to be had, so those out of work were seen as being lazy. Employers told you that you were no good by not employing you.

The direct issue was the loss of my baby. The indirect one was problems with my neighbours and my job.[24]

If I look back on what caused the depression and what caused me to try and take my life, it was quite normal, average things . . . a divorce, I had two children, I was three months pregnant when I left . . . holding three jobs down, mundane jobs, trying to keep it going really. I was worn out, absolutely worn out.[25]

In other words, despite the adoption of some medical terminology ('I'm diagnosed as manic-depressive', 'I was very psychotic at the time'[26]), service users tend to attribute their breakdowns not to *illness*, but to a variety of psychological and social *reasons*. The shorthand for this is a *psychosocial* understanding of mental distress; that is, a model which sees psychiatric breakdown as resulting from a mixture of *psychological factors* (mainly past and present relationship difficulties, and sometimes a spiritual crisis of values and beliefs), often accompanied by *social and financial problems*.

An eclectic psychiatric view would certainly see such factors as being relevant too; perhaps they were triggers for an underlying illness in rather the same way that stressful life events may lower your immunity to cancer. This is sometimes known as a vulnerability-stress model of mental illness, and is subscribed to by many psychiatrists. However, a survey of 516 service users emphasises the difference in viewpoint: 'It was not these factors which *led* to their problem; these *were* the problem. . . . Respondents saw their difficulties as meaningful in the context of their life experiences in regard to past disappointments, current dilemmas and future concerns.'[27] Their difficulties were complex and individual, and could not be reduced to simple diagnostic categories such as 'manic-depression' or 'anxiety neurosis'.

As many readers will be aware, dissatisfaction with what the psychiatric services offer has led to the rise of an increasingly active and vocal service user movement in recent years. Their protests make sense if there is such a mismatch between how service users and professionals view mental distress and the ways it should be dealt with. The above survey put it like this:

Being treated in a medicalised way, as if they had physical illnesses, formed the basis of negative evaluations and complaints on the part of most users in every aspect of their management. This ranged from a dislike of the aloof and cool attitude of psychiatrists during interviews whilst in-patients, to the rejection of physical treatments as a response to personal distress. In summary, the professional discourse and the lay discourse about personal distress are incompatible . . . In this light it is not surprising that our respondents felt misunderstood and aggrieved so often.[28]

It is consistent with these findings that service users described warm, caring attitudes and being treated with respect as the most appreciated aspects of their treatment. Counselling or psychotherapy was described as helpful or very helpful by almost three-quarters of those who had been offered it. On the other hand, a narrow focus on medication and diagnosis was disliked: 'They have a set diagnosis which they work to and treat [you] with ECT and drugs. They do not search out the reasons for your illness with you, so the illness just repeats again and again.'[29] Perhaps we should not be surprised that this survey found psychiatrists rated as the least helpful profession by one in five people, and the most helpful by only one in eight.

Other surveys of user views have produced similar results; for example, women who self-harm report that what they want above all is to be able to talk to someone who is sympathetic and supportive about their emotional and practical difficulties. What they are more likely to get from the psychiatric services is 'no help other than a hurried prescription for drugs' and dismissive or blaming attitudes; 96 per cent of them are dissatisfied with their hospital treatment.[30] Of those service users who spoke to the Mental Health Foundation, 401 said their main need when distressed was for 'someone to talk to', to be listened to and respected, to help them express and understand their feelings. This did not necessarily mean formal counselling sessions, although again these were rated very positively by those who had been offered them: 'Because I feel my mental illness had its roots in emotional damage . . . examining these things was more profitable than merely using drugs to contain it.' Although medication could also be helpful, people were clear about its limitations: 'A recurring theme is the failure of these treatments to take account of the whole person.' As one respondent put it, 'Medical treatments can be applied in an impersonal way, as though you are an object that needs re-moulding rather than a person with feelings and human needs.'[31] And a detailed investigation into the lives of discharged psychiatric patients uncovered the same themes in those trying to survive in the community. One person put it particularly clearly:

> A doctor treats a *patient* and he looks at it, he's patient-orientated and my contention is that I get mentally ill because of social problems . . . Although they tackle me and give me these injections and so on, it will continue to happen because of the social problems involved . . . If you like, I am the symptom of something outside, the cause is outside, whereas they would see the cause as me and if they solved me, solved my problem, then everybody else is all right. And so it's an eternal conflict!

As the interviewers noted:

> What participants looked for from psychiatrists was an approach that took account of their needs and concerns as persons, an approach in which . . . the prescription of anti-psychotic drugs was an adjunct to a psychosocial understanding of their predicaments rather than a substitute for such understanding . . . And it was here that their conflicts with the medical profession arose.[32]

If the above picture is accurate, and there is indeed an irreconcilable difference between what service users want and what the psychiatric system provides, between the *psychosocial* understandings and needs of those in distress and the *medical* assumptions and treatments of the professionals, then two results can be predicted:

1 recovery within the psychiatric system will be rare;
2 those who do recover will do so despite rather than because of their psychiatric treatment, and mainly with help from non-medical settings outside the psychiatric system.

There is evidence for both these predictions.

Anyone who has worked in psychiatry knows how unusual it is for people to recover completely and be discharged for ever. One psychiatrist who asked colleagues in a busy psychiatric unit to identify recovered patients for a research project collected only thirteen names in nine months, and even these people were still suffering from considerable problems.[33] Every ward has its complement of regular attenders who may have had up to twenty or thirty admissions over the years. The staff move on; the patients, on the whole, do not. Some of this can be attributed to the 'poor prognoses' of the 'illnesses' concerned, although there is intriguing evidence that 'schizophrenia', for example, has a much better outcome in non-Western, non-medical settings (see Chapter 10). The alarmingly high re-admission rate, as discussed in Chapter 1, confirms this depressing picture.

There has been remarkably little official interest in how service users do explain their recovery, if it occurs (although service users themselves have written on the subject[34]), but some patterns can be discerned. The people in the Mental Health Foundation survey had found alternative and complementary therapies very helpful, as well as a variety of coping strategies (exercise, keeping busy, having a regular routine, getting support from friends, and so on). Many of them found support from religious and spiritual beliefs. Others described how their lives were turned around by, for example, a stay in a therapeutic community. These are hospitals run entirely along the psychotherapeutic principles already described; a few of them exist in the NHS, usually under permanent threat of having their funds withdrawn:

> It was the most helpful psychiatric ward I was ever in. What made it so helpful was the ethos that we were all there to help each other. We had to agree to a written contract before we went in. We could leave at any time. No one took any drugs. The contract said some unusual things, for example, 'Free expression and exchange of views is desired so that we can learn about these reactions between people.' Also, 'The staff do not have all the answers, and they have their problems too. The patient is just as likely as the staff members to find a solution to one of the problems under discussion' . . . I was in this residential place for over three months, and came home transformed. It was like being brought up again. It was a lesson in love from fellow group and staff members. I carry the things I learned with me still.[35]

As we have already noted, not everyone wants or needs formal counselling or psychotherapy, and the woman quoted above, like many others in the surveys we have discussed, also found invaluable support from other service users and self-help groups:

> A friend's boyfriend had joined a self-help network . . . A few months later I hit a further low-spot of despair and went along to a meeting. I was greeted as an equal . . . No one was an expert; they'd all started where I was. Meetings were led in turn, all tasks were subject to election and time-limited, so all members quickly felt ownership

of the group . . . I cannot describe the difference between a self-help group based on mutual respect, and the mental health system where one set of people are the healers and get status and money for it, and another are the 'mentally ill', at the bottom of the hierarchy with less than equal citizenship, stigmatised, no power, barely enough money, seldom respected work, and sometimes no housing.[36]

Others echo these sentiments:

> I have the support of the tranquilliser project . . . and I work for them and we all help and encourage each other, support each other and it's brilliant. And you have to build back your self-esteem, your self-worth, it doesn't just happen . . . and I'm doing it now and it's fantastic.
>
> I had so much inspiration from other people who were further on [at a support group], and I really just got involved and started helping out there and becoming a bit more empowered . . . I just knew that's what I wanted to do, try and help other people in the way that that helped me.[37]

The survey of 516 service users noted that they tended to speak far more positively about voluntary sector provision (drop-in centres, clubs and groups and so on) than about the official services, because of the less formal and more equal relationships, the support from others in similar situations, and the chance to make an active contribution to the service.

The overall themes are by now very clear. A substantial proportion of users of the psychiatric services find them not only unhelpful, but actually damaging. The good work that does go on is undermined by the basic principles on which the service is run, which derive from the medical model of mental distress. Service users on the whole see their difficulties in terms that are not just different from, but incompatible with, these assumptions; this can be referred to as a psychosocial understanding of distress. Those who recover often do so despite, rather than because of, their psychiatric treatment, and with non-medical help from outside the psychiatric system.

All of this raises important questions such as: Why does psychiatry continue to operate in this way, if it is so unhelpful? Is there any evidence in support of these models and approaches? How can the situation be changed? However, before discussing these issues, we need to look at some further consequences of traditional psychiatric practice.

Chapter 3

The sick role

After everything that has been said so far, it may be hard to believe that the role of psychiatric patient has any advantages. Nevertheless, there are some people for whom it is the best available option in a desperate situation and who are prepared to go to considerable lengths to find their way into hospital. Once inside, they are often the most difficult and demoralising people to deal with. Typically they absorb enormous amounts of staff time and energy, acquire a whole assortment of diagnoses, run through every possible treatment, are discussed at numerous case conferences, and still fail to get better.

To understand how this comes about, we need to have a closer look at what it means to be called 'mentally ill' in our culture. First, we need to remember that being admitted to psychiatric hospital, or even having an appointment with a psychiatrist, is, to most people, synonymous with being mentally ill, a 'nutter' or a 'loony'. The very word hospital, with its complement of doctors, nurses, wards and medicines, implies that people who are admitted must be suffering from an *illness*.

Second, there are powerful cultural assumptions that go along with being diagnosed as ill. These have been summarised as:[1]

1 You are supposed to be unable to recover by a conscious act of will. You are not responsible for your disability, and 'can't help it'.
2 You are exempted from certain social obligations and commitments.
3 You are supposed to see being sick as an undesirable state, and want to get well.
4 You are seen as being in need of specialised help, which is obtainable by becoming a *patient*.

DOI: 10.4324/9781003095958-3

All of this applies to illness in general. Mental illness carries the additional implications that you have lost your reason, and are therefore probably unpredictable, impulsive and liable to behave in deviant ways.

What this adds up to is that the mentally ill person is *not responsible*. Absolute responsibility for that person therefore falls on the shoulders of the psychiatric staff and, in particular, on the doctors (who retain ultimate medical responsibility for a team's patients). To the extent that staff are influenced by the cultural image of mental illness, which is that of a Victim, they will be involved in taking absolute responsibility for, or Rescuing, their patients.

We have seen how this can be very destructive for people who are engaged in a genuine struggle to resolve their difficulties. However, for those who do not know how to resolve their problems, who cannot bear to face them and have few alternative ways of obtaining care, the illness role may be the most attractive option available. We saw how it was easier for Elaine's family to push her into the sick role than face up to their own part in her difficulties. Sometimes people in Elaine's position actively play along with this – it is easier for them, too, to accept an illness label. Sometimes they initiate the labelling process themselves by starting to act in a crazy way. Seeking help from an expert whose recommendations are to be followed obediently is a socially sanctioned way of dealing with all kinds of difficulties and distress, while the whole psychiatric set-up invites and reinforces crazy behaviour on the part of the patients.

Official entrance into the sick role is marked by receiving a psychiatric diagnosis and/or by crossing the threshold into hospital. Sick role players will therefore aim to get admitted, because they know that in the common cultural view this is equivalent to being mentally ill. One way of doing this is by getting admitted 'for assessment' or 'for observation', and then behaving in such a way that it is very difficult to discharge them. By this stage it is far too late for the doctor to decide that, on closer assessment, they are not ill at all. They now have a psychiatric history, and can tell people they come from St X's hospital. This is more than enough to label them as ill in the eyes of the general public, and they use the public, plus agencies such as the police and casualty departments, to put pressure on doctors to readmit them.

Once inside, there are benefits to be reaped which may, for the desperate, seem to outweigh the disadvantages. You can escape from painful conflicts and decisions outside. At the same time you can, if you play your cards right, gain care and asylum away from the pressures of the outside world, in a place where all responsibilities will be lifted from you. What is referred to by mental health workers as 'the community' – that is, everywhere that is not the hospital – often fails to live up to the cosy image that is implied. The community for many people is a bleak, lonely place of isolated bedsitters and queues in Department of Social Security offices. In contrast, the little communities that build up in hospitals, especially on long-stay wards in the old-style asylums in the days before hospital closures, can be lively and sociable worlds where people can find quite a comfortable place for themselves. One man contrasted his present existence, living in a vandalised flat with only his dog for company, with his previous stays in hospital:

> There is nurses to look after you all the time. Better facilities there than I have here – you can watch television and listen to the radio, go for walks round the grounds, go for a pint at night which I can't afford to do whilst I am paying rent for this place . . . They've got washing facilities, like washing machines and spin dryers, and you can go for a bath at any time you want, there's always hot water . . . I was getting three meals a day which I am not doing now and am surviving mostly on sandwiches till I get my electric on. This past four winters I have gone through hell, having no gas and electric.[2]

It is often unclear just how consciously sick roles are adopted. People who receive a psychiatric diagnosis are acutely aware of the expectations that go along with the role:

> The psychiatrist said I could use the hospital as an asylum, and I immediately thought of lunatics. I took that role on; 'Right, I'm a lunatic so I must be mad.' I broke some crockery on the ward because I thought if I am mad I can do that. That behaviour seemed to fulfil their expectations. It was an angry response; 'If they call me mad I will be mad.' . . . I met a friend who I still have, in that hospital, and we played at being mad by eating flowers and things like that.[3]

This is not to deny that these people are genuinely distressed – after all, such a desperate strategy implies an equally desperate situation in the first place – but to point out the inadequacy of medical model explanations of behaviour and reactions. 'Sick role' patients often end up trapped within this role and unable to break out of it even if it started off as more of a deliberate strategy. The nurses, the lowest members of the medical hierarchy, are the most likely to suspect game-playing while doctors are still juggling with treatments and diagnoses. Ultimately the only way to test out suspicions is to challenge the sick role. This is often very hard to do. But it is only by challenging the role that its hidden power is exposed, as Jeanette's story clearly shows.

JEANETTE'S STORY

Jeanette, a thin and unkempt women who looked much older than her forty-three years, had been very hard to cope with on the ward. She had good days and bad days but usually she would not get up, dress, wash, or eat without constant coaxing. She did not mix with the other patients or converse with the staff, except to say 'I don't know' or complain that the devil was making faces at her. Her difficult behaviour included incontinence, making strange grimaces, falling over (usually outside the nurses' office) and having to be picked up, and getting into the bath with all her clothes on. Her eyes were vacant, her movements slow and shaky, and her walk was slow and shuffling. She puzzled the doctors and frustrated the nurses.

It was difficult to piece together much information about her, but it was known that she had had an unstable upbringing as one of six children. Her first husband had been violent and her second an alcoholic. She had had various abortions, accidents and overdoses, and only one of her four children still kept in contact with her. Now she was divorced and living on her own. Jeanette's psychiatric career had started a few years previously, around the time of her divorce. She had been admitted to several other psychiatric hospitals, nearly always after a crisis in the community. The most usual routes into hospital were via the police or the casualty department. She would refuse to answer questions except with 'I don't know' or a vacant stare. Admission 'for observation' or 'for assessment' usually followed, with a query under the heading 'Diagnosis' in the files. Over the years, the following suggestions had been made: agitated depression; obsessional and neurotic personality; schizophrenia; personality disorder; depressive illness; pseudo-psychotic. She had also been given about ten different drugs, ECT, neurological tests and brain scans, none of which produced any improvement or threw any light on her problem.

When Jeanette moved house, she came into the catchment area of another hospital where, as described, her condition seemed to be steadily deteriorating. The familiar routine of changing drugs, ordering tests, and referring to other specialists for opinions was well under way with no obvious benefit at all.

Finally, the staff decided to take a new angle on the problems Jeanette was posing. Some of the nurses who had been involved with the tedious business of coaxing her through every step of the daily washing, dressing and eating routine had started to suspect that she might be exploiting her status as a mentally ill patient. They decided that they had two options: to stop trying to make her better in the face of her passive resistance and to transfer her to a long-stay ward, which was what she seemed to be angling for; or to challenge her sick role behaviour. They decided to challenge her role. The plan that was drawn up was: (a) that a date should be set for her discharge, and she should be informed of this and asked what help she needed to prepare herself and arrange accommodation and so on; (b) that the staff should consistently refuse to reinforce any of Jeanette's behaviour that fitted in with the idea of being ill – for example, they should not run to pick her up off the floor, or comment on her grimaces. Conversely, they should respond positively to responsible behaviour – for example, making an effort to hold a conversation with her when she turned up to meals.

It was predicted that if the staff suspicions were correct, Jeanette would switch from passive helplessness to active resistance in an attempt to restore the status quo. She would start behaving in a much more 'crazy' way to pressurise the staff into letting her resume the safer, more familiar role of mental patient.

Of course, it can be very hard for staff to put into action what might seem to be very heartless behaviour to a frail old lady – and Jeanette was always related to as an elderly lady, although in fact she was only in her early forties. The cultural view of mental illness which underlies nurses' training courses puts the emphasis on protecting and caring for patients, not confronting and challenging them. The distinction between being firm and Persecuting has to be made very carefully. Jeanette was not being denied help; in fact, the staff were prepared to go to considerable lengths to help her find somewhere suitable outside hospital and prepare her for greater independence. What they *were* denying her, in a firm but non-Persecutory way, was the option of a career as psychiatric patient under the guise of being mentally ill.

Any doubts that the staff might initially have felt about this plan were, however, dispelled as the predictions were rapidly fulfilled, confirming their suspicions and showing Jeanette's apparent helplessness in a very different light. She began smashing plates on the ward. In accordance with the plan, Jeanette was told that she was held responsible for this behaviour, that it was not acceptable on the ward, and that if it continued she would be discharged for twenty-four hours. Jeanette continued smashing plates. A place in a hostel was arranged for her, money was supplied, and a nurse was assigned to escort her to the bus stop. Jeanette's shuffling gait and shakiness had mysteriously disappeared – but as the hospital chaplain approached she suddenly collapsed on the ground in a heap. The chaplain stepped forward to offer this distressed lady assistance, only to be told briskly by the nurse that Jeanette was quite all right and was about to catch a bus. Meanwhile the local police, the casualty department, Jeanette's GP and her daughter had all been warned of possible trouble and told that Jeanette was to be treated not as ill, but as fully responsible for her behaviour.

That night, the psychiatrist on duty received telephone calls at regular intervals with news of Jeanette's progress through the town. At 1 a.m. the police rang; they had been called out after Jeanette had smashed the cupboard in her hostel room. Should they bring her into hospital? They were advised not to see this behaviour as a sign that she was crazy and needed admission, but to send her away. Several other police stations through the night, ringing in to say that they had a patient from X hospital who seemed to need admission, had to be given the same advice. So did the casualty department at 5 a.m. So did social services at 6 a.m. At 7.30 a.m., Jeanette's daughter rang in to report that Jeanette had arrived on the doorstep saying that she had no money; she was advised to take her in only if her behaviour was reasonable. A few hours before the twenty-four-hour deadline expired, Jeanette arrived back on the ward escorted by her daughter. She was once again docile, but the power and determination behind her supposed confusion, frailty and helplessness could no longer be doubted.

The staff had held admirably firm throughout the first skirmish, but Jeanette had not given up the fight. There were many further dramatic scenes both on and off the ward over the next few weeks. To cut a long story short, the staff held their ground and an all-round solution was reached when Jeanette accepted a place in a hostel for ex-psychiatric patients, run along family lines by a kind but very firm landlady who had clear rules for her tenants. They were expected to do their share of the chores, get out and about, mix with the other residents, and behave responsibly. Under this common-sense regime Jeanette, the formerly fragile, helpless patient, was transformed. She became sociable, outgoing and active. A few months later, one of the nurses was hailed in the street by a well-dressed, friendly, middle-aged woman. It was Jeanette, whose shuffling gait and blank expression had vanished.

Obviously, absolute consistency and firmness on the staff's part is crucial to a successful challenge. This is rarely achieved. More often, there is a mixed approach: some staff try to challenge the role while others reinforce it, with results like the following account.

ALICE AND GEORGE'S STORY

Alice Brown, aged forty, was admitted to hospital with a strange series of complaints. According to her husband, George, she had been throwing herself to the ground, hitting people in the stomach and trying to eat lumps of coal. At her assessment interview Alice sat in a rigid posture with glazed eyes fixed on the middle distance, answering 'I don't know' to all questions in a strange, vague voice. The consultant thought that her behaviour might be due to a brain tumour, and ordered a series of tests. On the other hand, it might be the sign of a psychotic breakdown, so he also prescribed the relevant drugs. In any case, he was certain that she needed to be in hospital.

One of the junior doctors, however, suspected that the underlying problem was a marital conflict. He and a nurse invited the couple to a joint session to see if they could get a clearer idea of what was going on.

George used the first half of the session to describe all the details of what he saw as his wife's mental illness. He answered all the questions addressed to his wife, insisted that she needed to be in hospital, and denied that there were any marriage problems. As the interview progressed, Alice became increasingly stiff and glassy-eyed. She professed in her strange, vague voice not to remember any of the incidents her husband described, including a recent one which involved her chasing him around the house with a broken bottle. The doctor found himself becoming irritated with both of them. Eventually he breached all the cultural assumptions about mental illness by bluntly insisting that, in his view, Alice was neither ill nor in need of hospital care, that she was quite well aware of her actions and (addressed to George) did not need George to speak for her.

The couple were both very startled. George protested, but the doctor held his ground, and gradually the whole tone of the interview changed. Alice reluctantly admitted to recalling some of the details of the chase. The nurse suggested that she had perhaps been feeling angry at the time. Alice confirmed this by producing a stream of accusations against her husband, changing as she did so from silent rigidity to furious resentment. George, though shaken, steadfastly maintained his position that he could not possibly blame his wife for irrational beliefs and behaviour that were obviously due to a mental illness. However, as the accusations continued, his annoyance became more and more apparent and soon the couple were in the middle of a blazing row ranging back over many years of accumulated grievances. The nurse commented that there was a great deal to be sorted out in the marriage, the couple were offered further meetings to help them do this, and both were sent home.

So far so good; but George and Alice were not going to be caught out that easily. A few days later, George by-passed the junior doctor and the nurse, who had agreed to be available in case of emergencies, and managed to arrange a home visit by the consultant. This, of course, was the best way for Alice to re-enter the sick role, and indeed after a few more bizarre symptoms had been described by George and demonstrated by Alice, she was readmitted for more neurological tests.

This put the junior doctor in a very difficult position. His attempts to tackle the problem at a marital level were being seriously undermined by the consultant going over his head to act in accordance with a medical model approach, and thus (in the junior doctor's view) colluding with both George's and Alice's desire to avoid facing up to their relationship difficulties. Whenever they wanted to avoid uncomfortable issues in marital counselling, they could choose an easy route into hospital again. At the same time, the doctor was very hesitant about challenging a senior colleague who had many more years of experience – and on whom, incidentally, he relied for a reference for his next job. He began to doubt his own judgement. Perhaps Alice really was ill after all, and needed a mood-stabilising drug to put her right.

The nursing staff, too, were left in an awkward position. Nurses do not generally decide who should be admitted and why; they have to stand by the psychiatrist's decisions. For at least some of them, being required to treat Alice as sick and in need of medication and her husband as irrelevant to the problem conflicted with their own observations and intuitions about the situation. Nevertheless, it is as rare for nurses to mount an effective challenge to a psychiatrist's decisions as it is for psychiatrists to provide an effective challenge to a patient's sick role. Nurses are left to work out their own unsatisfactory compromises on a day-to-day basis in the demoralising muddle of treatment approaches.

There were many more dramas over the next few weeks, involving the police (after Alice ran away from home in her nightdress), the casualty department (after she turned up there at midnight clutching an empty bottle of pills), and an assortment of Alice's and George's concerned relatives. An extremely complex history emerged of affairs, sexual problems and family feuds, all of which had previously been invisible behind the label of a randomly occurring mental illness. A consistent treatment approach was never arrived at. If the latest crisis landed Alice at the consultant's feet – and the couple seemed to be trying to ensure that it did – then more admissions, physical investigations and drugs were prescribed (with no improvement in Alice's mental state). The junior doctor and the nurse, meanwhile, tried hard to work on the relationship problems when the couple turned up for sessions, which they did not always do. Eventually the junior doctor's contract ended, he moved on to a different hospital, and the marital counselling was abandoned. After several more months of medical treatment something seemed to change and Alice stopped presenting herself to the psychiatric service, although no one knew quite how or why this had happened. It remains to be seen whether this apparent improvement will last.

Most commonly, however, there is little or no recognition of when or how sick roles are being exploited, with the danger that the person will follow an uninterrupted downhill path to chronic disability.

FAY'S STORY

Fay, aged sixty-three, had led a reasonably active and successful life until she was admitted to hospital, although she had always been a frequent visitor to her GP with various physical complaints. She had lived with her parents until her late thirties, but eventually married a man who took over most of the planning and decision-making for both of them. They had no children. He was nearing retirement, and she had already stopped work, when he developed an illness that was almost certain to kill him within a year. Fay became increasingly unhappy and preoccupied with physical complaints of her own. Her husband complained that he could not cope with her at home and, largely for this reason, she was admitted to hospital.

Having crossed the sanity/madness threshold, Fay rapidly deteriorated. On the first day, she evaded direct questions about her feelings and her husband's illness by voicing a string of complaints about backache and stiff legs; she seemed very unhappy, but was clearly spoken, rational and physically mobile. By the third day, nurses were reporting that she seemed to be 'picking up' some of the symptoms of the other patients on the ward. She had also started to limp. On the sixth day she refused to get out of bed, saying she could not walk. On the eighth day she refused to eat or drink. On the tenth day she told the doctor that she was mad.

To the psychiatrist, all this was confirmation of how right he had been to admit her in the first place. However, the nurses who had the day-to-day care of her insisted that she *could* walk, move and eat perfectly adequately, but just did not want to. Referral to an orthopaedic surgeon revealed no physical cause for her limp. The nurses were left with the thankless task of trying to restore Fay to an approximation of her state on first arrival, which entailed hours of coaxing her to eat, dress and take a few steps down the corridor, in the face of considerable passive resistance. She still refused to speak about her husband's impending death and became very agitated when the subject was raised, fending it off with renewed complaints about her aches and pains.

Fay became increasingly difficult to deal with. Sometimes she would emerge from the toilet extending hands smeared with faeces. Her husband's reaction was strange. The nurses noticed that on his visits he would urge her to sit down, take things out of her hands, and comment on how painful walking must be for her. What was his part in the whole set-up? Since no proper joint assessment was ever made, it is impossible to say, but it certainly looked as if he too had some investment in maintaining his wife's sick-role behaviour.

Three weeks after admission, Fay presented a pathetic picture. This formerly well-dressed woman sat trembling in a chair, her clothes and hair in disarray, slowly rubbing her stiff legs. Her face was closed off and vacant and her eyes were glazed. When approached she murmured in a small shaky voice, 'I've just got worse, mentally and physically, I don't know what's going to happen to me, it's a nightmare, my legs are so stiff, my back hurts, I can't walk properly, I'm going backwards all the time.' Asked about her husband, her trembling increased: 'I'm killing him – I can't cope with his illness – I just moan at him and drive him away – I'm so selfish – it's all my fault – I feel so angry inside, I don't know why – I'm terrified of what's going to happen if he dies . . . ' Despite the best efforts of the nursing staff, Fay continued to deteriorate mentally and physically. It is hard to imagine her ever being able to live independently again.

The stories of Jeanette, Alice and Fay bear all the hallmarks of people who have adopted the sick role. First, they had each been assigned to a bewildering variety of treatments and diagnoses, which in Jeanette's case came from several different institutions. The diagnoses varied wildly from organic (for example, brain tumour) to functional (agitated depression) while attempts at treatment ranged from ECT (Jeanette) to marital counselling (Alice) to physiotherapy (Fay). This is in marked contrast to the other people whose stories we have followed, who tended to get the same treatment throughout their hospital careers.

Second, they had all absorbed an enormous amount of staff time. While patients like Elaine and Susan tend to receive the most cursory discussions in the ward round ('Mrs Jones, a known depressive, was admitted again last night and has been started on anti-depressants. She had a good night's sleep and has been assigned to an occupational therapy programme'), many hours had been spent in fruitless debate about how best to manage Jeanette, Alice and Fay. Nurses had spent hours talking Jeanette and Fay through washing, dressing and feeding, and doctors had answered many midnight emergency calls on Jeanette's and Alice's behalf.

Third, there were the 'symptoms' which were both bizarre – eating coal, grunting, falling over, smearing faeces – and fluctuating, so that all three had periods when for no apparent reason they were rational and co-operative. These 'symptoms' did not fit clearly into any of the usual categories of mental illness – hence the difficulty in agreeing on a diagnosis.

Obviously, you cannot ask outright to come into hospital for an indefinite period in order to escape problems outside and with no commitment to confronting or resolving anything in your life. If you can find a way of entering the sick role, though, all this will be granted to you. To do this, you need to act in such a way that other people will see you as mentally ill and take you along to a psychiatrist, so that you can maintain your position of not being responsible for what is happening. If you are married, like Alice and Fay, you can use your partners in this way, especially if they are equally keen to avoid confronting the real issues. If your problem is a lot to do with isolation and loneliness, you may need to rely more heavily on agencies such as hostel staff, casualty departments and the police. Confronted by your Victim presentation, the psychiatrist will find it very hard not to do a Rescue and admit you.

Since mentally ill people are also seen, as we have noted, as unpredictable, violent and irrational, you will also be able to take advantage of your status by creating all sorts of havoc without being held responsible. For example, Alice, by presenting herself as sick, was not held accountable for chasing her husband with a broken bottle. It was also easier for him to see her behaviour as craziness, rather than as intense fury directed at him, so that he could take on the more comfortable role of concerned, sympathetic husband of a sick woman.

Of course, there are some disadvantages too. In keeping with the cultural assumptions about illness, you are supposed to see it as an undesirable state and to want to get well. You will be given all sorts of tests and treatments by the staff, which may be welcome in so far as they confirm your sick role, although you will also have to find a way of not benefiting from all this without arousing the suspicions of the staff. However, if the staff apply the most effective test of the genuineness of your illness and challenge your role, your resistance will become increasingly obvious. One strategy is to approach the psychiatric system from another angle, as Alice and George did when they bypassed the junior doctor to get to the consultant. Another is to raise the stakes in the game, and this shows very clearly the enormous hidden power of the sick role, and indeed of Victim roles of any kind. Thus, Jeanette and Alice were able to create huge crises in the community, knowing that the community would place enormous pressure on the doctors to comply with the cultural image of illness, take responsibility for them and admit them. Another powerful threat is that of suicide.

The other main disadvantage, from the patient's point of view, is that the reasons for the genuine distress which they are certainly experiencing cannot be openly expressed either, because it would give the game away. This distress often has a large component of anger. It became increasingly apparent that Alice was torn with fury, jealousy and resentment towards her husband, but presumably she could not bear to express this openly and face the conflict and the possibility of losing him. She therefore paid the penalty of having all her angry actions discounted and ignored by her husband and by most of the staff.

Jeanette's problems seemed to start around the time of her divorce, but she had to show her bitterness and anger at how life had treated her by indirect means, which still left her burdened with unresolved despair and resentment. Fay was perhaps faced with the most desperate dilemma. She felt totally unable to bear living without her husband. It was too painful to talk or even think about, and she resorted to expressing her distress in a way already familiar to her – through complaints about her physical condition. At the same time, she seemed to be overwhelmed with anger at being abandoned by him through death. But how could she express this rage to a sick man, or even fully admit it to herself? The result was terrible: she ended up driving him away even as he was dying, which only led to crippling feelings of guilt. This, at any rate, was what seemed to be going on. Looking to the future, the indications were that she would be quite unable to accept or mourn his death, but would remain paralysed by unresolved grief and anger.

From the staff point of view, these patients are extremely hard to deal with, no matter what line is taken. Even if the role is challenged, a consistent approach may be made impossible by the ever-changing rotas and shifts of doctors, nurses and students, to say nothing of the other patients. On top of this, staff will need to be able to tolerate the very high levels of anxiety that such patients create if challenged. In fact, the staff will be effective in direct proportion to the amount of anxiety they are able to bear. This is especially true of the psychiatrists, who will be held primarily responsible for the patient's behaviour by the community. They will need to withstand what will sometimes be intense pressure from relatives, GPs, the police and others, who may abuse and threaten psychiatrists who refuse to adopt their counterpart of the sick role and take total responsibility for a patient. Most psychiatrists do not like being addressed in this way, particularly by their medical comrades, the GPs, whom they often go to great lengths to keep happy. It is easier all round to admit the patient and let them and the rest of the staff bear the cost.

The category that includes Jeanette, Alice and Fay overlaps with the fourth group described at the beginning of Chapter 2, *those who use the hospital mainly to meet social or economic needs, or who come into hospital mainly for a break from stressful situations.* As we have seen, social problems are a factor in many people's crises, and social or respite needs are still, despite increased pressure on beds, the main reason for about one in ten admissions.[4] However, there is little evidence that psychiatric wards are tackling these problems. On the contrary, a recent report found that 'staff were aware that many patients left hospital with social problems that had not been addressed. Effectively, hospital stays patch people up before they are sent home again to the environment where their social problems originated, and where they are likely to resurface and provoke another crisis.'[5] The short-term benefits of warmth, meals and company are accompanied by the handicap of a psychiatric label, which certainly does not improve people's job prospects, and it is dishonest and humiliating to have to trade psychiatric 'symptoms' for shelter and company. Nurses, too, become frustrated at having to provide nursing care for people whose real needs are for something quite different. Neither is the use of hospital admissions for 'time out' very satisfactory; people whose main need is for a rest and a break end up acquiring a diagnostic label and a psychiatric history as well. Nowadays, when beds are reserved for the most seriously disturbed, wards are often so crowded and chaotic that there is little chance of recuperation.

However, while these ways of using the hospital are less common than they used to be, the psychiatric services have been slow to come up with alternatives. A model based on a greater appreciation of social factors in mental distress would see the development of supported employment and housing, social and self-help groups and so on as being just as important as diagnosis and medication – perhaps more so. Some community mental health teams do offer drop-in or day-centre facilities of this kind, and they can be extremely useful. The drawback of having such facilities attached to psychiatric services is that they still carry all the same 'illness' messages as before, even if this is not so overt. There is a danger of getting stuck in a 'patient subculture' from which it is very difficult to rejoin mainstream society:

> One difficulty if you have friends like that is that they tend to talk about medication and their symptoms all the time . . . It depresses you at times like that, you just don't want to talk about things like that, you want to talk about normal things everybody else talks about – sex, drugs, rock and roll or something, or horse racing . . . You want to break out of that mould of being part of a schizophrenic fellowship or whatever. It does get you down at times.

> It's a bit demoralising . . . You're sort of tied to the strings of the hospital, the apron strings of the hospital I suppose you could say, you're being treated like a child really, and you prefer to think, 'Well, I'd like to be independent and this is OK temporarily but I want to move on eventually and break away from all this.' (A man talking about his experiences of living in a hostel run by the psychiatric services.)[6]

The fifth category outlined in Chapter 2 consists of *people suffering from conditions of definitely physical origin*, such as head injury, the different types of dementia (such as Alzheimer's disease, Huntington's Chorea), and various others. It is essential to be able to identify the cases (more common in the elderly) where psychiatric symptoms turn out to be indications of an underlying organic disease. For example, memory and language impairment, visual hallucinations and 'schizophrenic'- type symptoms can be signs of a cerebral lesion, while brain tumours may give rise to depression, euphoria, anxiety or irritability. Poisoning by alcohol and other drugs and chemicals, vitamin deficiencies, liver failure and various other factors can all affect mental functioning.

The diagnosis of an underlying organic problem is often a very difficult one to make, and obviously it is essential for the psychiatric team to have access to someone with the medical expertise to carry out this kind of assessment, even if the need arises only rarely outside of work with the elderly. Whether or not it follows that only someone with medical training is competent to head the hospital team and make the final decisions about all in-patients is another matter. In fact, once the diagnosis has been made (and in many cases this is best done by a psychologist using psychological tests rather than by a doctor), medical science has very little to offer most victims of head injury or dementia, since there is no known cure. The most helpful interventions are behavioural (setting up groups to stimulate old people's memories, drawing up programmes to help with washing and dressing) and social (arranging attendance at day centres, organising laundry services, and brief admissions to care homes to ease the burden on relatives). Arguably, people with organic problems would be more suitably placed in separate rehabilitation services, rather than incurring all the stigma that goes with a psychiatric admission.

We can identify some important principles that apply to all categories of psychiatric problems by returning to the 'sick role' patients and asking: How can these situations be avoided? The key word is *responsibility*. The inability to take responsibility runs through all the assumptions behind the mental patient role, and it follows that the hospital staff, doctors in particular, are expected to take responsibility in their place. Thus the whole Rescue game starts up.

Yet it is not enough to tell people that they are responsible for their own problems and to dismiss them, as tends to happen in Persecution. Clearly, they are genuinely distressed and in need of some kind of help. What is needed is recognition that people suffering mental distress are responsible, capable agents *and* in need of help as well. The one state of affairs does not contradict or cancel out the other. This means that when they behave in a way that implies lack of responsibility they must be challenged. It also means that help must be given in a way that acknowledges the person's ability to take responsibility for him- or herself and his or her own life.

Let us look at how this would work in practice in the cases we have been discussing. First, attempts to force entry into the sick role, that is, to present oneself as irresponsible and as a Victim, will need to be blocked. Such situations can readily be recognised when the person first appears in front of the mental health professional (usually but not always a psychiatrist). Apart from the familiar hallmarks of bizarre symptoms, the involvement of other agencies and so on, the would-be patient presents him- or herself as having no responsibility for his or her arrival or behaviour, and refuses to make a direct request for anything. At the same time the professional feels a powerful pressure to Rescue or take responsibility for him or her. The covert request for admission needs to be blocked, and the various ways of denying responsibility (being vague, saying 'I don't know' or 'I don't remember', taking advantage of the role by hitting people or breaking things) need to be challenged.

Second, the offer of help needs to be addressed to a whole person living within a whole system of relationships and not just to a supposed illness, so that the person is still seen as a responsible agent. For Alice, this meant offering marital therapy. For Jeanette, it might have been an offer to find a suitable hostel or day centre where she could get support and make social contacts. For Fay, it could have been counselling to help her come to terms with her husband's impending death and plan for life on her own.

However, it is equally important that help should be offered in a *way* that implies the person's responsibility for making choices about his or her life. Thus, it is no use prescribing marital therapy ('I want to see you both weekly from now on') or a hostel place ('I'm arranging a bed for you in St John's Home'), rather like an alternative form of medicine. This does not acknowledge the person's ability and indeed right to consider the offer and perhaps refuse it. Since the person has not played an equal part in the decision, she or he may have no commitment to the form of help offered, and may express this by missing sessions, creating scenes in the hostel, and so on.

The offer, then, needs to be phrased in some such way as this: 'It seems to me, Mrs Brown, that you want to be admitted to hospital. I am not willing to arrange this, partly because I do not see you as having a mental illness, and partly because I don't think admission would solve your problems, which I suspect are to do with your relationships. What I am willing to offer is some sessions with both of you in which we could start to discuss how problems in your marriage might be contributing to your difficulties. This might well be painful, but I think it is the best way of helping both of you in the long run. We could start with two meetings to see how things go. Do you want to think this plan over?'

Since it is the *way* in which help is offered that is so important, it is possible to include forms of help that otherwise tend to imply illness and helplessness (medication, admission, and so on) in such a way that the person retains responsibility and the Rescue Game is avoided. Thus, instead of 'I am prescribing for you' (or, addressed to a relative, 'her'), 'some pills to take three times a day', or 'I think you/she had better come into hospital for a while', a psychiatrist might ask the person if she or he wants medication or admission. This simple step, which is nearly always omitted in psychiatric interviews, gives the person the opportunity to take a share of responsibility for what happens by making an explicit request. This request can then form the basis for negotiation between the two parties, during which the psychiatrist can make it clear that, in this case, medication or admission are not being seen as indicating the presence of a mental illness. Again, although psychiatrists often protest that they don't go around telling everyone that their problems are a sign of mental illness, they fail to appreciate that, unless they make a clear statement to this effect, the cultural meaning of admission and pill-taking will prevail.

The differences in approach might seem small, but they are crucially important. If the Browns, or whoever, accept the offer of counselling, then a major – perhaps *the* major – piece of work has been done. They will have shifted their attitude from blaming everything on an illness suffered by one person to acknowledging emotional problems in both, and the psychiatrist will have gained their active commitment to work on these problems. If, on the other hand, the Browns refuse, then at least the whole destructive, time-consuming Rescue game has been avoided.

Probably there will be some middle course. Several crises may have to be dealt with along these lines before the Browns are ready to take up the offer. At difficult points in the therapy they may switch back into the Rescue game, and the mental health team will need to stand very firm.

In summary, a *treatment contract*, based on *mutual consent*, needs to be drawn up and agreed between both parties. Doctors often claim that patients have consented to treatment. However, mutual consent involves a great deal more than a response of 'All right then' or 'I'll try anything' when someone recommends medication or admission. As in legal contracts, mutual consent implies that the person in distress has made an explicit request for help with a clearly defined problem; that the mental health professional has made an equally explicit offer of a clearly described and understood form of help; that the person understands the contribution he or she will be expected to make to treatment; and that he or she has accepted the offer.[7] Active involvement even in acute crisis is made possible by the use of Advance Directives, legal documents in which service users can set out a detailed account of how they wish to be treated in an emergency.

The Patient's Charter states: 'You have the right to have an explanation of any proposed treatment, including any risks involved in that treatment and any alternatives, before you decide whether to agree to it.'[8] Obviously, this is essential if consent to treatment is to mean anything. However, this ideal state of affairs is rarely found in psychiatry; 63 per cent of the 516 people in the survey discussed in the previous chapter felt that the reason for their admission was not adequately explained.[9] Where medication or ECT are concerned, people frequently complain that they were given no, or inadequate and misleading, information. This was true of around 70 per cent of people in the above survey. Typical comments were:

> Just told that I was to have anti-depressants and given them – no force but no choice given.

> What I was really unhappy about was, I wasn't told what it [ECT] would entail. I was just told to sign a piece of paper and that was that . . . I wasn't even really sure what it was.

The powerlessness of the psychiatric patient, who can under certain circumstances be detained (or 'sectioned' as it is termed) and forced to have drugs or ECT against his/her will, also makes it very hard for them to refuse what is offered. When coupled with desperation and a tendency to believe that 'experts' know best, much of what looks like agreement turns out to be simply fear and compliance:

> I wouldn't have known how to object, it wasn't on the horizon. You didn't disagree with doctors, you did what they said.

> He [the doctor] is the one with the power, he is the one ultimately that has the answer . . . If that's the only help you're getting, you've got to hang on to it.

> If you're at your wits' end and they've drugged you up to the eyes you don't question . . . you're not thinking straight anyway.[10]

In any case, objecting to your treatment does not always go down well with the staff, who may use pressure or coercion even when you have the legal right to refuse:

> I was threatened with ECT if I did not take Nardil.

> I was told that I would be sectioned if I didn't take the anti-depressants.[11]

I said immediately that I didn't want it [ECT], and I pointed out that the previous consultant . . . had said to me that she didn't think I was an appropriate case for ECT . . . and he [the consultant] got into a real huff basically and got up and walked out of the room . . . I felt absolutely devastated. I just burst out crying and didn't know what was going to happen to me, or whether they were going to section me, or what.[12]

If the principle of informed consent were adhered to, it would be an important step towards turning the people who use the psychiatric services from patients – a word which implies the sick role, a passive waiting on expert advice – into clients who are actively selecting and participating in their own treatment.

But this does not just apply to people like Jeanette, Fay and Alice. It applies to *all* patients/clients/service users and all psychiatric staff. We saw how the Rescue Game operated so destructively in the stories of Elaine, Susan and Linda, so that they were either pitied/ Rescued/seen as 'mad' or blamed/Persecuted/seen as 'bad'. The whole Rescue Game can be avoided by drawing up a proper treatment contract based on equality, mutual consent and a whole-person, whole-system under-standing of the situation. For example, when Elaine Jones (Chapter 1) was first referred to a psychiatrist, an elementary knowledge of psychotherapy should have been enough to recognize the very common pattern of breakdown in a woman who is trying to give to others when she has never been given to herself. Although a full understanding of the problem was only reached after several months' counselling, Elaine's breakdown could have been explained in simple terms to her and her husband after the first interview as the delayed effect of her emotionally deprived childhood coupled with current stresses in the family. This would have set the framework for the treatment contract. Elaine might still have been offered (not ordered) admission and/or medication, but with the clearly explained aim of rest and recovery from the present crisis so that the underlying issues could be tackled. Such a contract would have given the nurses and occupational therapists the necessary guidance to make their contribution to the treatment plan, perhaps helping her to choose relaxing activities instead of cooking, and encouraging her to take care of herself for a change. In the longer term, counselling sessions could have been offered to Elaine. The scene would also have been set for involving Elaine's husband and perhaps her whole family at some point. Fifteen years before the entrenched situation that we saw in the first chapter, Elaine and her husband might have accepted this explanation and offer with relief and understanding. Mr Jones might well have learned to make use of counselling too, with the probable result that his own difficulties would have become an equally important focus of treatment. And with luck, many of the destructive patterns that later emerged in their children would have been avoided.

It is vitally important that treatment contract negotiations start from a person's very first contact with the psychiatric services. The initial interview is of absolutely crucial importance. If the first meeting ends in a Rescue rather than a negotiated contract, if one person out of a system is labelled as the sick one, or if all the difficulties are attributed to an illness, then the whole direction of treatment has been set. Staff, patients and relatives will take up their positions accordingly, and it may be extraordinarily difficult to frame the problem in any other way at a later date.

It is equally important that the same messages are given throughout a person's contact with the psychiatric services. This is particularly difficult on the ward, where, as we have seen, such attempts will continually be undermined and contradicted by the overall messages of the medical setting. Even someone who is determined to retain as much of an adult role as possible will face an uphill struggle, as we saw from Linda Hart's account. Community work offers, at least in theory, the chance to work in more of a partnership. However, even here, this is limited by the extent to which staff are able to leave behind the assumptions that may have become deeply entrenched in training. As one community nurse put it:

> It's very hard for nurses to say that patients have to take responsibility for themselves. I think it stems back to the old idea that the nurse is someone who cares and who does things for people – and patients have expectations of you – they expect you to solve their problems and they find it hard to accept that sometimes you just can't.[13]

It may be thought very strange that these dangerous muddles occur routinely in psychiatry, and that in many places it is virtually unheard of for someone to be asked such simple questions as: Why are you here? What do you want help with? What contribution can you make to getting over your problems? How will we know when you are better? When do you want to leave? But to do so challenges the whole medical model on which traditional psychiatry is based. People who are sent to general hospitals with physical complaints are not expected to work out for themselves what the cause is, nor are they asked to decide what kind of treatment they want – these are questions for the doctors and nurses. Psychiatry as a branch of medicine is based upon the same principles, and the training that psychiatric staff receive makes it extremely difficult for them to view it in any other way.

However, there is an important limitation to the benefits of treatment contracts, informed consent, challenging sick roles and so on, important as they are. This is the fact that no matter how enlightened your hospital treatment is, the fact of receiving a psychiatric diagnosis is enough to assign you to a mental patient role, with all its stigmatising implications, in the eyes of the wider community. A recent MIND survey, *Not Just Sticks and Stones*,[14] found that people with a psychiatric history face prejudice in all areas of life, including being shouted at, threatened, physically attacked in public (47 per cent); being harassed, intimidated or teased at work (38 per cent); being dismissed or forced to resign from a job (34 per cent); being turned down by an insurance or finance company (25 per cent); and having decisions about custody or access to children unfairly influenced (27 per cent). They said things like: 'The gangs on the estate got to know I was a psychiatric out-patient so I was teased and harassed.' 'My children were teased both at school and on the streets near my home about my condition. I was referred to as a "psycho".' Local reaction to community mental health facilities is frequently characterised by similar levels of intolerance and ignorance, with people expressing quite unfounded fears about violence and threats to children: 'Public resistance and hostility towards the siting of projects for people with mental health problems in or near their own communities is becoming more common, increasingly powerful, and is often successful in preventing the location, or forcing the closure of much needed facilities.'[15] As Liz Sayce from MIND has argued, the term 'stigma', which tends to locate the problem in the individual, is insufficient to describe the range of difficulties that service users face. By using the term 'discrimination' instead, we shift the focus to the collective unfair and oppressive actions of others, and the need to change them by a variety of means, including legislation and public education.[16]

Peter Barham and Robert Hayward have vividly documented the enormous struggle that former psychiatric patients face in trying to find their way back from the sick role, or from 'patienthood' to 'personhood', and to build some sort of meaningful life for themselves in the community.[17] For these people, who had had severe breakdowns and an average of six admissions each, there is the dilemma of how much to tell other people:

> If I meet somebody who isn't or hasn't been in hospital, then you don't mention that you're psychiatric and hope to God that nobody

else mentions it in your family or whatever that meets them later. Because the attitude from people, some of them . . . you can tell they're embarrassed and don't know what to say or anything . . . They think it's terrible . . . it's taboo, you mustn't talk about it.

I have actually avoided getting into relationships because of the difficulty I would have in explaining what I'd been through, and what it all means, to someone . . . If I met someone in a pub or club or whatever, and I liked her, if I felt that she'd never known anything about mental illness, never experienced anything to do with it, I'd avoid talking to her . . . because it would seem pointless to me. I'd just stop it dead.

There is the difficulty in getting a job, and the demeaning nature of the 'rehabilitation' on offer instead:

I went for a job just recently at a local bakery and I saw a lady there who interviewed me. And as soon as I mentioned – I put it as nicely as I could – that I had had a nervous breakdown . . . and that I was well over my troubles – her face dropped and her attitude completely changed. I could tell it wasn't my imagination and of course I got the letter in the post a few days later saying 'Thanks, but no thanks.'

Taking little sticky tabs off an X-ray file over and over again all day long . . . it was just soul-destroying. You could never tell yourself you were doing a job doing that.

Along with unemployment goes poverty and all the limitations it imposes:

Certainly money can make a lot of difference to what you can do and what you can't do because you certainly can't take part in . . . any kind of social life, without a certain amount of money . . . You know, I'd like to go to the theatre or the cinema or to concerts or something, and I could have made friends that way if I'd had the money, because friends, I think, are important to your life.

Housing is often very poor:

It was a right grotty place. We shared three to a room . . . They had a cooker that didn't work, the place was like a pigsty . . . The bannister railings were half falling off.

There was also a painful struggle between wanting to have meaningful work and rejoin and make a contribution to society, and the limited expectations imposed on them by their psychiatric label:

> I find it a very inadequate existence at the moment. I could do with a sense of purpose, of actually doing something . . . I've got nothing to get up in the morning for, it's a matter of some-how passing the day, day to day, and it's very depressing . . . That's why more challenge, and more stress in that sense, would do me good not harm. There's a strange kind of sub-culture [of other psychiatric patients] where they say, 'You haven't got a job have you? How did you get a job? You're a mental patient!' – because I'm known as a mental patient not as a technician or a college student or something . . . There is that kind of prejudice there and I do it myself.

Overall, in the authors' words, 'an impoverished conception of what [they] can reasonably do and hope for – of [their] significance and value – have been brought to merge in a painful experience of exclusion and worthlessness'. In the words of two of the participants:

> With schizophrenia you are not living, you are just existing . . . I am labelled for the rest of my life . . . I think schizophrenia will always make me a second-class citizen. I go for an interview for a job and the anxiety builds up . . . I haven't got a future.

> I get so depressed because I sometimes feel as though I have no future. I just think I'm going to be a psychiatric patient for the rest of my life with no social life and not much money . . . To try and be accepted, that's it. It's as though you've got to try and be accepted by people, to be normal.

As the authors point out, these are not the *natural* consequences of a psychiatric breakdown, but the *social* consequences. To give someone a diagnosis in psychiatry, unlike in general medicine, is to introduce them into a role and a life of stigma, social exclusion and discrimination which would be a struggle even for the emotionally resilient. The challenge is to tackle this outside as well as inside the psychiatric system. This raises questions such as: What exactly are we doing when we 'diagnose' someone as 'mentally ill'? Are there alternatives? We shall start to discuss these issues in the next chapter. But first we shall consider the question of whether the treatment contract approach has anything to offer people who are most out of touch with reality, or in simple terms, mad, and who might seem to be the most suitable candidates for medical-style Rescuing and intervention.

Chapter 4

The treatment barrier

WHERE FAMILY RELATIONSHIPS ARE SO INTENSE AND ENTANGLED THAT ONE PERSON IN THE SYSTEM BREAKS DOWN VERY SEVERELY

Jenny's story

Jenny Clark was a 20-year-old student of hairdressing, living at home with her parents. Her brother, several years older, had left home to marry and her younger sister was away at teacher-training college.

Unlike her more outgoing brother and sister, Jenny had never had many friends of either sex. She found it very hard to talk to people, and at school had sometimes been teased for her slight stammer when she was nervous. She did not seem to be settling in very well at college either. Most evenings and weekends were spent at home, despite the rather tense atmosphere there. Her mother had been brought up in a deeply religious Catholic family in a small town in Ireland. She had met her English husband, her first boyfriend, when she was a shy and inexperienced 19-year-old, and moved to England with him. Over the years the couple became disenchanted with each other and ended up living almost as strangers in the same house. With the failure of her marriage, Mrs Clark's children became even more important to her. She only spoke of her husband with bitterness and resentment, and he withdrew into himself and became the butt of family jokes. Neither of them had friends locally, and he spent his time either at work or out fishing while she kept the house in immaculate order.

DOI: 10.4324/9781003095958-4

During her second year at college, Jenny started to retreat into herself even more. Quiet and obedient all her life, Jenny had never caused her parents any trouble. Her brother and sister had been the ones who got into rows about staying out late and not helping around the house. Jenny's mother often said that she lived only for her children; and since she saw many of her own attitudes and characteristics in Jenny, they had been particularly close. Now, though, there were clashes between them for the first time when Jenny flouted various family rules and cut herself off from the activities she and her mother used to do together. She stopped talking to her parents, refused to answer the telephone, and sometimes did not go into college. Mrs Clark couldn't understand why Jenny locked herself away in her room for hours listening to music. As the weeks passed, she became more and more concerned. She even began to fear that Jenny was going out of her mind. In the end, she called in the family GP.

The GP thought that Jenny was very confused and unhappy rather than mentally ill. Jenny sat staring miserably at the floor while the GP, who fortunately had a good relationship with her, tried to coax a few words out of her. Slowly and hesitantly, Jenny opened up. Her whole life was a hopeless failure, she said. She had never fitted in at school. The other girls ridiculed her and none of the boys ever asked her out. She had hoped college would be different, but it was turning out to be even worse. Everyone else had their little groups of friends and she was left on the outside. Anyway, no boy would ever want to go out with someone who had such big hips and freckly skin. She wasn't even sure if she wanted to do hairdressing anyway, but what else could she do? It was all her parents' fault. No wonder she had no friends when they never mixed with anyone and had such old-fashioned ideas. Living at home in that atmosphere was enough to make anyone miserable. If only they would try to understand her, but her mother just interfered and her father was worse than useless. No, she didn't want to move out – she just wanted to be able to live happily with them. Her secret ambition, she confided, was to be a film star. She had been practising expressions and poses in front of the mirror in her room.

All this information was pieced together over several sessions. Jenny, driven in her mother's car since she refused to go out on her own, was being seen by the GP for twenty minutes or so after surgery once a week. The GP saw her as struggling with many common adolescent problems about finding her own place with her contemporaries, planning her life and separating from her parents, and he encouraged her to start reversing her retreat from the world. Jenny gradually became more at ease with the doctor and took a few tentative steps – ordering some books for college was one, and telephoning a girl she had been at school with was another. She still clung to the idea of being a film star, despite a complete lack of acting ability or experience, and she refused to contemplate the possibility of leaving home. The whole idea of boyfriends and sexual relationships was terrifying to her. Nevertheless, progress was being made. After confiding many bitter memories of being teased and ridiculed at school, she discussed with the GP how she could handle such situations differently. One day there was a breakthrough. Jenny came to the surgery on her own, by bus. She had drawn out some of her savings and bought herself a new, fashionable pair of boots. She was going to the cinema with a girlfriend that weekend, and was more cheerful and confident than the GP had ever seen her. He told her how delighted he was, and privately anticipated tailing off their meetings.

This was not to be. The next evening, he received a frantic telephone call from Mrs Clark, who said that Jenny was refusing to come down to meals and she was sure her daughter must be going crazy. The GP dismissed this idea, advised Mrs Clark to leave Jenny's food in the oven for her, and promised to bring the subject up with Jenny the following week. Mrs Clark did not seem at all reassured. The next day there was a similar telephone call. Mrs Clark insisted that Jenny hadn't eaten for two days, that she was pacing round the house muttering to herself in a crazy way, and that she needed to see a psychiatrist. The GP agreed to call round that evening. The atmosphere was extremely tense. There was no sign of the strange behaviour that Mrs Clark had reported, but Jenny was more openly angry with her mother than he had ever seen her. She furiously accused her of forcing her to eat fattening food when she was trying to diet, and of generally treating her like a baby. Mrs Clark yelled back that anyone who could say such things must be crazy – Jenny had never behaved like that before – she must be ill. The GP tried in vain to help them reach some kind of compromise, but feelings were running too high. He withdrew, telling them they would have to sort this one out themselves, to which Mrs Clark retorted that he was useless at his job, and anyone could see that Jenny was ill.

It was the on-call GP who received the next telephone call later that evening. By the time she went round, Jenny was extremely agitated and unable to sit still for a second. As the GP opened the door, Jenny seized her coat and rattled off a long speech about how much she hated both her parents, how her mother had suffocated her all her life and never let her grow up, and how everyone treated her like an idiot. This was interspersed with such strange remarks as: 'I can fly out of here any time I want, you know. I know the GP is really married to me. I know everything.' Simultaneously, Mrs Clark tried to engage the GP's attention by yelling her version of events – that Jenny was crazy and dangerous and needed to be taken away, just as she'd been trying to tell people for months. A furious screaming match broke out as Jenny shook her fists and let rip with pent-up resentments against her mother: 'I hate you! You just want to keep me like a child! You never leave me alone!' while her mother retaliated at the top of her voice with 'You're crazy! You're mad! You should be locked away!' As the accumulated family tensions of many years exploded round his head, Mr Clark hovered ineffectually in the background, wringing his hands and remonstrating feebly with both of them.

The GP felt totally out of her depth and also was alarmed by some of Jenny's bizarre remarks. She decided that the best thing to do was to call in the psychiatrist and the duty social worker. When these two people arrived at the house, they accepted Mrs Clark's word that Jenny was violent and agreed that she was also deluded, a danger to herself and in need of hospital treatment. Forms were signed for Jenny's compulsory admission, and an ambulance was called. Struggling desperately and shouting that she was sane, Jenny was physically forced into the ambulance and taken to the admission ward of the local psychiatric hospital. Here she refused to submit to a medical examination, telling the doctor angrily: 'I'm perfectly sane. I don't need to be in hospital.' She was injected with a powerful tranquillising drug and put to bed.

The next morning, Jenny was stunned, scared and bewildered. One of the nurses came to talk to her as she sat dazed and silent on her bed. There was no sign of the furious struggle of the previous night, nor did she make any bizarre remarks. Instead, she was trying to make sense of the catastrophic event that had befallen her. She asked anxiously: 'Does being in here mean I'm mad?' She refused to see her parents when they visited, saying she hated them. Later in the day her dazed bewilderment was replaced by open distress and agitation. She refused her medication, accusing the staff of trying to drive her mad, and so she was held down and injected instead.

Over the next few days, Jenny slowly lost her hold on reality. Partly due to the side-effects of the large dosage of drugs, the bright young woman was transformed into a shuffling creature with slurred speech and vacant eyes, a trace of saliva escaping from her half-open mouth. The heavy sedative effect was accompanied by a restlessness that kept her constantly on the move, up and down the ward, muttering under her breath and intermittently pulling up her nightdress to show the nurses her supposedly too-large hips. From time to time she had outbursts which could perhaps have been seen as a frantic protest against her situation, but were interpreted by the staff as further evidence that she was sick and needed to be controlled. Thus, when she threw food and plates around, tried to escape from the ward, swore at the doctors, slammed doors and hurled herself to the floor, more medication was produced to sedate her, in spite of her frantic cries of 'I don't want that stuff! You're just trying to slow me down!' At other times, it seemed as though her previous worries were all appearing in a distorted form. For instance, she told the staff that Prince Charming had spoken to her from the television and was going to visit her that night. She announced that she was a film star and then that she was pregnant. Once she asked anxiously if she had killed her family, and then told one of the doctors: 'I'm only three years old.'

The Clarks, who visited each evening, were desperately upset to see their daughter in this state. When Jenny agreed to see her, Mrs Clark put her hair in ribbons and fed her sweets, though the visits sometimes ended with Jenny swearing and shouting at her mother.

After several weeks, Jenny was judged to have improved; that is, although far from her previous self, she was more often bemused and passive than furious and resistant. She was allowed home on leave, where she was visited by a community nurse. He found that Mr Clark had once again retreated into the background, while Mrs Clark's entire time was devoted to caring for her daughter. Jenny was constantly exhorted to brush her hair nicely, to eat up her food like a good girl, to sit quietly in her chair, and so on. Jenny made feeble protests at some of these instructions, but at the same time seemed unable to let her mother out of her sight, trailing after her from room to room asking: 'I'm a good girl, aren't I? You're not cross with me, are you?' Mrs Clark became openly furious at any suggestion that it would be helpful to encourage Jenny to be a little more independent. As far as she was concerned, the doctors were entirely to blame for not listening when she first thought Jenny was going crazy. As for Jenny, she looked terrified at the suggestion that she might one day want to go out into the world again and perhaps have a job and friends of her own. 'No, no,' she said, quickly retreating into her fantasy world. She picked up one of the pictures of film stars which littered her bedroom floor and wandered round the room, saying in the childlike voice that had now become habitual: 'I want to look like her. I want to be like her.'

We will leave Jenny there. There are several possible outcomes for her and others who, like her, are diagnosed as 'schizophrenic'. ('Schizophrenia' refers, not to a split personality, but to a state where a person loses hold on reality and may suffer from delusions and hallucinations.) She may make a good recovery after one breakdown, as about a quarter of sufferers do, and resume a normal life. She may go on to have repeated breakdowns and admissions, spending as much time in hospital as out of it, as happens to another quarter of people so diagnosed. Or some kind of compromise situation may be reached whereby she manages to stay out of hospital most of the time, but settles for a limited existence at home, friendless and partnerless, never quite able to break away from her family to establish independence and an identity of her own.

A number of factors seem to have contributed to Jenny's breakdown. Always more sensitive and introverted than her brother and sister, she had found it especially hard to overcome the disadvantages of an upbringing in a socially isolated and conflict-ridden family. All the same, she had the usual desires of young women her age for friends, boyfriends and an attractive appearance. It was not very surprising that she lapsed into despair at achieving none of these, although in retrospect her very unrealistic ambition to be a film star might have sounded a warning note. However, the interesting fact is that the crisis blew up just when everything seemed to be going better at last.

Jenny was more closely identified with her mother than the other two children, and hence had a more intense and complex relationship with her. Out of the three children who had come to mean everything to Mrs Clark after the failure of her marriage, only Jenny was still at home. It was at the point when real separation became an issue, when Jenny seemed to be about to grow away from her anxious, obedient child self and her family and step into the outside world, that Mrs Clark's genuine concern over her daughter's unhappiness seemed to be replaced by a more desperate fear that Jenny might abandon her. In a common (though not universal) pattern, the first 'schizophrenic' breakdown is precipitated by the threatened separation of a child from a parent (usually the mother). Hence, first breakdowns occur most frequently between the ages of seventeen and twenty-five, when young people are involved in the struggle to establish their identity and separateness from their families.

Of course, separation causes conflicts and arguments in most families, but in some the struggle takes on a particularly intense quality. Typically, the child or young adult has been unusually unseparated up until this point. Like Jenny, he or she is often described in such terms as 'good as gold', 'never a moment's trouble', 'couldn't bear to be apart from us', and this is seen by the parents as normal and desirable rather than worryingly lacking in the protests and disagreements by which healthy children start to establish themselves as separate individuals.

After many years of 'good' behaviour, there typically follows a stage where the child, rather belatedly, starts to act in a manner that is seen as 'bad': getting angry, answering back, disobeying rules, and so on. Most parents are able to bear this period of estrangement until the transition from a child–parent to a more adult–adult relationship is achieved, but if a parent's whole identity and life is bound up in the child, then the prospect of challenge and separation may be intolerable. The 'bad' behaviour constitutes an unbearable threat which has to be seen as being beyond the bounds of reason; crazy; mad. The 'bad to mad' route by which people end up in hospital was seen in embryonic form in such cases as George and Alice (Chapter 3). It is the counterpart of the 'mad to bad' route by which patients get pushed out of hospital again. By labelling 'bad' behaviour as crazy, the message that the parent cannot bear to hear can be discounted. Thus, the Clarks did not have to consider whether there was any truth in Jenny's accusations about them. As Jenny became more independent, the threat to the family set-up increased. So, rather than welcoming Jenny's progress, Mrs Clark became more and more terrified and her accusations of craziness escalated. Many first admissions for 'schizophrenia' occur not as the result of a considered decision to seek psychiatric help, but during a huge crisis when life-long tensions erupt in a terrifying maelstrom. The parental or family view and the child's view become polarised as each side is involved in a desperate struggle for self-preservation. Either Jenny's (extreme) view of her mother's possessiveness and her father's uselessness will win, and the family will be forced to face up to the element of truth in these accusations, with catastrophic results for the present family set-up; or her mother's equally extreme view, that Jenny is simply mad, will prevail, with equally catastrophic results for Jenny.

At this crucial crisis point, the psychiatric services are called in. From an outsider's point of view, there is perhaps not much distinction to be made between Jenny's behaviour and her mother's. Each was screaming equally unpleasant things at the other ('I hate you!' versus 'You should be locked away!'). However, for reasons that will be discussed more fully later, the psychiatric staff almost invariably take the parental/family side. Thus it was Jenny and not her mother who was described as verbally aggressive, violent and a danger to herself. (No actual evidence of violence to another person was ever produced, either in or out of hospital, but it is a frequent accusation from relatives and is almost always taken at face value by the professionals without investigation.) The crisis is over when the professionals yield to the considerable pressure to designate the nominated member of the family as the crazy one, and have confirmed this status by the ritual of diagnosis, admission and medication. Whatever craziness there is in the family has then been officially located in one member, and the rest can breathe a sigh of relief. The child, however, will have been defeated in this crucial battle to assert identity and independence, possibly for ever.

Once the line has been drawn between the mad and the sane, all future remarks and behaviour will be classified accordingly. Thus, the account that appears under 'Previous history' in the medical notes will probably be derived entirely from the parents and will be treated as the true version of events. A typical example might read: 'Mother dates the patient's illness back two years when she changed from being quiet and well-behaved to being aggressive, resistant and rude. Parents have managed this as best they could until stress over exams triggered the present breakdown.' Here, the delayed emergence of normal adolescent behaviour is described, and accepted, as illness, with the final breakdown attributed to some external event. Meanwhile the patient's point of view is discounted, because, after all, the patient is mad. At best, it might appear under the heading 'Sample of patient's speech', where Jenny was recorded as saying: 'I am all right. I don't need any medical examination. I don't know why people are making a fuss of me.' Such statements are noted for diagnostic purposes only and their meaning is ignored.

The catastrophic effect on a sensitive young woman like Jenny of finding yourself compulsorily detained in a psychiatric hospital, feeling abandoned and betrayed by your family, can hardly be over-estimated. Your sanity depends on being able to make some sense of this appalling event – but the powerful drugs that Jenny was immediately given made it very hard for her to think this through. She was very aware of the numerous cues that told her she was deemed to have crossed the threshold into madness: the hospital surroundings, the doctors and nurses, and more subtle cues such as the tone of voice used to address her. However, her cries of 'You're trying to drive me mad!' were either discounted or taken as further evidence of madness. Some of the nurses privately thought there was some truth in her complaints about her parents, but they saw their main job as nursing a sick young woman through her illness. They had only the parental version of the events leading up to her admission to go on and were not trained to intervene in family conflicts, so they did not share their reactions with her. When Jenny did lose her hold on reality, they were even less able to make sense of her strange statements about Prince Charming, being pregnant, killing her family, and being three years old. Such remarks were simply recorded in the notes as 'delusional thinking'. Looked at from another angle, Jenny's desire to find a partner, her fear of the consequences of sexual relationships, her terror of losing contact with her family and her acknowledgement of her childlike state can all be recognised in these statements. Most of us speak in metaphors: 'I wish I could meet my Prince Charming', or 'I could murder my family'. Some people who break down take the process a stage further and start living their metaphors instead. As Linda Hart put it at one of her lowest points: 'I suppose the difference between sanity and madness is akin to the difference between a simile and a metaphor. One is like, the other is. I'm is at the moment.'[1] However, doctors and nurses are not trained to understand or decode such messages, and thus it was Jenny and not the psychiatric staff who earned the comment in the medical notes: 'Has no insight. Does not understand what is said to her.'

The hospital environment, as we have seen, tends to reinforce all of a person's most childlike aspects, which is particularly damaging for someone like Jenny whose very problem centres around the struggle to grow up and achieve adulthood. Thus she had to go to bed and get up at specified times, ask permission to have a bath, stay in her nightgown, and comply with various other ward regulations. In a tragic repetition of the situation in her family, her rebellion against these rules, against taking her drugs and against the very fact of her containment, was seen not as healthy assertiveness or understandable protest but as further evidence of her illness. The more she struggled, the more entangled she became.

But it would be misleading to describe Jenny simply as the helpless victim of her family. During the home visit after her discharge, the symbiotic nature of the relationship with her mother was very clear. Neither could separate from the other. If Mrs Clark was terrified of Jenny abandoning her, Jenny was equally terrified of being abandoned. The unhappy result whereby each was tied to the other was a way for each of them to avoid their deepest fears. In retrospect, this pattern could be traced back to before the breakdown. If Mrs Clark had not been able to promote Jenny's independence, Jenny had never been willing seriously to consider the possibility of leaving her. The fantasy of being a film star had never involved moving away from home.

It would be equally mistaken to doubt the Clarks' genuine care and concern for their daughter. Mrs Clark's reactions and behaviour were the result of her desperate attempts to find a solution to her own impossible dilemmas. The departure of her daughter would threaten her psychological survival and leave her facing the emptiness of her marriage and life. The position of Mrs Clark, and of the shadowy figure of Mr Clark on the edge of the family, will be considered in future chapters.

This analysis of the experience of a girl diagnosed as schizophrenic and her family is an extremely contentious one. The same events might be described from a medical point of view along the following lines:

> This young woman showed a pattern of increasing withdrawal typical of the early stages of schizophrenia. When she became floridly

psychotic, compulsory admission to hospital was necessary and the appropriate medication was given. After a few weeks she was sufficiently improved for discharge. Her progress will be monitored closely, and it is likely that she will need to be maintained on medication for some time.

While there is often informal recognition of the relevance of family relationships, reflected in such comments from the nurses as: 'She/he is fine as long as mother/father isn't around', or 'I think we've got the wrong one in here', the orthodox psychiatric view is that 'schizophrenia' has a genetic biochemical cause, the cure for which will ultimately be revealed by medical research. This theory is often stated as a fact, for example:

Schizophrenia . . . is caused by a biochemical abnormality in the brain.[2]

Schizophrenia is a disorder of brain chemistry that may be brought on by stress.[3]

Schizophrenia is a physical disease of the brain, probably caused by a combination of genetic and other factors.[4]

As we have seen in earlier chapters, the orthodox medical view describes anything else going on in the patient's life under some such general heading as 'environmental stress' which merely acts as a trigger for the underlying 'illness'. To put forward an alternative view is to be accused of ignorance of the research and heartlessness towards the suffering of patients and their families:

Advances in the understanding of the biological basis of schizophrenia have left most of the philosophical objections to the medical view of it as an illness . . . looking distinctly old hat.[5]

You only have to live with someone who in fact is going mad to realise that it's not your narrow, pinched refusal to tolerate the discourse of the mad that's at fault, but that actually people are ill. I think that a great deal of harm was done to the families and to the ill themselves by the great sixties denial of mental illness.[6]

If the existence of schizophrenia is denied, it is no wonder that sufferers . . . are not taken seriously, and denied care and treatment even when they ask for it.[7]

These three writers are referring to the last period when it was acceptable to see family relationships as having a role to play in severe psychiatric breakdown, the 1960s.

However, one can occasionally find an admission from within the medical establishment that the prevailing theories are not as well founded as is claimed. These two quotes come from the *British Journal of Psychiatry*, the flagship journal of the Royal College of Psychiatrists:

> Although the concept of schizophrenia has been in existence for nearly a century . . . there has been no identification of any underlying causal pathology.[8]

> In some quarters schizophrenia has gained the reputation of a graveyard of research. Few findings stand the test of time, most of the pieces of this particular jigsaw seem to be missing, and it is not easy to make sense of those that are available. Even 'hard' scientific findings fail to be replicated.[9]

There is a similar mismatch in media reports, where optimistic findings are constantly heralded: 'Anti-viral drugs could stop mental illnesses', 'Breakthrough in acid tests brings hope on schizophrenia'.[10] The inevitable failure to live up to these promises is only documented rarely, as in 'Scientists seeking genetic link to mental illness draw blank',[11] leaving lay readers with the impression that the medical science's answer to the problem of 'schizophrenia' is only just round the corner.

In summary, we have the strange situation in which 'schizophrenia' is described and treated as an illness with an organic cause although none has ever been discovered. This, of course, is a status it shares with almost every other condition in psychiatry, since only a very small minority (for example, senile dementia, Korsakoff's syndrome) have a known physical origin.

The significance of this cannot be overstated. What is at issue for the psychiatrists is the whole basis of their claim for domination of the field of mental health. They are under threat from other professions which have developed effective counselling approaches for so-called 'neurotic' disorders such as anxiety and milder forms of depression, while the new community mental health teams are often managed by senior nurses, not doctors. 'Schizophrenia', one researcher has argued, 'functions as the prototypical psychiatric disease.'[12] If patients like Jenny are not suffering from a condition of physical/biochemical origins, then the whole necessity for a medical training and approach is thrown into question, and the position of psychiatrists becomes untenable. Psychiatry would then become, in the words of one critic, 'something very hard to justify or defend – a medical speciality that does not treat medical illnesses'.[13]

It is not surprising, then, that the issue of what causes 'schizophrenia' is the most controversial in psychiatry, and that the search for proof of its genetic/biochemical origins has become its Holy Grail.

THE CAUSES OF 'SCHIZOPHRENIA'

The following account of the flaws and limitations of current research into the causes of 'schizophrenia' applies equally strongly to other supposedly biologically based psychiatric problems such as manic depression. By highlighting the elementary logical errors underlying every single study, I hope to spare readers the extremely tedious task of trying to digest this mountain of research themselves.

Diagnosis

Any scientific investigation must start from a precise definition of what is being investigated. If we cannot agree what we mean by 'schizophrenia' (or any other psychiatric diagnosis), we shall not be able to say who has it and who does not, and studies will be bound to produce variable and inconsistent results. An obvious difficulty here is that since there are no physical tests (blood counts, X-rays and so on) for this hypothetical illness, diagnosis has to be based on reports and observation of *behaviour* and *experiences* (hearing voices, being withdrawn and so on). But although it is relatively easy in principle to describe the normal functioning of the human body, and thus to draw the line between the physically well and the ill, there are no absolute and agreed standards about what constitutes 'normal' behaviour. Such judgements depend on context and culture. It is not surprising, then, to find that psychiatric diagnosis is notoriously unreliable, with variations in usage between different doctors, different hospitals and different countries.[14]

In response to this problem, there have been numerous attempts to standardise the criteria for applying psychiatric diagnoses, which are summarised in the *Diagnostic and Statistical Manual–IV** (drawn up in America) and the *International Classification of Diseases–10*** (the British version.) However, even if *reliability* in applying a particular diagnosis could be achieved, this is not the same as establishing its *validity*. To illustrate this, let us consider the concept of Father Christmas. We could certainly draw up very precise and reliable terms for identifying him – long white beard, red cloak, sack of presents and so on – but does this mean he actually exists? Whatever we may have been told as children, the answer is clearly no. In the same way, agreement about who merits the diagnosis of 'schizophrenia' in no way provides evidence that this hypothetical disease actually exists.

In fact, there are numerous other anomalies that confirm the suspicion that in talking uncritically about 'schizophrenia', we are not dealing with a valid concept at all. The so-called 'symptoms' of the illness seem to cluster together fairly randomly, so that two people with the same diagnosis may have none in common. The diagnosis doesn't predict either the course or the outcome of the 'illness', and often has no clear relationship to treatment.[15] As one well-known critic puts it: 'Taking all this evidence together, it is difficult to see why modern researchers continue to take the concept of "schizophrenia" seriously.'[16] (I have indicated my own reservations about the term by using it in inverted commas throughout this book.)

The logical conclusion of these arguments is that investigations based on a concept that is not valid are bound to produce invalid results. Undeterred by 'this massive flaw in every single study undertaken',[17] researchers have produced a mountain of inconclusive and contradictory findings which can be summarised under the following headings.

Genetic explanations

It is accepted as fact in psychiatric circles that there is a genetic contribution to 'schizophrenia', although since identical twins, who inherit the same genes, do not necessarily both develop the condition, it is acknowledged that environmental factors must also play a part. The risk of breaking down is usually put at about 10 per cent for the child of a 'schizophrenic' parent.[18] Of course, the fact that something 'runs in the family' could equally well be explained by environmental factors such as parenting styles or poverty. To eliminate possible environmental contributions, a famous researcher called Franz Kallmann in the 1950s looked at identical twins who had at least one 'schizophrenic' parent and who were raised separately. Another, Seymour Kety, in the 1960s and 1970s, looked at the risk for adopted children in general. Their claims for a substantial genetic contribution are widely quoted even today, despite subsequent revelations of extremely dubious methodology. Kallmann, a firm believer in eugenics and compulsory sterilisation for psychiatric patients, had taken advantage of the flexibility of the concept to include 'suspected untreated schizophrenics' and had even diagnosed people, in some cases after their deaths, on the basis of third-party reports. Kety's sample included people with 'uncertain borderline state' and others; without this strategy the results would have been insignificant. Reviewers who have taken a detailed and critical look at these and other classic studies have concluded that a genetic contribution to 'schizophrenia' is at best unproven:[19] 'That the reported studies are riddled with methodological, statistical and interpretational errors has been repeatedly demonstrated.'[20] In fact, it would make more sense to cite them as evidence of environmental rather than of genetic factors.

A recent and more rigorously designed investigation from Finland tried to disentangle the effects of genetics and environment by comparing 155 adopted children, whose biological mothers had been diagnosed as 'schizophrenic', with a second group of adopted children whose mothers had not been so diagnosed.[21] The children in the first group did turn out to have more diagnoses of 'schizophrenia' and other severe psychiatric diagnoses; this is consistent with a genetic explanation. However, a close look at the data revealed that the situation is more complex than this. The children of mothers who had been diagnosed as 'schizophrenic' became disturbed *only if they had been brought up in adoptive families which were themselves rated as disturbed*. In other words, all children – even those who were presumed to be carrying some genetic tendency to develop 'schizophrenia' – did well in emotionally healthy adoptive families. Two important conclusions may be drawn: one is that the *quality of family relationships* may be the critical factor in leading to, or protecting from, serious psychiatric breakdown; the other is that, as the researchers themselves suggested, any inherited component may be a non-specific predisposition, such as general sensitivity to the environment, which it would be neither possible nor desirable to eliminate. 'If this turns out to be the case, the diagnosis of schizophrenia as a specific disease entity may also need revision.'[22]

One day, when the Human Genome Project has completed its massive task of decoding all the genes that go to make up human beings, there will presumably be some definite answers to these questions. In the meantime, the possibility of identifying a specific gene or genes for 'schizophrenia' has raised all sorts of anxieties about antenatal screening, embryo selection and related moral dilemmas. There are good logical reasons why we do not need to be too worried. Remember that we are talking about forms of *behaviour*, and not 'illnesses'. As a speaker from the Genetic Forum in London says: 'The idea that human behaviour can be explained at a molecular level is patently rubbish.'[23]

Biochemical explanations

It will be useful to bear the above quote in mind while we consider the evidence that 'schizophrenia' has some biochemical cause in the brain. There has been no shortage of suggestions for the guilty chemical, including noradrenaline, prostaglandin, endorphins, amino acids, acetylcholine and histamines.[24] The currently favoured candidates are dopamine and serotonin. Once again, we can apply logic to ask: (a) has any consistent link between a diagnosis of 'schizophrenia' and unusual levels of a particular chemical or neurotransmitter been found? The answer is no; and (b) if such a link were to be found, would this tell us anything about the causes of 'schizophrenia'? Even setting aside for a moment the problem of the validity of the concept under investigation, the answer is, probably not. Let us say, for the sake of argument, that it has been established that people with a diagnosis of 'schizophrenia' have raised levels of dopamine in their brains. It is perfectly possible that the mental state is causing the physical one, rather than vice versa, in the same way that fear increases heart rate, or anxiety leads to ulcers. (For example, it has recently been established that prolonged stress during combat can cause actual physical damage to soldiers' brains.[25]) It is equally possible that the association is due to some third factor, as when the presence of certain metabolites in the urine of hospitalised patients (the so-called 'pink spot' test, which caused a lot of excitement at the time) was shown to be due to the excessive tea drinking that is a part of institutional life.[26] The most common third factor is, of course, medication, although few studies take the elementary step of allowing for its powerful and widespread effects on patients' brains.

Two other common arguments deserve brief attention. It has been suggested that because neuroleptic drugs block dopamine and seem to help in the treatment of 'schizophrenia', then, by a form of backwards logic, 'schizophrenia' must result from overactivity of the dopamine system. This is rather like arguing that headaches are caused by a lack of aspirin.

The fact that substances that increase dopamine production, such as amphetamines, can also produce 'schizophrenic'-type symptoms has also been put forward in support of the dopamine hypothesis. This is like arguing that because caffeine can cause anxiety, anxiety must be caused by caffeine.

At the end of this overview, we may be in a position to agree that, in the words of a classic paper, 'Given that schizophrenia is an entity which seems to have no particular symptoms, which follows no particular course and which responds to no (or perhaps every) particular treatment, it is perhaps not surprising that . . . research has so far failed to establish that it has any particular cause.'[27] Or, as another critic put it, 'No single cause, medical or psychosocial, will ever be found for such a vast and diverse array of "symptoms". It is time to act on the recommendation that research on "schizophrenia", and the term itself, should be abandoned.'[28]

This is *not* to deny that there exist many very distressed people who have unusual and frightening experiences, cause great anxiety to those around them, and are in urgent need of some kind of help. Rather, it is to reject the concept of 'schizophrenia' as an explanation of those experiences.

Equally, it is *not* to deny that we are bodies as well as minds, or that there are biological and brain events that correlate with all aspects of our mental states, whether these are 'normal' or 'abnormal'. The problem arises when one aspect of our biology is arbitrarily elevated into the primary 'cause' of other aspects of our functioning, and used to justify the categorising of certain experiences as 'illnesses', with all the consequences we have discussed.

Moreover, as we have seen, what any medical approach crucially fails to address is the *meaning* of so-called 'schizophrenic' experiences. Personal meaning is the first and biggest casualty of the biomedical model. All the biological research in the world will be unable to enlighten us about what Jenny's failure at college meant to her, or why Linda's father's death affected her so profoundly. One psychiatrist who has worked with such people for many years believes that 'the biochemical research still being financed in the field of "schizophrenia" may well be the symbol of our obstinate attempts to *deny that human distress and confusion can take this form.*'[29]

Psychotherapeutic explanations

Paradoxically, despite the hostility noted earlier (p. 75) towards psychotherapeutic models of severe mental distress, they are much better supported by the evidence than the medical one. For a brief period in the 1950s and 1960s, during the so-called 'anti-psychiatry' movement, these theories were widely discussed and researched, athough their impact upon mainstream psychiatry was limited. Since a thorough overview could fill a whole book, I will present a brief synopsis with references for those who wish to read further.[30] (The strong evidence for social factors in 'schizophrenia' will be discussed in Chapter 10.)

Over the years, recurring relationship themes have emerged during the course of work with individuals with a diagnosis of 'schizophrenia' and their families. Professionals using a whole variety of different psychotherapeutic approaches (psychoanalytic, existential, systemic, humanistic and cognitive-behavioural, for those familiar with the terminology) have all reported difficulties in the following areas:

- extreme separation difficulties between parent and child;
- blurred boundaries in relationships;
- identity confusion;
- confused and contradictory family communications;
- emotional and physical/sexual intrusiveness;
- difficulty in dealing with anger and sexuality;
- severe marital problems;
- social isolation.

Is all this coincidental or irrelevant?

Because of the sensitivity of the subject, it is worth spelling out some of the implications of arguing that these findings point towards a causal role for family relationships in the emergence of 'schizophrenia'. This does not imply that they are the *only* causal factor, as we shall see in this and later chapters; nor does it mean that such explanations are relevant in *all* cases, since the label of 'schizophrenia' is, as we have seen, fairly randomly applied. Nor, again, do we need to imply that parents may be in some way to blame: after all, parents are themselves partly the product of their own parents' attitudes, and so on in an infinite regression, and families are themselves shaped by powerful external pressures that may be beyond their control. We also need to acknowledge the considerable burden that carers carry; a survey by the National Schizophrenia Fellowship (NSF) found that over two-thirds had suffered health problems as a result, and other research describes the 'sadness, anger, guilt and self-reproach, anxiety, loneliness, fatigue, helplessness, shock, relief, yearning and numbness' that relatives go through when a family member is diagnosed as having a mental illness.[31]

Having said all this, the model that consistently emerges from this large body of research and practice is one in which parents, due to psychological problems that may date back several generations, are unable to facilitate their infant's very early development of a sense of identity and separateness. The child's sense of him- or herself becomes inextricably linked with the parents' identity and difficulties. Problems come to the fore when separation becomes an issue in adolescence or early adulthood. Because of the crucial role that the child has come to play in the parents' fragile psychological adjustment, any moves that he or she makes towards independence, and particularly the expression of anger or sexuality, are very threatening. However, since these difficulties are largely out of awareness and are in conflict with the parents' genuine love and concern, they can only emerge in the form of confused and contradictory communications. The child, torn between overt and covert messages, lacking a secure sense of identity and isolated from healthier outside influences, has no room to manoeuvre. He or she may resort to expressing in metaphor what cannot be said openly. This, as we saw in Jenny's case, carries the danger of being labelled 'mad'.

A striking confirmation of the role of such factors in severe breakdown can be found in the tragic story of the Genain quadruplets, who became the focus of perhaps the most detailed investigation ever undertaken into one family.[32] These four identical girls, born in America in the 1930s, were all diagnosed as 'schizophrenic' in their early twenties, providing researchers with a unique opportunity, as they thought, to confirm the role of genetic influences: 'When one first learns that the quadruplets are both monozygotic [that is, genetically identical] and schizophrenic, one can hardly help but wonder what further proof of a genetic aetiology [cause] of schizophrenia anyone would want to have.'[33]

However, the picture that emerged was not so simple. Every possible physical and psychological investigation into the quads was carried out, and family, friends, neighbours, colleagues, teachers and others were all interviewed at length. Tape recordings of Mrs Genain alone amounted to several hundred hours. The picture emerged of a violent, alcoholic, sexually abusive father and a mother who could not allow her daughters to express any anger, upset or independence of thought or feeling. The quads, virtually forbidden to mix outside the family, were timid, confused and terrified, and unable to make the transition into the adult world. In such an environment, breakdown would seem to be almost inevitable. In fact, the results gave clear evidence for the causal influence of family relationships in the emergence, the timing, the form and the outcome of the condition. Parental attitudes of control, emotional over-involvement and intrusiveness were implicated in the *development* of the condition, while parental hostility was related to *outcome*. Thus, the most favoured quad was eventually able to marry and have children, while the least favoured of her sisters spent most of her life on a locked ward. Moreover, each quad appeared to represent, and to manifest in her 'symptoms', a particular aspect of her mother's difficulties; for example, Hester seemed to be acting out her mother's repressed anger and sexuality. However, these intriguing and important findings have not been followed up. Indeed, a recent textbook actually summarises the study as providing 'compelling evidence for a genetic base for schizophrenia'.[34]

If disturbed family relationships do play a crucial role in the development of 'schizophrenia', it follows that psychotherapy of various kinds may, in at least some cases, be the most effective way of helping people. A few clinicians still carry out psychotherapeutic work with clients diagnosed as 'schizophrenic', starting from the belief that even the most bizarre experiences can be understood as meaningful responses to extreme relationship difficulties, and that real recovery (not just symptom relief) can, in some cases and with a great deal of hard work on both sides, be achieved. However, such work is usually carried out in an extremely hostile environment, since, in the words of one leading therapist: 'Schizophrenia is now generally believed to be an organic disease like diabetes or cancer . . . [Psychotherapeutic models] . . . are looked on as relics of antiquity, even of the age of magic and witchcraft.'[35]

For reasons of space, a sample of the large literature contradicting such a position is listed in the notes section for this chapter.[36] A particularly important recent project comes from Finland, where 'schizophrenia' is conceptualised as the result (among other factors) of family conflicts, identity confusion and separation difficulties. A nationwide project has been set up based on this model. Immediately after the first admission, all members of the family are invited to a meeting in which they are helped to 'conceive of the situation rather as a consequence of the difficulties the patient and those close to them have encountered in their lives than a mysterious illness the patient has developed as an individual'. Treatment plans are flexible, depending on the individual's needs and his or her progress, but might typically consist of a year or so of family therapy in order to promote separation, followed by long-term individual therapy. Group and couple psychotherapy is also available, as is practical help with social needs such as job-hunting. Medication is used at the minimum dosages and often discontinued altogether after a year. Follow-up studies show a reduction in symptoms, in-patient days and disability pensions, and many people have been able to return to work.[37] Similar projects have been set up in Norway, Denmark and Sweden.

Summary

This rather lengthy overview of the traditional medical assumptions about 'schizophrenia' has been necessary because of the crucial implications for the whole practice of psychiatry. Using 'schizophrenia' as the 'prototypical psychiatric disease', we have reached the startling conclusion that not only is there no evidence for biological causes, but that it makes no logical sense to assume that such an illness exists at all. This means that a whole branch of medicine is based upon unsupported hypotheses and logical errors; that research which incorporates such assumptions is bound to be flawed, and probably fruitless; that medical cures for psychiatric breakdown are not only unavailable but unattainable; and that those who are said to be suffering from such illnesses will be at best unhelped by psychiatry, and at worst will have their difficulties and distress disastrously compounded. Meanwhile, because of vested interests, important evidence that might throw light on the psychological and social roots of mental distress has to be discounted and ignored. These are themes to which we shall be returning throughout the book.

TREATMENT APPROACHES TO 'SCHIZOPHRENIA'

In the remaining part of this chapter I should like to look briefly at four different approaches to 'schizophrenia' in the light of the discussion so far. The first two are relatively recent concessions towards incorporating *relationships* and *personal meaning* into the psychiatric understanding of 'schizophrenia'. Although widely recognised by mainstream psychiatrists, they are, as I hope to show, limited by their need to avoid a fundamental challenge to medical model assumptions. The other two are alternative approaches, one carried out within the psychiatric system and one outside it. Both see 'schizophrenia' as part of a whole person in a whole system of relationships, not just as a disease entity. The second presents a particularly powerful challenge to traditional psychiatry.

Family management

A well-known psychiatrist, Professor Leff, and his colleagues have carried out thorough and much-quoted work with people diagnosed as 'schizophrenic' and their families.[38] They rated patients' relatives on a number of scales for such factors as hostility, over-involvement and critical comments, and found that about half the families scored highly on these measures. (Note the similarity to the attitudes identified in the Genain family.) This was referred to as High Expressed Emotion, or High EE, while the other families were characterised by Low Expressed Emotion, or Low EE. They found that the likelihood of relapse after a first 'schizophrenic' breakdown was greatly increased if a patient lived with a High EE family. Leff and his colleagues therefore put together a package of educational talks, groups for relatives, and family sessions, to try and reduce the level of EE and hence the rate of relapse in these families. The approach is a commonsense, practical one in which the professionals try to help patients and relatives to reduce the amount of time they spend together, to build up separate social lives, to deal with arguments around the house, and so on. All the families succeeded in reducing the level of EE or at least spending less time together, and this significantly reduced the rate of relapse in the patients, especially if medication was taken as well. Interestingly, though, overinvolvement – which included such factors as overprotectiveness, excessive self-sacrifice and an inability to lead separate lives – hardly changed at all. Meanwhile a comparison group received standard NHS treatment, that is, there was no help or advice for the relatives, and the relapse rate was much higher.

The work of Leff and other well-known figures in the field has been widely accepted in psychiatric circles. Other clinicians have developed their own versions,[39] Family Management (FM) teams have been set up in many British and American cities, and the Thorn Diploma has been established to train psychiatric nurses in the approach. The work certainly has its useful aspects. However, in my view, much of its success can be attributed to its skill in providing a framework in which psychiatrists can admit the relevance of psychological and relationship factors in 'schizophrenia' while keeping within the medical model and avoiding the whole controversial issue of what caused the breakdown in the first place. The Family Management view is that stress, as measured by EE, only triggers *relapse* in a condition that is described to patients and relatives as 'an illness, that is, having a biological basis'.[40] Clinicians emphasise that they do not describe their work as family therapy, since they 'do *not* view the family as in need of treatment . . . Our aim is to help the family cope better with the sick member who is suffering from a defined disease.'[41] This so-called 'vulnerability–stress model' is currently the most popular way of conceptualising 'schizophrenia'.

It is, of course, somewhat tricky to maintain that family attitudes play a part in causing relapse but have nothing to do with the development of the problem in the first place. The standard response is to say that High EE is *caused by* the stress of coping with the patient, though some of the FM work itself seems to contradict this:

> Evidence exists linking one emotional attitude we found to be influential, with maternal overprotectiveness antedating the onset of

schizophrenia . . . overprotective attitudes were more commonly shown by mothers of children who later developed schizophrenia than mothers of control children . . . This suggests that the overprotective degree of involvement develops very early in the child's life, and indeed we have anecdotal evidence of this from several of our families.[42]

Separation is always the big issue . . . for some families it was possible to work towards hostel placement, in others the intensity of closeness was so great that the focus had to be on small issues. In one family, for example, months of work was spent on helping a mother and daughter negotiate the daughter's washday.[43]

Some of the thumbnail sketches of the families involved in the study confirm how blinkered it is to treat one member of the family as ill while ignoring what is going on around them. Thus:

The patient, a man of twenty-three living with mother, stepfather, and a younger brother, suffered a first attack of schizophrenia. Mother had always seen him as the weaker of her two sons and appeared to have been overinvolved with him virtually from birth. He slept in her bed till the age of fifteen.

The patient, a woman of twenty-four, lived with her parents and siblings. Both parents were highly critical of her, particularly her father . . . She returned home. After a few days her father had a furious row with her and ordered her to sleep in a shed in the garden. Several days later she suffered a return of auditory hallucinations.[44]

Critics have noted that the central controversy about cause and blame has not been resolved in this work, but simply ignored: 'Blame is avoided only at the expense of conceptual clarity – by declining to address the issue of aetiology [causation] altogether.'[45] This avoidance is essential if Family Management is to avoid a storm of protest and the embarrassment of undermining the medical assumptions on which it rests. However, as I have argued elsewhere,[46] this results in contradictions both in theory (it is argued that patients can cause disturbance in relatives, but not vice versa) and practice (families are told there is nothing wrong with them, but they need to change to avoid relapses).

One consequence of retaining a medically based approach is, as we have seen before, the loss of meaning. American psychoanalyst Michael Robbins sees vulnerability–stress models as being particularly insidious in this way, since they are disguised as an appreciation of psychological factors while denying their personal meaning and causal significance in people's lives.[47] What is all the High EE about? Why is separation so hard in these families? How and why did the overinvolvement start? None of these questions can be addressed or answered within this model. Perhaps this explains why, despite international acclaim, its achievements are actually quite limited: 'Patients appear better but not well . . . relatively few patients appear to achieve independent living and full employment.'[48] One service user has suggested that what is needed is not so much a family *management* programme as a family *separation* programme.[49] Or, to put the point another way: 'Are the identified patients being encouraged to achieve genuine growth and independence, or do they merely end up having their "illness" more successfully "managed" within the confines of the family system?'[50]

Cognitive approaches

I want to look briefly at another recent mainstream approach which believes that there is value in looking at the *content* of the beliefs and experiences of those with a diagnosis of 'schizophrenia', rather than simply categorising them as 'symptoms'. This has been a taboo area in psychiatry for many years: doctors and nurses have been advised 'not to go along with the patient's delusions and hallucinations; on the contrary, the patient should be encouraged to ignore them'.[51] Recent cognitive-behavioural work, developed mainly, but not only, by clinical psychologists, has come up with a range of techniques that involve a close examination of unusual beliefs and experiences.[52] These fall into two main categories: first, behavioural interventions such as distraction, relaxation, stress management and so on (the Hearing Voices Network, as described pp. 96–99, has identified a similar range of coping strategies); second, patients are encouraged, in a series of therapy sessions, to challenge and test out some of the underlying assumptions behind their beliefs, and hence modify them. For example, the theory states that people with a diagnosis of 'schizophrenia' may be particularly prone to make illogical leaps in their thinking – perhaps jumping to the conclusion that people are plotting against them on very little evidence, or taking things out of context. They may also be inclined to attribute internal processes, such as their own thoughts, to external sources, such as voices coming from someone or somewhere else. By a process of sensitive discussion, education and reality-testing, more rational ways of interpreting the world can be introduced, with a consequent reduction in 'symptoms' and general levels of distress. An example gives the flavour:

M is a 34 year old married woman of Iranian origin with a three-year history of schizoaffective disorder. Onset followed the dissolution of her first marriage and was marked by visual hallucinations of the Islamic prophet Masuma and accompanying auditory hallucinations in Arabic . . . The voice was ever-present and offered advice on her functioning as a housewife (eg telling her to try new recipes), mother (eg telling her when to change a nappy), and wife (eg advising her how to please her husband). M felt great reverence for the voice and it directed the majority of her behaviour. To most observers, including her husband, M was increasingly undermined by her voices and was losing all confidence in her own judgement . . . Dependence was also reinforced by fear that if left alone she might fail in her different functions as wife and parent. Belief 3, that she could not think without the voice, was weakest and therefore tackled first. The main piece of evidence was that the voice was involved in all day-to-day decisions. However, a detailed diary revealed that over a week 58% of her actions were voice-driven, 32% were self-governed, and 10% represented a rejection of the voice's advice. M was impressed by this result . . . Belief 2, that the voice helped her through personal difficulties, rested on two points: that it gave good advice and that it predicted the future. However, discussion clarified that the predictions had high probability – perhaps that the husband would be home at the usual time. The most potent advice was novel recipes. However, questioning revealed that none of the ingredients was actually new and a subsequent test involving the husband confirmed that the recipes were not novel but rather variations on one theme. The main evidence that the voice was a prophet was that it spoke in Arabic, directed her to pages of the Koran, and knew her thoughts. M acknowledged that this evidence was equally consistent with the view that the voice was self-generated . . . Therapy lasted 18 weekly sessions, some involving her husband, and conviction in all four beliefs weakened considerably over this time . . . M volunteered that the voice was less intrusive and regarded it more as an irritation.[53]

Obviously this work can be very effective and is undoubtedly an advance on offering medication as the only treatment. How much of a challenge it will ultimately pose to traditional medical assumptions is as yet unclear. As Mary Boyle has pointed out: 'The new approaches have often maintained medical language and theoretical frameworks. The term schizophrenia is often used, or if not, terms such as disorders, symptoms or psychopathology may be substituted.'[54] Cognitive approaches complement medical ones in that they too locate the problem within an *individual*, who is said to be defective or irrational in some way. There is a danger of conceptualising treatment as a kind of fixing of a faulty machine, while the rigid barrier between 'mad' and 'sane' (or, in its cognitive version, between 'rational' and 'irrational') is maintained. The closer we come to admitting that 'madness' is understandable and even rational in its context, the greater the need to 'call into question the primacy of the medical model . . . [and] ask uncomfortable and threatening questions about the ways in which culture, social structures and individual families are involved in the development of "madness".'[55]

For these reasons, it is not a surprise to find that content and context are attended to only in a limited way within a cognitive model. We can see from the example that many questions are left unaddressed. For example, M's husband seems to have been enlisted in treatment primarily in order to supply more information about his wife's 'faulty' thinking, while more searching and threatening issues about the relationship and the power dynamics between the couple have gone unexamined. What did the breakdown of her first marriage mean to M? Did she perhaps have to create an external adviser to cope with her sense of failure? What factors in her own upbringing had made her vulnerable to this? Why did she have such a limited conception of being a good wife and mother? How was Mr X contributing to these expectations? What part did cultural issues play? Exploring these questions might have led to a view of M's 'symptoms' as rational, functional and meaningful within her personal situation, and to solutions that involved change at a whole-person, whole-system level, not just a cognitive one.

Crisis intervention

Dr R.D. Scott, a former NHS psychiatrist, spent many years working with those who are diagnosed 'schizophrenic' and their families. In contrast to Leff, he is particularly concerned with the whole process of how someone comes to be labelled as 'schizophrenic' and admitted to hospital in the first instance, and the events that lead up to this crucial moment. His stance is very different from the orthodox one, but his findings will not come as a surprise to readers who have followed the arguments of this book so far.

Scott punctures the myth that it is psychiatrists who diagnose 'schizophrenia' and other psychiatric problems.[56] In almost every case, he points out, the diagnosis has already been made by ordinary lay people who have selected one member of the group or family as the sick one. These lay people then put the psychiatrist under enormous pressure to rubber-stamp this diagnosis while at the same time insisting that it is *he* who is making the diagnosis and not they. ('You're the expert, doctor. He must be ill or he wouldn't be here.') But if as the 'expert' he or she refuses to go along with this diagnosis and to say what they have told him or her to say, then the situation may become very tense and threatening. We saw how Mrs Clark had decided that Jenny was crazy at a very early stage, was furious with the GP who refused to go along with this diagnosis when the crisis blew up, and eventually found a doctor who was willing to do so.

Scott sees the purpose of this manoeuvre as 'avoiding mutual and unbearable pain between two or more family members',[57] which threatens to come to the fore during a crisis point in the family's life. If the doctor complies with the relatives' expectations and agrees to label the person as mad and take total responsibility for him or her, then:

> he will be forced to draw a line which rigidly divides the ill from the well; human relationships are then maintained in a severed and disconnected state. The parents deny that forms of relationship threatening to themselves are relationships; they are seen as forms of disturbances in the patient. Thus, symptomatology is maintained by the conventional approach whilst relationship issues are depersonalised and evaded.[58]

Scott calls this event, the drawing of the sick/well line, 'closure', and notes that 'the point at which inner disturbance in the family, which may have been present for many years or even generations, becomes officially located as being disturbance in one member . . . brings relief from uncertainty – now they know what the trouble is'. At the same time, 'the cost is frightful. What happens may result in the permanent . . . crippling of one or more lives.'[59] After closure has occurred, there is an impenetrable barrier to dealing with issues in the relationship between the patient and others. Scott calls this the 'treatment barrier'.

The operation of the treatment barrier can be detected in the other cases we have seen; it was very hard for Elaine or her therapist, for example, to untangle the relevant relationship difficulties since all the problems had been officially located in her 'illness'. What seems to distinguish those diagnosed as 'schizophrenic' and their families from other patients is the intensity with which the dramas are played out, and the rigid finality of closure when it occurs. A further result of the treatment barrier is that the identified patients, even if genuinely needy, can at the same time exploit their sick role status rather as Jeanette, Fay and Alice did. Scott again:

> In our experience the power of the role . . . of mental patient is tremendous. It is a power which patients freely use: many times our patients have presented themselves at a police station, 'I'm from Napsbury'. They want a free ride back. I might tell the police officer, 'It is very kind of you to offer transport, but I think it would be better to let him increase his self-reliance by finding his own way back'. The chances are that the patient still arrives by police car, or else the patient may phone a relative who gets on to me and accuses me of negligence and cruelty. It is practically impossible to let a patient be responsible, and they know it.[60]

He also presents evidence that, although patients are seen by their parents as fitting the cultural image of mental illness, that is, as being confused and unable to take responsibility, the patients often see themselves as controlling, while also being aware that others do not see them as possessing this power.[61] This is added confirmation of the secret power of the Victim role.

So how can closure and the creation of the treatment barrier be avoided? Or, to put the same question a slightly different way, how can one avoid this particular variation of the Rescue game? With people labelled 'schizophrenic' the question is, if anything, even more crucial than with other patients, since closure is even more final and absolute. The answer, though, is the same. Essentially, it is to resist the pressure to treat the identified patient as the helpless Victim of a disease process; to refuse to collude with hiding the relationship issues under the label of an illness; and to negotiate a proper treatment contract rather than taking complete responsibility for the patient and the 'illness'.

Scott has shown that all this is possible, even with those patients who are most out of touch with reality and apparently most suitable candidates for a medical model-style Rescue. He and his team started to do

> something we had never dared to do before: challenge the role of the mental patient. At the group meeting in the admission ward we, as a team, would not take the medical counterpart of the mental patient role, but instead adopt an approach in which we might say to a patient, 'You must want something from us since you do not leave.

If you could tell us about this we might be able to help'. We do not accept denials of agency, and we remain unresponsive to psychotic [that is, crazy] types of explanation. In this way psychotic ideas can sometimes be undercut in one session revealing more real issues, the hurts, despair, conflict with others.[62]

Similarly, relatives were asked why the children came into hospital with an equally firm refusal to accept that it was entirely the result of a doctor's decision. This simple policy led to a drastic reduction in psychotic behaviour, length of admissions and use of sedative drugs on the wards, but not without cost to the staff: 'The use of the approach has required staff to withstand a high degree of anxiety. It cannot be used by individual staff members, but requires a team organised from top to bottom.' The case of George and Alice, where only one unsupported doctor and nurse were prepared to challenge the mental patient role, illustrates this point. Again, Scott warns that breaking these unwritten rules meant that 'relatives, and patients too, have tried threatening us with the highest authorities'.

It became obvious that if this approach was to work properly, not only for people diagnosed 'schizophrenic' but for all types of patient, then the psychiatric team would need to organise itself in a radically different way. Usually, there are a number of different routes into hospital (via casualty, the police, GPs). The person designated as the sick one will probably be seen at the hospital, so that it is impossible to get a true picture of the home and family situation, or else admissions will be arranged over the telephone without the doctor seeing the prospective patient at all. If a short home visit is made, it is merely to rubber-stamp the diagnosis that, as we have seen, will already have been made by relatives, neighbours and other lay people.

Scott and his colleagues realised that there had to be a cohesive admission team prepared to travel out to homes, hostels, bedsits, or wherever the problem was and to spend as much time as was needed to get a proper picture of the whole situation and every individual's part in it. Since at the start of the new approach 90 per cent of their admissions were by crisis, the team had to be available twenty-four hours a day, seven days a week, so that the confusions created by having several routes into hospital were avoided. The staff also had to be readily available for some weeks or months after the initial crisis visit, to do follow-up work and give advice and support as necessary. The crisis intervention team consisted of a psychiatrist and a social worker, and it guaranteed to be on the doorstep within two hours of receiving a call from a GP, the police or, more rarely, members of the public. The team believed that the first contact with the psychiatric services was crucial and could determine the whole future pattern of events. A crisis was not an unfortunate event that had to be defused as quickly as possible by removing the supposedly sick person; rather, it was a unique opportunity to do vital therapeutic work, as tensions that might have been dormant and hidden for years erupted into the open. But if this chance was not seized and used, closure would occur and the conflicts would be sealed off, perhaps forever, as one member of the family embarked on the career of mental patient.

On a crisis visit, the first task was to reduce the tension and build up a complete picture of the background to the crisis. Then some sort of mutual understanding and agreement about what was going on had to be reached. If this turned out to be a couple or family issue, then the focus would shift to couple or family counselling, perhaps followed up with further meetings over the next few weeks. Whatever the outcome, the same therapist would be involved throughout to co-ordinate the treatment. If one person was admitted to hospital, then great care was taken to ensure that this was not done in such a way that one person was labelled as the 'sick one' with all responsibility for him or her being handed over to the doctors.

In Jenny's case, the team would have needed to sit with the family until the immediate uproar died down, rather than defusing the situation by certifying one member and forcibly removing her. When a measure of calm had been achieved, they would have started piecing together the events leading up to the crisis, this time taking Jenny's viewpoint into account as well. They would have tried to build up a full picture of the background: Jenny's difficulties at school, the Clarks' unhappy marriage, the role the other children played in the family, Mr and Mrs Clark's own background, and so on. This might well take several hours, rather than the half-hour or so that would be needed for a quick decision to admit one member. They would have worked towards a mutually agreed view of the problem as something in which the whole family was involved, so that even if admission were still necessary, the way would have been open for more work on the family issues. Regular family meetings might have been arranged for the next few months, while the hospital staff would have been informed about the background and encouraged Jenny to talk about her feelings and frustrations instead of just medicating her. In other words, there would have been a proper treatment contract rather than a Rescue.

Leaving the sheltered world of the hospital was an eye-opening experience for the team. Scott and his staff realized that following normal psychiatric practice had meant that we hardly knew anything about the lives of our patients and their families . . . We have discovered things that amazed us. We began to find out about life and it was not always pleasant. But at least it was preferable to that awful sense of arrested life that goes with closure.[63]

The team had anticipated resistance to the new approach; in fact, there was what Scott described as a 'bloody revolution' within the hospital, which found its very existence threatened by the dramatic fall in admissions. The climax of the struggle was an inquiry into the medical and nursing practices on some of the wards, which put the continuing existence of the crisis intervention team and its philosophy under threat. The team survived, but the rigidity of the nursing hierarchy meant that nurses could never be part of it.

The new approach demanded much from the staff. Scott speaks of:

the distress all members experienced when brought face to face with the realities of human relationships. When the presenting 'madness' is penetrated and the anguish and desperation is laid bare, it takes a strong stomach to continue with one's endeavour . . . Roles tend to become blurred in the dust and murk of the coal face and the release of emotion that is often encountered is no respecter of status or discipline.[64]

Truly, it is safer and easier to stay in the hospital with the old routine of medication and admission.

Over a period of several years the number of sudden emergency calls dropped, and, perhaps because GPs had been educated to look for underlying issues, people were more likely to come along to ask for help with relationship problems than with mental illnesses. More recently, closer links with voluntary agencies and other resources and a greater awareness of the effects of sex roles have influenced the way the service operates.

The crisis service still exists, although to what extent it operates as a true crisis intervention team depends very much on the attitudes of the current consultant and his/her staff; obviously, it is possible to visit homes and meet relatives and yet when you get there still be doing the same diagnosis–prescription–admission routine as before. A study of one of the original teams over a two-year period showed that admission rates were halved, with first admissions being reduced by up to 60 per cent. The resulting reduction in the number of beds enabled several wards to be closed with a saving of several hundred thousand pounds of NHS money a year.[65] More recent research also confirms that crisis services are cheaper than the alternatives.[66] Less tangibly, the new approach was felt by Scott's team to be vastly more productive and satisfying than the old one. However, it does present a strong challenge to orthodox psychiatry; indeed, Scott came up against active resistance from official bodies when he tried to give lectures and submit articles on his work. This is perhaps why, despite their many therapeutic and financial advantages, more than thirty years on, Barnet hospital is still almost unique in offering a comprehensive crisis service to all potential admissions. Even here, the service 'remains controversial, appears to be under constant review and is being eroded by financial restrictions'.[67]

Most current crisis services seek to offer alternatives to hospital for acute need, thus avoiding the criticism that they are, in the words of one service user, 'merely getting me to an unsatisfactory destination a little more efficiently'.[68] Over a hundred such projects now exist, varying from walk-in self-referral centres to safe houses offering sanctuary for a few days or weeks. Some of these resources are available twenty-four hours a day, others on a more limited basis, or only for people with certain types of difficulty (such as drug addiction). Some are part of the NHS, while others are set up and run by voluntary organisations or service users themselves. Service users have for many years called for community-based crisis teams backed up by alternatives to hospital and run along psychosocial lines. With the reduction in hospital beds, the advantages of crisis intervention have become more apparent, which may explain why it is coming back into favour as a key element of the present government's plans for mental health services.

The Hearing Voices Movement

In 1987 a Dutch psychiatrist, Marius Romme, was struggling to help one of his patients, Patsy Hage, who heard intrusive and distressing voices. She challenged him to take them seriously as a real experience for her. In a novel move, both psychiatrist and patient appeared on a national television programme asking other people with similar experiences to contact them; 450 people who heard voices responded, and this became the start of a series of studies of voice-hearers and their experiences.[69]

Hearing voices is, in standard psychiatric practice, one of the primary symptoms of 'schizophrenia', and as such leads almost invariably to diagnosis and medication. However, to their surprise, Romme and Sandra Escher, a science journalist who works with him, discovered that significant numbers of people who hear voices function well in society without needing psychiatric help. What distinguishes them from people diagnosed as 'schizophrenic' is not the presence or absence of voices, but their ability to cope with them. Those who had escaped the attention of psychiatry had developed various techniques such as setting limits to when they would attend to the voices, talking back to them, listening selectively to the more positive voices, and so on; in other words, instead of feeling terrified and powerless in the face of their experiences, they took an active, constructive stance in which the voices were accepted as an important and even valuable part of their lives. They also tended to understand their voices in spiritual, mystical, psychoanalytic or paranormal rather than medical terms. The contrast with psychiatric explanations, which are highly pathologising and alarming, offering only the passive solution of taking medication, is obvious.

Romme and Escher also explored the relationship between hearing voices and the individual's life history. A number of themes emerged. Both psychiatric patients and non-patients reported traumatic events, particularly bereavement and sexual or physical assault, which seemed to precipitate the voice-hearing. For example:

> Hannah, a 31 year old woman, was sexually abused by her father. As far as she could remember this experience continued until her eleventh year. Her father brutally raped her and threatened to kill her . . . She explained that as a child she used to talk to herself and that she was unable to accept the memories from this time. When she gets 'flashbacks' of this unhappy time she hears the voice of a small child telling her 'you know this really happened'. The voice of the small child then reminds her of what occurred and she responds by telling the voice, 'this is a really terrible thing you are telling me.' She also has periods when she hears many voices and they do not only speak about the abuse. She recognises among the voices, the voice of her mother. As a child, Hannah recalled that she used to talk about herself in the third person as a means of preventing the flood of bad memories she experienced . . . [70]

Romme and Escher now believe that such voices are a normal human reaction to stress and an important part of the individual's coping strategies. For example, Hannah's voices could be understood both as drawing attention to emotional traumas that urgently needed resolving and as a development of her earlier defence of talking about herself in the third person. (Linda Hart, whose story we read in Chapter 2, had a similar understanding of her own voices.) Since they are a normal human variation, they cannot be 'cured' any more than, say, left-handedness, but they can be accepted, managed and learned from. This can be achieved within a trusting relationship with a mental health worker or a support group of other voice-hearers who will help the individual to develop coping strategies and to discover the *meaning* of the voices in the light of his or her life situation and experiences:

> It is a good idea to begin with a comprehensive inventory of the number of voices, their gender, age and characteristics, to whom they belong, how they are organised, what influence they have on the hearer, what they say, how the hearer reacts to this, what has happened since they were first heard, and so on. The supposed identity and way of speaking of the voices might reflect the persons represented by the voices. The content mostly indicates the themes which the person has difficulty expressing in daily life. The triggers might point to troublesome emotions or situations the voice-hearer cannot handle . . . And the time when the voices were heard for the first time often shows traumas or interactions with others that made the voice-hearer quite powerless.[71]

Ron Coleman spent thirteen years in the psychiatric system with a diagnosis of 'schizophrenia' before finding help through the Hearing Voices Network. He is now a freelance trainer promoting this approach nationally and internationally. His dominant voice

> was that of a Dundee priest who had sexually abused him when he was 11. It would tell him he was responsible for the abuse and had led a good man into sin. As a result, he would burn himself, often pouring lighter fuel over his body. [He] was diagnosed as a chronic schizophrenic in 1984. He was prescribed medication to stop him hearing voices, but it failed to do so. 'Whatever conventional treatment I was given, from tranquillisers to electroconvulsive therapy, I still heard the voices', he recalls. 'The doctors only succeeded in making me too numb to make sense of them.' Finally he got help, from an organisation called the Hearing Voices Network in Manchester. 'They helped me to enter into a dialogue with my voices and negotiate with them', he says. 'I identified six other voices apart from the priest. I realised the most disturbing ones where exploiting my weaknesses, reinforcing my doubts and fears. The priest's voice played upon my Catholic guilt, making out that I was not the victim of abuse but the perpetrator. With the help of support workers I was

able to replay what had happened and recognise my own innocence. Although I still hear the priest occasionally, he's only a minor voice now.' Another distressing voice was that of his first lover, Annabel. 'She had committed suicide and her voice would tell me to join her', Mr Coleman says. 'Sometimes she would sound seductive and at other times angry, but I learned this depended on my mood.' After bereavement counselling, he has gradually come to terms with Annabel's death . . . 'On the anniversary of her death I was able to recall her as a memory and not a voice.'[72]

Hearing Voices self-help support groups have been set up in many British cities. We can see that their existence and, even more so, their success are a powerful challenge to psychiatry's most fundamental assumptions. A primary 'symptom' of 'schizophrenia' turns out to be a normal and relatively common aspect of human experience; interventions, for those who need them, are best supplied not by professionals but by self-help groups; and the key to coping lies not in standard psychiatric theories and treatments, which actually make the situation worse, but in *exploring meaning in a trusting relationship*. Once again, we find ourselves echoing the themes of earlier chapters.

It remains to be seen how psychiatry will react to this challenge. One commentator has outlined the possible responses: ignoring the work; dismissing its conclusions; attacking Romme's personal and professional credibility; and if these fail, absorbing the approach into mainstream psychiatry while stripping it of its more radical aspects:

> What may happen is that through Romme's work, hearing voices becomes less significant in the diagnosis of schizophrenia . . . People who work in psychiatry and the general public will understand the experience of hearing voices a little better. Treatment for people who hear voices will be more varied and appropriate but there will be no great long-term changes. The temptation is to concentrate on the short-term benefits of developing self-help groups, coping strategies and on exploring the experience at the expense of creating a political movement of people who can change, for good, the position in society of people who hear voices.[73]

The aims and struggles of the service user movement, of which the Hearing Voices Network is a part, are described in Chapter 11. In the meantime, we can look at psychiatric theory and practice from yet another angle: that of sex role expectations on both women and men.

Chapter 5

Women's and men's role problems and psychiatry

For most of the past fifty years, more women than men have been admitted to psychiatric hospitals,[1] although the trend has gradually changed so that since 1990 there have been slightly more male than female admissions.[2] However, many of the problems that bring people into contact with the psychiatric services – depression, eating disorders, agoraphobia, anxiety, self-harm – are found far more frequently in women than men. A closer look at the roles women are expected to fulfil in our culture is necessary to understand why this is so. I shall follow this with a discussion of the neglected topic of how the mental health of men, too, is affected by sex role pressures.

Let us backtrack a little and look again at the 'depressed housewife', who is a common recipient of psychiatric treatment. We saw in Chapter 1 how Elaine's depression was treated as something separate from her family, her upbringing and her life and role as a woman. Her dilemma, unravelled in therapy, went something like this:

- She had adopted the traditional woman's role of wife and mother.
- She had devoted her whole life to giving to others. Her own needs were not fulfilled.
- She believed it was selfish to have anything for herself. She could not ask for what she needed.
- She resented not getting what she needed.
- She could not express her resentment and felt she had no right to protest about her situation.
- She broke down through giving out far more than she received.
- She blamed the whole situation on herself.

In a much quoted study, Pauline Bart[3] traced these and similar themes in over 500 American women aged between 40 and 59 who had come into

DOI: 10.4324/9781003095958-5

hospital for the first time with a diagnosis of depression. Theories have been put forward which suggest that the increase in depression in woman around this age is due to the hormonal changes of the menopause or other biological factors. A special diagnosis has been coined for the problem: 'involutional melancholia'. Bart, though, wanted to try and understand the problem from the point of view of women's role expectations. She talked to women whose breakdown had occurred shortly after a child had left home or got engaged or married, and discussed what this had meant to the mothers. She found that the women in her survey saw their most important role in life as mothers and homemakers, and that they had thrown themselves into these roles with a completeness that left very little time for themselves or a life outside the family. Being deprived of this role by the departure of their children was devastating:

> It's a very lonely life, and this is when I became ill, and I think I'm facing problems now that I did not face before because I was so involved especially having a sick child at home. I didn't think of myself at all. I was just someone that was there to take care of the needs of my family, my husband and children.

As another of the women said:

> I don't feel liked. I don't feel that I'm wanted. I don't feel at all that I'm wanted. I just feel like nothing. I don't feel anybody cares, and nobody's interested, and they don't care whether I do feel good or I don't feel good. I'm pretty useless.

These women had nothing to do, nowhere to go, and no source of confidence or self-esteem apart from the bitter memory of having been such devoted mothers. Often, there was a sense of betrayal and of resentment against the departed children. This could not be openly acknowledged and was turned inwards into despair. The loneliness was accentuated by the fact that dissatisfactions in their marriages could no longer be hidden behind relentless activity: 'My whole life was that because I had no life with my husband, the children should make me happy . . . but it never worked out.'

The irony is, as Bart points out, that these women arrived in their position by doing what was expected of them by their families, their friends, the media and society in general. To an even greater degree than some of their contemporaries, they had embraced the traditional female destiny of finding fulfilment solely through being wives and mothers. But because identity, purpose and self-esteem were all dependent on having others around to care for, they were empty and bereft when those others departed.

We saw in Chapter 1 how the hospital characteristically responds with an unquestioning reinforcement of the traditional values that led to the problem in the first place. Psychiatrists, particularly male ones, often find these women as bemusing and frustrating as the husbands who suddenly find themselves with a weepy, despairing woman on their hands, and the tone of their letters often betrays this. Thus, one of Elaine's psychiatrists wrote to her GP: 'I spoke to her husband who seemed a fairly reasonable person, he had put up with Mrs Jones's relapses with relatively good humour and only occasionally criticised her for the difficulties she produced for the family'; while in the opinion of another: 'She has many vague fears about the future . . . she really is too imaginative.' Exasperation and lack of comprehension on the part of the husbands or partners is to some extent understandable; what is less excusable is the failure of the professionals to bring any greater degree of understanding to the situation. Apart from this, such women tend to be pushed to one side in the hospital as they are in life. They are viewed as cured if they manage to force themselves to take up their old roles as wives and home-makers, at whatever cost to themselves. Not believing that they deserve any better treatment, they pass through the psychiatric system without protesting or attracting the kind of attention that has been paid to less common but more dramatic conditions like 'schizophrenia'.

None of this is meant to imply that it is a mistake for women to follow the traditional path of marriage and motherhood. Where this can lead to problems, though, is first, if it is a forced choice because it is the unquestioned thing to do and other options are not easily available; second, if these roles are carried out at the expense of the woman getting what she needs for herself, so that she is giving out of her own neediness and always putting herself last; and third, if the role of wife and mother is idealised by society while at the same time wives and mothers are devalued, unsupported and blamed in reality.

These themes have been developed by other writers. In her classic book, *Women and Madness*, published in 1972, Phyllis Chesler argued that women are in danger of being labelled as mad either when they take the devalued female role to extremes – for example, becoming excessively anxious, weepy and dependent – or when they reject the traditional role by, for example, being seen as too aggressive.[4] The trap is illustrated in a well-known study by Dr Broverman and her colleagues in 1970,[5] which has been confirmed by subsequent research.[6] Seventy-nine psychiatrists, psychologists and social workers, both male and female, were given a questionnaire consisting of pairs of descriptions, for example, 'very emotional–not at all emotional' and 'not at all aggressive–very aggressive'. They were asked to tick the descriptions that represented healthy male and healthy female adult behaviour. They were also asked to tick the descriptions that fitted their idea of healthy adult behaviour (sex unspecified). The results showed that the professionals' ideas of what constituted a healthy mature male were very similar to their idea of a healthy adult. However, healthy, mature women, in their view, should be:

> More submissive, less independent, less adventurous, more easily influenced, less aggressive, less competitive, more excitable in minor crises, having their feelings more easily hurt, being more emotional, more conceited about their appearance, less objective, and disliking maths and science.

As the authors comment: 'This constellation seems a most unusual way of describing any mature, healthy individual.' The trap awaiting women who come into contact with the psychiatric services is obvious. On the one hand, being independent, assertive and adventurous is seen as abnormal and discouraged in various ways. On the other hand, the more excitable, emotional, dependent behaviour that is expected of women is also seen as unhealthy, because the standard of emotional health is virtually the same as the idea of the healthy adult male. Either way, the woman loses.

Other evidence confirms that women with less conventional lifestyles and attitudes may fare particularly badly in psychiatry, often receiving the overt or covert message that they should not deviate from traditional female norms. For example, gay women have reported that their sexual orientation is either ignored, viewed as the 'cause' of their problems, or seen simplistically as the result of factors such as sexual abuse. They experience widespread ignorance, harassment and judgementalism within the psychiatric services.[7] Women make up 20 per cent of the population of special hospitals like Broadmoor and Rampton, as opposed to 4 per cent of the prison population. One explanation is that aggression, violence and drug-taking are judged much more harshly in women, and are more likely to lead to diagnoses such as 'psychopathic personality disorder' rather than a straightforward prison sentence because they are seen as contrary to appropriate female behaviour.[8]

How much has changed in the thirty or so years since Bart, Broverman and Chesler carried out their classic studies? There have, of course, been enormous challenges to women's traditional roles, with knock-on effects for men, and this may explain both the changing ratio of male to female admissions and the changing patterns within particular disorders (for example, more men reporting eating disorders and more women presenting with alcohol problems). One recent study found that women in their forties become more confident as they grow older and as their children leave home, branching out into education, new jobs and new relationships.[9] Other surveys have found that some of the changes are more apparent than real, and that both sex and class differences in the conditions of work still apply; for example, even women employed outside the home still do an average of nine hours more housework a week than their partners. They 'continue to carry a dual burden: the husbands have in effect one job where they have two'. In addition, 'the role that most women play as mother/housekeeper still significantly affects their career opportunities . . . their promotion prospects, job security and earnings potential are still much more restricted than are men's'.[10] Equal sharing of household tasks is only practised by 1 per cent of couples.[11] More than twenty years after the Equal Pay Act, women's average pay is only 80 per cent of men's. Pay levels are also affected by stereotyped work choices: for example, 92 per cent of hairdressers are women. 'Stereotyping feeds people into a cycle of inequality which is not limited to the first job.'[12]

All this needs to be set in the context of a society in which being female means you are more likely to find yourself struggling with various situations which are known to be linked with mental health problems. These include poverty (which is greatest among single parents, black women and older women); being a victim of domestic violence; caring for children and dependent relatives with little support; childbirth; and being a victim of sexual abuse. These factors interact with a woman's social class and race, with both working-class and black/ethnic minority status increasing socioeconomic hardship and the risk of psychiatric diagnosis.[13]

The picture, then, is complex; but it is certainly the case that traditional roles and expectations are still influential, particularly among older women and those from working-class backgrounds. There is also evidence to support the contention of earlier writers that women who break down are likely to be those who have adopted a more traditional woman's role. A famous study of working-class women in Camberwell, London, found that a quarter of them could be diagnosed as suffering from depression. Factors such as being confined to the home looking after young children and having no outside employment made them more vulnerable to depression.[14] A large survey on minor tranquilliser use found that most of the people who filled in the questionnaires were 'more readily identified by their normality than by their problems'. They described themselves as 'being happily married with two children, living in houses as owner-occupiers and enjoying an average standard of living'. This strongly suggests that there is something very unsatisfying about the lives that ordinary, average women are expected to be content with.[15] A review of possible causes of depression (diagnosed twice as often in women as in men) concluded that the peak incidence in women aged 20–40 who are married with children is best explained by 'the particular problems of young mothers in developed Western societies, where families are nuclear and geographically mobile, extended family support is uncommon, and a woman with children is particularly dependent on the quality of the relationship with her partner'.[16]

Of course, not all the women who contact the psychiatric services fit the 'depressed housewife' picture. However, Susie Orbach and Luise Eichenbaum, co-founders of the Women's Therapy Centre in London, have argued that all women, whether psychiatric patients or not, share at a very fundamental level the struggle to come to terms with the conflicts and dilemmas of the woman's role. The 'depressed housewife' syndrome is just one manifestation of the confusions in which all women are caught up. As they explain, it is not a simplistic case of helpless women being victimised by wicked men. The dilemma is far more subtle and complex, and in fact it is mainly through the mother–daughter relationship that the female script is handed down from one generation to the next. The following exposition is paraphrased from their book, *Outside In, Inside Out*.[17]

The central feature of the traditional woman's role is that she must be a wife, mother and homemaker, and must take care of others emotionally. All these roles involve deferring to others, putting them and their needs first, 'not being the main actor in her own life'. She must live through others and shape her life through her partner (who must be male). There are various consequences to this. Because women are not seen as important individuals in their own right, because their work is often repetitive and undervalued ('just a housewife', or a carer for elderly relatives, or else a secretary, cleaner, shop assistant, nurse, childminder, all of which involve serving other people), they come to feel that they are insignificant, unworthy and undeserving. Again and again, women put themselves down, hesitate to speak up for themselves, run down their achievements. Moreover, they come to believe that their inadequacy is unique to them, that everyone else is managing far better, and in their isolation they take this as further proof of their worthlessness.

In order to take care of others emotionally, a woman has to develop exquisitely sensitive emotional antennae. Empathising with others, picking up their feelings, intuiting reactions and sensing emotional atmospheres all become second nature for most women. They can tell at a glance what mood their partner, child or boss is in, and they become experts at guessing what is needed and supplying it. Here again, though, a woman must put herself last and not expect the same care for herself, and she is left with a deep feeling of being unappreciated and uncared for.

These lessons in how to be a woman have to be learned mainly from another woman, mother, who has herself learned them as the daughter of her own mother. Here, a number of contradictory impulses come into play. If mother gives birth to a boy, he is clearly different, other than, separate from mother by virtue of his sex. If the child is a girl, however, mother will identify much more closely with her. Inevitably the feelings that mother has about herself at a very deep level will be *projected on to* the baby girl. In other words, because mother identifies so closely with her baby daughter, she will tend to see the baby more as an extension of herself than as a separate being. She will see parts of herself in her daughter, and some of her deep feelings about herself – her neediness, her wish to be cared for, her insecurity – will, without her being aware of it, be superimposed upon her baby. This leads to a very complicated situation. Mother wants to fulfil her daughter's needs and give her satisfaction and contentment, but it is very difficult for her to do this when her own needs have not been fulfilled. The sight of her daughter's neediness and vulnerability reminds mother of the needy, vulnerable parts of herself, which she has had to shut off in order to carry on her role of caring for others. This results in a sort of push–pull inconsistency in the mother–daughter relationship. When mother can see her daughter as a separate person, she can be responsive and loving and give her daughter the sense of security and well-being that she needs. At other times, it is as though the boundary between them dissolves and mother experiences her daughter and herself as having the same feelings, thoughts and desires, almost as if she were an extension of the same person. When this happens, mother finds herself relating to her daughter in the same way as she relates to the locked-away, needy, little-girl part of herself which she has never come to terms with, and she ends up withdrawing from her daughter at one moment and becoming overinvolved the next.

The effect on the daughter is very confusing – as it was when mother played out the same drama as a daughter to her own mother. What she learns is that it is all right to be needy, but not too needy; that she can strive for a fuller and more satisfying life than her mother, but that it is dangerous to go too far towards independence; that she can get emotional care and attention, but never quite as much as she needs; that she must seek happiness with a man, but must ultimately expect to be disappointed; that she must leave her mother to start her own family, but that all the same she should never quite separate from her: 'A son is a son till he takes a wife, but a daughter's a daughter all her life.' As daughter receives these crucial lessons in how to be a woman and how to set limits to her hopes and desires, she suppresses the parts of her that she has learned are unacceptable: the emotional cravings, and the anger and disappointments that come from never quite getting what she wants and needs in her first and most important relationship:

> She comes to feel that there must be something wrong with who she really is, which in turn means there is something wrong with what she needs and what she wants. A process of feeling inauthentic develops. She feels unsure in her reactions and distanced from her wants. This soon translates into feeling unworthy and hesitant about pursuing her impulses. Slowly she develops an acceptable self, one which appears self-sufficient and capable; one that is likely to receive more consistent acceptance . . . she comes to feel like a fraud, for an external part of her is developing which is different from who she feels she is inside.[18]

Since the daughter never feels secure in herself at a deep level, she lacks the confidence to make a full separation from her mother. The world outside seems tantalising but frightening, rather than a place that is full of exciting possibilities. Inside herself the daughter may never quite feel that she knows where she begins and mother ends; she may sometimes feel as if she is carrying mother around inside her. Both mother and daughter may need to stay close to each other so that neither loses their fragile sense of who they are, and this may make it very hard for daughter to join together with a partner later on. And if she has a daughter of her own, the whole cycle continues.

With all this in mind, we are in a better position to appreciate the intense separation difficulties of Jenny and her mother, Mrs Clark. What we know about Mrs Clark suggests that her way of relating to her daughter was a consequence of finding herself in the same trap described by Orbach and Eichenbaum and experienced by the women in Bart's article. She had followed the traditional path to marriage and motherhood under the influence of social and cultural expectations and a romantic dream. She had transferred a dependency on her family to a dependency on her husband without any intermediate exploration of herself as an individual. When the dream turned sour, she found herself trapped in a failed marriage by her strong conviction that divorce was wrong, isolated in her neighbourhood, and with no interests outside the home. She invested everything in her children, and particularly in Jenny, who was most like her and the last child still at home. For Mrs Clark, Jenny's threatened separation faced her with unbearable isolation and emptiness. At a psychological level, Mrs Clark and Jenny were so tied up in each other's identity that separation threatened their very survival. In some cases, this turns out to be literally true. As we saw, medical model psychiatric treatment does not promote separation; instead, it legitimises the sick role so that proper separation need never occur. But Scott found that if family work was carried out which enabled the child to separate, the effect on the involved parent, usually the mother, could be devastating, confirming the two-way nature of the bond. Although many parents were eventually able to let their child go and find new fulfilment in their own lives, some mothers developed crippling mental or physical problems themselves after their child's departure.

Women who take advantage of the sick role, like Jeanette, Alice and Fay in Chapter 3, are often struggling with women's role problems too. As we saw, they may be trapped in unhappy relationships without the confidence or opportunity to find alternative ways of living their lives. The sick role may be one of the few ways they can find care, attention and a role for themselves, while also allowing them to vent the anger and frustration that women find so hard to express directly.

There is a further consequence to the traditional family set-up where it is the mother's role to do most of the child-rearing: she tends to blame herself, and to be blamed by others, for any problems that the children have. This is very unfair, and prevents any analysis of why mothers are placed in such an impossible situation in the first place. It also ignores the role of the father, who plays an equally important part, if only by his absence or distance. The position of Mr Clark and of fathers in general will be discussed later (pp. 122–9).

In the meantime, we can trace the themes we have identified so far in some of the psychiatric problems that are found mainly in women.

ANOREXIA NERVOSA AND BULIMIA NERVOSA

The fear, dislike and sense of alienation that women with eating disorders feel for their bodies are only an exaggerated version of attitudes shared by nearly all women. 'Most women today are so figure conscious that in terms of averages it is normal to have a distorted body image.'[19] Up to 90 per cent of women restrict their diet to some extent,[20] while about one in eight college women use vomiting or laxatives to control their weight at least occasionally.[21] Worries about weight are well established in a third of girls aged only nine.[22] About 5 per cent of women meet the criteria for an eating disorder, numbers having risen rapidly since the 1960s.[23]

Anorexia and bulimia are currently found most commonly in the middle and upper socioeconomic classes. It is women in these classes and of this generation who are suffering most severely from the conflict between following the traditional and the newer but equally daunting expectations of women. They are unable to work out a middle path for themselves when faced with contradictory sets of messages that have been summarised as: 'Be thin, but feed others; Be educated, but sacrifice your training in order to nurture others; Be both, be mother and career person, be superwoman.'[24] It is, of course, impossible to be independent, tough, powerful, successful, assertive and *at the same time* self-sacrificing, sensitive, nurturing and family-centred. As a broad generalisation, anorexics tend to react to this dilemma by trying to opt out of it altogether, starving themselves until they return to a childlike physique with no breasts, hips or menstrual periods. Bulimics tend to be women who have apparently achieved many of the ambitions of the 'new woman' – they are often unusually intelligent, attractive and successful – but inside, hidden from the world, they are caught between the old and the new roles, and express their anguish and confusion in alternate bingeing and vomiting.

Here is the story of Angela, a 19-year-old student who lost weight very rapidly during her first year at university.

Angela's story

Like all women at some level, Angela was closely emotionally involved with her mother, a housewife who suffered from anxiety and depression. Angela's upbringing was quiet and sheltered, and she, like her parents, was a practising Roman Catholic. The last words of Angela's grandmother (her mother's mother) to Angela were, 'Be good and look after your mother.' This hardly needed saying, since Angela was already devoting her life to these two aims. Angela and her mother could tell what the other was feeling at a glance, and a circle of anxiety quickly developed where each was panicking about and trying to reassure the other. Angela's main desire was to please others, but despite constant striving she felt herself to be unworthy and wicked. This was reinforced by an interpretation of Christian ideas which led her to believe that it was sinful to upset your parents, to be angry, or to cause anyone else to get angry.

When Angela went to university, she was faced with a whole new set of demands and expectations. She seemed to be surrounded by confident, outgoing girls who wore make-up, went to parties and had boyfriends, all things which were alien and alarming to her. At the same time she felt that these were things she ought to do, indeed had to do, if she was to fit in and be liked. If everyone else was expecting this of her, they must be right. Unable to say no for fear of upsetting people, Angela found herself committed to half a dozen different societies and activities. Somewhere along the line she had picked up the idea that very soon she had to be independent, which was the last thing she felt inside. She interpreted being independent in a black-and-white fashion as competing successfully in this hectic world, making all her decisions entirely on her own, and never leaning on her parents again because to bother them would be wrong and they might be upset or angry. There was also the idea that at some point she had to have a husband and children, although this too seemed a terrifying prospect.

Pushed and pulled by contradictory messages and expectations, unable to trust her own feelings or to say no to any of the demands placed on her, Angela felt her life was getting increasingly out of control. One of the few areas of her life over which she could exert some control was her eating. By rigorously limiting her food intake and starting a punishing exercise programme she gained a temporary feeling of achievement and power. The battle to subdue her body and her physical appetite also reflected her profound belief, reinforced by her religious ideas, that her real self was unworthy, selfish and full of dangerous desires that had to be beaten down. The only time that she could allow herself to eat without feeling greedy was when her nails turned blue and pains ran up and down her legs.

When Angela came for therapy during her vacation, she weighed around five stone. Part of her treatment contract was an agreement that she would try to put on a pound a week in weight. The discussions, which sometimes included Angela's parents as well, centred around the meaning of Angela's self-starvation. On the one hand, her extreme thinness seemed to be one way in which she could demonstrate what she felt she should not be expressing openly: that she still wanted care, protection and attention from her parents and felt very much like a little girl inside. It was a way of retreating from the whole world, which seemed so frightening to her. On the other hand, starving herself was one of the few ways in which she could protest and rebel against everything that she felt was being forced upon her. In a way, it was her own bid for autonomy.

The same conflicts were evident in Angela's struggle to put on weight again. At first, she only felt safe if her parents determined exactly how much she needed to eat to put on a pound that week. She had no confidence in her ability to determine her own food intake, or her life. If she did dare to estimate for herself how much she should eat, she was terrified of getting it wrong and suddenly putting on ten pounds, since her sense of control was as precarious in her eating habits as in her life. Progress was made when Angela was able to assert herself a little more with parents and friends, paralleled by her ability to decide what to eat even if it did not coincide exactly with her parents' wishes. She gradually came to appreciate that independence did not have to be the terrifying position of total competence and responsibility that she had visualised. She could move slowly towards it and move back again as she needed, rather as she was slowly putting on weight but retaining the right to stay the same weight for a week, or even drop a little, to reassure herself that she was still in control. Therapy took many months, during which Angela pursued a slow and sometimes erratic path towards greater self-confidence and autonomy.

Once again, the issues that all women, anorexic or not, have to struggle with can be seen in Angela's story: separation from mother; achieving autonomy; compulsive caring for others; rejecting one's own feelings and needs; problems with asserting oneself and expressing anger. Angela's story also illustrates women's difficulties with having good things for themselves. Angela could only allow herself to eat if other people gave her food, or were eating as much as she was; it seemed too greedy to reach out and take food for herself. Paradoxically, although most women are suffering from some variation of not getting enough for themselves emotionally, they often feel that they are already too greedy and selfish. They apologise to therapists for taking up too much time when there must be more deserving people to be seen; they take on other people's problems but do not ask for support in return because 'so-and-so has got enough on her plate already'.

Angela's retreat from the world was paved by the current obsession with the shape and size of women's bodies. Being thin has come to represent not only beauty, success, happiness and acceptance, but also certain *moral* qualities like self-control, strength and diligence. It is no exaggeration to say that Western cultures, in which the standard of beauty is the supermodel who meets the weight criteria for anorexia,[25] have developed a phobia of fat. All the qualities that we find least acceptable have been projected on to body fat, with even six-year-olds worrying about looking fat in swimming costumes.[26] Eating disorders are almost unknown outside Western industrialised nations.

How is anorexia treated in the psychiatric system? Large areas of the UK have no comprehensive eating disorders service at all, or else offer only a very limited range of therapies, according to a 1998 survey by *Health Which?*.[27] Mental health staff with limited experience in the area often fall back on a crude version of a behavioural approach: that is, the 'symptom' (loss of weight) is seen as the problem. Treatment is directed towards removing the symptom, that is, persuading the patient to put on weight, and when she (or more rarely he) has done this she is regarded as cured and is discharged. A woman who was forced through such a regime describes how it feels to be on the receiving end:

> Some crazy system of rewards and punishments was put into operation. If I gained x amount of weight I might be allowed certain so-called *privileges*, things that for any other person would be basic human rights and taken for granted, such as using the lavatory alone, having a bath in privacy and having visitors . . . Unfortunately the nursing staff seemed to have no concept of the fact that I was not wilfully refusing to eat, but that my whole body was screaming silently NO. Any efforts to force me to eat were threatening to rob me of the only identity I had found for myself, the only real achievement I was making as an individual in my own right. Though my stomach had shrunk with lack of food I was presented with dinner plates piled high

with stodgy potato, tough lumps of over-cooked liver and boiled cabbage. When I just could not/would not eat, I was force fed. It became the norm that every mealtime I would be held down by two members of staff, one pinning my arms behind the chair whilst the other mechanically shovelled food into my mouth . . . [28]

The very narrow definition of the problem allows psychiatrists to claim success for these methods; they certainly do make people put on weight. Their wider effects are less beneficial. Anorexia is all about control; to the anorexic, the rigid control she maintains over her weight is her only defence against chaos and despair. To have this defence seized from her as large amounts of food are virtually forced down her is terrifying for her. Not surprisingly, many anorexics try to retain some control of the situation by any means left to them, such as secret vomiting or drinking large quantities of water before weighing sessions. This has earned them a reputation for being devious and manipulative patients, and Persecution may result. Since the underlying issues are not resolved, anorexics often lose weight again as soon as they are discharged, and may spend months or years being shuttled in and out of hospital to be fattened up and released again.

Treatments which focus solely on weight gain are falling into the same trap as the anorexic herself; they are treating her body as an object, as something separate from her as a person, to be forced into one shape or another without any regard to what this means for the young woman herself. Rather than helping the anorexic to accept and make friends with her body, the hospital may view it as a problem, an enemy, that has to be beaten down, the only difference being that the hospital wants it to be fat whereas the anorexic wants it to be thin. This in its turn is a reflection of the way society presents women's bodies as objects to be manipulated into the correct shapes to sell consumer goods, attract men, display the latest fashions, and so on. In addition the situation where powerful male doctors decide what is to be done to her body may echo and reinforce her fears about sexual relationships, that this is another area where she will feel used and out of control. The same attitudes underlie much of the academic research on anorexia, for which young women may be recruited to have electrodes attached to their hands, pulse and blood pressure taken, and haemoglobin and urea and cholesterol checked, in order to aid the classification of anorexics versus bulimics, dieters versus vomiters, without any regard to the person to whom the body is attached.[29]

As we have seen before, standard psychiatric treatment not only fails to help but actually reinforces the underlying problems, which this woman came to see as a need to express anger and to rebel against the expectations set for her:

> Any anger I felt towards the violent treatment I was receiving, together with my enforced isolation, was considered a symptom of my mental illness and I was promptly prescribed large doses of tranquillisers . . . I had to suppress my anger when I was a child, it was never allowed expression in my family . . . and ironically even in a psychiatric ward expressing justifiable anger was not acceptable . . . In a paradoxical way, starving myself was the only thing that was keeping me alive – my search for my Self . . . there was a great fear that if I gave up my struggles I would be . . . forced to play both femme fatale and housewife and child rearer – all smiles and sweetness, never expressing any of my feelings of anger, desperation or fully realising my power.[30]

SELF-HARM

Self-harm is the deliberate infliction of damage on one's own body by cutting, burning or scratching with needles, razors, cigarettes, broken glass or other means. Although precise figures are hard to obtain, it appears that self-harm is an under-reported and growing problem which is found mainly in women.[31] It should not be confused with attempted suicide. Women who self-harm have described it as a desperate attempt to cope with unbearable inner pain that may date back to loss, rejection, neglect and physical or sexual abuse in childhood, or rape and abusive relationships as an adult.[32] Although women may feel intense shame at their actions, they also find that self-harm is a way of expressing and relieving overwhelming feelings and helping them to survive:

> I'd go for a while, then it would build up again and eventually I would explode like a volcano, smashing everything in sight. Only when the blood poured out of me was I able to let go and cry.

> I became trapped in a world of my own, suffering the hurt and pains in silence. Cutting was my only release from the unbearable chaos inside me.

> Sometimes at night I would walk for hours in the rain wondering why I'd been born so bad, useless and ugly. The only way I found of coping was to self-harm.[33]

Women who self-harm have described their greatest needs as being for someone to listen, accept, respect and help them to explore their underlying problems and release their pain and anger in different ways. They have rarely found this kind of help from the psychiatric services. Overviews by both professionals and service users[34] remark on the Persecutory responses that self-harm can evoke: 'Staff feelings fluctuate between rage, sympathy, guilt, solicitude and the urge to retaliate'; 'Over and over again women told us of being criticised, ignored, told off, dismissed as "attention-seeking", "a nuisance" or "wasting time" . . . These attitudes reinforce the self-hatred and desperation which contributed to their need to self-injure.' As in the case of eating disorders, the nearest thing to psychological help that is offered may be a simplistic form of behaviour therapy, in which women are encouraged to replace self-harm with more constructive outlets for their feelings, or to substitute positive thoughts about themselves for negative ones. While this may be of some use, it is much too superficial to get to the roots of the problem and can (as we have seen before) be used to justify punitive practices like ignoring women's distress on the grounds that this will somehow 'reinforce' their problems. (Thus, one book advises staff to 'reduce care, empathy and concern as much as possible for the period immediately following the infliction of the wound'.[35]) Medication and ECT can also serve as a means of expressing the staff's punitive feelings while leaving the real problems unaddressed.[36] As one survivor of self-harm notes: 'Women's self-injury may . . . be a means of expressing emotions and reactions (such as anger and defiance) which are not socially acceptable for women.'[37]

SEXUAL ABUSE

Sexual abuse only began to be recognised as a widespread problem in the late 1980s, although it has probably been occurring just as frequently for generations. Surveys indicate that about one in eight women are victims of sexual abuse in childhood,[38] with the figure rising to as much as 50 per cent in women who use psychiatric services.[39] Among the recognised long-term consequences are eating disorders, substance abuse, self-harm, anxiety and depression, as well as more general difficulties with relationships, self-esteem and sexuality.[40] Women with a diagnosis of borderline personality disorder often report a history of child sexual abuse as well.[41]

These facts pose two rather embarrassing questions which are usually ignored. First, how did all this trauma in the early lives of women psychiatric patients go undetected by professionals for so long? Although embarrassment and shame may make it hard for women to reveal such events, a large part of the responsibility must lie with a system where professionals do not have the training or time to explore such issues (see Mary's account later in this chapter), and where the basic model does not even acknowledge the central importance of psychological factors in breakdown.

Second, what implications does the widespread occurrence of abuse have for a medical model of mental distress? Large numbers of women with psychiatric diagnoses turn out to have experienced events which make the so-called 'symptoms' of their 'mental illnesses' (low mood, despair, self-destructiveness, dislike of their bodies, fearfulness and so on) seem like entirely understandable reactions to the traumas that have been inflicted on them. Beliefs that are labelled as delusional can also, in my experience, reflect experiences of sexual abuse in a disguised form. Four out of five people with the diagnosis of 'borderline personality disorder' are women, and 68 per cent of them have experienced child sexual abuse; it has been pointed out that the 'symptoms' of this disorder correspond almost exactly to known reactions to abuse.[42] What sense does it make to see all these women as suffering from illnesses with biological causes, as opposed to traumas with psychological consequences? The response from psychiatry has been as predictable as it is unconvincing. Child sexual abuse is said to 'increase vulnerability to adult psychiatric illness' rather than throwing doubt on the concept of illness itself,[43] in the same way that, as we saw in Chapter 4, psychological stresses in 'schizophrenia' are acknowledged only in the limited role of 'triggers' of an underlying biological condition.

Mental health professionals now routinely ask new clients/patients about sexual abuse, and some services offer individual or group counselling with staff who are experienced in working in this area. In other places:

> contact with unresponsive and unhelpful [professionals] is likely to replicate and perpetuate women's previous experiences of their abuse not being recognised and accepted by others . . . This, in turn, may lead to the maintenance of substance abuse, psychotic symptoms or self-harm on the part of the woman, and high use of mental health services.[44]

Sometimes the parallels between treatment and abuse are disturbingly close. A woman survivor of sexual abuse described her experience of ECT like this:

It certainly felt, 'Do what you like', and that's something I felt as a child, that I had no power, there was no way I could stop anyone doing whatever they wanted to me, so rather than get hurt I'll let them do it and maybe they'll like me . . . especially because it was men doing it, the men actually operating the machinery or whatever, and I can remember it was men putting the needle in . . . And then just sort of lying there, feeling really frightened and yet completely passive. So it was like all trapped, all my emotions were trapped.[45]

Psychiatric hospitals may be very unsafe places for women to be, with a high proportion of severely disturbed people crammed into a small, under-resourced ward due to bed closures. Being on a mixed ward with little privacy is unpleasant for anyone, but especially so for a woman who has a history of sexual abuse. Women have reported experiences of sexual comments and jokes, flashing, unacceptable touching and rape in psychiatric hospitals.[46] It is increasingly recognised that professionals too may exploit female in-patients and out-patients by starting sexual relationships with them.[47]

To summarise the arguments of this chapter so far: it is hard to draw very precise conclusions from the existing statistics on mental health problems in women. Figures may be influenced by women's greater willingness to report emotional distress as well as by policy factors (for example, restricting admissions to diagnoses such as psychosis, which have a more even sex distribution). There is evidence that both these factors are operating.[48] Nevertheless, there is a clear general trend, emerging from both hospital and community surveys, for women to suffer more frequently from depression, anxiety, eating disorders and self-harm. We have discussed a number of possible and not mutually exclusive reasons for this:

1   Women's position in society may make them more vulnerable to certain types of breakdown. We can include under this heading poverty, low-paid and low-status jobs, lack of support in child-rearing, isolation within the home, increased vulnerability to domestic violence and sexual abuse, social pressures on weight and appearance, and the conflicting expectations of women's changing roles. All of these will be compounded by the additional discrimination suffered by black, gay and older women. It is not hard to see how such pressures might reasonably be experienced as depressing and anxiety-provoking, with eating disorders and self-harm serving as a desperate attempt to survive and cope.

2   The internal, psychological aspects of women's roles may also make them more vulnerable to emotional breakdown (rather than, say, violence or alcoholism) when they are under stress. Caring for others may be at the expense of emotional care for themselves; younger as well as older women may carry a deep sense of neediness and unworthiness; and it may be very hard to acknowledge or express the anger that is necessary to change their situations. Clashes of expectations about women's changing roles lead to conflict and confusion both for white women and for black and ethnic minority women who have their own cultural influences to take into account as well.

3   Finally, definitions of 'mental illness' may themselves be influenced by sex role expectations, with women being seen as 'mad' if they either display too much traditional 'feminine' behaviour, or conversely, deviate too far from traditional 'feminine' norms. The fear, weepiness, lack of confidence, dependency, helplessness, and preoccupation with appearance associated with depression, anxiety and eating disorders would fall into the former category, while any type of violence or aggression, including self-harm, is more likely to lead to a diagnosis of personality disorder in women than men. The example of a proposed new diagnosis of 'Masochistic Personality Disorder' for DSM III R* is revealing. This new type of mental disorder could apparently be detected by behaviours such as 'Remains in relationships in which others exploit, abuse or take advantage of him or her / Rejects help, gifts or favours so as not to be a burden on others / Responds to success or positive events by feeling undeserving / Repeatedly turns down opportunities for pleasure.' American feminists responded by demanding the inclusion of another new psychiatric syndrome, 'Delusional Dominating Personality Disorder', characterised by 'Inability to derive pleasure from doing things for others / Tendency to feel threatened by women who fail to disguise their intelligence', and so on.[49] Their point, of course, was that it is male standards of behaviour that are being taken as the norm here, with female behaviour not only taken out of its social context but designated as 'mad'.

Psychiatric services vary, and women may be lucky enough to be referred to one of the innovative projects designed specifically with their needs in mind. Unfortunately, it is more likely that their treatment will reinforce the problems that they come along with by acting on the same assumptions that led to the problem in the first place. Certain psychological and social pressures lead to difficulties, and the psychiatric team applies the same pressures, only more forcefully, to solve them, with medication, ECT, or a crude version of behaviourism as tools.

What most women with psychiatric diagnoses need is, first, to be helped to see that they are only part of the problem, and second, to get angry enough about it to make some real changes. The medical model cannot allow for this. Diagnoses are attached to individuals – there is no such thing as a medical diagnosis that includes a partner, children, parents or wider society as an equal part of the problem. Thus the woman's belief that it is all her fault, which is preventing her from seeing possible changes and solutions, is reinforced.

It has to be borne in mind that most psychiatric staff receive virtually no training in counselling or psychotherapy. Doctors and nurses do particularly badly in this respect. They are even less likely to have had any specialist training in helping with mainly female problems such as anorexia, post-natal depression, being a victim of rape or sexual abuse or of a violent partner, or having an abortion or a miscarriage, let alone learning to look at psychiatric problems from the point of view of women's roles. It is only to be expected, therefore, that psychiatric staff will unwittingly reinforce the values of the society they come from, since they have not attained any higher degree of critical awareness than their patients. The more subtle messages of the psychiatric system are in line with all this. The most powerful, high-status and well-paid indivduals will be the predominantly male consultant psychiatrists, descending through the ranks to the lowest-paid, low-status, predominantly female nurses, occupational therapists, secretaries and domestics.

Nurses are the staff who are most exposed to the day-to-day stress of caring for patients and usually know them best, yet they have least say in their management. Very little provision is made for caring for the carers; support groups and places where they can talk about *their* distress are not seen as necessary to the job, while many of them find that their earnings will hardly stretch to outings, new clothes, holidays or treats for themselves. In doing such a difficult job for so little recognition or reward, caring for others and yet not being adequately cared for themselves, they find that they are in the same dilemma as their female patients. Like these patients, they may accumulate frustration and anger at the exploitation and powerlessness of their position. However, they find it extraordinarily hard to use their anger constructively to assert their rights and opinions, individually or collectively, with the people further up the hierarchy, and in this too they resemble their female patients. Although there is usually much private grumbling among the nurses about the psychiatrists and their decisions, it is rare for them openly to challenge and disagree, however strongly they feel. There is a danger that, for a few, disillusionment and demoralisation may take the form of venting their frustrations by Persecuting the bottom layer of the hierarchy, the patients.

In looking at the plight of women within the psychiatric system, we find ourselves echoing the themes of earlier chapters. Despite an abundance of biological theories for the characteristic patterns of mental distress suffered by women, ranging from the nineteenth-century belief that hysteria was caused by the womb wandering round the body to more recent suggestions that hormonal changes may account for post-natal depression, or that there may be a gene for depression carried on the X chromosome, no hard evidence has been forthcoming.[50] However, 'treatment' continues to consist primarily or exclusively of medication and ECT, despite considerable support for the importance of *psychosocial* factors in women's distress and calls by women themselves for a *psychosocial* approach to their problems. The underlying philosophy of the medically based psychiatric approach can be summarised as tending to *remove* power and control from the woman, to *deny* her feelings, and to *ignore* the meaning behind her actions. These are the very circumstances that are likely to have led to her breakdown in the first place. A vicious circle is set up: the woman hates herself and often harms herself; the psychiatric system all too often ends up Persecuting and harming her too; and the problem that brought her into contact with the services in the first place is reinforced, with yet more admissions and medication as the consequence. Some comments by service users illustrate what can happen:

> The psychiatrist I was seeing on the NHS told me that I was suffering from depression and immediately prescribed anti-depressants. The emphasis seemed to be on getting me 'back to normal' as he put it – never mind the fact that I was actually desperate to change my life and didn't want to go back to just passively accepting things. I was 29, married with two small children. My husband was extremely successful and I was supposed to reflect his glory . . . I was an educated, intelligent, articulate, responsible person and I didn't want to spend the rest of my life existing in somebody else's shadow.[51]

Mary's difficulties stemmed from sexual abuse as a child:

> I wasn't getting anything constructive to help me face my problems. I took another overdose so I was sent upstairs and my clothes were taken away from me because they said I was a danger to myself. They

didn't figure out why I was taking overdoses but I wasn't with anyone long enough to tell them. I would need to get to know someone before telling them about sex. You got to know a doctor for a few days and then they wouldn't be there . . . You felt you were abnormal and this was the place for abnormal people, and yet they're not abnormal people when you get to know them, just normal people with a problem that perhaps just needs listening to. But you've got to find out what the problem is first – that's the hard part. The whole system is that you've got to conform, but when you think about it, the ones in here are non-conformists . . . The general impression was that you go out and you come back in again, you're never completely free of the place . . . I lost six months of my life in there . . . I was scared to go out because everyone knew I'd been in the psychiatric hospital. I moved house to get away from the stigma, and I never hear from my old friends and schoolfriends any more . . . I just wanted someone with a bit of time, I needed someone to visit me at home perhaps, give me some moral support or arrange some help at home . . . To get worse when you go into the place – there's got to be something wrong somewhere, hasn't there?

This woman was finally offered an alternative, after an in-patient admission:

Therapy changed things enormously for me, in fact completely . . . [Otherwise] I would have been sent to a psychiatrist, I would have been labelled, quite possibly hospitalised, and I think my own self-esteem and the battles I'd fought over these years would just have been lost at that point and I would have given up on myself, and the system would have engulfed me like it does with many women, and that could have been me for the rest of my life. I think because women are asked to repress so many things that are natural to us, asked to repress violence, anger and any strong emotion and actually brought up to be passive, and when that passivity clashes with the social norms, or her lack of passivity, that's when she comes into contact with the psychiatric services. And then the usual route is always drugs . . . I think on the whole women get categorised very fast, and get treated in a very stereotyped way.[52]

WHAT HAPPENS TO MEN IN THE PSYCHIATRIC SYSTEM?

A great deal has been written on the way women are dealt with by psychiatry, and very little on what happens to men. Tragically, they often fare equally badly. Once again, much can be understood in terms of the different but equally powerful sex role expectations placed on men. Jim Read describes his own experiences:

> It seems to me that being male in this society is very tied up with being strong, independent, successful, decisive, knowing what you're doing and so on, and everything about having a mental health crisis seems to be the opposite of that, so my major preoccupation when I needed some sort of help was to try and cover up, and act as if I was OK, which I was actually quite successful at doing for some time. But of course I didn't deal with any of the problems, and so they built up. I think actually when I did end up in the mental health system it felt like a very female experience. It felt like I'd almost lost my maleness by taking tranquillisers, being diagnosed as being depressed, going to a mental hospital, being quite passive . . . The way I tried to deal with things at that point was to get a job. I saw it all very much in terms of, if I get a job I'll be all right. I didn't think of it in terms of having to sort myself out in some way, and I think that was partly because I had no way of thinking about or expressing myself emotionally, which again I think is quite a male thing . . . and if someone were to ask me how I felt, which actually they very seldom ever did in psychiatric hospital anyway, I probably wouldn't have had a clue how to answer . . . There's a number of things I notice about men in the mental health system. One is that I think we have a number of ways of expressing the fact that we're distressed which means we might end up somewhere other than the mental health system, and sometimes our distress can come out in some quite dangerous and frightening ways for other people, and then society responds by trying to lock us up, or stop us from doing what we were doing, and it's very difficult to see someone, for example, who molests children or is violent to his wife as someone who needs help.[53]

The characteristically masculine needs to compete, succeed, provide and be strong, while suppressing the awareness and expression of most feelings except anger, have been traced back to men's early upbringing and the consequences for the little boy of having, in a traditional family set-up, the woman as the main carer.[54] Other important early figures – childminders, nursery nurses, primary school teachers, and so on – are usually female too. It is comparatively easy for a little girl to learn the important lesson of what it means to be a girl, even if this is at the expense of later difficulties in achieving independence; she gets this experience directly from her first and most intense relationship with her mother. A boy, on the other hand, needs to reject much of the close attachment to and identification with mother that makes up the very earliest stage of life, in order to learn what it means to be a boy and enter the world of men. It has been suggested that this difficult and painful shift in his relationships and attitudes can feel like rejection and abandonment by the first woman in his life, his mother. The blow is made doubly hard by the fact that everything that goes along with that feminine world – closeness, touch, feelings, intimacy – is also being defined as out of bounds. He is cut off not only from his mother but from his own 'feminine' side, on pain of rejection by male peers and standards. The end result is that the little boy, and later the little boy inside the grown man, is left with an unfulfilled longing for the intimacy he once had, together with a deep suspicion of the kind of closeness that might awaken his buried emotions and make him vulnerable again. Fear of intimacy is particularly strong in men who, as little boys, experienced their mothers as overwhelming and humiliating them. This may occur as a result of the mother's own sex role problems – her lack of emotional boundaries and her over-investment in relationships with her children in order to meet her own needs.

The traditional father is ill-equipped to heal these wounds. Physically and/or emotionally absent for much of the time, he cannot offer a secure alternative model or identity for the little boy. (A recent survey revealed that many men spend as little as fifteen minutes a day with their children.[55]) This painful gap in men's relationships with their fathers is a prominent theme in recent literature from the men's movement. Masculinity has to be defined negatively, by the need to detach oneself from and deny the feminine. The whole dilemma is sealed over and probably lost to consciousness behind the pursuit of male activities, many of which seem designed to block out uncomfortable feelings – drinking, over-work, and so on. As Jim Read suggests, the only acceptable outlet for pain and distress as an adult may be in the form of violence and aggression, against the self and others.

These are generalisations which do not apply to all individuals and cannot explain all of men's mental distress. Gay men and black men face additional pressures and discrimination. Moreover, as we have already discussed, roles are changing for both sexes. Nevertheless, this account does give us a way of explaining the characteristic patterns of male, like female, psychiatric breakdown as representing an extreme version of traditional sex role expectations. Thus, men are more likely than women to receive a diagnosis of alcoholism or drug addiction, which can be seen as ways of *blocking out* feelings, in contrast to the more typically female pattern of being *overwhelmed by* feelings. More men than women are said to have 'personality disorders', which include such 'symptoms' as anger and hostility, emotional distance and aloofness, lack of concern for others, isolation and self-destructiveness. Suicide rates in men have always been higher than in women, and have increased dramatically in recent years.[56] It has been suggested that violence against oneself is one of the few ways out for men who find it hard to express and deal with their feelings or ask for help.[57]

Another possible outlet, as Jim Read noted, is aggression and violence against others. Without seeking to excuse rape in any way, we can see it 'not so much as a deviant act as an over-conforming act. Rape may be understood as an extreme acting out of qualities that are regarded as supra-masculine in this and many other societies: aggression, force, power, strength, toughness, dominance, competitiveness.'[58] A similar analysis could be applied to other forms of criminal behaviour. Since men are more likely than women to be seen as *responsible* for deviant behaviour, they may end up being labelled as bad rather than mad, and sent to prison rather than psychiatric hospital. In this ultra-macho environment, they too will find that the 'solution' consists of a heavy reinforcement of the conditions (in their case, toughness, brutality and a denial of emotions) that led to the problems in the first place:

> Once a label has been affixed, men as a group are in some respects dealt with more harshly than women. This is especially true at the interface between psychiatry and the criminal justice system. Men are over-represented in the most stigmatised and policed part of the mental health system, the 'special hospitals'.[59]

The penal system enforces discipline with particularly brutal and widespread forms of psychiatric abuse. Prison psychiatrists have a range of terms such as 'aggressive', 'subversive' and 'psychopathic' which can be used to justify the imposition of large doses of medication on this very powerless group: 'Any step out of line by a prisoner is usually regarded as problematic and medicalised leaving the prisoner vulnerable to various types of "treatment" designed to produce a docile, conforming individual and, ultimately, a docile, conforming prisoner population.'[60]

Earlier, we looked at some of the socioeconomic pressures that impact particularly heavily on women. The obvious parallel for men is unemployment. Studies have found significant increases in symptoms such as anxiety, depression, insomnia, irritability, lack of confidence, listlessness, inability to concentrate and general nervousness in unemployed men, as well as alcoholism, raised blood pressure and heavier smoking,[61] while the alarming rise in men's suicide rates, particularly in the age group 15–24, has occurred in parallel with rises in unemployment.[62]

There are obvious reasons why life on the dole should be depressing: less money and all that it entails, lack of structure to one's life, and so on. However, this is not a complete explanation: a small subgroup of the unemployed manage to keep active and enthusiastic and to create goals and opportunities for themselves. Nor does it explain why the association between psychological well-being and paid employment fails to hold for women as a group, although single women and principal wage-earners do show a similar pattern of effects. At least part of the harmfulness of unemployment comes from the way it is perceived by the individual, and this is where men, whose identity is so closely tied up with work, are hit so hard. Loss of this role is 'an existential and not just an economic problem. If such a man is hit by unemployment and cannot find a new role in life he is confronted with loss of both working faith and identity.'[63] Discussing the rising numbers of men admitted to hospital with depression, two psychiatrists commented:

> Important changes in gender roles have occurred over the last 20 years. These include a decrease in the number of men in full time work and an increase in the number of women in both part time and full time work. For men, the resultant loss of status as sole financial provider for the family, the perceived loss in social status, and the consequent social isolation could all be considered risk factors for depression.[64]

Acquiring a psychiatric diagnosis will certainly not improve a man's chances of getting a job, while the 'Industrial Therapy' that may be offered instead is a demeaning parody of meaningful employment: assembling boxes or packing for a few pounds a week.

We can see that men, like women, have characteristic stresses in their external lives and internal psychology and that they too will experience and express distress in ways that are shaped by sex role expectations. In addition, men, like women, may find that recent changes in roles have complicated the picture by exposing them to conflicting demands: 'For men now there is conflict between the need to be strong, the macho image and the need to be the caring, new man. Role conflict is very important in the search for identity', in the words of one psychologist.[65] A large recent survey identified a crisis of masculinity in many young men, who have low self-esteem, do badly at school and work, and resent the increasing success and confidence of young women.[66]

Men as well as women can self-harm, develop eating disorders and be victims of sexual abuse. All these are under-researched areas in men, which may make the problems harder to admit to and find help with. For example, 'the experience of sexual abuse for a man is evidently incongruent with his need, implied by societal values, to be masculine. This incongruence is likely to lead to denial and dissociation from the abusive experience', according to two psychologists; boys who are abused by men may become very confused and fearful about their later sexual identity and possible homosexuality, and may feel intensely ashamed about the powerless and passive role into which they were forced.[67] As a result, sexual abuse in men may be widely under-reported. However, men who were sexually assaulted either as children (at least one in twenty) or as adults (about 3 per cent[68]) are very much more likely to end up in contact with mental health services.

Eating disorders in men seem to be on the increase, and this may be linked to role conflict and to recent emphasis on body size and shape in men, although for men fitness and muscularity (as shown by a 'six-pack' stomach) is more of a concern than thinness *per se*. These pressures are especially strong in the gay community, and gay men seem to have a greater risk of developing eating problems.[69] Rejection of the traditional expectations placed on men may be relevant here, as we saw earlier with women:

> The family I was born into was an industrial working class one, in a steel and coal community. Much as I respect the generations of people before me, it is the expectation to conform to certain concepts of manhood and womanhood which were and still are problematic to me . . . Eating distress is just another symptom of the conflicts between the individual, and a group which is reflecting cultural norms . . . For many of us, these issues are linked to a conflict about gender roles and sexuality . . . Questioning the values that were being handed on to me, re-defining myself, led to me being seen as a suitable case for treatment . . . I was given a major tranquilliser, an anti-emetic, vitamins, iron and potassium. I was a prize specimen. I was allowed out, after putting on four and a half stones in weight, to be the

'normal weight for a man of my build'. What more could I, or they want – Normality! So I was out, with all the same problems that faced me before . . . One thing had changed though – my social status. I was no longer an anonymous person with a private life; I was a psychiatric case.[70]

We can see that men, like women, can run into trouble not only by over-conforming to sex role expectations but also by deviating too far from them. A particularly clear example is the 'treatment' given in the 1960s and 1970s to 'cure' gay men of their homosexuality, which was defined as a mental illness until 1973. Hundreds of men were admitted to psychiatric wards and subjected to aversion therapy, consisting of electric shocks and nausea-inducing drugs. The consequences included severe anxiety, depression, lifelong trauma and attempted suicide; some died through inhaling their own vomit during 'therapy'.[71]

Another important way that men may feature in the psychiatric system is as the hidden other halves of the problems that bring women along. Frequently, as we saw in Elaine Jones's story, the woman who is identified as the 'sick one' is in fact carrying the problem for both partners or even for the whole family. This is to be expected if women are socialised to be more in touch with their feelings and more able to ask for help. There are signs that Mr Jones, although not officially ill, had been through his own form of torment. He had spent the greater part of his life shackled to a poorly paid job to fulfil his responsibilities as family provider, and had had many years of stress over his wife's depression. The rest of his background is unknown; the professionals who treated his wife did not see it as relevant. Mr Jones was left to deal with his fear and his despair in the traditional masculine way: silently, and on his own. This left him in an impossible position. Not only was he ground down by the enormous burdens he had carried over the years, but he was also completely unequipped to adapt to his wife's greater assertiveness and her need for him to respond to her on an emotional level.

Shadowy and poorly understood male figures have been glimpsed in the background of several of the stories from earlier chapters. Fay, who adopted the sick role, had a husband who seemed to have some investment in keeping her sick. What this investment might have been was never investigated or discovered. Very little was known about Mr Clark, the father of Jenny Clark who was diagnosed as 'schizophrenic'. Mrs Clark may, like many women, have tried to deal with the deep sense of neediness inside her by a search for 'Mr Right', the fantasy figure who would at last fulfil her needs, understand and cherish her and give meaning to her life. Popular culture – magazines, books, music, advertisements, films – conspires to promote this hope at every turn. Of course, no one can fulfil all these unconscious hopes, since she is expecting something of a man that in the end she has to find ways of doing for herself, but her future partner is particularly ill-equipped for the task she has unwittingly set him, because he cannot deal with his own needs and feelings, let alone with hers as well. Thus, heterosexual relationships are set up to contain a great deal of disappointment. The woman who has, in effect, been asking her partner to Rescue her, may turn to Persecuting him – ridiculing him, pushing him to the edge of the family circle and seeking fulfilment in her children instead. This drama seems to have been carried out in Jenny's family. However, Mr Clark's situation was ignored by the hospital as it was in the family. Although he was cut off from real closeness with his children, his role was extremely important if only because of its absence, which contributed to the damaging lack of balance in family relationships.

Then there are the more sinister male figures of Linda Hart's violent father and the uncle who subjected Mary to sexual abuse. Again, we have to remember that only people who have themselves been brutalised are capable of acting so brutally, though this does not absolve them from responsibility for their actions. Men who behave like this are full of the buried grief, loneliness and fear which go along with the harshest imposition of the male role.

Here is an example of a man who, as the result of being brutalised in his early childhood, cut himself off from his own feminine side and created a caricature of the macho man. But his inability to come to terms with his feminine aspects was reflected in his obsession with and hatred for women, which he eventually took to its logical extreme:

> M4 rapist John Steed created a macho-man image which girls found irresistible – but behind the façade lay a dark secret. Steed hated women and enjoyed sex only when holding a victim at the point of a knife or the barrel of a gun. Steed, a physical fitness fan, built up his muscles during endless weight-lifting sessions. He loved driving fast cars, which he stole to impress women. His screen idol was the rough detective Dirty Harry, played by Clint Eastwood. 'He could never have any human relationships', said 45-year-old Sheila Steed (his mother). 'Even as a toddler he could never let anyone cuddle him. His father used to beat him, and I remember on his first day at school he went off without as much as a goodbye.'[72]

In summary, we can see that even if men in distress avoid being either ignored or sent to prison, they are no more likely than women to find the help they need in the psychiatric system. Instead, in parallel with women, they face 'a vicious paradox, where men are punished for either over-conforming to, fighting against or just having problems with the stereotypes of masculinity. And at the same time, their treatment pressurises men to behave according to the stereotypes that caused the problems in the first instance.'[73]

The wider messages of medical model psychiatry are equally unhelpful. The belief that uncomfortable feelings, like the symptoms of an illness, should be suppressed and eliminated, rather than expressed and worked through, is damaging for both sexes, but for men it coincides particularly unfortunately with the messages they have already been given. More generally, the whole practice of psychiatry is based on traditionally masculine values. In order to present it as a legitimate branch of medical science, there has to be an over-riding emphasis on labelling, categorising and medicating, rather than a more 'feminine' exploring of feelings and relationships. Prestige in psychiatric circles is gained by research and publication in respectable, scientific, objective fields, and psychiatrists may be able to carve out a distinguished career for themselves while having no aptitude whatsoever for forming therapeutic relationships with their patients. The only other approach to have gained a firm foothold in psychiatry, cognitive-behaviour therapy, is also of a goal-oriented, symptom-removing nature.

None of this is meant to imply that the more 'masculine' values and approaches are mistaken or useless, and nor is a more 'feminine' or psychotherapeutic approach the answer to everyone's problems. What is needed is balance, since lack of balance is as damaging in a whole system as it is in an individual person. What is also desperately needed, and almost completely lacking, is awareness of gender issues in theory, training and practice. Without this, the psychiatric system will continue to reinforce and perpetuate all the most damaging aspects of our societal expectations of men and women.

Chapter 6

The professionals and their training

One of the problems that arises in trying to describe the day-to-day practice of psychiatry to people outside the business is that they find it hard to understand how such obviously inappropriate treatment can be handed out while commonsense attempts to help people to talk and to understand their home situations are ignored. Not all psychiatry is of this nature; we have seen some examples of good practice, and more will be given in Chapter 11. Unfortunately, these are the exceptions. Yet the great majority of psychiatric staff are dedicated and hard-working people with a genuine wish to help the people they are paid to care for. So how does it come about that the results are often so damaging? A partial answer is supplied by looking at the training that different mental health professionals receive, which, as I hope to show, actually makes them less rather than more able to help people in mental distress. Setting this in the context of a brief history of psychiatry and examining the role of the drug companies may provide further clues. First, though, it is time to look at the psychiatric system from the point of view of the professionals.

PSYCHIATRISTS

Psychiatrists are doctors who have followed the basic five- or six-year medical training and then chosen to specialise in psychiatry, rising up the medical hierarchy from Senior House Officer to Registrar, Senior Registrar and possibly, in the end, Consultant. Consultant psychiatrists are at the head of the traditional hospital-based psychiatric team, where they have the power to admit, discharge, and prescribe medication or ECT. All of these can, in certain circumstances, be carried out 'under section' or against a patient's will. They also decide on the diagnosis and make the ultimate decisions about treatment plans. Their position is somewhat

DOI: 10.4324/9781003095958-6

different in the new community mental health teams, which are generally managed by nurses. However, this erosion of their influence under the implementation of community care is likely to be balanced by new powers to follow up patients in the community.

There is a widespread misconception that a psychiatrist is a bearded man who asks you to lie on a couch and free-associate about your dreams while he offers Freudian interpretations of your remarks. This is actually a better description of a psychoanalyst in private practice. Medical training, with its emphasis on biology and factual knowledge, probably discourages more psychologically minded candidates from entering the profession:

> Concentration on school-leaving attainment in science subjects may lead to negative selection as far as potential interest in psychiatry is concerned. The present restrictive entrance requirements . . . act to screen out schoolleavers who have the general interest in literature, philosophy and the arts which often accompanies what may broadly be called a psychological orientation.[1]

Once on the course, this emphasis is reinforced. Over the last twenty years there has been a shift towards 'neuroscience, such as the basic brain sciences of neuroanatomy, neurophysiology, neuropathology and neuropharmacology. Much importance is also attached to genetics and psychopathology . . . The social sciences have a limited role in the education of psychiatrists, and the humanities have no role at all.'[2] As a result, psychiatrists are, in the words of one of them:

> brought up to see personal counselling as slushy, crazy and useless . . . Everyone expects them to be fully skilled in modern bio-scientific medicine. Counselling is too lowly a subject to get into the lecture programme. Anyway, it cannot be learned through lectures alone. So there just isn't time in a massive curriculum to learn both aspects of the job. For psychotherapy it has taken major effort to gain a minor foothold in the training of psychiatrists and in NHS services. People as people are not really placed reliably at the centre of psychiatry's concerns. As a trainee I thought I was 'person-centred' but now I can see that I too listened to patients while primarily on the lookout for symptoms of psychiatric conditions . . . The missing basic skill with people was and is simultaneously taken for granted and denigrated.[3]

Another psychiatrist notes that an interest in psychotherapy and counselling may actually be an obstacle to career advancement: 'Most psychiatric trainees . . . will recognise, for example, the feeling of uncertainty about whether to express an interest in psychotherapy before a psychiatric appointments committee.'[4]

Junior psychiatrists arrive at their first jobs, having had only eight weeks' teaching on psychiatry, to be faced with a bewildering series of patients, many of whom are long-term attenders inherited from a succession of previous post-holders. They are expected to pick up the relevant skills on the job, with every grade below consultant officially described as a training post. However, while going out on placement is an important part of all mental health workers' training, no other profession gives its trainees such enormous responsibility (diagnosing, arranging admissions and so on) from day one. Consultants vary in their willingness to offer supervision and support during this time. Having to move to a different post every six months does not help continuity of care for the patient or of learning experience for the junior doctor.

Psychiatrists, like clinical psychologists, tend to come from very different social backgrounds than their patients. Three-quarters of applicants to medical school have professional parents and only 1.1 per cent are drawn from unskilled backgrounds.[5] White candidates for medical school are twice as likely to be offered a place as black ones.[6]

Psychiatry is a very low-status speciality in medicine, and recruitment is a problem. At the top end of the scale, about 450 consultant posts are currently vacant, and many doctors take early retirement because of the increasing stress and bureaucracy of the job.[7] The shortfall in applicants is made up by overseas-trained doctors who fill about half of all posts, mostly in the lower grades. Some are excellent, but many are poorly equipped for the job. As one psychiatrist writes:

> It is clear that many doctors from overseas come here without any intention to take up the subject. They come here to obtain a higher qualification in medicine, surgery, or obstetrics, but because they have little money and are at a disadvantage when competing with home-trained graduates for the better training posts they have to be content with taking positions in less well-endowed hospitals, posts that British medical graduates would not touch under any circumstances.[8]

One writer describes the resulting dilemma:

> Having chosen a field he is least interested to work in, befuddled by the terminology of dynamically-oriented psychiatry, perplexed

by the anxiety-provoking interview of an acute admission ward, lacking fluency in the English language, let alone familiarity with the English culture and idiom, the postgraduate tries hard to put on a bold front.[9]

(Equally serious problems can arise when white doctors try to understand the difficulties of black and ethnic minority patients: see Chapter 10.) Attracted from abroad by the promise of receiving postgraduate training, these doctors may find themselves forever stuck in the lower ranks of psychiatry while patient care suffers. The other group who, for different reasons, find it hard to move up the medical hierarchy are women who want to combine a career with a family. They often take up part-time posts as clinical assistants, but it is very difficult to move from there to a consultant post.

There are, however, considerable rewards for those who stay the course. In all medical specialities, NHS consultants are permitted to supplement their basic £45,000+ salary with half a day of private work. In addition, a third of them receive a so-called 'merit award' of up to £55,000 a year given on confidential grounds by a group of other consultants at a total cost of £104 million to the NHS. This system is currently under review, and is likely to be replaced by a more open one which includes votes from patient representatives and employers.

Traditional psychiatrists stick closely to the diagnosis, admission and medication routine, perhaps with some claims to be doing low-key supportive counselling as well. While pressure on beds may allow little time to do anything else on the wards, it has been pointed out that 'hospital-trained doctors are ill-prepared for working in community-based teams, and their detached . . . approach is increasingly out of touch with clinical and consumer demand'.[10] A minority of other doctors, as we have seen from earlier chapters, attempt a more innovative approach. Many junior doctors in particular are very aware of the limitations of their training and are eager to fill the gaps if the opportunity presents itself. A promising development is the plan for three new medical centres which will specifically aim to attract trainees from a wider range of academic, personal and cultural backgrounds.[11]

PSYCHIATRIC NURSES

Psychiatric nurses follow a three-year higher education programme, approximately half of which is made up of formal teaching, the rest being spent in various placements. There is a foundation course with basic medical input – anatomy, physiology, neurology and so on –followed by more specialised training which includes psychology, psychiatry, sociology and social policy.

Before the introduction of the 1982 syllabus, the training was much more closely based on general medicine, in which the patient was seen as someone suffering from a physically-based illness which it was the nurse's job to cure by taking over from him or her and dispensing the correct medical treatment. The current syllabus places greater emphasis on social factors, personal development, community work and developing relationships with patients, and nurses are encouraged to draw up goals for their own group of patients. This is done according to the 'Nursing Process', a treatment-planning exercise derived from general medicine, in which problems are summarised under such headings as Needs/Problems, Intervention/Strategy, and Goal/Expected Outcome. Although it is essential to draw up a treatment plan for patients, a format which is suitable for physical illness (Problem: Patient has bed sores. Intervention: Turn the patient hourly. Expected outcome: Cure the bed sores, and so on) is not always so appropriate for emotional distress. Moreover, it is rarely integrated into the overall treatment policy laid down by the psychiatrists. Although the importance of counselling is acknowledged, it is generally true that anything other than the most basic counselling skills have to be acquired after qualifying – if, that is, one can manage to get funding to go on the relevant courses.

Low pay, low status, too much paperwork and (for women) poor promotion prospects have led to a recruitment shortfall and high drop-out rates from training and of trained nurses in all branches of nursing. Office work takes up 20 per cent more of a mental health nurse's time than in the mid-1980s, while patients may spend as little as 4 per cent of their day in direct contact with ward staff, according to recent research.[12] Although more training places have been promised, some of the gap has to be filled by overseas staff.

The position of a qualified psychiatric nurse is in some ways a difficult one. Although the work can be very satisfying, nurses' contributions tend to be undervalued by other staff, by relatives who will ask to see 'the doctor' for preference, and by patients themselves, many of whom hold a strong faith in the magic words of the psychiatrist even if the latter has only been in psychiatry a matter of months as opposed to the nurse's several years. Close day-to-day contact with the long-term and readmission cases on whom everyone has given up can induce a sense of failure.

One researcher has described how the innate contradictions of the psychiatric system – simultaneously removing responsibility from patients and expecting them to help themselves, paying lip-service to psychosocial factors within a model that denies their relevance – 'trapped the nurses into actions which they felt quite ambivalent about and which they subjectively experienced as quite distressing'. Thus:

> the younger nurses, in particular, often expressed concern about the control-oriented ethos of their daily activities and spoke of their desire to develop more effective therapeutic relationships with their patients. They often tried to do this by singling out a few specific patients for special attention. Unfortunately, the wider environment of the mental health system often doomed these attempts to failure. When this happened the nurses often reacted quite defensively and blamed patients for lacking the motivation to change, without examining the wider context in which the patients' acts took place . . . [These reactions] were often subtly encouraged by the more experienced staff, who tended to reinforce the younger nurses' incipient cynicism even while they paid lip service to the ideal of more individualised care.[13]

The chance to work in the community was often greeted with enthusiasm until similar tensions and stresses emerged in dealing with long-term attenders in this setting as well. Lacking a comprehensive critical analysis of the system, ('Nurses' insights tended to form a piecemeal and individualised critique of discrete problems . . . rather than a coherent analysis of the whole range of factors influencing ward life'), demoralisation and Persecutory attitudes can develop even in the most committed nurses.

Traditional nurses stick mainly to the basic tasks of ward management, pill-dispensing or, in the community, giving slow-release injections of medication. Others try to become more involved with ward groups, counselling individual patients, and seeing relatives, although pressure to discharge patients as soon as possible often means that there is little opportunity or encouragement for such activities on the ward. The move to community care has created new opportunities for developing counselling, family therapy, group work, rehabilitation and other areas of interest, and for taking on team manager roles in new and less medically oriented community mental health centres. There are also new responsibilities associated with the Care Programme Approach and Supervision Registers (see Chapter 7). Community Psychiatric Nurses (CPNs) undergo an extra year of training, and have established themselves, not without opposition, as a fairly independent profession. Since they can receive direct referrals from GPs they can build up their own caseload and style of working away from the hospital by basing themselves in clinics and surgeries and visiting people in their homes, in addition to their traditional role of administering medication by injection.

However, the central paradox of the nurse's position remains: a supposedly independent and skilled professional whose ideas and autonomy are still, in the words of one student, 'overruled and over-shadowed by the spectre of the medical model. Psychiatrists brought the model with them and they still hold all the power . . . The mismatch between what nurses believe and what they are actually required to do is such that it can never be resolved so long as mental health services continue to exist in their present form.'[14] This may account for the contrast described by one nurse tutor

> between the way in which mental health nurses saw themselves and the way in which they were seen by service users. For example, in the literature of the user movement, service users often describe mental health nurses as aloof, inaccessible, punishing and as colluding with the use of controversial treatments such as depot injections and ECT. However, the nurses I spoke to tended to describe them-selves as being empathic, flexible, adaptable and able to respond therapeutically to even the most severe forms of mental distress.[15]

This tutor believes that the close alliance with medical psychiatry undermines any attempt to be genuinely client-centred, and leads to a naive view that patients can be 'empowered' simply by introducing a few counselling techniques into the care plan.

HEALTH CARE ASSISTANTS/COMMUNITY CARE WORKERS

Wards may have as few as two or three trained nursing staff on duty at any one time, with health care assistants (formerly known as nursing assistants) carrying out many of the basic practical tasks. Although some have National Vocational Qualifications (NVQs), the main requirements for the job are a mature attitude, an interest in mental health, and willingness to work in a team. Paradoxically, although pay and status are low, it is health care assistants who are often in closest daily contact with patients and may get to know them best. While some are excellent, inexperience and poor supervision means that they are in danger of finding themselves out of their depth in complex situations with the more challenging and disturbed patients. The consequences are rarely discussed in ward rounds, but are often very destructive all round.

The equivalent role in the community is carried out by the community care worker. Again, these are mostly people without formal training who offer practical support to people with mental health problems in order to help them to live as independently as possible in their homes or in supported accommodation. This could include helping with finances, housing problems and general life skills, in accordance with care plans drawn up with the rest of the psychiatric team. Although community care workers deal directly with the social needs that are a central factor in many people's problems, they tend to be undervalued by mainstream psychiatry.

OCCUPATIONAL THERAPISTS

The two- or three-year occupational therapy training course includes some medical input – anatomy and physiology – as well as basic psychology and sociology, and equips occupational therapists to work with the physically disabled, older people and people with learning difficulties as well as with psychiatric patients. The emphasis is on helping people with their difficulties through meaningful activities and occupations. For some people, this might be acquiring daily living skills such as shopping, cooking and budgeting. For others, self-confidence and self-esteem may be best promoted through looking at work and leisure opportunities, or through social skills training, or through learning how to deal with anxiety or anger. Training courses teach communication skills rather than formal counselling. Although occupational therapy is a popular career choice, there is a shortage of training places and about 15 per cent of all posts are unfilled. Occupational therapy helpers, untrained people with practical skills and an interest in psychiatry, supplement the trained staff in some hospital departments.

Occupational therapists can feel undervalued by doctors and other staff, who use them merely to divert and occupy patients and do not appreciate the contribution that they can make from their often very detailed first-hand knowledge of the patients and their difficulties. They are often faced with limited space and resources to carry out their work. However, the profession is achieving a higher profile with its increased emphasis on theory and research to underpin practice, and with an enhanced role in assessing and meeting needs and acting as key workers in the community.

CLINICAL PSYCHOLOGISTS

This profession is relatively small in numbers. Unlike psychiatrists, psychologists do not have a medical training; their preferred model is the 'scientist-practitioner' who applies research-based psychological techniques to mental distress. Clinical psychology is seen as a desirable option for psychology graduates and courses are heavily oversubscribed. Successful (and mostly middle-class, white and female) applicants follow their first degree in psychology with a three-year training course consisting mainly of placements in hospitals, clinics and community teams. Carrying out therapy under supervision is a very important part of training, although some courses still insist that cognitive-behaviour therapy is the only respectable approach, with other forms of psychotherapy being regarded with suspicion.

The main areas in which psychologists work are psychiatry, learning difficulties, the prison service, with the elderly and with children. Their position in psychiatric hospitals is rather ambiguous. On the one hand, they do not have the power and influence of the psychiatrists, which can lead to very frustrating situations in in-patient work if patients are suddenly discharged or put on medication or transferred to another ward in the middle of a treatment plan. On the other hand, psychologists do not have the same rigid professional hierarchy as doctors and nurses; since they can accept referrals directly from GPs, they can build up their own independent caseload and work fairly autonomously in the community. Many psychologists choose to avoid the difficulties inherent in hospital-based work by doing this, although there has been pressure on the profession to join community mental health teams and prioritise those with more severe difficulties.

Traditionally, psychologists have special expertise in psychological testing (assessing IQ scores, brain damage, personality characteristics, and so on) and in research and cognitive-behaviour therapy. Nowadays most psychologists have expanded their role to become involved in other fields instead or as well, with a majority describing themselves as 'eclectic' in orientation (that is, drawing from a number of different psychotherapeutic approaches as appropriate). They may offer various kinds of therapy to individuals, families, couples and groups, train and supervise other staff, and help to develop new therapies and services. For example, several prominent figures in family management and in cognitive therapy with psychosis (Chapter 4) are psychologists. Although a substantial minority of clinical psychologists are sceptical both of medical-model and of scientist-practitioner approaches to mental distress, it is comparatively rare for them to use their confidence and status to speak out; the profession as a whole appears to feel that its interests are not best served by offending psychiatrists.

SOCIAL WORKERS

All qualified social workers follow a general training course, usually two years long, which equips them to work in a wide variety of settings: local authority area teams, residential units, hostels, hospitals, probation, and so on. The course covers such areas as law and criminology, social policy, welfare rights, and work with older people and those with learning disabilities as well as people with mental health problems; and students do projects and supervised placements (which take up about eight months of the course) in the area in which they wish to specialise. Practical training in communication, assessment and intervention skills are a standard part of the course.

The general orientation of social work training is sociological and psychological rather than medical, and the emphasis is on the client in his or her social context. Understanding social inequality is an important aspect of the training, and students learn to recognise and try to redress the impact of discrimination based on class, culture, gender, disability, age and sexuality. Social workers are expected to become involved not only with service users themselves but with their families and relevant agencies, and to know about local community facilities and resources and how to access them. Partly because of their training and partly because of the kind of people who are attracted to the job in the first place, social workers as a group tend to be less favourably disposed towards the use of physical treatments in psychiatry and to be more concerned with psychological and social interventions, interagency teamwork, and service users' rights. Although social work has a middle-class image, initiatives such as having access courses for members of ethnic minorities and the educationally disadvantaged help to attract students from a broad range of backgrounds. Life experience is valued, not simply academic qualifications. The majority of entrants are women, although men are disproportionately represented at management level.

The role of the social worker has changed in recent years to include much more report-writing, form-filling and general bureaucracy. Nearly all social workers are now expected to undertake additional training to become Approved Social Workers who, along with psychiatrists, have a duty to assess people for compulsory detention in hospital. These statutory responsibilities, along with acting as key workers for the care plans that are now compulsory for all mental health service users, mean that there is very little time for carrying out counselling or psychotherapy.

PSYCHOTHERAPISTS

'Psychotherapist' is a general term for anyone who practises psychotherapy of any kind, whether they are doctors, nurses, social workers, or whatever. There are a very few posts in the NHS of 'Psychotherapist' or 'Consultant psychotherapist', and they are usually filled by psychiatrists who have trained in psychotherapy for several years in addition to their medical training, and who tend to be very much influenced by psychoanalysis (that is, in-depth individual therapy over several years). However, the average psychiatric patient needs something a good deal more flexible, informal and commonsense than in-depth individual analysis, involving relatives and practical forms of help as necessary. This means that even where psychotherapy is available on the NHS, it tends to operate as a sort of fringe benefit for articulate middle-class patients without having much influence on the general ethos of the hospital.

Counselling psychologists, who have a first degree in psychology and further training in counselling, are the most recent professionals to enter the mental health field. They often work within clinical psychology departments, and offer counselling for a range of clients and difficulties.

ART THERAPISTS AND MUSIC THERAPISTS

These two new professions are still very small in numbers. People with a degree or diploma in art or music follow this with a postgraduate course (one year for art therapists, three years for music therapists) which teaches them to use these skills therapeutically with individuals and groups. The orientation is a non-medical psychotherapeutic one, with painting and music used as tools to reach, communicate with and understand the whole person and his or her feelings.

GENERAL PRACTITIONERS

Although not part of the hospital-based psychiatric team, GPs have an extremely important role, since it is they who act as the gateway to psychiatric treatment by deciding whom to refer; and equally importantly, it is they who actually deal with the vast majority of mental health problems in the community. Although psychological difficulties of various kinds take up almost a third of a GP's time,[16] only 3.5 per cent of cases diagnosed as psychiatric by GPs are referred to psychiatrists. This decision is influenced as much by factors such as the patient's reluctance and the length of the waiting list as by the severity of the problem.[17] Most people with psychiatric problems, therefore, manage to get along somehow with the help of their GP, who often knows the person and his/her family very well and tends to take a more commonsense view of mental distress than the psychiatrist.

GPs follow the basic five- to six-year medical training with two years of six-month placements in hospitals, which might or might not include a psychiatric hospital, according to choice, and one year as a trainee in a GP practice. Although courses, especially the newer ones, do include some counselling training, this is likely to be fairly elementary; and of course, the six to ten minutes allotted to each patient leaves very little time to go into problems in any depth. One result is a tendency to reach for the tranquilliser/anti-depressant as a quick solution, although there are some very good GPs around who do somehow manage to make time for a more psychological approach to people in emotional distress. Many GP practices buy in counselling sessions from private counsellors for people who need extra time and support.

VOLUNTARY WORKERS

Statutory mental health services are complemented by a wide range of voluntary provision, which is often more flexible and innovative and less institutionalised, working in partnership with service users. It includes, among many other possibilities, day and drop-in centres, hostels and supported housing, telephone helplines, crisis centres, advice work, tranquilliser withdrawal, counselling and self-help groups. Local health authorities sometimes have contracts to buy in certain services, for example places at a day centre; indeed, Conservative government policy envisaged the voluntary sector replacing some existing state services altogether.

Voluntary workers come from a whole variety of backgrounds and experiences (including that of having received psychiatric treatment themselves) and are generally given training as part of the job. Surveys show that service users particularly appreciate the informality, support, sense of equality and opportunity to contribute that characterises voluntary agencies.[18]

CONCLUSION

It can be seen that in each profession the more traditional staff tend to see themselves as members of a hierarchy with a definite but limited role which is primarily to do with diagnosing, testing, organising, or carrying out practical, medical or administrative tasks. The new-style staff, particularly those who are community- rather than hospital-based, see themselves as operating more independently and, often in the face of considerable opposition, have moved towards a broader and more psychotherapeutic role with the traditional tasks of their profession being subordinate to this. Since it is the most powerful (psychiatrists) and numerous (nurses) professionals who receive the least psychotherapeutically oriented training, such skills are most likely to be possessed by the more recent, more peripheral and less influential professions.

Of course, ward management, testing, prescribing, report-writing and so on all have their value, but when these skills are not grounded in a psychosocial understanding of people's feelings, relationships and social circumstances, there is a danger that the whole-person, whole-system approach will be completely lost, with the kind of results that we have seen. The medically-based training of doctors and nurses in particular encourages them to override their natural commonsense reactions and see their charges as patients with illnesses, rather than as people with problems. Not only are most mental health professionals not trained to see people in a whole-person, whole-system way, they are actually *trained not to do so*. All of this means that, as we have seen throughout the book so far, although every member of staff may be doing the best job they can within the limitations imposed by their own training and the institution itself, the results can still be disastrous.

Some changes have taken place along with the three-fold increase in community mental health teams (CMHTs) in the last decade. CMHTs can be loosely defined as consisting of a mixed group of professionals (most commonly community psychiatric nurses and social workers, but often with input from psychologists, occupational therapists and psychiatrists as well) who offer a range of services outside the hospital. Most CMHTs are based in ordinary buildings in the local community. They vary in size, personnel and services offered, but generally aim to be local, comprehensive, accessible and non-stigmatising, and to provide a more holistic model of care which takes social and personal needs into account as well as medical ones. Their work may include individual, family and group counselling, drop-in sessions, support for carers, and practical help with daily activities like cooking and managing money, as well as the more traditional monitoring of medication. Bed closures mean that most will be seeing a high proportion of clients who fall under the heading of 'severe and enduring mental health problems', for whom admission used to be the only option. A few CMHTs have their own beds, but most rely on the hospital for back-up if crises are uncontainable within the community or occur outside office hours. Along with the new structures goes a general philosophy of care that 'explicitly values egalitarianism, role blurring and a surrender of power to lower-status workers and service users'.[19] This, of course, can be anxiety provoking as well as liberating for staff who are used to more traditional ways of working: a recent survey found that 'overall, staff are emotionally over-extended and exhausted'[20] due to lack of resources and lack of clarity about their own and the team's roles and responsibilities. Another review noted that training is still dominated by the desire of each professional group to define its own role and boundaries, rather than the need for all disciplines to work together towards agreed common goals.[21]

The most important question is how far this change of policy on the delivery of mental health care reflects a change in the underlying model. Are we seeing a genuine shift in the underlying philosophy, or are we simply delivering treatment in a different setting and in effect institutionalising people in the community? In practice, the answer is usually a bit of both. As we have seen, professionals who hope to escape the limitations of medical-model, hospital-based treatment quickly find the same tensions and frustrations compromising their work in the community as well.

Related to this is the whole question of the role and future direction of the various professions. For example, should mental health nurses, as one professor of nursing argues, be developing their role in monitoring medication, cognitive-behavioural interventions and perhaps even genetic counselling,[22] or should they, in the words of another professor, be offering 'a more humanised approach to health care and genuine empowerment'?[23] *Working in Partnership*, the 1994 report of the Mental Health Nursing Review, recommends a number of desirable changes, such as improving nurses' awareness of the racial and cultural needs of service users; including service users and relatives in service planning and research; and recording and acting on people's wishes when they are in crisis.[24] *Pulling Together*, a report by the Sainsbury Centre for Mental Health, extends similar recommendations to all professions, with particular emphasis on service users' desire for 'a more holistic understanding of their lives, an empathy with their distress and a consequent reduction in their use of pejorative labelling and categorisation of people's experiences', in contrast to their present position as 'passive recipients of a care model they find deeply unsatisfactory'.[25] We return to the theme of earlier chapters, the contrast between service users' desire for a *psychosocial* understanding of their difficulties and the primarily *medical* model of the professionals, which means that, paradoxically, mental health staff are likely to be found helpful in inverse relation to their status, power, salary and length of training, with voluntary workers getting the most favourable rating of all.

The argument is clear: the psychiatric system will be able to offer real help and healing only to the extent that it is able to move away from the divided-function, medical-model approach to one where a psychosocial, whole-person, whole-system understanding of people's problems underlies the training of all the different professions, and where the promotion of this approach is seen as everyone's role and responsibility. This, of course, has profound implications for the relationship between the professions and, at a broader level, for the role of psychiatric staff in relation to society as a whole. One nurse believes that her colleagues should 'begin by challenging the language of the hospital and go on to challenge the views of its masters',[26] while a nurse tutor calls for the nursing profession to 'acknowledge the link between social injustice and mental distress, by supporting political campaigns against poverty and all forms of discrimination . . . Truly client-centred approaches also require participation in a struggle against social injustice.'[27]

All this raises the important question of how, if it is so unhelpful, the underlying medical-model philosophy has come to exert such a powerful influence on the training of mental health professionals. To answer this we need to look briefly at the history of psychiatry over the last 200 years.

Chapter 7

A brief history of psychiatry

THE OFFICIAL ACCOUNT

The conventional account of the history of psychiatry goes something like this: despite some ups and downs and false starts, there has been slow but steady progress from the unenlightened days when lunatics were untreated or even tortured in places like Bedlam for the amusement of the public to our present more advanced state of knowledge. During the nineteenth century there was a gradual shift from a primitive view of madness as caused by supernatural agencies to a more sophisticated medical view, with psychiatry becoming accepted as a standard part of medical training.

The era of 'moral treatment', under the influence of Pinel in France and the Tukes in England, ended some of the worst excesses of the early attempts to treat madness, although unfortunately not all the old habits were eradicated, since the new asylums built in every county quickly became overcrowded. More liberal polices in the 1930s encouraged the setting up of local out-patient clinics and after-care facilities for former patients, and the mood of optimism was increased by the discovery of new treatments such as insulin coma therapy (no longer used) and ECT. The 'drug revolution' of the 1950s, when several new classes of drugs were synthesised, enabled many of the most disturbed patients to be discharged into the community, or at least to spend long periods outside hospital, and the number of patients in psychiatric hospitals fell accordingly.

Psychiatry is now accepted as just another branch of medicine, and patients can avoid much of the stigma associated with the old asylums by attending psychiatric units attached to district general hospitals. Of course, much still remains to be done; 'progress in this branch of medicine has been slow, but the difficulties to be contended with – professional apathy, public prejudice and the inherent complexity of the subject – have been

DOI: 10.4324/9781003095958-7

very great',[1] but psychiatry can rightly be proud of its achievements to date. 'The treatment of psychosis, neurosis and schizophrenia have been entirely changed by the drug revolution. People go into hospital with mental disorders and they are cured' (Sir Keith Joseph introducing the 1971 White Paper, *Hospital Services for the Mentally Ill*).

Some such summary appears at the start of most standard textbooks on psychiatry. The alternative and far more controversial account is presented by writers such as Andrew Scull, who, in his closely researched book *Museums of Madness*, argues that to regard nineteenth-century lunacy reform as 'a triumphant and unproblematic expression of humanitarian concern is to adopt a perspective which is hopelessly biased and inaccurate: one which relies, of necessity, on a systematic neglect and distortion of the available evidence'.[2] He presents a rather less reassuring picture of the history of early psychiatry in terms of the medical lobby's struggle for power and control of the field.

AN ALTERNATIVE ACCOUNT

The first moves to segregate the insane from the rest of society came in the seventeenth century with the setting up of private madhouses. Charitable voluntary asylums began to appear in the eighteenth century, although the mad were equally likely to find themselves in workhouses or jails. For most of the eighteenth century the madhouses were run privately by people from many different backgrounds – the clergy, and other less respectable individuals hoping to make money out of the business. It was widely believed that madness was caused by witchcraft or sinful behaviour. Scull describes how, seeking to enter this profitable field themselves, the medical profession, which up till then had taken very little interest in insanity, began to claim that it was a disease like any other for which the usual remedies of purges, vomits, bleedings and coloured powders, which of course only they could administer, were the cure. Many were highly respected medical men, and since recovery seemed to occur spontaneously in about one-third of cases anyway, doctors were able to claim success for treatments which were not really any more effective than anyone else's.

Throughout the nineteenth century the doctors manoeuvred to gain acceptance for their views on madness and to control the way it was treated. Given their lack of genuine expertise on insanity, this was a difficult task. The most serious obstacle was the growth of what was called 'moral treatment', which was developed by a lay person, William Tuke, and his colleagues at an asylum in York. The word 'moral' meant something equivalent to 'emotional' or 'psychological', and implied a compassionate and understanding approach to sufferers from mental distress. Tuke had investigated the various remedies recommended by the medical profession, which included bleeding, blisters, evacuants and medicines of all kinds, and found that all were either useless or positively harmful, with the possible exception of warm baths for melancholics. From then on, the visiting physicians at York only attended to bodily illness, while the lay people who were in charge of the day-to-day running of the institution developed a new approach in place of the harsh physical remedies. Lunatics were seen as essentially human, although distressed, and in need of kind and respectful management and cheerful and homely surroundings. Externally imposed medical remedies like purges and physical restraint had no place in helping lunatics regain their dignity and self-control. They were to be treated as far as possible as if they were in full possession of their wits, with the firm and confident expectation that they could return to more acceptable behaviour. This, for the Victorians, meant re-education in the socially approved virtues of industry, self-control, moderation and piety. Patients were expected to conduct themselves respectably at the regular lunatics' balls, and to work diligently in the kitchens, the bakery, the gardens and the hospital farms. The recovery of women in particular was defined in terms of their willingness to undertake cleaning, sewing and laundry in a spirit of decorum and obedience. Nevertheless, this regime was undoubtedly more humane than the previous one, and many recoveries were reported. Its fame spread, and one physician wrote:

> The . . . Quakers have demonstrated beyond contradiction, the very great advantages resulting from a mode of treatment in cases of Insanity much more mild than was before introduced into any Lunatic Asylum at home or abroad. In the management of this institution, they have set an example which claims the imitation, and deserves the thanks, of every sect and every nation.[3]

Not surprisingly, this view was not shared by most of his colleagues, whose claims to possess special skills in the treatment of the insane were being threatened. Prominent doctors responded with such assertions as: 'The disease of insanity in all its shades and varieties, belongs, in point of treatment, to the department of the physician alone . . . the medical treatment . . . is that part on which the whole success of the cure lies',[4] and 'Direct medical remedies can never be too early introduced or too readily applied.'[5]

Indeed, the doctors had a very difficult task reasserting their authority in the face of a popular approach based entirely on the idea that common sense and humanity, which any lay person might possess, were the curative factors. The exponents of moral treatment who took over the York Asylum from Dr Best, one of the most famous medical experts of the time, could hardly have been less flattering about the events of his reign. One of them, a magistrate called Higgins, pointed out that after Dr Best's departure the number of patient deaths per year fell from twenty to four. He observed scathingly that:

> amongst much medical nonsense, published by physicians interested to conceal their neglect, and the abuses of their establishments, it has been said, that persons afflicted with insanity are more liable than others to mortification of their extremities. Nothing of the kind was ever experienced at the institution of the Quakers. If members of the royal and learned College of Physicians were chained, or shut up naked, on straw saturated with urine and excrement, with a scanty allowance of food – exposed to the indecency of a northern climate, in cells having windows unglazed – I have no doubt that they would soon exhibit as strong a tendency to mortified extremities, as any of their patients.[6]

There was concern that:

> the management of the insane has been in too few hands; and many of those who have been engaged in it, finding it a very lucrative concern, have wished to involve it in mystery, and, in order to prevent institutions for their cure from becoming more general, were desirous that it should be thought that there was some secret in the way of medicine for the cure, not easily found out.[7]

This in fact was written by a doctor, who recommended that the best safeguard against future abuses was to ensure that the care of the insane was not left to any one group of experts, medical or otherwise, but that asylums should be constantly supervised by lay people. Or, as Higgins remarked sarcastically: 'Who after this will doubt the efficacy of my medicine – visitors and committees? I will warrant it superior even to Dr Hunter's famous secret insane powders – either green or grey – or his patent Brazil salts into the bargain.'[8]

So, having failed to oust the new regime, those doctors who found their position threatened by it had to find some way of turning it to their advantage. An approach specifically developed to be carried out by lay people did not seem a very promising place to start. But Scull shows how the very open-mindedness of moral treatment and the honesty and modesty of its claims made it vulnerable to takeover bids by the medical profession. Tuke and his followers had not protected their position in the usual way by forming organized groups of workers with special training or entry qualifications. At the same time they openly admitted that 'as we . . . profess to do little more than assist Nature, in the performance of her own cure, the term *recovered*, is adopted in preference to that of *cured*'.[9] This left a gap into which the medical men could step with claims (however unfounded) of new remedies which really did cure insanity. At the same time they revived the use of cathartics and tried to take over the administration of warm baths to melancholics, arguing that such techniques were by no means 'of so simple and straightforward a nature as might be at first sight conceived' and really needed to be supervised by medically trained professionals. Something that worked to their advantage was the fact that Tuke and his colleagues, although rejecting medical remedies, had still kept to much of the actual language of medicine – 'patient', 'treatment', and so on – which implied an illness model.

By the early nineteenth century, the doctors had gained enough ground to win an important battle and to deal the reform movement a serious blow. They successfully argued against legislation that would mean that the growing number of public asylums came under the strict supervision and control of a board of lay people who would have the power to investigate patients' treatment, forbid harsh practices and order any patient they considered sane to be discharged. Doctors insisted that only medical experts could undertake this task satisfactorily, and consolidated their victory with a spate of medical articles and complicated lists of diagnoses. Around this time, lectures on the treatment of insanity became part of the normal medical training. Moral treatment was too widely known and highly regarded to be dismissed, but the doctors were now in a position to propose a compromise which at first sight seemed very reasonable. Both moral and medical methods had something to offer; indeed, a knowledge of moral treatment was an important part of a doctor's expertise, but the best results could be obtained by using a combination of both approaches. What this did, in fact, was to reduce the status of moral treatment from a whole philosophy of care to a mere collection of techniques, while the doctor, as the only one who understood both approaches, was left firmly in charge of the whole enterprise. Towards the second half of the nineteenth century the first medical journals appeared, devoted to the theme that 'Insanity is purely a disease of the brain. The physician is now the responsible guardian of the lunatic and must ever remain so.'[10]

Of course, this still left the doctors with the big problem of actually demonstrating that there was a physical basis for mental illness, but despite their confident assertions that this was the case, no proof was forthcoming. This did not stop them from applying all sorts of bizarre and unpleasant physical treatments; in fact, they did so with all the more enthusiasm, hoping to find successful remedies to back up their claim to possess special skills and knowledge. At various times, these remedies included 'hypodermic injections of morphia, the administrations of the bromides, chloral hydrate, hypocymine, physotigma, cannabis indica, amyl nitrate, conium, digitalis, ergot, pilocarpine',[11] thirty-four different emetics, and fifty different purgatives, sudden immersion in cold water or pouring ten to fifty buckets of icy water on patients' heads, anointing shaven heads with vinegar, or raising blisters on the head and neck and rubbing salves into the pustules, applying ants or leeches to the skin, whipping with stinging nettles, making incisions in the skin, applying red hot pokers simultaneously to the head and the soles of the feet, drilling holes in the scalp, putting patients in revolving chairs that could be rotated so fast 'that a healthy, rational man would lose everything in his stomach in five minutes', applying restraining masks to the face, putting patients on a treadmill for up to forty-eight hours, ordering baths in thin gruel, milk or even gravy,[12] and many other even more bizarre devices. But although there was no shortage of theories to explain how these remedies were supposed to work (icy water was said to cool heads that had been made feverish by congestion of the blood, while emetics were justified by the belief that there was a close link between insanity and abdominal disorders), the proportion of recoveries to admissions remained distressingly low.

By now it was very obvious that these methods were not producing cures. This would have been more of a threat to the medical profession's position and claims with regard to insanity if the asylums had not, by this time, become so extremely useful to the communities they served. Any troublesome person could be sent there, whether insane, or old, infirm, poor, delinquent, simple-minded or simply inconvenient to their families and neighbours. The inmates were in no position to complain, and the local officials found the arrangement too useful to worry very much about the validity of the doctors' claims, although it was convenient to be able to reassure oneself that sending people to the asylum was really in their best interests too. Meanwhile the asylums grew . . . and grew . . . and grew. The 1845 Lunatic Asylums Act made it obligatory for every county and borough in England and Wales to provide enough asylum space to serve the local population, but however huge the asylums were, they never had enough space for the increasing number of so-called lunatics. The vast Victorian buildings, more like small towns than hospitals, with their chapels and farms, fire brigades and smithies, laundries and bowling greens, sometimes contained over 2000 inmates. Very few of them ever left the walls of these asylums again. The disappearance of the ideals of moral treatment was visible in the architecture:

> the wards are long, narrow, gloomy and comfortless, the staircases cramped and cold, the corridors oppressive, the atmosphere of the space dingy, the halls huge and cheerless. The airing-courts, although in some instances carefully planted, are uninviting and prison-like.[13]

About half of these places have closed in the last ten years.

Since by now, as one asylum superintendent noted, 'it is totally impossible there to do more than know [the inmates] by name', it became increasingly difficult to maintain the fiction that such 'treatments' as cold water shocks and tranquillising drugs were being used for therapeutic reasons, rather than merely to control and discipline the inmates. Depriving them of tobacco and recreation and keeping them on starvation diets also helped to maintain order. But there was one advantage of the increased numbers: doctors could now claim that their enormous workload prevented them from achieving the cures that were really within their power, although at the same time they firmly resisted the appointment of lay administrators to free them to give more attention to their patients.

Over the last hundred years, the medical profession has continued to consolidate its monopoly over the treatment of the mentally distressed. A highlight was the discovery around 1900 that syphilis was the cause of general paralysis of the insane, which affected a large group of patients, and seemed to give hope that a physical basis would soon be found for all the other types of mental distress. This has yet to happen but, as before, this has encouraged rather than diminished the search for effective physical treatments. Asylums, or 'bins' as they are sometimes known, were increasingly criticised for their harsh, overcrowded and impersonal regimes, but there was little change until the Mental Treatment Act of 1930 started the gradual shift away from large institutions and towards out-patient and community services, in line with the general expansion of state welfare.

The 1930s also saw the introduction of three new treatments which were seized upon with enthusiasm.

Insulin coma therapy

As well as controlling diabetes, insulin was thought to have a calming effect on psychotic patients. It was believed that the best results were obtained by using extremely high doses which put 'schizophrenic' patients into life-threatening comas, closely supervised by trained staff in special units. Thirty to forty comas constituted a complete course, and magical results were claimed. Patients, however, experienced intense fear, as well as ravenous hunger and a feeling of suffocation, and a proportion of them actually died. It was not until twenty years later, by which time it was widely used, that a thorough study showed that the insulin itself had no therapeutic effect at all,[14] and that any improvements had to be attributable to the attention and expectations surrounding the treatment rather than to the treatment itself.

Electric shock treatment (also called electro-convulsive therapy or ECT)

The dramatic claims made for insulin coma therapy were subsequently attached to ECT, still very widely used today. Electricity was used inter-mittently throughout the early history of psychiatry, for example, by John Wesley in the eighteenth century, who declared that from his shock machine 'hundreds, perhaps thousands, have received unspeakable good'.[15] In the 1930s, on the basis of an inaccurate belief that 'schizo-phrenia' and epilepsy never occur together and must be incompatible conditions, drug-induced convulsions were introduced for 'schizo-phrenia'. Unfortunately for the patients, the seizures were often violent enough to fracture spine, ribs and limbs, and in addition the drug produced a terrifying aura such that 'the majority soon grow to fear the injections, and a few reach a pitiable state of apprehension and alarm'.[16] One solution was to induce the fits while the patient was actually in an insulin coma. Later, epileptic-type seizures were induced by passing an electrical current through the head. The following rather chilling account describes how Cerletti and Bini, the Italian inventors of ECT, administered it for the very first time in 1938 to a tramp found muttering incoherently in a Rome railway station:

He started to sing abruptly at the top of his voice, then he quieted down . . . It was quite evident to all of us that we had been using a too low voltage. It was proposed that we should allow this patient to have some rest and repeat the experiment the next day. All at once the patient, who evidently had been following our conversation, said clearly and solemnly without his usual gibberish: 'Not another one! It's murder!' I confess that such explicit admonition under such circumstances, and so emphatic and commanding, coming from a person whose enigmatic jargon had until then been very difficult to understand, shook my determination to carry on with the experiment. But it was just this fear of yielding to a superstitious notion that caused me to make up my mind. The electrodes were applied again and a 110-volt discharge was applied for 1.5 seconds. We observed the same instantaneous brief, generalized spasm, and soon after, the onset of the classic epileptic convulsion. We were all breathless during the tonic phase of the attack, and really overwhelmed during the apnea as we watched the cadaverous cyanosis of the patient's face . . . Finally, with the first stertorous breathing and the first clonic spasm, the blood flowed better not only in the patient's vessels but also in our own . . . He rose to sitting position and looked at us, calm and smiling, as though to inquire what we wanted of him. We asked: 'What happened to you?' He answered: 'I don't know. Maybe I was asleep.' Thus occurred the first electrically produced convulsion in man, which I at once named electroshock.[17]

'Regressive ECT', in which convulsions are invoked twice daily until the achievement of regression, a state 'characterised by complete helplessness, confusion, mutism etc., and by neurological signs of altered cerebral activity', was sometimes used to treat 'schizophrenia'. It was said to aid ward management by making patients more docile, resulting in a dramatically reduced need for sedation, restraints and solitary confinement.[18]

Cerletti himself later came to believe that ECT should be abandoned. This has not happened; ECT is currently described as the treatment of choice for severe depression, and is given to about 11,340 patients a year in Britain. A muscle relaxant and an anaesthetic are always administered, unlike in the early days of its use, thus avoiding the risk of fracture, but it remains a controversial procedure.

Psychosurgery

Finally, and occasionally used today, there is psychosurgery. In its more primitive form it involved the removal or destruction of nerve fibres in the frontal lobe of the brain in an operation known as the 'standard leucotomy'. This involved:

> making a burr hole in the side of the head, above and in front of the ear, inserting a cutting instrument, sweeping it in an arc and thereby dividing as much white matter as possible. The same procedure was then repeated on the opposite side of the head. This operation was extremely crude in that at post-mortem there was found to be extreme variation in the positioning of the cuts.[19]

The technique was later refined, although, given the complexity of the brain and our limited knowledge about its functioning, it is still impossible to be at all precise about the effects one wishes to achieve.

As with every new technique, psychosurgery was initially hailed as a wonder treatment, and was used for a wide variety of problems: 'schizophrenia', alcoholism, learning disabilities, depression, anxiety, phobias, personality disorders, for shell-shocked war veterans and even for problem children. Approximately 50,000 lobotomies were performed in America between 1936 and 1955, many at the untrained hands of a particularly enthusiatic American professor of neurology, Walter Freeman, who sometimes carried out twenty-five such operations a day.[20] According to him, the best results were obtained with women, black people, Jews, and those with simple occupations. He extolled lobotomy's potential for controlling society's misfits: 'Society . . . justifiably distrusts the thinker . . . Lobotomised patients make rather good citizens.' One of his victims was Frances Farmer, a rebellious film star with communist sympathies. Another was one of John F. Kennedy's sisters who had mild learning difficulties. Neither they nor anyone else ever recovered from the devastating after-effects, including seizures, aggressiveness and other undesirable personality changes, intellectual impairment, a general emotional blunting sometimes dubbed 'zombie-ism', and even death. More unusual after-effects were suffered by Egaz Moniz, the Portuguese neurosurgeon credited with the invention of psychosurgery. Not only was he awarded the Nobel Prize for this innovation, but one of his lobotomised patients, presumably not so impressed by his achievements, put an end to his career by shooting him in the spine.

By the 1950s, reservations were finally being expressed: 'Is quieting a patient a cure? Perhaps all it accomplishes is to make things more convenient for those who have to nurse them . . . It disturbs me to see the number of zombies that these operations turn out,' in the words of the Director of the New York State Psychiatric Institute.[21] The introduction of chlorpromazine, the first major tranquilliser, in 1952, marked the end of the period of mass lobotomies. Psychosurgery is now restricted to the very occasional case where someone suffers from severe obsessional neurosis or is a serious management problem. There are about twenty-six such operations a year in England and Wales.[22] Whether such drastic interventions are ever justified is still open to question, although its supporters would argue that in very severe suffering it is a valid option.

The nadir of psychiatry's activities was reached with the little-known story of its involvement in the eugenics movement in Nazi Germany. Laws allowing the compulsory sterilisation of those said to be suffering from hereditary disorders, mainly mental 'illness' and learning disabilities, had been applied to about 400,000 German and 30,000 American victims before the outbreak of World War Two. After the start of war, a secret programme of mass killings of German psychiatric patients began; there were about 100,000 deaths, mostly in gas chambers in strategically located psychiatric clinics across the country. Psychiatrists, including leading doctors and professors, were asked to compile lists of those said to be unworthy of life on the basis of a brief look through their case files, while the official cause of death was taken from a list of possible conditions, such as strokes or pneumonia, matched with age, sex and prior symptoms. Standard letters of condolence were sent to relatives. Although some doctors tried to save their patients by falsifying the diagnosis or transferring them to other hospitals, open protest was very rare. Meanwhile, in occupied France, an estimated 40,000 psychiatric patients were allowed to die through malnutrition and hypothermia. After public disquiet and the courageous speeches of a few churchmen had brought the official psychiatric euthanasia programme to a halt in 1941, both the equipment and some of the doctors were redeployed in concentration camps where the experience they had gained in gassing was used, as all the world knows, against the Jews. Dr Eberl, the first commandant of Treblinka, had previously been the medical superintendent of an asylum involved in killing its patients. Even after this date, 100,000 of the remaining asylum patients were deliberately starved to death.[23]

In Britain in 1948, the NHS came into being. At the time, there was virtually no special training for psychiatrists and the profession itself hardly existed, although there were specialist mental health nurses. The mental hospital population peaked at 154,000 in 1954, and out-patient facilities gradually took over much of their work.

The next landmark in psychiatric history is the 'drug revolution' of the 1950s and 1960s.

THE DRUG REVOLUTION

Drugs of various types have been used in psychiatry since the nineteenth century, but in the 1950s and 1960s several new classes of medication were developed and became the basic tools of modern psychiatry. They are known under two different names, the generic name and the brand name, the latter being the same basic product marketed and packaged by a particular drug company. Since 1985 many brand name drugs are no longer available on the NHS, and the cheaper generic version is prescribed instead. The new drugs are:

1   The neuroleptics, also known as anti-psychotics or *major tranquillisers*. As the name suggests, these have a very powerful sedative effect, and are mainly used on patients who are thought to have a psychotic illness such as 'schizophrenia'.
2   The *anti-depressants*, of which there are three main types. The monoamine oxidase inhibitors, or MAOIs, were developed first but are less frequently prescribed because they interact dangerously with certain foods such as cheese, chocolate and bananas. The more recent tricyclic anti-depressants are now used for preference. Newest on the market are the selective serotonin re-uptake inhibitors, or SSRIs, of which Prozac is the best known example.
3   *Lithium* is a simple salt that does not fit into any of the above categories, but is thought to be effective in controlling severe mood swings ('manic depression').
4   The benzodiazepines, such as Valium and Librium, also known as *minor tranquillisers*. These drugs are mostly used to relieve panic and anxiety, although some are used as sleeping pills.

The major tranquilliser chlorpromazine was developed first by a French pharmaceutical (drug) company. The company that originally synthesised it had been looking for a drug that could be used in surgery to slow the pulse, heart rate and other bodily functions. When marketed in the USA, in what has been described as 'an at times almost frantic search for therapeutic applications with which (a) to convince the Federal Drug

Administration to allow marketing of the drug; and (b) to persuade American physicians to prescribe it',[24] it was considered as a general sedative, a treatment for itching, or control for nausea and vomiting. But it was promoting its use with psychotic patients that really hit the jackpot. It obviously met a need, because just over a year later an estimated two million psychiatric patients in the USA were receiving this major tranquilliser.

The usual claims for miraculous results were made, although it is still unknown how these drugs actually work. It is a widely accepted part of the official history of psychiatry that the introduction of the major tranquillisers brought about a decline in the population of psychiatric hospitals by enabling many chronic patients to be discharged and others to stay out of hospital for long periods between admission. Certainly the two events occurred at about the same time, but Scull and others have pointed out that both in the USA and in Britain numbers had begun to fall *before* the new drugs appeared on the market.[25] In Britain, the Open Door Movement had led to the unlocking of wards, allowing male and female patients to mix and improving visiting arrangements. Therapeutic communities, where staff and patients worked together to break down the roles and rules of the old institutional way of life, were established with a radically new, psychotherapeutic understanding of mental distress. Breaking down hierarchies of authority, encouraging emotional expression, making decisions by consensus, and seeing the patients themselves as important sources of help and healing were the themes of the new settings. This wave of postwar innovation and optimism preceded the new drug treatment in many places; if the major tranquillisers were a factor, they were not the only one, and certainly not the most important one.

The first anti-depressants to be introduced, the MAOIs, were discovered accidentally when certain drugs used in the treatment of tuberculosis were found to have a mood-elevating effect. Following a favourable report on their effect on chronically withdrawn patients in 1958 there was a flood of studies and trials (over 1300 in three years) and widespread enthusiasm about their use. Subsequently the tricyclic group became the usual first choice instead. They were discovered accidentally during trials to develop new major tranquillisers, to which they are chemically very similar. While they were heavily promoted as different and improved versions, there is little evidence that they were superior to the originals.

In 1988, Eli Lilly introduced the first of the selective serotonin re-uptake inhibitors, Prozac (fluoxetine). In fact, their action resembles that of a minor tranquilliser more closely than an anti-depressant,[26] but in the wake of the scandal about benzodiazepines they were marketed as a non-addictive, safer and more effective alternative to the tricyclics. Six years later, Prozac had become a household name and was earning its manufacturers $1.6 billion a year.[27] However, there is emerging evidence that SSRIs can have both side-effects and withdrawal effects.[28] Over 21 million prescriptions for anti-depressants are written annually in Great Britain,[29] and the market is growing rapidly.

Lithium salts were once used for a variety of ailments, especially gout, but lithium was first suggested as a remedy for the over-excitement of manic patients in 1949 by a doctor who was investigating the toxic effects of injecting uric acid into guinea-pigs.[30] In order to carry out this experiment, he first had to make the uric acid soluble by adding lithium salts. The result was that the animals became 'extremely lethargic and unresponsive'. Although, as he himself commented rather apologetically, 'it may seem a long distance from lethargy in guinea-pigs to the excitement of psychotics', this did not deter him from administering lithium to ten manic patients. Miraculous improvements were claimed, although he failed to mention that three of the patients suffered severe toxicity, and one died. By the 1960s the new treatment was widely used in Europe, although it was slower to catch on in America. One writer has suggested that this 'was due to a lack of enthusiasm on the part of the pharmaceutical companies. Lithium carbonate is such a simple substance that it cannot be patented . . . The profit margin for manufacturers is therefore a good deal lower than with other products.'[31] One solution to this problem has been to sell lithium in a special slow-release form.

In the 1960s, the first minor tranquillisers appeared on the market. One such tranquilliser was initially promoted as a cure for alcoholism,[32] although it is now known that the two substances are very dangerous in combination and can lead to a dual addiction. The emphasis shifted, via what has been described as 'the slickest and most effective marketing campaign in the history of pharmaceuticals',[33] to selling minor tranquillisers as a simple, non-addictive remedy for anxiety, panic and other vague and hard-to-define complaints that pose such a problem to GPs and psychiatrists. Promoted in this way the minor tranquillisers (like the major tranquillisers before them) seemed to promise a desperately needed solution to a hitherto enormous and time-consuming problem. Many hard-pressed doctors prescribed them after interviews of less than ten minutes, often without telling patients what they were or warning them about side-effects, and people could obtain repeat prescriptions from receptionists for years on end.

The first hints of trouble started to emerge in the late 1970s, when researchers began to uncover some of the less beneficial effects of these drugs. However, there was little public or professional awareness of the true scale of the problem until a *That's Life!* TV programme of June 1983 reported the stories of three people who had become dependent on tranquillisers, precipitating jammed switchboards and over 3000 letters from people recounting similar experiences.[34]

The 1960s also saw the emergence of the so-called 'anti-psychiatry' movement, along with a general wave of political unrest and protest throughout society. Although its impact on actual practice was limited, it became possible for a brief period to question many of psychiatry's fundamental tenets. A central figure was R.D. Laing, a Scottish psychiatrist who rejected the category of 'schizophrenia' and argued, in writings that became required reading for students and political activists, that so-called 'symptoms' made sense in the context of family relationships. Later he broadened his criticisms to include the whole of a society in which, in his words: 'The statesmen of the world who boast and threaten that they have Doomsday weapons are far more dangerous, and far more estranged from "reality" than many of the people on whom the label "psychotic" is affixed.'[35] His conviction that what we call madness is ultimately meaningful and understandable is as relevant and contentious now as it was then. The same could be said of the ideas of Thomas Szasz, an American psychiatrist who totally refuted the concept of 'mental illness'. The mind, he argued, cannot be 'sick' in any but a metaphorical sense (like economies, for example). There is no such thing as 'schizophrenia', and the continuing search for brain lesions to justify incarcerating and drugging people whose behaviour upsets us is 'the greatest scandal of our scientific age'.[36] We saw in Chapter 4 that anti-psychiatry critiques are now generally seen as mistaken, irrelevant and damaging.

The new drug treatments paved the way for the next important development from the 1960s onwards: the move from the old Victorian asylums to small psychiatric units attached to district general hospitals. The impetus came partly from the increasing amount of evidence that the asylums were actually creating, rather than curing, the problems that their patients demonstrated. It was 'beyond question that much of the aggressive, disturbed, suicidal, and regressive behaviour of the mentally ill is not necessarily or inherently a part of the illness as such, but is very largely an artificial by-product of the way of life imposed on them'.[37] Since Enoch Powell's impassioned 1961 speech against the 'isolated, majestic, imperious . . . and daunting'[38] asylums, there has been a policy of reducing hospital beds and eventually closing down the old asylums altogether.

The process has speeded up in the last twenty years with, in England, a loss of nearly half of all NHS mental hospital beds between 1983 and 1993.

At first sight the creation of new units in district general hospitals seems to be a very positive step. Patients and their visitors no longer need to travel miles to vast, grim buildings out in the country, but can instead call in at the new units for out-patient treatment or stay a few days as an in-patient, in the same way as they come in to the general side of the hospital for X-rays or operations. But although these units do have some advantages, they can also be seen as a further victory in the medical profession's campaign to establish psychiatry as just another branch of medicine, to be assimilated with its new drug treatments into the traditional medical world of wards, beds, nurses and medicines. (Most of the examples in this book are taken from one such unit.) The objections were summarised in a World Health Organization report in 1953 which discussed the American experience:

> In much modern writing on the subject it is taken as axiomatic that psychiatric wards in general hospitals are the most desirable form of provision for psychiatric medical care . . . but, as the committee has emphasized, the psychiatric hospital does not do its job best by imitating the general hospital. Too often the psychiatric wards of a general hospital are forced by the expectations of the hospital authorities to conform to a pattern which is harmful to their purpose. Patients are expected to be in bed and nurses are expected to be engaged in activities which resemble general nursing. The satisfactions of neurological diagnosis are enhanced by the prestige in the general hospital of clear-cut physical pathology, to the detriment of interest in the average psychiatric patient whose case does not exhibit such features . . . the more the psychiatric hospital imitates the general hospital . . . the less successful it will be in creating the atmosphere it needs.[39]

COMMUNITY CARE

The so-called 'community care' movement in fact dates back to the 1960s, but it is only with the large-scale reduction in beds and movement of patients into the community in the last decade or so that it has attracted so much public attention and controversy. As we saw in the previous chapter, most health authorities now try to base psychiatric services as far as possible in local facilities such as GP surgeries, clinics and newly set up Community Mental Health Centres, rather than operating entirely from hospitals, although nearly all still retain some hospital beds for acute need.

The community care movement gained its force from its appeal to both would-be reformers and to government economists. Reformers saw it as a chance to reject a medicalised model of psychiatry in favour of a more psychosocial approach in which professionals could work together as equals in teams that would not necessarily be headed by psychiatrists. However, there is a widespread suspicion that the main appeal of community care was the opportunity it provided for cutting costs under the guise of humanitarian reform, with relatives bearing most of the resulting burden. Three-quarters of the mental health budget is still spent on hospitals, leaving community resources severely stretched. Hostels run by voluntary organisations, private owners or local councils vary widely in quality, even if they have spare capacity, and there are not enough 24-hour crisis services to fill the gaps left by bed closures.

The public outcry about community care, heavily reinforced by sensationalist media reporting and by relatives' organisations like SANE, is based on two main concerns. First, there is the belief that closing the asylums means that large numbers of vulnerable people are being thrown out on to the streets. This is erroneous. Only 2 per cent of the homeless on London's streets have ever been long-stay psychiatric patients.[40] Follow-up studies show that most people discharged after asylum closure settle successfully into group homes or supported housing in the community, where they describe themselves as much happier than before; less than 2 per cent are lost to the services.[41] All the available evidence shows that properly funded community services are an improvement on hospital care on all variables, and are much preferred by service users.[42] The reason there are so many homeless people on the streets is high unemployment coupled with a lack of affordable housing; and the reason that some of them subsequently develop mental health problems is that this is a very stressful way to live.

Second, there is anxiety about the apparent danger of being murdered by a raving, unsupervised madman. As we saw in Chapter 2, such a fate is statistically highly unlikely and has not become any more of a risk since community care was introduced. Moreover, the few people who do commit such crimes do not come from the mostly elderly, damaged and institutionalised population of ex-asylum inmates, but from the so-called 'revolving door' patients whose care has posed problems ever since the move away from long-stay asylum incarceration in the 1930s. However, inquiries after several high-profile and tragic incidents have revealed a dismaying lack of co-ordination between the various professionals, with no one willing to take overall responsibility and a severe shortage of facilities (both in-patient and out-patient) for those in greatest need of support and supervision. This is not an indictment of community care *per se*. Unfortunately, the subsequent enactment of a complicated set of additions to mental health legislation has addressed only the first half of the problem.

In 1990, social services departments were given the main responsibility for the effective implementation of community care plans, and it is their job to assess the needs of discharged patients and to ensure that appropriate services are provided under what is called the Care Management Process. Confusingly, a separate initiative in 1991 called the Care Programme Approach placed the same obligation on health authorities. Their plans might be as simple as providing regular medication, or as complex as a range of social, psychological and medical interventions co-ordinated by a key worker (probably a social worker or community psychiatric nurse). In the minority of cases where someone is thought to be a significant risk to themselves or others, they can be put on a Supervision Register which is meant to ensure that they do not fall through the system.

Not surprisingly, the existence of two parallel processes has resulted in considerable confusion about the roles and responsibilities of the various professionals and agencies, and even if a clear discharge plan is agreed upon, there is no guarantee that the resources will be available to fulfil it. In the face of continuing public pressure, Supervised Discharge was introduced in 1995. This applies only to patients who have been on section (that is, admitted compulsorily to hospital). This small group of people who are said to suffer from severe mental disorder can be required, after leaving hospital, to live at a specified address and attend at specified times for medical treatment, occupation or training. Their nominated 'supervisor' has the power to convey them to the relevant clinic or other facility, or to authorise someone else to do so. There was opposition to this bill from a number of professional and service-user organisations, who argued that it amounted to unjustified power of arrest. It was widely felt that this significant increase in restrictions on discharged patients is no substitute for appropriate care and resources. However, the bill stops short of actually compelling discharged patients to continue taking medication.

The current Labour government, inheriting this controversial mess, commisioned a 'root and branch' review of the whole situation. New national standards for mental health care include 24-hour helplines and round-the-clock crisis teams, and extra beds in hospitals, hostels and supported accommodation. Although this is described as drawing a line under community care, in fact there is to be no return to the asylums, and the plans meet some of the long-standing demands of those who argue that community care has not been given a fair trial.

Community treatment orders (CTOs) are the most controversial aspect of the new Mental Health Act. These will provide, for the first time, the means by which people can be compelled by law to continue their medication even outside hospital. This development can be seen both as a reaction to unfounded public fears about community care, and as a means of extending medical influence and the medical model into the community. Critics believe that compulsory medication is a very poor substitute for meeting people's social and psychological needs, and will have damaging effects on relationships between professionals and service users, perhaps leading to the most needy people avoiding contact with psychiatric services. Moreover, as we will see in Chapter 8 , the word 'treatment' as applied to psychiatric drugs is somewhat misleading; the neuroleptics that are most likely to be the subject of CTOs are essentially powerful sedatives, helpful to a few, causing distressing side effects to most, and physically damaging to a substantial proportion. In this light, decisions to come off medication may be seen as entirely rational. The debate about CTOs might more accurately be phrased, 'should psychiatric patients be forcibly sedated in the community?'.

CONCLUSION

Psychiatry is at present in a state of transition and confusion. In hospitals, psychiatrists and the medical model still dominate treatment (although consultants have had to concede much of their political power over resources and service development to the new breed of NHS managers). When virtually all admissions are acute and bed occupancy is running at over 100 per cent all over the country, so that urgent new cases may have to be moved to distant facilities or shipped out to private hospitals at NHS expense, there is little opportunity to do anything except diagnose and medicate. In community settings, psychiatrists are much less influential, and a broader model of care is often available. However, the possibility of being censured at an inquiry into the homicide by or suicide of a patient on a register has led to more defensive practice, with an increased emphasis on diagnosis and risk assessment. Meanwhile, the growing trend towards 'assertive outreach', or persuading people who are reluctant to engage with psychiatric services to keep up their treatment (that is, medication), can be seen as simply extending the medical model into the community.

The new requirement for 'evidence-based medicine', while sensible in principle, seems in practice to be operating in favour of standard medically based interventions such as Family Management teams.

Meanwhile, the biggest challenge of all to traditional psychiatry is growing in strength and numbers. The service user/survivor movement (described in greater detail in Chapter 10) is a loose coalition of people who have been on the receiving end of psychiatry and found the experience deeply damaging. Many are totally opposed to the medical model of mental distress; they are campaigning not for an improved system of psychiatric care, but for a radically new one based on totally different assumptions. The emphasis on accountability and consumer satisfaction has also opened up a new role for service users as representatives on management and service development committees, while outside the NHS they are setting up their own independent facilities. It remains to be seen how far the movement will be able, or allowed, to challenge and change the practices of traditional psychiatry.

The alternative history of psychiatry highlights some remarkable parallels between the nineteenth-century issues, as described by Scull and others, and present-day ones. Now, as then, psychiatry is devoted to proving that mental distress has a physical origin, although there has been no sequel to the discovery that syphilis causes general paralysis of the insane; now, as then, this has increased rather than diminished the search for effective physical treatments to back up the psychiatrists' claims, although explanations of how they work are as speculative as ever and the number of cures remains distressingly low; now, as then, there is no shortage of jargon and obscure lists of diagnoses to give the whole field of psychiatry an air of authority and special expertise. Community care has been one of the most serious threats to medical domination of psychiatry since the era of moral treatment, but the overall outcome has so far been somewhat similar: traditional psychiatry has been diluted rather than fundamentally altered, and we have been left with a change of *location* rather than a change of *model*. As we saw with moral treatment in the nineteenth century, this reduces a whole philosophy of care to a set of add-on interventions, while the medical model remains the basic approach. Meanwhile modern psychiatry's main claims to success are either inaccurate (for example, that the major tranquillisers enabled chronic patients to be discharged) or consist of belated recognition of the harmfulness of some of its earlier treatments:

> British psychiatry . . . has earned itself a distinguished record for its exploration of the aetiological role of social factors in psychiatric

illness. The work of researchers in Britain showed that many of the psychiatrical and behavioural features exhibited by chronic mental hospital inmates owed more to the manner whereby such patients were treated than to the actual illness[43]

or represent a return to the ideals of moral treatment while staying just within the medical model (for example, the Family Management work, which shows, not very surprisingly, that patients diagnosed as 'schizophrenic' do better in a supportive atmosphere that is not too hostile or critical).

The drug revolution of the 1950s and 1960s seemed to provide the validation, awaited since the early nineteenth century, of psychiatrists' claims to have special knowledge and expertise in the treatment of the mentally distressed. It certainly convinced many people – see Sir Keith Joseph's speech earlier in the chapter – and medication remains the mainstay of treatment for the more severe forms of mental distress. But are modern physical treatments for psychiatric patients a genuine advance on the previous ones? To what extent, for example, can the seventy-plus minor tranquillisers and the equal number of major tranquillisers currently on the market be said to be an improvement on the thirty-four emetics and fifty purgatives of the nineteenth century? Is the shock of ten ECTs essentially different from the shock of ten pails of icy water? Or are these just the latest versions of moves in the same old game? These questions will be considered in the next chapter.

Chapter 8

Physical treatments and the role of the drug industry

Note: No one should come off psychiatric medication without taking expert advice.

It is impossible to evaluate the true impact of the new drug treatments of the 1950s and 1960s without taking a close look at the role of the pharmaceutical (drug) industry in psychiatry.

Pharmaceutical companies are among the most powerful and profitable on earth. In fact, they have been ranked the first or second most profitable industries in the world in most years since 1955,[1] and are outstripped only by the international arms trade.[2] Their global annual sales amounted to $256 billion in 1994, or more than the total health expenditure of all developing countries plus the former socialist economies of Europe;[3] the last decade in particular has been 'a golden age for drug companies . . . it was hard to be a drug company and not make money'.[4] Britain has had its share of this success: its four largest companies have carved out a 10 per cent global share[5] becoming the UK's second-largest foreign earner after North Sea Oil.[6] In Britain, enough minor tranquillisers were distributed in 1981 to allow for thirty tablets for every man, woman and child in the country.[7] The major tranquillisers are a similar success story for the drug industry: an estimated 150 million people take them world-wide.[8] Drug companies spend around £5000 a year on every GP in Britain or £150 million a year in total[9] to promote their products and the annual NHS drugs bill is around £6.3 billion.[10]

Where such enormous sums of money are involved, drug companies have a very strong vested interest in selling the chemical solution to mental distress. Of course, this does not necessarily mean that their products are of no value. However, it does mean that where there is a conflict between public service and making money and between giving accurate information and making sales, it is not always the worthier motive that carries the day.

DOI: 10.4324/9781003095958-8

The particular structure of the pharmaceutical industry means that huge profits are virtually guaranteed, regardless of economic recessions and competitive market forces. The industry is half way to being a monopoly: the top thirty drug companies in the world control more than 60 per cent of the market.[11] Moreover, there is strong evidence of unofficial agreements between the various companies to fix their prices at very similar levels, since they would all lose out if there were a price-cutting war.[12] Instead, companies tend to specialise in different fields, so one makes antibiotics while another produces tranquillisers or contraceptives. Another factor that limits competition and thus keeps prices high is the system of granting patents. A company which discovers a new drug is, in many countries, granted a patent for a certain length of time (ten years in Britain) during which it alone can manufacture and sell its new product. When the patent expires, any company can make and sell the drug under its generic name. However, an effective campaign will ensure that the brand name remains in doctors' minds, so that even when the patent runs out doctors will automatically continue to prescribe the brand version (although the introduction of annual drugs budgets for hospitals and GP practices in 1992 has increased price-consciousness on the part of prescribers, and GPs are encouraged to prescribe generically as often as possible). Another result is that other drug companies pour enormous proportions of their research money (one estimate is 75 per cent)[13] into producing what are known as 'me-too' drugs – products that are just different enough from the patented one to earn their own patents. Although heavily promoted as new, exciting and different, such products are virtually indistinguishable in practice from the original one and merely add to the confusing choice of drugs facing the doctor (around 6500 in Britain). The official justification of the patenting system is that it allows companies time to recoup the enormous costs of research: for each product that reaches the market, about 10,000 compounds will have been discarded along the way, and the industry claims that it costs an average of £125 million to develop a new drug.[14] However, the overall effect, again, is to limit competition and keep prices high. The drug companies have a number of ways of maintaining this happy (for them) state of affairs, some less admirable than others. Their front line consists of the drug company sales people or 'drug reps' (one for every seven GPs in Britain) who are trained to promote their company's products on their regular visits to surgeries and hospitals. Other methods can be summarised under three main headings.

ADVERTISING

Drug companies spend vast sums of money on advertisements in medical journals and on the free drug-firm literature that GPs receive through the post, estimated by one researcher at thirty-five journals and fifty advertisements for each doctor every month. The range of problems for which a chemical solution has been proposed is enormous: one minor tranquilliser was initially recommended not only for alcoholism, anxiety, tense muscles and cardiovascular problems,[15] but also for tricky cases such as the 'always weary', 'psychic support for the tense insomniac', and even to create 'a less demanding and complaining patient'. Another was said to be of use for, among other things, the college student whose 'newly stimulated intellectual curiosity may make her more sensitive to and apprehensive about unstable national and world conditions'.[16] Faced with a cure looking for a disease, the drug industry has been ingenious in defining new illnesses and hence new applications for its products. The minor tranquillisers in particular 'have been promoted as solutions to almost every state which falls short of total serenity'.[17]

Drug advertisements are notorious for presenting women in a stereotyped and unflattering way. In 1983, after a lengthy search through medical journals, two investigators could find only two advertisements that depicted a woman as the doctor or therapist. More typical were those such as the one which:

> portrays the tear-streaked face of an attractive young blonde woman who is said to be suffering from 'copelessness'. Medication, it is suggested, will help her pull herself together and apply herself to needed tasks. These advertisements strongly suggest that inability to function in a traditional female role, inability to cope with being a woman and with women's tasks, need to be treated with medication.[18]

Even today, advertisements have slogans such as: 'Next time you see a depressed patient, ask her which shade of lipstick she wears', illustrated by a smiling, immaculately made-up woman who has been cured by anti-depressants.

In Britain it is illegal to advertise prescription drugs directly to the patient, though discreet leaking of new findings may encourage people to ask their GP for the latest wonder-pill such as Viagra (for impotence) or Aricept (for Alzheimer's disease). In America, 'direct-to-consumer' selling has been growing since the Food and Drug Administration (FDA) lifted its moratorium in 1985, so that TV advertisements and magazines like *Reader's Digest* now urge people to 'Ask your doctor about Nicorette' and many other products as well. Although the FDA insists that advertisers must give a fair summary of risks and benefits, such information is usually put in the small print which few people read and still fewer understand.

INFILTRATION

This term refers to the many subtle and not-so-subtle strategies by which drug companies ensure that their products form the background to just about every medical activity. Gifts stamped with the company and product name – pens, blotters, clocks, paperweights, calendars, notepads, textbooks, pencil cases, name stamps, files, paperclip holders, leaflet displays and so on – are given out to medical students and fill the GP's office. Free samples are handed out by the drug reps, while doctors have been given watches, microwaves, televisions and all sorts of consumer durables as a reward for prescribing certain products. Doctors have been offered money for every patient they treat with a certain drug in a 'research trial' which has the underlying aim of getting patients switched to the new product. Drug companies lend or give equipment to surgeries and hospitals. They provide films and publications for medical training. Senior doctors and their spouses have been funded to fly to conferences in exotic places, with trips, amenities and entertainment laid on – and, of course, the relevant company's products prominently displayed. 'Drug lunches', at which food far superior to that of the average hospital canteen is served after a film about the wonders of some new pill, are a regular feature of hospital life. Drug companies underwrite the cost of meetings, seminars and conferences in return for the opportunity to put their name on the programme and send their drug reps to set up stalls at the event. They make contributions to party political funds.[19] 'Major companies run highly sophisticated intelligence departments; they routinely analyse individual doctors' prescribing habits, and systematically collect detailed information about the views of "opinion formers" and leaders of the profession. In the process, companies help doctors with the right opinions to become more prominent, isolating independent critics at the same time.'[20] In 1997 the Department of Health announced a clampdown on gifts as an inducement to buy products, and only inexpensive items which have some relevance to the world of medicine are now allowed. However, even if doctors remain fairly cynical about particular claims and tactics, the overall effect is to create a culture where the solution to a patient's problems is assumed to be a chemical one.

It is alarming to realise how crucially the drug companies are involved even in apparently more-objective information about their products and medical issues in general. Medical journals rely on funds from drug advertisements and may not be able to afford to offend the industry. These journals may also have editorial boards whose members have drug company affiliations.[21] They often publish supplements, in the same format as the parent journal, which are sponsored by drug companies and not subjected to the same rigorous process of peer review.[22] Health journalists are inundated with publicity for new products, and freelancers have been offered money to get stories placed in national magazines.[23] In America, celebrities testify to cures and doctors go on media tours without disclosing that the drug companies are training and paying them to do so.[24] Drug companies fund foreign fellowships and underwrite the cost of television programmes. In 1992 the Royal College of Psychiatrists launched its 'Defeat Depression' campaign which urged people to visit their GP for the chemical cure for this common 'illness'; it was supported by drug company money. Drug companies give money to patient organisations, who in turn lobby for more resources to treat their conditions.[25] Some of the doctors who are members of the Standing Medical Advisory Committee and the Committee on Safety of Medicines, which are meant to give the government independent advice on drug licensing, also have substantial shares in drug companies.[26] One of the main international doctors' pocketbooks on drugs (*Monthly Index of Medical Specialties*, or *MIMS*) relies on information supplied by the companies themselves. It does not, contrary to popular belief, generally list adverse effects, and editions for Third World countries where regulations are less strict may include products that are banned elsewhere.[27]

Astonishingly, it is an offence punishable by two years in jail to reveal any of the information on which the Medicines Control Agency bases its decisions about drug licensing in this country. In fact, both it and the Committee on Safety of Medicines carry out their work in almost complete secrecy.[28]

In some countries the companies themselves supply the pharmacology teachers for the medical schools. This has particularly tragic implications for the Third World; for example, $400 million worth of anti-diarrhoeal drugs are prescribed globally, often to parents who can barely afford to buy them, and yet most of the five million children who die of diarrhoea every year could be saved by a simple and cheap mixture of water, sugar and salt.[29] But since there is no profit in this for the drug companies, there is no incentive to teach it to medical students.

Two particularly important forms of influence deserve a separate mention. One is the extent to which drug companies fund research in universities, hospitals and medical schools, so that investigations into non-drug and non-medical approaches are much harder to get off the ground. Once in this powerful position, other forms of manipulation are then open to them:

> They fund projects with a high likelihood of producing favourable results . . . They exclude products that may compare favourably with the sponsor's own. Sometimes, only favourable data are released to investigators . . . Negative studies may be terminated before they are ready for publication . . . Corporate personnel may seek to control the content and use of the final report, including the decision not to publish.[30]

Thus, the whole arena of research is shaped towards biomedical models and treatments.

A second form of influence, outlined by psychiatrist Dr David Healy in a recent book,[31] is the way in which drug companies are actually involved in 'making views of illnesses' and 'selling diseases' in order to create markets for their products. Thus he describes how, in the wake of the minor tranquilliser scandal of the 1960s, the pharmaceutical industry 'discovered' depression, hitherto thought to be a rare disorder, and paved the way for the promotion of the SSRIs. Their action is in fact similar to anti-anxiety medication such as Valium, but with current fears about dependence it makes more marketing sense to sell them as anti-depressants. Other new 'illnesses' which have been highlighted by scientific meetings, journal supplements and so on in recent years include panic disorder, obsessive compulsive disorder and social phobia. This is not to deny that people may genuinely suffer from panicky feelings, extreme shyness or whatever. However, the decision about how to describe (and hence treat) their difficulties is driven largely by business, not scientific, considerations. Healy gives a fascinating historical overview of the complex interaction between psychiatric categories and drug development and promotion. For example, 'social phobia' only made its debut as a psychiatric disorder in the 1980 version of DSM*, but is now said, in drug-company sponsored conferences, to affect up to 5 per cent of the population. By a fortunate coincidence, one of the new SSRIs is said to be particularly effective in treating it.

This category shades over into the next one:

CORRUPTION

Dr John Braithwaite, who has investigated this subject in depth, found that 'corporate crime is a bigger problem in the pharmaceutical industry than any other'. To start with:

> My own research found evidence of substantial bribery by 19 of the 20 largest American pharmaceutical companies. There is evidence of bribes being paid to every type of government official who could conceivably affect the interests of pharmaceutical companies: bribes to cabinet ministers to get drugs approved for marketing; bribes to social security bureaucrats who fix prices for subsidized drugs; to health inspectors who check pharmaceutical manufacturing plants; to customs officials, hospital administrators, tax assessors, political parties, and others.

Safety testing procedures provided further examples of fraud:

> Rats die in trials on new drugs and are replaced with live animals; rats which develop tumours are replaced with healthy rats; doctors who are being paid 1,000 dollars a patient to test a new product pour the pills down the toilet, making up the results in a way which tells the company what it wants to hear.[32]

Other scandals abound. Drugs that have been banned in the West can be 'dumped' in the Third World by strategies such as changing the name, altering the formula slightly, setting up a factory in a country with less strict regulations, and so on.[33] Drugs which are regarded as too high-risk for testing in the West can be tried out in the Third World instead.[34] Latin American health ministers are 'almost invariably rich with wealth which comes largely from the international pharmaceutical industry'.[35] The list goes on. Moreover, the very power which enables the companies to act in this way makes it hard, if not impossible, to bring them to account. When the *Daily Mirror* serialised a book called *Health Shock* which was critical of the drug industry, 'constant phone calls at home, threatening cables, and telexes sent to the *Mirror*'s chief lawyer and editor put immense pressure on the newspaper'.[36] In the thalidomide disaster the company never admitted liability, nor was a court judgment ever passed on it; the trial dragged on for two and a half years and the company then settled out of court. Dr Braithwaite writes: 'To my knowledge at least, the thalidomide disaster led to not one successful prosecution nor one successful private law suit in a court of law anywhere in the world.'[37]

At the same time, Braithwaite pointed out that many, indeed most, drug industry executives and employees are honest, idealistic and highly committed to responsible business conduct. Fraud flourishes in this situation partly because of the complexity of the organisation – most people have no knowledge of or contact with corrupt conduct – and partly because employees are only involved in doing their own small piece of the work to the best of their ability. For example, the quality control manager's job is to ensure that the drug has no impurities, regardless of whether it actually does more harm than good. So, 'the difference between socially responsible and corrupt companies is that in the former, ethical questions are everyone's business'.[38]

All governments have tried to keep the NHS drugs bill down through voluntary agreements on price control, and the newly established National Institute for Clinical Excellence (NICE) has the job of judging whether new, more expensive drugs are genuinely more effective than old ones and whether or not they should be available on the NHS. However, the threat of combined opposition from the medical profession (who want to preserve their clinical freedom to prescribe what they think best) and from the drug industry has been a serious impediment. Following a recent agreement to cut the price of branded drugs, drug companies have increased the price of some commonly used generic drugs by up to tenfold, while others have mysteriously become unavailable or in short supply.

One recommendation made in 1982 by the Informal Working Group on Effective Prescribing, known as the Greenfield Report, was that pharmacists should automatically dispense the cheaper generic version of any drug unless the doctor specifically indicated a preference for the brand version. The drug industry successfully argued against this policy (generic substitution) on the grounds that there would be 'far-reaching and damaging effects on the welfare of patients, the national economy and even on the practice of medicine'.[39] However, governments find that there are compensations to this awkward dilemma. The increasing power of the drug industry means that it contributes around £2 billion a year to the balance of trade by exporting its products[40] – far more than could be saved on the drugs bill. The government, the medical profession and the drug industry each benefits from the co-operation of the other: 'British government policy is that medicines should help people *and* the national economy to get better and stay well: too bad if these objectives conflict.'[41]

New physical treatments in psychiatry all tend to go through predictable cycles of opinion. The initial discovery is accidental: 'A clinician has used a drug for the treatment of psychiatric patients, usually on quite false theoretical grounds, and found clinical effects that he had never predicted.'[42] The treatment is initially greeted with cries of wonder and delight, and a flood of reports glowingly describe its safe and miraculous action in all sorts of previously problematic conditions. One of the first minor tranquillisers to be developed was said at various times to give symptomatic relief in alcoholism, allergies, angina pectoris, appendicitis, asthma, behavioural disorders in children, depression, skin problems, glaucoma, hypertension, intractable pain, childbirth, menopause, motion sickness, petit mal epilepsy, stuttering, typhoid fever and half a dozen other ailments.[43] And here is an American psychiatrist extolling the effects of the new major tranquillisers on institutional life:

> A transformation has occurred in mental hospitals in the past two decades that defies description. Visit one today. You will be impressed by the serenity you observe and feel. Flowers, curtains, paintings, music, fresh air, comfortable tidy lounges make a pleasant environment for clean, tranquil patients being offered a myriad of therapies.[44]

Here is another psychiatrist extolling lithium:

> Manic depression, this spectacular disease, now has an equally spectacular cure. Lithium is the first drug in the history of psychiatry to so radically and specifically control a major mind disorder . . . It is truly spectacular to watch this simple, naturally occurring salt . . . return a person in one to three weeks from the terrible throes of mood-swing to normalcy.[45]

And again, a psychiatrist recommending ECT for, among other things, heroin withdrawal, colitis, psoriasis, schizophrenia, and the pain associated with back ailments and cancer: 'Surely shock treatment represents one of those medical miracles that the *Reader's Digest* likes to write about.'[46] Similar claims were made in 1898 for a new drug that was safe, non-addictive, effective in controlling pain and in infant respiratory ailments, and a cure for morphine addiction. It performed so heroically that it was named heroin.[47]

Even if claims are more moderate, 'Almost without fail, new medications are believed to have fewer or more benign side-effects than their predecessors.'[48] After a while it becomes clear that the new treatment is neither as effective nor as widely applicable as was first claimed, but it is still viewed as very useful in a more limited range of situations and becomes one of the standard tools of psychiatry.

Finally, evidence begins to mount that the treatment is either useless, of very limited use or even positively harmful, and has just as many disadvantages as the intervention it replaced. The treatment is abandoned, and the whole cycle starts again with something else. Lobotomy and insulin coma therapy are two examples of this process. Barbiturates were once widely prescribed where minor tranquillisers would be used now and amphetamines were recommended for as many different disorders as the minor tranquillisers in the early days of their use, but especially for depression before the advent of anti-depressants. It is now recognised that both these classes of drugs are highly addictive and very dangerous in overdose and they are Controlled Drugs under the Misuse of Drugs Act of 1971.

The current favourite physical treatments in psychiatry can be seen as occupying various positions in this cycle. The minor tranquillisers have taken a severe knocking as their very serious drawbacks (withdrawal symptoms and the like) have become apparent. ECT and the major tranquillisers are somewhere in the middle stage of the cycle; although their limitations are acknowledged, at least to some extent, they are still widely and routinely used. However, sources other than the official ones of psychiatry textbooks and medical journals (which, as we have noted, may not always be as impartial as one would wish) provide some disquieting evidence about their effects. Meanwhile, we are offered new hope in the form of up-dated versions of anti-depressants (such as Prozac) and major tranquillisers: 'The importance of these new anti-psychotic drugs . . . is their lack of side-effects. The new drugs also have a great advantage in that they treat both the positive symptoms, which include delusions, hallucinations and abnormal thought, as well as the negative symptoms – depression, social withdrawal and lack of drive.'[49]

It is at this point in the cycle, when there is a new 'cure' to promote, that you will see the frankest official appraisals of the previous miracle, thus: 'If treatment made them feel like a zombie, removed their sexual desire, did peculiar things to their breasts and increased their girth to an unacceptable size, it is not surprising that they failed to co-operate.'[50] The occasional reports of the effects of psychiatric medication on 'normals' also paint an alarming picture. For example, a woman who was accidentally prescribed a neuroleptic 'took three months to recover . . . "My mother thought I was dying"',[51] while a doctor who took a dose of a neuroleptic as an experiment reported: 'It was awful. I like to be in tune with myself, but I felt in complete discord, as if I had ingested a portion of hell . . . the side-effects were so distressing that one's concentration was entirely taken up by it . . . I was reduced to a nervous wreck . . . Actually, I was suicidal – I made no plans but I did feel that death would be better than what

I was going through . . . I now prescribe neuroleptics with great care.'[52] However, as we shall see, emerging information suggests that once again the new versions will turn out to have at least as many drawbacks as the older ones.

It may be useful to consider each of these treatments in more detail. Comments from service users are taken from the Mental Health Foundation's 1997 report *Knowing Our Own Minds*,[53] except where otherwise indicated.

MINOR TRANQUILLISERS

There is now widespread public and professional awareness of the potential dangers of these drugs and many GPs and psychiatrists have altered their prescribing habits accordingly, although they are still frequently used (18 million prescriptions in 1997[54]). Some people find them useful for short periods of time or during particular crises: 'Valium takes the edge off my panic and agitation. Helps me think more clearly and feel more confident to go out and get involved in the things I want to do.' There are fewer long-term users than in the late 1970s, when prescriptions peaked at 30.7 million a year and some people had been taking them for ten years or more.[55] The majority of these people were women (as were the users of barbiturates and amphetamines). Misinformed by the drug companies, doctors handed out tranquillisers to their anxious or panicky patients with the assurance that they were not addictive. The pills sometimes seemed to help for a while until other symptoms developed. Not realising that these symptoms were in fact *caused by* the drugs, the natural assumption to make was that the illness was getting worse. The solution suggested by the equally ignorant doctors was often to increase the dosage, and the effects on the patient and her or his family life continued: 'I'm afraid I feel that those years were wasted. I floated through everything. I missed a lot of my children's upbringing, I've forgotten so much. Looking back it was like being in a cocoon.'[56] 'I didn't feel I was fit to take my children out alone as I had panic attacks, sweating, and peculiar breathing. Very antisocial, completely different person in fact. Couldn't concentrate on conversations with people.'[57]

Coming off the pills often led to even worse problems, and again, since the tablets were supposed to be non-addictive, these were mistaken for a return of the original problem. Not everyone suffered withdrawal symptoms. For those who did, though, cutting down was a nightmare; indeed, a leading psychiatrist has said that it can be worse than coming off heroin.[58] Another psychiatrist notes that 'benzodiazepine withdrawal is a severe illness. The patients were usually frightened, often in intense pain, and genuinely prostrated.'[59] Symptoms may last for many months, with devastating effects on all aspects of the person's life.

Minor tranquillisers may have other consequences too. They may lead to drowsiness, lack of co-ordination and sexual dysfunction. They disrupt memory and learning,[60] and increase the risk of accidents and injuries. (A recent study in the *Lancet* estimated that they account for at least 1600 road accidents, including 110 deaths, every year in the UK.[61]) Taking these medications during pregnancy may result in babies who show withdrawal symptoms. In elderly people, the side effects can be confused with dementia. More rarely, their use has been associated with depression, psychosis, paranoia, and outbursts of rage and violence.[62] Halcion, thought to be one of the worst offenders, was banned in Britain in 1991 after allegations that Upjohn, the firm that manufactured it, had concealed crucial information about its effects.[63] The question of whether minor tranquillisers can lead to permanent damage to the brain is still unresolved.[64]

The current recommendation of the Committee on Safety of Medicines is that minor tranquillisers should be used for a maximum of four weeks and only for a limited range of problems, for example, for anxiety or insomnia that is 'severe, disabling and subjecting the individual to extreme stress', and not for mild anxiety or phobic or obsessional states. The Committee warns that 'withdrawal symptoms can occur with benzodi-azepines following therapeutic doses given for *short* periods of time'.[65] In 1988, 13,000 people, represented by more than 2000 firms of solicitors, planned to take legal action against drug companies based on 'the mass of evidence showing that the medical profession and the drug companies knew many years ago that there were major problems with these drugs, but did not act in their patients' interest to limit the damage they were likely to cause'.[66] Six years later, legal aid was abruptly withdrawn due to the huge costs, and the case collapsed. In America, drug companies have paid out billions of dollars in compensation to patients damaged by their products, but no such action has ever been won in Britain.

The newest anti-anxiety drugs, such as buspar, have been promoted as highly effective without creating dependency. In fact, there is very little information on their effects for periods longer than a few weeks.[67]

MAJOR TRANQUILLISERS

The major tranquillisers, or neuroleptics, are seen as psychiatry's most effective treatment for 'schizophrenia'. 'Neuroleptic agents have, since the mid-1950s, proven to be the most consistently effective compounds in the treatment of acute and chronic schizophrenic patients.'[68] Sometimes referred to as 'antipsychotics', they have become a routine, almost automatic, remedy in psychosis and relatively little effort has been made in psychiatry to use these medicines selectively: 'One might search for a long time to find a diagnosed schizophrenic who has never been treated with a neuroleptic drug',[69] although even the official literature accepts that not everyone benefits from them. They are also sometimes recommended to control mania (when a person becomes restless, supercharged with energy and very 'high'), and to relieve severe anxiety.

The major tranquillisers do not cure 'schizophrenia' or anything else, but some people find that they do make distressing experiences more bearable: 'The drug blocks out most of the damaging voices and delusions and keeps my mood stable.' In making an overall assessment of their value the questions that need to be asked are, first, at what price these benefits are bought; second, to how many people this applies; and third, how they are actually used in day-to-day practice.

The major tranquillisers are not pleasant drugs to take (see Linda Hart's vivid description in Chapter 2). The general sedation which can reduce mental distress has its downside: 'The high dose . . . deadened me emotionally leaving me very demotivated and I spent three years mostly sleeping and watching TV'; 'The dosages depressed me and made me feel my motivation, ideas and whole autonomy being forcibly removed.' Restlessness (akathisia) is one distressing effect, sometimes accompanied by acute anxiety, which can persist even after discontinuing the medication. ('It may not mean much to you but I feel squishy inside in the morning. Kind of jittery-like. I just don't feel comfortable . . . I used to work in an office but I can't do that any more. I just can't sit all day).[70] Other possible effects are blurred vision, weight-gain, impotence and loss of libido, constipation, loss of concentration, apathy, depression, dry mouth, sensitivity of the skin to sunlight, tremor, breathlessness and dystonias or sudden, unco-ordinated movements of the head and neck caused by muscle spasms. In addition there are three potential consequences, pseudo-Parkinsonism, tardive dyskinesia and neuroleptic malignant syndrome, which are far more serious.

Pseudo-Parkinsonism

Some people taking major tranquillisers, especially if they are on a high dosage, experience the very unpleasant symptoms of Parkinson's disease, which include a mask-like face, an open and dribbling mouth, shaky hands and shuffling walk. More medication (anti-cholinergic drugs) may be prescribed to control these symptoms. However, this has two disadvantages: one, that these drugs themselves have side effects like constipation, dizziness and blurred vision; and two, they may increase the risk of developing an even more serious condition, tardive dyskinesia.

Tardive dyskinesia

Tardive dyskinesia (TD) is characterised by uncontrollable movements of the lip, tongue and face, fidgeting hands, tapping feet, rocking backwards and forwards, grunting, and other bizarre involuntary mannerisms. If the major tranquillisers are stopped as soon as the first signs are detected these movements generally disappear. Often, though, the symptoms of tardive dyskinesia only emerge when a patient cuts down or stops his or her medication – sometimes weeks or months later. Again, the movements may generally fade, but some people are left with a permanent, irreversible disability for which the only 'treatment' is to go back on the major tranquillisers again. The trap in doing this is that, although the symptoms of tardive dyskinesia will be once more masked, in the long term the drugs will increase the neurological damage that led to the problem in the first place.

In accordance with the cycles of opinion that we have already discussed, the risks attached to these new wonder-drugs were hardly mentioned for many years – indeed, the major tranquillisers were described as 'among the safest drugs available in medicine'.[71] Some writers have argued that there has been a semi-deliberate cover-up of the facts of tardive dyskinesia by the professionals, leading to an 'almost total denial of the phenomenon in the 1950s and early 1960s'.[72] The preface to the first book on the subject (published in 1980, by which time the drugs had been on the market for over twenty-five years) noted that 'the majority of psychiatrists either ignored the existence of the problem or made futile efforts to prove that these motor abnormalities were clinically insignificant or unrelated to drug therapy'.[73]

Patients are frequently not informed about the risk of developing TD, nor have prescribing habits altered in the light of this danger.[74] It is still very hard to get accurate figures on how many people will develop the condition; one estimate puts the rate at 38 per cent after five years, rising to 56 per cent after ten years.[75] One drug company has put the risk at only 3–6 per cent, which would still mean that between five and ten million people worldwide have tardive dyskinesia.[76] Others have argued that this is a serious underestimate and that the true figure for irreversible tardive dyskinesia since the major tranquillisers were introduced is nearer 86 million.[77] This would make it 'among the worst medically-induced disasters in history'.[78]

Neuroleptic malignant syndrome

About 1 per cent of people on major tranquillisers will develop this little-researched reaction, which is characterised by muscle rigidity, difficulty with breathing, rapid heartbeat and fever. Neuroleptic malignant syndrome (NMS) leads to death within a few days in up to a third of cases. In addition, there have been regular reports since the 1960s of sudden, unexpected death from unknown causes in people taking major tranquillisers. There are no accurate figures on fatalities associated with psychiatric drugs, although Malcolm Lader, a professor of psychopharmacology, has estimated that there may be one such death a week.[79] A recent report in the *British Journal of Psychiatry* identified two other ways in which neuroleptics may contribute indirectly to increased mortality rates in those diagnosed as 'schizophrenic': by causing rigidity and thus reducing overall activity levels; and by overwhelming the body with side effects when more than one neuroleptic is used at once.[80]

Three further consequences of using major tranquillisers, seldom addressed in the literature, deserve a mention. The first is the stigma that results from the changes in appearance and behaviour described on p. 79. People affected in this way look odd and crazy, with their blank faces, grimaces and shuffling walk. As well as being distressing to them, their relatives and other patients, this is a serious hindrance to being accepted back into everyday life. Although any member of the public who took a stroll round a psychiatric hospital might conclude that these bizarre mannerisms, together with the pervasive apathy and listlessness of the patients, were the result of mental illness, in fact they are caused by the treatment.

The second damaging consequence is that this apathy (the inevitable result of taking such powerful sedatives) undermines people's ability to take advantage of social programmes and work training, especially since there is evidence that the major tranquillisers impair learning ability.[81]

The third and very important hazard is that withdrawal from major tranquillisers may cause psychiatric symptoms to rebound to a higher level than they would otherwise have reached; in other words, in some circumstances the treatment may actually cause the problem for which it purports to be the cure. Almost universally unaware of this possibility, psychiatrists regard sudden relapses when major tranquillisers are reduced or stopped as a sure indication that the drugs are playing an essential role in keeping the condition under control, and prescribing is started up again. Failure to take this phenomenon (known as tardive psychosis) into account means that many research studies on drug withdrawal give a misleading impression of the efficacy of these drugs. Again, as with tardive dyskinesia, a vicious circle is set up. Continuing the drugs may mask the psychiatric symptoms again, but only at the expense of worsening the underlying problem, so that patients 'must remain on neuroleptics for the rest of their life regardless of the natural course of the illness'.[82]

The possible explanation for tardive psychosis is complex and has been well summarised by Warner.[83] Briefly, he argues that the drugs create an artificial sensitivity in nerve cell receptors which can lead to very serious consequences if the drugs are stopped: to tardive psychosis if the sensitivity occurs in one set of nerve pathways, and/or to tardive dyskinesia if it occurs in another set. Warner believes that for people with a poor prognosis, the benefits of the major tranquillisers may still outweigh the disadvantages. However, he argues that for the 50 per cent or so of people whose prognosis is good (that is, their breakdown came on suddenly and after an identifiable stress, or later in life, and they were previously functioning well), 'drug withdrawal may worsen the course of an other-wise benign condition and drug maintenance therapy may increase the risk of psychosis, cause side-effects, or, at best, prove worthless'.[84] In support of this statement he quotes various studies comparing drug and non-drug treatment in patients with good and with poor prognoses, which demonstrate that patients with good prognosis actually do worse (in terms of symptoms and readmission to hospital) on major tranquillisers than without them. Conclusions such as: 'Antipsychotic medication is not the treatment of choice, at least for certain patients, if one is interested in long-term clinical improvement' were drawn by the investigators.[85] Another recent reviewer has also concluded that the usefulness of major tranquillisers for the majority of people with a diagnosis of 'schizophrenia' is far from established.[86]

The Family Management literature also throws an interesting light on this question; a careful look at the figures suggests that for patients living in Low Expressed Emotion families, drugs may not give any additional protection against relapse.[87] Since half of all patients have Low EE relatives, and half of the remainder can be converted to Low EE by family intervention, this suggests that major tranquillisers may actually be unnecessary for a majority of people diagnosed as 'schizophrenic'. (Incidentally, it also suggests that the drugs 'work' not by correcting some biochemical imbalance, but by sedating someone to the point where they are indifferent to their relatives' hostility.) However, when I made this point in a journal article, it was dismisssed out of hand.[88]

A more outspoken critic of psychiatric drugs and of major tranquillisers in particular is American psychiatrist Peter Breggin.[89] He argues that major tranquillisers have no specific effect at all, and that their impact is not only on the dopamine systems but on nearly all other biochemical reactions in the brain as well. In fact, he believes that they achieve their effect by disabling the brain in a manner similar to the lobotomies that they replaced; indeed Heinz Lehmann, who wrote the first American article on major tranquillisers, drew this parallel at the time, describing them as 'a pharmacological substitute for lobotomy'.[90] Among the evidence Breggin cites in support of his argument is the very high rate of generalised brain disease and dementia in patients with tardive dyskinesia, the frightening implications of which have been played down or ignored by investigators.[91] He also quotes various studies whose disturbing conclusions ('It is also clear that the antipsychotic drugs must continue to be scrutinized for the possibility that their extensive consumption might cause general brain dysfunction'[92] and so on) have somehow been overlooked in subsequent research and review articles. A recent review article echoes his concerns; it summarises the parallels between the effects of lobotomy and of major tranquillisers, in particular the characteristic apathy, loss of initiative, indifference to environmental stimuli and impairment of intellectual functions.[93] This syndrome certainly made institutions easier to manage: a historical overview suggests that neuroleptics gained favour mainly because of their 'outstanding ability to stupefy agitated inmates as well or better than electric shock, insulin coma, and lobotomy'.[94] The idea that the drugs had a specific anti-psychotic effect did not emerge until several years after their introduction.[95] The (disputed) view that these powerful compounds somehow facilitated the emptying of the asylums by enabling patients to live in the community emerged later still.

In the light of all this evidence, it is a matter of great concern that the major tranquillisers are used so routinely, in such high doses, and often in such dangerous combinations. In spite of the 1993 'Consensus Statement on the Use of High Dose Antipsychotic Medicine' issued by the Royal College of Psychiatrists, significant numbers of patients are being prescribed these drugs at above the highest recommended levels. There is also evidence that many will be taking more than one antipsychotic at a time, a hazardous practice that is contrary to official guidelines.[96]

Even more alarming is the use of major tranquillisers on groups of people for whom they are often clearly inappropriate, such as the elderly and people with learning disabilities, whose mental functioning may be further impaired as a result. One survey found that a quarter of nursing home residents were taking neuroleptics, usually for completely unjustified reasons such as to reduce wandering and 'uncooperation'.[97] It is often alleged that these drugs are used for purposes of control in prisons.[98] In such cases the line between treatment and control becomes dangerously blurred. Another worrying trend is emerging in Australia, where drug company sponsored 'education' campaigns are urging GPs, school counsellors and parents to be alert to the signs of 'early psychosis' in schoolchildren and to start them on 'preventative' doses of neuroleptics,[99] despite the fact that the so called 'symptoms', such as belief in telepathy and clairvoyance, are widely found in normal high school students.

It is the neuroleptics that will be involved in most cases of compulsory treatment in the community. In parts of America, where 'assertive outreach' or taking active steps to follow up people with long-term problems is a growing trend, benefits can be dependent on taking your daily dose of medication.

Dramatic claims are currently being attached to so-called 'atypical' (and much more expensive) neuroleptics such as clozapine and risperidone. Clozapine has actually been around since the 1960s, but fell out of favour after a number of deaths from agranulocytosis (a sharp drop in white blood cells.) Re-launching it as a remedy for 'treatment-resistant' psychosis, without the undesirable side effects of the other major tranquillisers, has been a successful marketing strategy, leading to newspaper headlines like 'Mentally ill refused "too costly" superdrug' ('cuts suicides by 80% . . . hundreds of patients have been able to live a relatively normal life'[100]). Such statements are not supported by the facts; akathisia, tardive dyskinesia, NMS and so on have all been reported, while the evidence for improved effectiveness is weak.[101] Patients also have to have weekly or fortnightly blood tests to check their white blood cell count. Nevertheless, as we have already noted:

> the much-publicised introduction of 'new, improved' drugs creates the impression that there is unequivocal *progress* in treating psychosis.

This in turn reinforces the dominant biopsychiatric idea that 'schizophrenia' represents a genetically predisposed . . . brain disease, which, at this state of our knowledge, best responds to chemical intervention.[102]

ECT (ELECTRO-CONVULSIVE THERAPY)

ECT is given in a designated room where the patient lies on a bed and is given a general anaesthetic and a muscle relaxant. Padded electrodes are placed on her or his head and an electric current, about enough to power a lightbulb, is passed through the brain, causing an epileptic seizure lasting approximately 20–90 seconds. The patient will probably wake up confused and with a headache, and will need to rest for about an hour afterwards. Standard length courses of ECT consist of four to twelve individual shocks given a few days apart.

The official current view of ECT is that, although no one knows exactly how it works, 'there is substantial and incontrovertible evidence that the ECT procedure is an effective treatment in severe depressive illness'.[103] In fact, 'over 8 out of 10 depressed patients who receive ECT respond well to it'.[104] It is often said to reduce the risk of suicide. Moreover, it said to be 'among the safest medical treatments given under general anaesthesia'. Although there may be some temporary memory loss, 'as far as we know, ECT does not have any long term effects on your memory or intelligence'.[105] A British review article came to similar conclusions, and although noting 'the widespread conviction by former patients that their memories have been permanently affected', dismisses these effects as neither serious nor extensive and attributes the complaints to a 'heightened awareness of normal failings . . . It is well known in other contexts that there is little correlation between subjective complaint and objective impairment where memory is concerned.'[106] Nor is ECT unduly distressing to receive, according to one frequently quoted study, which concludes that people find it 'a helpful treatment and not particularly frightening'.[107] The *ECT Handbook* states that it may also be useful in mania and 'schizophrenia', and occasionally in Parkinson's disease, neuroleptic malignant syndrome, catatonia and epilepsy as well.[108]

The Department of Health collected no data on ECT between 1991 and 1999, and up to 1991 only supplied figures for the total number of treatments administered in a given year, not the actual number treated, let alone their gender, age or ethnic origin. Despite its poor public image, attributed by one authority to the activities of a 'loose coalition of expatients, civil libertarians, religious cultists, consumer advocates and medical opportunists',[109] ECT is widely used: 105,000 individual treatments a year in England in 1991, representing about 22,000 people.[110] Usage has declined since then, with the 1999 figures indicating that about 66,000 individual treatments, representing about 11,340 people, take place each year.[111] This varies from region to region, with the most recent survey showing that twice as many treatments are given per head of the population in the North-West as compared to London. Other sources indicate different rates in different hospitals, with some using it up to seventeen times as much as others.[112] Variations between individual psychiatrists are even greater, ranging in one sample from one to forty-two patients over a three month period.[113] The new figures confirm that women are twice as likely to receive ECT as men, and that women over 65 make up by far the largest single group of those who are given ECT. A similar pattern emerges for those given ECT under section (that is, compulsorily); in the period 1991–2, 73 per cent were women, ranging in age from 15 to 94, with a steep rise for women over 60. Thus, 'substantial numbers of middle-aged and elderly women are being detained under the Mental Health Act and are having ECT in circumstances where they are either refusing or are unable to consent.'[114]

International variations in ECT usage are also very striking. It is rarely used in Italy, Japan, Germany, the Netherlands and Austria. In America, ECT is making a comeback after years of decline, although the typical recipient is no longer the young black male 'schizophrenic' in a state hospital but an elderly depressed white woman being treated privately. However, even this is subject to astonishingly wide variations, with different metropolitan areas using ECT at rates between 81 patients per 10,000 population, and none at all.[115] Unmodified ECT (that is, without anaesthetic or muscle relaxant) is still sometimes carried out in India, Greece, Turkey, Japan, China and some African countries.

ECT is one of the most controversial subjects in psychiatry. Readers will by now not be surprised to learn that official and unofficial views are polarised, ranging from 'an eminently safe . . . procedure which has saved countless lives'[116] to 'a barbaric and destructive process which delayed our opportunity to deal with the real issues of our distress'.[117] As with medication, the picture may be distorted by vested interests; for example, ECT in America is 'the most profitable procedure in psychiatry',[118] enabling a doctor who gives ECT to an average of five patients a week to add around $150,000 to his yearly income.[119] Richard Abrams, author of the standard textbook on ECT, is co-owner with another ECT researcher of a company that makes ECT machines.[120] Richard Weiner and Harold

Sackheim, two prominent authorities on ECT, have admitted that such companies have contributed to their research funding.[121] Nearly all the educational videos on ECT are made by the companies who make the machines.[122]

The theory and practice of ECT is problematic even in its own terms. The variations noted above suggest that it is certainly not being prescribed according to objective and standardised medical guidelines. Either a lot of people are missing out, or a lot of people who are getting it shouldn't be. Although the Royal College of Psychiatrists claims, 'We now know a great deal about ECT, how and why it works',[123] and their factsheet for patients states confidently that 'repeated treatments alter chemical messages in the brain and bring them back to normal',[124] such assertions are just as misleading as the equivalent ones made for medication. Abrams admits that 'Modern ECT researchers . . . do not have any more of a clue to the relationship between brain biological events and treatment response in ECT than they did at the time of the first edition of this book – which is to say, none at all.'[125]

In the last twenty years the Royal College of Psychiatrists has carried out three large-scale surveys of the practice of ECT, but even the most recent one found that there were still serious deficits, with only one-third of clinics meeting College guidelines (which only half the psychiatrists had ever heard of).[126] For example, junior doctors were often poorly trained and supervised, and some clinics used machines which did not allow a sufficiently wide range of current to be delivered, so that patients with a low seizure threshold risked receiving too high a dosage. Since, in the words of one of the investigators, 'cognitive function is liable to be more impaired the more the stimulus exceeds just the minimum needed to cause a fit which can vary 40-fold between patients', it follows that brain damage is unavoidable for an unknown number of people at clinics whose identity is a secret.

Frustrated by this failure to raise standards, a former president of the Royal College of Psychiatrists took the unusual step of warning doctors about the dangers of relying on guidelines and exhortations to maintain good practice, and citing the example of ECT as a potential scandal waiting to erupt.[127] In the previous year, John Gunnell MP presented a bill that would require the collection of detailed national statistics on ECT, give legal powers to uphold guidelines and limit its use under compulsion. It was talked out in March 1998 and has now been dropped.

It may be useful to summarise the ECT debate under two broad headings.

Does it help?

There is very little good-quality research on outcome after ECT. One exception, which compared real and simulated ECT, found that patients whose depression included delusions and physical retardation did show benefits from ECT at four-week follow-up, but that this difference had disappeared at six months.[128] Thus, there was no evidence of effectiveness for the majority of depressed patients, and even very severe depression 'may have a favourable outcome with intensive nursing and medical care even if physical treatments are not given'.[129] Psychiatrists themselves admit that one of the chief limitations of ECT is its high relapse rate. In fact, there are no controlled studies showing that ECT has any benefits for longer than four weeks. This fact is never disclosed to patients or relatives. Nor is there any good evidence for the common claim that ECT prevents suicide, according to a number of studies and reviews.[130]

The views of people who have had ECT are as polarised as those of everyone else, but 43 per cent in one recent survey and 30 per cent in another had found it helpful or very helpful.[131] They made comments such as: 'Depression lifted very quickly after six treatments'; 'Lifting mood. Physical benefit, e.g. eating and sleeping improved.'[132] This raises the question of how it works in these cases. Placebo effects may be a partial explanation; that is, as with insulin coma therapy, the associated ritual, attention and expectations may be more important than the treatment itself. Support for this theory comes from the story of the hospital whose machine, unknown to staff, was broken and had not been delivering a current for two years; no one had noticed any diference in the results.[133] Other theories depend on your view of what ECT actually does to the brain. Obliterating painful memories, either temporarily or permanently, will obviously bring some short-term relief: 'It helped me forget painful memories of the past which were depressing me.'[134] Such gaps are sometimes welcome to relatives: 'Mr Karr expressed pleasure to the research interviewer that ECT had made his wife forget her hostile outbursts against him.'[135] Whether or not this is the kind of 'cure' that psychiatry ought to be aiming for is, of course, debatable, and if underlying issues have not been resolved, repeated rounds may be necessary to maintain the 'improvement'. The still occasionally employed practice of giving 'maintenance' ECT every few weeks for years on end was introduced for exactly this reason.

Some critics, notably the American psychiatrist Peter Breggin, have pointed out that four weeks is the usual duration of the artificial euphoria that typically follows a closed-head injury.[136] This brings us on to the next heading:

Does it do harm?

The benefits reported by some people obviously have to be balanced against the possible drawbacks, which, as we have seen, are officially described as minimal and short-lived. Alternative accounts are less reassuring. It is worth noting that the idea that ECT causes brain damage was first introduced not by its critics but by its advocates; indeed, textbooks of the time openly stated that this was how it worked. The ECT patient 'secures his re-adaptation to normal life at the expense of a permanent lowering of functional efficiency. He may, in the language of chess, be sacrificing a piece to win the game.'[137] A common contra-indication for ECT was that the patient had an intellectually demanding job; this did not apply to housewives, who were deemed to be less in need of their full brainpower. Such ideas were not particularly contro-versial in comparison to some of the other physical treatments that were in vogue, for example, forcing psychiatric patients to breathe nitrogen until they collapsed, or freezing them into a coma by packing them in ice.

However, after 1947, when a committee of America's most eminent psychiatrists expressed grave doubts about the abuses of ECT, there was a dramatic change of attitude.[138] From that date, according to Peter Breggin, there was a tendency for reviews and textbooks either to fail to mention research which warned about serious brain damage, or else to misrepresent its conclusions, while evidence quoted in support of the use of ECT was often unsound or misleading. Breggin gives a number of examples from different areas.[139] He points out that Cerletti and Bini, the Italian inventors of ECT, had to abandon their early experiments on dogs' brains because of the severity of the resulting damage. Among a number of animal studies which supported these findings was an extensive and widely ignored investigation by Hartelius, who reported that even on conservative criteria ECT can produce irreversible brain damage. In the field of clinical reports, accounts of patients who have been left with considerable memory problems are not included in reviews. Breggin claims the same is true in the fields of human autopsy studies, human brainwave and neurological studies and MRI scans. He also points out that the older studies may actually underestimate the degree of damage, since it is necessary to use a stronger current nowadays in order to overcome the effects of the anaesthetic. However, after a time, misleading conclusions about the safety and efficacy of ECT acquire the status of accepted facts and are quoted unquestioningly in reviews and textbooks.

Breggin points out that immediately after ECT the patient suffers from the same acute confusional syndrome that occurs after any trauma to the brain, whether the result of epilepsy, strangulation, suffocation, blows to the head or lobotomy. She or he is confused and disorientated, has impaired judgement and insight and all intellectual functions disrupted, and may display shallow or inappropriate emotional reactions. The patient may have a severe headache, nausea, and a feeling of being out of touch with reality. This acute stage wears off over the next hour or two. The more serious effects do not disappear so quickly, if at all, and Breggin presents evidence that although longer courses of treatment produce more severe damage, it can also occur after standard length courses.

The commonest effects are loss of memory for events that took place before the ECT was given (retrograde amnesia) and/or loss of memory for events that occur after the ECT (anterograde amnesia). Memory loss (reported by 74 per cent of ECT patients in one study)[140] may span all areas of life experience. Thus, people may be unable to recall educational and professional experiences; films, books and plays; important social events such as birthdays and family gatherings; names and faces of friends and acquaintances; household details such as how to do the chores and where things are kept; familiar locations such as the layout of the local shops or town; what happened to them in hospital; inner thoughts and feelings; and public events such as elections and news stories.[141] Obviously this can be extremely distressing:

There are a lot of blanks that have to be pieced together for me. Sometimes when I get very frustrated and angry, I ask my husband or father to tell me different things that I've known since childhood, like my relatives and uncles, and what my children's names were, and where they were and what they did. I always had a very good knowledge of this because I had been the one in the family who kept in communication and kept the family aware of each other's doings . . . But I cannot go back and feel the feelings I had then. I told my sister one day that I don't remember the things shown in the pictures from my honeymoon, but I can see a happy female in the photographs. The experience is lost. I have the data that somebody gave me, I have the pictures, and therefore I know it did occur. But the actual physical feeling of being there – no, it's gone.[142]

Even when I was depressed my garden was a wonderful solace. Now it's as if the flowers are cardboard cut-outs, or as if I'm watching them on TV. I can't *reach* them.[143]

I can't remember when they [her children] started junior school, I can't remember when they left infant school. Now those are things you remember, they're highlights . . . and I'm quite resentful really to think that my ex-husband has got more memories of my children and did pretty well nothing to help.[144]

It's a void, I can't describe it, and there's also a feeling of something fundamental that I don't even know what it is missing . . . just like an intrinsic part of me that I feel isn't there and it once was . . . Part of me feels like there was a real death of something, something died during that time.[145]

The situation is complicated by the fact that those patients who are most severely impaired tend to complain the least. Like sufferers from senile dementia, they tend to confabulate – that is, to cover up the gaps in their memories by faking recollections or by denying difficulties which later show up on neurological and psychological tests. Some conceal their difficulties out of shame or embarrassment, while others have been accused of exaggerating. The loss of autobiographical memory and its devastating consequences have been documented in a series of seldom-quoted studies. The researchers concluded that 100 per cent of the ECT recipients they tested had sustained at least some permanent memory loss, even though some of them denied it.[146]

Breggin argues that patients may also be left with a more general permanent impairment, such as difficulty in understanding what is heard or read, in doing simple sums, in concentrating, in learning new tasks, and in many other areas. In other words, ECT may, in some cases, and particularly in large amounts, result in severe, global and permanent brain damage. As in other cases of head-injury, there may be impairment in any or all areas of mental, emotional and behavioural functioning. In summary, Breggin sees ECT, as he sees major tranquillisers, as a slightly more sophisticated form of lobotomy. In his view, 'There can be no real disagreement about its damaging effects. The only legitimate question is: "How complete is recovery?"'[147]

Even if cognitive impairment is minimal, patients may still find ECT psychologically traumatic. In the words of Abrams: 'Doctors . . . have shown remarkably little interest in their patients' views of the procedure',[148] although the available surveys have all identified a minority of people (ranging from an eighth to a third) who have very strong reactions against it.[149] I investigated the experiences of twenty people who said they had found ECT distressing.[150] A variety of themes emerged from their accounts, including feelings of terror, shame, humiliation, failure, worthlessness, betrayal and degradation, and a sense of having been abused and assaulted. ECT seemed to confirm that they were bad and mad: 'It was like I was a non-person and it didn't matter what anyone did to me'; 'It felt like I had been got at, yes, bashed, abused, as if my brain had been abused. It did feel like an assault'; 'At that time I was completely convinced I was being punished for something . . . I thought, well, I must have done something wrong to be treated like this'; 'You dread it, your heart starts beating, here we go again. Horrible, absolutely terrifying'; 'I was deeply, deeply ashamed of having ECT . . . this was real serious stuff, this was a mad person.'

Although these people's problems had clearly been compounded rather than relieved by ECT, the resulting distrust of psychiatric services left them less able to ask for help than before: 'I knew the only way I could get out was by being insignificant . . . by being a very good patient, and it worked. I wasn't any better, I felt quite terrible.' This obviously raises the possibility that some apparently successful outcomes are simply conformity and a fear of confiding one's true feelings to professionals.

All the people I interviewed believed, in retrospect, that ECT could have been avoided if the practical and emotional support that they needed had been available instead. Echoing other service user surveys, they believed that since there were *reasons* for their depression, ECT was obviously not going to be the answer: 'It's short-term relief . . . obviously until you find a solution to the problem it's just going to recur and you're going to keep on having ECT'; 'To be treated physically for something that isn't a physical complaint . . . I do object to that for emotional, psychic, spiritual problems.' Similar points were made by a group of older women who had been given ECT.[151]

Finally, ECT may increase mortality rates. Deaths from ECT are officially put at only one per 50,000 treatments (or about 10,000 patients) by Abrams.[152] This is implausible, since the overall risk for general anaesthesia alone is usually put at 4.5 deaths per 10,000 patients. In fact, several studies show that ECT patients, especially the elderly, have significantly higher long-term mortality rates from a variety of causes.[153] Official statistics are hard to come by, but one estimate is one death per 3–4000 in younger patients.[154] In Texas, where all deaths that occur within fourteen days of ECT have to be reported, the figures for the over-65s were 1 in 200. Most of these were due to heart problems.[155]

Since arguments in support of ECT are well represented in every psychiatric textbook, I will give the last words to the opposition. ECT

Anonymous is a campaigning organisation set up by survivors of ECT. Among the many cogent points it makes are these:

> If a woman is presented at an emergency room in a confused state from an accidental electric shock to the head, perhaps from a short circuit in her kitchen, she would be treated as an acute medical emergency. If the electrical trauma had caused a convulsion, she might be placed on anti-epileptic drugs to prevent a recurrence of seizures. If she develops a severe headache, stiff neck and nausea, a trio of symptoms typical of post-shock treatment patients, she might be admitted for observations to the intensive care unit . . . Yet in other parts of the same hospital other women might be receiving identical shocks, with identical results, under the guise of 'treatment', and rather than being helped to recover, will be booked in for more of the same two or three days later.[156]

John Friedberg, an American neurologist whose opposition to ECT nearly destroyed his career, summarises the arguments against ECT succintly:

> From a neurological point of view ECT is a method of producing amnesia by selectively damaging the temporal lobes and the structures within them . . . Assuming free and fully informed consent, it is well to reaffirm the individual's right to pursue happiness through brain damage if he or she so chooses. But we might well ask ourselves whether we, as doctors sworn to the Hippocratic Oath, should be offering it.[157]

A newcomer on the horizon is TMS, or Transcranial Magnetic Stimulation, which induces electrical currents in localised areas of the brain by using magnetic fields. The principle is the same as ECT but without a convulsion or general anaesthetic. The first articles claiming beneficial effects have started to appear, along with admissions that ECT does, after all, have substantial drawbacks,[158] although nothing has been done to establish the safety of TMS.

ANTI-DEPRESSANTS

Most cases of depression (which, it has been estimated, account for around 10–20 per cent of surgery visits)[159] are treated by GPs without being referred on to the psychiatric team. Anti-depressants are the commonest treatment offered. Since the bad publicity about minor tranquillisers, they are sometimes prescribed for anxiety as well. It is not known exactly how they work, but they are generally believed to be most effective in severer cases. Their value in milder depression, where they are widely prescribed, is less certain, especially since many of these episodes lift of their own accord in about three weeks – the same length of time that it takes for the drugs to start working. Although they were felt to be more helpful than other physical treatments in the Mental Health Foundation's survey, studies suggest that only about a third of patients overall will benefit from them.[160]

As always, the benefits of these drugs have to be weighed against the disadvantages. The older MAOI group are used less often because of their potentially dangerous interaction with some foods. The tricyclics are chemically very similar to the major tranquillisers and share some of the same side effects (sedation, concentration difficulties, confusion especially in the elderly, dry mouth, blurred vision, reduced sexual interest, and so on), although tardive dyskinesia does not seem to be a risk. They are particularly dangerous in overdose, accounting for about 400 deaths (or about 15 per cent of all drug deaths) a year.[161]

The anti-depressants are not pleasant drugs to take, and in fact an estimated 50 per cent of people fail to complete the prescribed course.[162] Despite the official line that these drugs are not addictive, some people do experience withdrawal symptoms (stomach cramps, depression, restlessness and so on from the tricyclics; headaches, shivering, and panic from the MAOIs) especially after taking the drugs for longer periods of time. The symptoms can be mistaken for a re-emergence of the original problem and lead to further prescribing.

The predictable hype about new drugs reached unusually high levels with the introduction of Prozac (fluoxetine), the first of the SSRIs. In the wake of the minor tranquilliser scandal Prozac seemed to promise an effective and non-addictive alternative, with fewer side effects, and rapidly became the most widely prescribed anti-depressant in the world.[163] In an alarming development, enthusiastic advocates like American psychiatrist Peter Kramer have recommended extending its use to the non-psychiatric population – people who are sensitive to rejection, have low self-esteem, or simply lack pleasure and motivation in life – along with extravagant claims that they can become 'better than well'. He has coined the phrase 'cosmetic psychopharmacology', or chemical improvement of the personality, to describe this process. In an update of the sales pitch aimed at female tranquilliser users in the 1960s, he even claims that Prozac is 'a feminist drug – liberating and empowering', enabling today's woman to cope with her demanding modern lifestyle.[164]

Readers will by now not be surprised to learn that early claims for the SSRIs seem to be unfounded. A number of studies have concluded that they work no better than the older (and far cheaper) anti-depressants, and produce different, rather than fewer, side effects.[165] There has been no systematic evaluation of their use in depression for periods longer than six weeks, and certainly none for the types of problem described by Kramer.[166] More worryingly, Charles Medawar of the consumer organisation Social Audit, who has written extensively on psychiatric drugs, believes there is emerging evidence that SSRIs are at least as addictive as the minor tranquillisers.[167] Very high numbers of adverse effects have been reported under the British 'yellow card' system; while in America, Prozac has triggered more adverse reaction reports than any other prescription drug ever. It has also been implicated in violence and suicidal impulses, a risk apparently known to the manufacturers for over 20 years.[168] Medawar argues that the 'non-addictive' message, heavily promoted to the general public as part of the Royal College of Psychiatrists' 'Defeat Depression' campaign, relies on a shifting of the goalposts whereby dependence is now only said to be present if tolerance (needing higher and higher doses of the drug to get the same effect) is present *as well as* withdrawal symptoms on stopping, and *as well as* at least one of a list of other symptoms such as neglect of alternative interests. Dependence on prescibed drugs has thus been defined almost out of existence. Medawar's attempts to stop history repeating itself by raising the matter urgently with the Department of Health have, as of 1999, met with little response.

LITHIUM

Lithium is prescribed for manic depression – a condition where a person suffers from severe mood swings, becoming either very high or very low or sometimes both in turn. It can be used to abort a manic episode, although major tranquillisers do this job more quickly. Mostly, though, it is used prophylactically, that is, to prevent further episodes occurring, and may be taken for many years or even for life. In a common pattern, recent studies have found lower rates of effectiveness than initial studies.[169] In fact, a review article in the British Journal of Psychiatry argued that 'follow-up studies suggest that the natural history of bipolar disorder has not improved since the introduction of lithium, and patients who are taking lithium appear to be little better than those who are not'.[170]

Lithium was initially said to produce 'no unwanted effects on mood or behaviour'.[171] In fact, there are a number of possible side effects, ranging from mild sleepiness or nausea to more serious hand tremor, weight gain, kidney damage, muscle weakness and confusion. The latter may be a sign that the lithium level in the blood, which has to be monitored very carefully by regular blood tests, is too high and needs regulating to reduce the risk of intoxication and of permanent neurological damage or death. There is evidence that abrupt withdrawal can lead to a sevenfold increase in the risk of relapse.[172]

HOW DRUGS AND ECT ARE USED IN PRACTICE

Textbooks on psychiatry give very little idea of how drugs and ECT are actually used in day-to-day practice. It is unusual for a psychiatric in-patient to be on no medication at all. (The commonest drugs in psychiatric hospitals are laxatives, taken by about one-quarter of patients to combat the constipating side effects of the rest of their medication.)[173] As we have seen, many patients will be taking medication at doses above the maximum recommended levels, or in potentially dangerous combinations. We also saw that ECT is frequently given by poorly trained and unsupervised staff using outdated equipment.

The decision to try someone on a particular treatment is often not based on the officially recommended indications, but is a function of the staff's desperation or the length of time the patient has been around. As one writer admitted in an unusual burst of frankness, the policy for chronic patients is that 'everybody is tried with everything worth trying as a new effective drug'.[174] Caffeine and nicotine from constant tea drinking and cigarette smoking, which punctuate the day in institutional life, form a background to the prescribed drugs.

Much of this use of drugs and ECT can more properly be described as treatment for the doctor, the staff or the ward than for the individual patient. Heavier sedation when there is a shortage of staff obviously makes the ward easier to manage, but is not necessarily in the best interests of the patients. With out-patients, writing a prescription is the accepted way for a GP or psychiatrist to bring a consultation to an end and, if necessary, fend off a problem that the doctor does not know how to deal with. (As one woman in a survey on minor tranquillisers said: 'I feel that, essentially, when a doctor prescribes a pill for me, it's to put *him* out of *my* misery.'[175]) In the same way, the standard response to a report in the ward round that

Mrs Smith or Mr Shah is no better is to suggest a change in the medication and move on to the next patient. This game can be played literally for years, so that long-standing patients may have been tried on twenty or thirty different drugs in various combinations with little or no improvement in their condition. In the short term, this is far easier than trying to unravel the complex mixture of psychological and social factors that contribute to mental distress, but as MIND points out, 'no treatment programme will be successful unless it offers the patient the support he needs to come to terms with his personal crisis'.[176] Many community mental health teams now offer a much wider range of approaches, but recent pressure on beds means that hospital-based treatment is even more likely than before to consist solely of medication and ECT. This, as we saw in earlier chapters, is a profound source of dissatisfaction for service users, who tend to see their problems in psychosocial not biomedical terms, and to want physical treatments to be an adjunct to, not a replacement for, a broader understanding of their difficulties.

All patients, except a very few of those who are compulsorily detained in hospital, have the right to refuse treatment, and before treatment can begin they must give legally valid consent to it. The law on this issue is complicated, but involves three main elements:

1 patients must be given information on the nature and purpose of the treatment and any serious side effects, though this need not be an exhaustive list of every possible risk;
2 they must be able to understand the nature and purpose of the treatment;
3 their consent must be given without undue force, persuasion, or influence being brought to bear on them.[177]

There is evidence that these conditions are frequently, even routinely, disregarded, as we saw in Chapter 3. In hospital, decisions about medication are made by the staff during the ward round and patients may simply be presented with the pills at the evening drug round without being involved in any discussion about the matter. As we have seen, doctors are unaware of many of the more serious hazards for which evidence has been presented in this chapter, but they frequently fail to pass on even such information as is well known to them – for example, the risk of tardive dyskinesia with major tranquillisers. More than half of voluntary patients in hospital are unaware that they have a right to refuse treatment.[178]

Perhaps most influential is the combination of the whole psychiatric set-up, where the staff so clearly wield the power and make the decisions, and the tendency of the average psychiatric patient is to believe that doctors and other experts know what is best for him or her. This, coupled with the confusion and despair that brought the person into hospital in the first place, means that it is both difficult and comparatively rare for people to question or refuse the treatment that has been prescribed. In practice, then, the distinction between having treatment voluntarily or compulsorily is often very blurred. In addition, the very nature of physical treatments can prevent people complaining about side effects. We have noted that ECT patients may be unaware of memory loss that shows up on tests, while the passive indifference and unawareness that tardive dyskinesia sufferers display towards their bizarre movements has been noted by several researchers.

Some of these points were illustrated in the accounts we heard in earlier chapters. Elaine was the classic example of someone who was tried on everything (major tranquillisers, minor tranquillisers, ECT, lithium and both types of anti-depressants) over a fifteen-year period in an attempt to solve her problems – everything, that is, except a move away from the medical approach itself. Linda Hart was on very high levels of medication, which depresssed and terrified her and caused severe side effects. The 'sick role' patients collected a whole chemist's shop of pills between them as the staff became increasingly desperate. Jenny Clark was put on a very high dose of major tranquillisers immediately upon her admission, although at that point she was bewildered and upset rather than irrational, and it could be argued that she fell into the category of patients who do best without these drugs. The powerful sedatives prevented her from working through and making sense of what had happened to her, but when she protested she was held down and injected. The resulting side effects (blank face, shuffling walk and stiff movements) were deeply distressing to her, her family and the other patients on the ward. Mary, who had been sexually abused as a child, did not know she was to be put on medication until it was handed to her from the drug trolley. She was given no explanation about what it was for or what side effects she might experience and was too unassertive to ask, besides being intimidated by the threats directed at other patients who tried to refuse their medication. Nor did she ask for or receive full information about the effects of ECT, although several years later there were still gaps in her memory. It took her three years, during which she suffered severe withdrawal symptoms, to come off her tablets and lose the weight she had gained while she was on them.

The issue of compliance – getting patients to take the treatment – has come to the fore along with public anxieties about care in the community.

The reluctance of many service users to take psychiatric medication is frequently attributed to 'lack of insight about their illness', or even seen as a symptom of the illness itself. It will by now be apparent that such reluctance may be rooted in entirely rational considerations and fears. Workers on the helplines set up by the mental health charity SANE say:

> The consensus we have found from all these thousands of callers is quite overwhelming . . . Almost all our callers report sensations of being separated from the outside world by a glass screen, that their senses are numbed, their willpower drained and their lives meaningless . . . In the anonymity of phone calls to SANELINE, even the most deluded person is often extraordinarily articulate and lucid on the subject of their medication . . . The negative parts are perceived as quite often worse than the illness itself . . . The price of quelling the more acute symptoms of psychotic illness is high, and perhaps too high.[179]

However, those who wish to reduce or come off medication often find themselves battling not only with withdrawal effects but also with their doctors:

> You're having an old battle with your doctor – 'I want to come off my medication!' 'Oh, if you do you'll become ill again.' You have to be really strong, you have to say 'Look maybe I won't become ill again' . . . I'm going through it at the moment. While you're on medication you're always going to be sleepy or ill or not perform like you used to be able to perform.[180]

In the place of measures such as compulsory treatment in the community, MIND argues that we need to move away from simplistic and misleading concepts like 'compliance' which are 'extremely problematic . . . and cannot be squared with concepts such as informed choice: a person having access to the range of information they require in order to make their own decisions about their lives'.[181] Instead, we need to be thinking in terms of *alliance*: a constructive partnership between prescribers and individuals based on trust, openness, respect and full information.

SUMMARY

So, are these treatments a genuine advance on the emetics, rotatory chairs and so on of the nineteenth century? My personal answer is a qualified 'yes' in theory, but a regrettable 'no' in practice.

The qualifications to the 'yes' should by now be obvious. Drugs and ECT are not the miracle cures that drug companies and doctors sometimes claim and that patients sometimes hope and ask for. 'Drugs are tamed poisons';[182] they all have potential side effects and their usefulness depends on balancing the risks against the benefits in each individual case. As we have seen, there has been a general tendency to underestimate the former and overestimate the latter; indeed, a recent book argues that there is no convincing evidence that any psychiatric drugs at all are substantially superior to placebos.[183]

In psychiatry, unlike in general medicine, there is no such thing as a physical treatment that cures a particular condition, nor is it known precisely how any of these treatments work. They were all discovered by accident, and although, in the words of one psychiatrist, 'such is the stuff of advance in many medical disciplines . . . when all advances are made in this way it is fair to doubt the scientific status of the subject'.[184] The decision to use them on psychiatric patients at all, let alone to promote them as, say, anti-psychotics rather than anti-depressants, or anti-depressants rather than anxiolytics, was driven by chance or by business rather than scientific considerations. Hence, the *post hoc* explanations for their 'effectiveness' are entirely bogus: 'There is no known lowering of serotonin in depression. These drugs didn't come about by rational design . . . No one for whom Prozac has been prescribed has ever had their serotonin levels checked to see if they really are suffering from what the drug supposedly corrects',[185] 'These drugs . . . might better be described as a chemical bull in a china shop, unpredictably interfering with a wide array of body systems including the heart, the digestive tract, the brain and the sexual organs.'[186]

Contrary to the dramatic claims, there has been little progress in drug treatment in the last thirty years: 'The best any of these drugs have done is to substitute one side effect for another.'[187] The most that they can claim to do is reduce some of the 'symptoms' of distress, although here again the pros and cons have to be carefully weighed against each other:

> If ECT reduces the pain of events only by helping the patients to forget them, or if tranquillisers make people able to handle their

emotions only by leaving them with no emotions to handle, then talk of a 'cure' becomes rather ironical. In that sense, after all, death 'cures' everything.[188]

These benefits have to be carefully balanced against the risk of actually exacerbating the 'symptoms' the drugs were supposed to relieve, and of causing sometimes irreversible damage to a range of brain and body functions.

Nevertheless, they can play a useful role as part, but only part, of the help that is offered to people in mental distress. These people may wish to make an informed decision that, say, they want to use minor tranquillisers to tide them over a crisis, or that major tranquillisers do help them cope with hearing voices, or that anti-depressants will help to keep them going while they uncover the roots of their distress in counselling.

In practice, as we have seen, physical treatments are used in a far from ideal way. The same quality that makes them potentially more valuable than rotatory chairs and so on, that is, their ability to affect the mind, also makes them potentially more dangerous. A genuine straitjacket is preferable to a chemical one in that it does at least leave your mind free, and its effects end when it is untied. The cumulative side effects of drugs and ECT as they are used at present – the physical damage to individual patients, the 'sick-role' implications that they carry, the undermining effect on social and psychotherapeutic approaches, the shaping of research and treatment by drug companies, the reinforcing of unsubstantiated medical claims about mental distress, the individualising of problems with psychosocial roots – have, in my opinion, far outweighed the benefits. In fact, I would go further. The accumulated physical and psychological damage inflicted on millions of the world's most vulnerable and powerless people over the last sixty years in the name of 'treatment' surely represents the biggest hidden scandal of the twentieth century.

Medical model psychiatry needs to use and claim success for physical treatments in order to maintain its credibility. Paradoxically, it is this same need and the resulting overuse and misuse of physical treatments that has made them into far more of a liability than an asset. Only a move away from the medical model approach will enable physical treatments to find a limited but genuinely useful role for themselves as one aspect of the help that some mentally distressed people may choose to receive.

Chapter 9

Resistance in the system

It may be useful to review the arguments that this book has presented so far. We have seen how psychiatry not only fails to address emotional and relationship problems, but actually reinforces them, for lack of a whole-person, whole-system way of understanding them. By using a medical label to 'Rescue' people, it takes responsibility away from them, encouraging them to rely on an external solution which is rarely forthcoming, and then blaming them for their continuing difficulties and powerlessness. The personal meaning of people's distressing experiences and the psychological and social origins of their difficulties are obscured by turning them into the 'symptoms' of an 'illness' located within one individual; the resulting treatment barrier keeps both patients and staff stuck and undermines alternative approaches such as psychotherapy. The medical approach reinforces sex role stereotypes, and brings with it a stigmatised and marginalised identity which creates a huge barrier to re-entering mainstream society. Instead of the emotional and practical support which they actually want and need, service users are mainly given medications and ECT, none of which produces cures, and all of which have a high probability of being unhelpful and extremely unpleasant, and possibly of causing permanent physical damage. Moreover, the medical model of mental distress which is used to legitimise this disastrous state of affairs is completely unsupported by the evidence, leaving traditional psychiatry with no justification for either its theories or its practices.

Put like this, it is hard to see why, given that the great majority of mental health workers are motivated by a genuine wish to help, psychiatry stays the way it is. We have discussed some partial answers to this question. Some patients and relatives may welcome the relief from guilt, blame and painful self-reflection that a medical explanation offers. For other people with limited options, the 'sick role' of medically based psychiatry may provide an escape from desperate situations. The general public has no

DOI: 10.4324/9781003095958-9

particular wish to challenge the view that psychiatric patients are primarily a medical responsibility, or to welcome them into their own localities. The training that the various professions receive is also a factor, and this training is itself one result of another factor: the enormously influential position that the medical model approach has carved out for itself over the last 200 years, very much to the advantage of the powerful medical profession and the even more powerful drug industry. And politicians of all persuasions have an interest in seeing mental distress as stemming from biological rather than social factors; in arguing, for example, that mental illness causes homelessness rather than, as the evidence actually suggests, that homelessness leads to mental breakdown. Further clues can be found by looking at what happens when people working within the system attempt to challenge it: 'If you want to know how things really are, try to change them.'[1]

Of a number of accounts of reform in psychiatric institutions, perhaps the most fascinating and readable is Jan Foudraine's *Not Made of Wood*.[2] Dr Foudraine is a Dutch psychiatrist who was trained in the traditional way:

> Of my time as a clinical medical student I can only recall that I struggled with mounting admiration through the thick tomes written by clinical psychiatrists on 'psychoses'. What the various authors had committed to paper by way of expert knowledge, observations, minute and subtle descriptive accounts, and how they larded these with a great mass of profound philosophical thinking and theorizing, often made my head reel. I nearly became convinced that . . . my intelligence was too limited to enable me to cope with such profundities. As a clinical medical student I helped to collect 'schizophrenics' from the various wards, whom we . . . then interrogated about their delusions, hallucinations, mental blocks, thought-disturbances, and whatever else had to be investigated. In short, we would inquire how their 'craziness' was getting on; and they (who had gone through all this before) would show us how crazy they were . . . Tranquillizers had made their appearance; I prescribed them. From time to time I pressed the button of an electroshock apparatus.[3]

Gradually he moved away from the belief that the psychotic person was qualitatively different and suffering from some kind of disease, although 'I discovered that this latter idea was a delusion entertained by a lot of psychiatrists and very much harder to tackle than the "fantasies" of people I met in the psychiatric institutions'.[4] Appointed to a small ward for chronic 'schizophrenic' patients in America, he began to try to understand and encounter them as 'people like you and me . . . Just people in profound, existential need, dire need . . . and for that reason all the more human';[5] and to confront and change the ward system within which they had lived for up to twenty-five years. Although these patients had more long-term and serious problems than most, the issues that arose for the staff and the psychiatric institution itself are the same everywhere and the following extracts will focus on these aspects of the reforms.

On his arrival, Foudraine found a very traditional set-up. The staff hierarchy descended from the top ranks, who issued the general decisions and orders and were furthest away from the patients, down to those with most patient contact, the low-salary, low-status nurses, while right at the bottom of the hierarchy were the patients themselves. The chronic and apparently hopeless condition of these patients had led to profound demoralisation on the part of the lower-status staff, who, perhaps as a way of coping with their despair, had lapsed into what Foudraine calls 'physical disease ideology', the belief that the patients were suffering from incurable physical illnesses and that nothing much could be done for them anyway. The staff spent as much time as possible with each other behind the closed doors of the nurses' office. The layout of the shabby and badly designed ward contributed to the generally depressing atmosphere. The whole approach encouraged passivity on the part of the patients, who had their meals served, clothes sorted, and pocket money doled out by the staff.

After some months Foudraine started to introduce reforms designed to give the patients more responsibility, and 'from that moment on the chaos was complete'. It will not be a surprise, recalling what happened when Jeanette was challenged (Chapter 3), to hear that the patients resisted extremely strongly. What is of particular interest, though, is how these changes highlighted the need of the *staff* to carry on in the traditional way. As their roles changed, they experienced extreme anxiety about what they should be doing instead: 'Again and again they would come to me and ask: "What should I do? I don't know what I should do anymore" . . . The loss of their former role was such an enervating experience that for a time they felt themselves and their function to be without meaning or purpose.' The temptation to step in as before was sometimes overwhelming: 'They simply did not believe that these activities could be taken over by patients; and it became obvious as time went on that *they themselves were unwilling to give up* a great part of them.' For example, a woman called Mrs Care, who had taken over one of the most difficult patients when her daughter left home, found it extremely hard to encourage her to do things for herself. Other staff were afraid of losing their jobs if the patients became too independent.

It was even worse when the nurses were asked to take a further step towards breaking down the staff/patient barrier and stop wearing uniforms: 'The white uniform was for me the crowning glory of my career. I had done all my training, I had got my diploma, for this.'[6] The loss of status and security that was implied was too much for many of the staff to bear. At times they hated Foudraine, and he learned later that they had held secret meetings in which they planned to resign *en bloc*.

When Foudraine insisted that the patients should take a share of responsibility for the cleaning, 'the result was a ward in a state of total squalor', and this plunged Foudraine into conflict with the wider institution. The attitude of the rest of the hospital had up till then been characterised by amused tolerance: 'They used to call us "that crazy bunch at Rose Cottage" . . . sometimes they would say, "He's crazy. Has he cured anybody yet?"'[7] However, a hygiene inspector who toured the ward during its worst stage of 'thoroughgoing pollution' took a more serious view, and for a while the whole hospital came under threat of closure.

In fact, this crisis seemed to serve as a turning point for the ward staff who, faced with the threat from outside, started to rally round in defence of the new regime. Further reforms were introduced, although not without difficulty. There was the breaking of the rule that patients should never carry keys, and the decision that they could take responsibility for ordering the drugs. One nurse described her initial reaction to this:

> At Hillside [her previous place of work] nobody touched the medicine cabinet but me. But then the head nurse came and said, 'No, Cathy will do that'. Cathy then came and ordered the drugs. It made me feel kind of useless. I thought: Here I go through three years of nurse's training and I can't even order drugs.[8]

Then there was the decision to make the medical notes and the daily nursing reports public, so that patients could listen and, if necessary, add and correct. An even more radical step was to banish medical words like hospital, patient, doctor, sick, illness and so on, and hopefully eradicate with them the medical-model view that seemed to Foudraine to be keeping both staff and their charges so stuck, and change it to an educational model:

> I forbade the 'patients' to use this language anymore and proposed calling them 'students' . . . Rose Cottage I described as a 'school for

living'; and Julia was instructed to make a large board with the words THIS IS A SCHOOL FOR LIVING and to hang it on the wall of the room. The 'Nursing Office' sign we changed to 'Educational Office'. I asked the staff to go along with the experiment and named them 'assistant educators'. I told the new-born 'students' that the name 'hospital' had been an especially unhappy choice and made my apology for this. In short, I told them that we in Rose Cottage had come together in a 'school for living' where they, the students, could learn what had gone wrong with their lives and how things could be made different . . . I told my baffled group of newly baptized 'students' and the personnel that there was no such thing as 'mental illness', that it did not exist, and that it would be better for them to regard themselves as *ignorant* about themselves and the forming of relationships with others.[9]

Although this idea was far from welcome to many of the 'students' and some of the 'educators', it gradually took hold and made a dramatic difference to the atmosphere of the ward.

The whole experience took two years, and by the end the results were remarkable. All the patients, hitherto regarded as dangerous and incurable, had made dramatic improvements, and several were able to leave hospital after decades in psychiatric institutions and to lead relatively independent lives outside. The changes on the ward were no less startling. Not all the staff could cope with it. But others said:

To me the patients were just vegetables. They stayed that way for about a year after our programme started. First you had to get the staff on your side: So long as we were still against you, nothing could alter. But now there's a feeling of a breakthrough. I can talk much better with everybody. How should I put it? On a different level. There's a different feeling about. In the old days we all had our jobs mapped out. It was really rather easy. Now there's something happening every minute and yet the nights are much more peaceful . . . Now instead of patients I can see people.[10]

The barrier between staff and patient, the 'healthy' and the 'sick', had to a large extent been broken down, and the growth of the staff was parallel to, and necessary for, the growth of the patients.

It has only been possible to touch briefly on some of the main points of Foudraine's tale, which is well worth reading in full. These extracts do, however, highlight some of the universal themes of attempts to reform the psychiatric system (and systems in general). As Foudraine notes, the aims are often very similar: '"democratizing", changing the vertical organizational structure into more horizontal forms, promoting co-responsibility and giving a bit of real encouragement to the category of people who form the lowest echelon in the institution's chain of demand.' The results are often similar too:

> More often than not the reformers are lone operators . . . and what they achieve are minimal modifications in the psychiatric institution. The reformers struggle against a mountain of opposition, and when, disillusioned or not, they eventually depart, the organization often rapidly sinks back into its bureaucratic, hierarchical, doctor-knows-best structure.[11]

Staff resistance comes from three main areas. First, and most straight-forwardly, the staff need the patients quite as much as the patients need the staff, if only because their jobs depend on it. Foudraine found that by getting staff to encourage responsibility and independence in the patients, he was asking them to cut off the branch they were sitting on – a fact that was well understood by the patients. In fact, he believes that in a different setting, 'a lot of the usual staff of a psychiatric institution *are indeed superfluous and so will be out of a job* . . . if the psychiatric institution still has a future – which I doubt – there is every reason drastically to *reduce* the size of the staff, and not – as we are so often told – to increase it.'[12]

Second, the staff may need the patients to be and to continue to be patients for their own personal reasons. Foudraine's Mrs Care was apparently dealing with her women's role problems by finding a substitute daughter in one of the most helpless patients after her own daughter left home. Other factors which may make it very hard for staff to allow patients to develop into competent and confident adults include the need to maintain a sense of importance and control; to feel useful and wanted; and to avoid confronting your own fears and 'crazy' parts by locating them all in other people.

Third, there is the complicated issue of *identification with the system*. It is impossible to work within any system, the psychiatric one in this case, without to some extent becoming part of it, and thus having an investment in its continued existence. This comes about partly through the training process, and the longer and more arduous it is and the more power and status accrues to you at the end, the greater will be your investment in keeping things as they are. In psychiatry this applies most strongly to doctors, but, as Foudraine found, certainly not only to them.

At a more fundamental level individuals within the system will adopt, without always realising it, the views of the system in which they work. Its unquestioned assumptions and values become their unquestioned assumptions and values. The medical model on which the psychiatric system is based has penetrated very deeply into the minds of psychiatric staff (and indeed of the general public as well.) We unthinkingly and automatically use vocabulary that implies this model: *mental illness, patient, treatment, diagnosis, symptom, remission, prognosis,* and because our language shapes our thought, it therefore seems self-evident that mentally distressed people need to be dealt with by *doctors, nurses, medication, wards, clinics, hospitals.*

Sometimes the identification is owned at a conscious level; thus, psychiatrists write books and articles in defence of a particular viewpoint (the medical model versus the psychotherapeutic model versus the social model and so on). More often, and more difficult to challenge and change, the assumptions have taken root much deeper, so that the member of staff is no longer aware that she or he is indeed making assumptions, that this view is only one of a number of possible views that she or he might hold. The assumptions have become an intrinsic part of the person's whole way of thinking: she or he '*knows*' that this is the way the world is. The phenomenon has been described by the anthropologist Evans-Pritchard: 'He cannot think that his thought is wrong.'[13] Foudraine's staff illustrated this point. For them it was – initially at any rate – *obviously* crazy to expect the patients to help with the chores. It was *obviously* ludicrous to start calling them 'students'. For psychiatrists it is *obvious* that certain types of behaviour and experience are caused by an underlying 'mental illness'. It follows that these people are *obviously* in need of medical treatment, and that it is a psychiatrist's duty to provide this, even if the people themselves resist it. Patients come into hospital because it is *obvious* that doctors must know what is best for them, and once in hospital it is *obvious* to most staff, patients, relatives and members of the public that they must be mentally ill or else they wouldn't be there in the first place. As Scott puts it:

> All people who work in a public service work in a psycho-political field which I term the 'System' . . . To a greater or lesser extent staff internalize the System into their thinking and seeing and in doing so they lose their own shape as persons. To the extent that this happens we will find that they see illness and chronicity rather than the healthy parts of the patient's personality, and that they are then liable to feelings of hopelessness. They become trapped in the System.[14]

The extent to which identification has occurred is not usually apparent until (as with 'sick role' patients) there is an attempt to challenge the underlying assumptions, and then the strength of the resistance and anxiety that is stirred up, even in apparently more enlightened members of staff, gives a clue to the power of the forces one is dealing with. The danger is that, if the assumptions go unchallenged, staff will inevitably act out and pass on, largely at an unconscious level, those aspects of the system which they have incorporated into their own way of thinking. Thus Foudraine's staff, with their unquestioned belief that the patients were suffering from incurable physical illnesses, behaved and treated the patients as if this were so, and the patients absorbed this belief as well and behaved accordingly. Another of the staff's unquestioned assumptions was that the patients were incapable of taking responsibility for themselves, and this contributed to a style of working that actually made the patients less responsible and more helpless. Thus, the assumptions become self-fulfilling prophecies; people who are treated primarily as patients, with all that the term implies, will come to live up to this image and the staff's beliefs will be further reinforced. The final irony is that the staff themselves fall into their own trap. As Foudraine notes, psychiatric nurses and aides *'begin gradually to react with just as much chronic schizophrenic behaviour as the patients with whom they have to deal'.*[15] In dehumanising others, they become dehumanised themselves.

There have been a number of examples of the consequences of identification with the system in earlier chapters. For instance, we saw how staff who have never questioned their assumptions about men's and women's roles but have instead accepted them as self-evident facts about the way the world is, will draw up treatment plans that reflect and pass on these assumptions. The fact that the internalised values of the system are passed on unconsciously makes them, from the patient's point of view, particularly hard to recognise and challenge, and for that reason all the more powerful. If the messages were made explicit ('We at St John's Hospital believe that a woman's place is in the home'; 'Your treatment will be based on the assumption that your job is more important than your emotional life') then at least the person would have a chance to evaluate them and decide whether or not she or he was in agreement. As it is, disagreement has to appear in the form of unresolved symptoms – continued inability to cope with the chores; persistent panic attacks on the way to the office – which are labelled by both staff and patient as illness. The patient has been mystified – confused about the origins of her/his distress by a powerful message that has not been made explicit. Mystification on the part of the patient is the logical result of identification with the system on the part of the staff. The final result is to reinforce the tendency of patients to internalise their oppression, as the phrase goes. Instead of being enabled to locate a significant portion of their problems where they belong, in externally imposed conditions and expectations, they adopt and impose those same conditions on themselves, and the messages that they receive about being inadequate, defective, abnormal and inferior are translated into actually *experiencing themselves* as inadequate, defective, abnormal and inferior.

Having spelt out some of the many personal, professional, business and political interests that are united against a move away from the medical model of mental distress, we should not be surprised to find numerous examples of the denial and suppression of dissenting views within psychiatry. I outlined some common tactics in an article that met with widespread recognition from other professionals:[16]

> *Ignoring or discounting non-medical input* The contributions of non-medical staff are rarely acknowledged and their work is often regarded as a kind of fringe recreational activity ('doing painting' with the art therapists or 'keeping occupied' with the Occupational Therapists). This assumption was betrayed by one consultant who, after hearing an OT's detailed description of one woman's progress in group therapy, commented, 'That's all very well, but we really need to start treating her depression.' Selective lack of awareness of what other team members are really doing enables doctors to maintain such beliefs as, 'Psychotherapy doesn't work with schizophrenics/ obsessionals/personality disorders.'
>
> *Attributing all improvement to medical intervention* Since medi- cation is constantly being adjusted, any change for the better will be bound to coincide with a new dosage and can be attributed to it. Conversely, progress in counselling is ascribed to other factors. When I reported a very successful outcome to a long period of therapy with one in-patient, the consultant commented, 'These conditions do go into remission sometimes.'
>
> Belief in medical interventions is also maintained by *disqualifying the counter-evidence*. If ECT appears to 'work', it will be used again. If it doesn't 'work', then it will still be used again in case it 'works' the next time. There are no circumstances which would count as indications against its use. This is in marked contrast to non-medical interventions, where a single failure (e.g. a family who did not respond to family therapy) will be quoted for years to come.

Quoting important-sounding research For example, 'It's been proven that schizophrenics have lesions in their brains.' This frequently bamboozles non-medical staff, who may not realise that there is no proven correlation, that even if there were it would not necessarily indicate a causal link, and that any research based on a dubious concept like 'schizophrenia' is seriously compromised from the start . . . And psychiatrists will not hesitate to undermine your ideas with the dismissive remark, 'That's only a hypothesis.' You will not be thanked for pointing out that the theory that mental distress has a physiological cause is also 'only a hypothesis'.

The category error This is the technical term for an error of thinking identified by the philosopher Gilbert Ryle, who described an American tourist being shown round all the various individual parts of Oxford University – the library, the colleges, the lecture halls – and then asking, 'But where's the university?' This kind of error underlies a great deal of psychiatric thinking. I recall a long discussion in which I attempted to show that all of a certain young woman's behaviour – her anger, her changeable moods, her distrust of staff – could be understood in the light of her statement that she had been sexually abused. The consistent response was, 'Yes, but she may also have a manic-depressive illness that needs to be treated.'

The category error is part of a more general *complete inability to comprehend alternative viewpoints*, which runs deeper than simple disagreement. For example, my occasional confession of disbelief in the concept of schizophrenia was invariably met by responses such as, 'But in the case of Mrs Jones the diagnosis was clear cut', or 'But people have a right to know what's wrong with them.' The idea that one might not subscribe to this thought system at all is incomprehensible to many. On another occasion, a group of staff argued that instead of stepping up the medical interventions to a very depressed woman, it would be more appropriate to offer support, understanding and containment while she struggled through her personal crisis. This carefully thought-out offer was rejected by the consultant with the words, 'We can't just stand by and do nothing.' There are various issues here: the deeply-held conviction of some staff that they always have to 'do something', however inappropriate, unwanted or damaging; the equally strong belief that only a medical intervention counts as 'something'; and the total inability to grasp the nature and value of what was being offered instead.

Clinical psychologist David Harper has provided a fascinating analysis of the rhetorical strategies that professionals use, probably unconsciously, in order to maintain their belief in the effectiveness of psychiatric medication in the face of evidence to the contrary.[17] Rather than question their practice, or the assumptions upon which it is based, their accounts draw on a flexible range of explanations such as: the patient is a non-responder; there are obviously odd exceptions; we don't know; because the patient is chronic; because the patient is on too low a dose; because the patient is on too high a dose; because the patient is on the wrong drug; because the patient is on too many different kinds of drugs; because the patient has not been compliant with their medication; because the patient has been wrongly diagnosed; because some of the patient's problems are due to manipulative behaviour. He argues that although common phrases such as 'chronic' and 'non-responder' do not actually *explain* anything, their *effect* (and, at some level, their *purpose*) is to remove responsibility from the professionals and from the medication and locate the problem in the patient, thus avoiding a threat to the orthodox biological accounts of mental distress.

Some of the tactics outlined above can be explained in terms of personal or professional defensiveness, ignorance of the alternatives, and narrow training leading to identification with the system. However, in my article I went on to argue that, beyond all these reactions, 'there is a point at which dissenters from the orthodoxy are told not only that they are wrong, but that *such views should not be held or expressed at all*'. Ironically, a psychiatrist provided an example of exactly this phenomenon in a response to my article. Under the title 'The re-emergence of antipsychiatry: psychiatry under threat', he recorded his horror that I would

be teaching the next generation of clinical psychologists that mental illness does not exist . . . Unfortunately, in many community mental health services, it is not accepted that the psychiatrist has more authority than other team members . . . Antipsychiatry, with its rejection of the concept of the existence of mental illness, is thriving in the nonmedical professions that make up the major part of our community mental health services. The rejection of all things medical in psychiatry is contributing to the failures of community care . . . This is a managerial, professional and training issue which needs to be addressed by the Department of Health, the appropriate professional bodies and by managers of the providers of psychiatric services as a matter of urgency.[18]

The active suppression of alternative points of view is, of course, completely incompatible with the supposedly 'scientific' basis of psychiatry, but completely predictable if psychiatry actually serves the purposes of all the vested interests we have outlined. Sociologists and social constructionists have long argued against the notion that we can arrive at simple, straightforward 'truths' about the world, or that there can be such a thing as an impartial, objective search for knowledge. Ideas arise within, and are shaped by, historical, social and political contexts, and are supported or opposed by groups or individuals (consciously or unconsciously) in accordance with their own desires and interests. Whether or not one accepts this as a valid account of human enquiry in general, there is plenty of evidence for the existence of such a process in psychiatry. Thus, 'Psychiatric thought more closely resembles political ideology than it does science in that it is presented and certified by a power elite, the psychiatric establishment, who promote and propagandize their views as official dogma and who dismiss, exclude and persecute dissenters.'[19]

Let us be clear; upholders of the orthodoxy have every right to their own views. What they do not have the right to do, and cannot do without undermining their claim to be part of a legitimate scientific enterprise, is impose their views on others, and attack and suppress those who put forward critiques and alternatives. Nevertheless, this frequently happens. We have already seen some examples earlier in the book: the difficulty Scott had in getting his views heard; the angry dismissal of ideas about family aetiology in 'schizophrenia'; the power of drug companies to shape and control what research areas are investigated, published and promoted; the sacking of John Friedberg for his criticisms of ECT; and the omission of disturbing evidence about drugs and ECT from official accounts.

Pressures may be exerted in all kinds of ways and settings. The first line of defence is to act as if the counter-evidence does not exist; thus the Soteria project's successful psychosocial approach to 'schizophrenia' (see Chapter 11) has quite simply been omitted from most reviews, although the team has published over thirty-eight articles in four languages on the subject. It eventually lost funding and had to be closed down because, in the words of its founder, psychiatrist Loren Mosher, it had committed 'the four deadly sins – demedicalizing madness, de-hospitalizing people, de-psychopharmacologizing, and de-professionalizing'.[20] There has been virtually no interest in the Scandinavian psychotherapeutic approach to psychosis (see Chapter 4) even after it was reported in the *British Jourrnal of Psychiatry*.

The second line of defence is attack. If controversial books are not entirely ignored, they may be reviewed in tones which are quite inappropriate to a genuine scientific debate about ideas. The review of Peter Breggin's *Toxic Psychiatry* in the *British Journal of Psychiatry* says that the book 'resorts to hyperbole and cant to argue the position. Sweeping statements such as "shock treatment is on the rise and elderly women are being targeted" abound and show the author's paranoid position . . . He even disputes the illness status of schizophrenia and manic-depression . . . this screed is so badly written, so simplistic, so vitriolic.'[21] In an acrimonious correspondence about a meticulously researched book which criticises the concept of schizophrenia, another reviewer described it as 'a destructive and unhelpful diatribe against the medical model . . . Dr Boyle's protests sound like those of flat-earthers faced with overwhelming evidence that the earth is round.'[22] The reviewer also made the common accusation that dissenters are indifferent to people's suffering: 'Schizophrenia . . . cuts sufferers off from society, causes untold pain and distress and leads to a failure to fulfil life's potential. The condition will not "go away" because Dr Boyle or anyone else wants it to.' Criticising the orthodoxy is, of course, not at all the same thing as denying that people are suffering and in need of help; nevertheless, it is a common rhetorical device to conflate the two. Thus, in response to a letter calling for a greater appreciation of the psychosocial causes of mental distress, Marjorie Wallace, chief executive of SANE, wrote: 'If the existence of schizophrenia is denied, it is no wonder that sufferers . . . are not taken seriously, and denied care and treatment even when they ask for it.'[23]

Other tactics are even cruder. Unwelcome findings may be shouted down ('Any challenge to the value of ECT is aggressively suppressed. I was astonished to experience the vehement hostility of a meeting of the Royal College of Psychiatrists listening to Eve Johnstone presenting the results of the Northwick Park trial, seen by the meeting as undermining the effectiveness of ECT', as one psychiatrist reported[24]). Careers may depend on the espousal of the 'correct' ideas: 'a psychiatric registrar . . . had been interested in "anti-psychiatry" ideas. He had been warned, however, that it would not be in the best interests of his career development if he was seen as being too closely associated with such ideas. It was suggested that he should develop a more "biological" approach to his work.'[25] Departments may become tainted in the same way: 'I have been told that the University Department in Sheffield does not have a good reputation because of its antipsychiatric stance.'[26] Patients' Councils, established to represent service user interests in psychiatric hospitals, have faced huge battles; when one council known to me raised the issue of the frequent use of ECT on a mother and baby unit, the workers were told their job descriptions would be changed and all advocacy work in the hospital would be banned. The editor of the monthly journal for clinical psychologists found himself in serious trouble for publishing articles questioning the use of ECT.[27] Peter Breggin has described how the National Alliance for the Mentally Ill, the main relatives' organisation in America, has, in alliance with the pharmaceutical industry and the American Psychiatric Association, lobbied against the funding of research into psychosocial factors in mental distress and made personal attacks on those who disagree with them. He writes that in the United States 'it is nearly impossible to teach at a university without giving lip service to the ultimate need for psychiatric drugs and electroshock. It is increasingly difficult to publish anything that questions the fundamental propositions and approaches of biological psychiatry.'[28] Thomas Szasz, a professor of psychiatry and one of the most outspoken critics of the medical model of mental distress over the last forty years, was banned from teaching psychiatric trainees because of opposition from his colleagues. Two of his supporters were sacked and found themselves barred from other appointments; one had a book turned down after opponents put pressure on the publisher.[29] The list of examples could be extended almost indefinitely.

Finally, if the first two strategies do not work, a third and more sophisticated manoeuvre is to disarm critics by assimilating aspects of different approaches without actually changing the basic medical standpoint. Thus we say in Chapter 7 how nineteenth-century doctors, threatened by the success of moral treatment, adopted some of its ideas themselves and then claimed that only they, as people who understood both medical and non-medical approaches, were qualified to be in charge of the whole enterprise. What this did was to reduce moral treatment from a whole philosophy of care to a mere collection of techniques. Psychotherapy has met a similar fate; while more enlightened psychiatrists agree that it has a part to play, this psychotherapeutic understanding is an addition to, not a replacement for, the medical model. Similarly, Family Management (Chapter 4) allows for the influence of family relationships in 'schizophrenia' but only as the trigger of an underlying biological 'illness'. Currently there is a danger that the newly acceptable crisis intervention philosophy will be hijacked by 'assertive outreach' teams with a highly coercive, drug-orientated agenda.

Individual systems are only cogwheels within larger ones, and it is impossible to introduce real changes in the former without affecting the latter. This is as true at an individual level (thus, Elaine Jones's own psychological changes affected the whole family set-up) as at an institutional level (Foudraine's innovations brought him into conflict with the rest of the hospital). Ultimately, the system that the more radical reforms come up against is the society in which we all live, and this is what happened to Scott and his team. Taking a closer look at what happened will illustrate this point and will also demonstrate the most important and fundamental reason why the psychiatric system resists reform and remains the way it is.

In Chapter 4 we saw how Scott's reforms caused what he described as a 'bloody revolution' within the hospital, which found its very existence threatened by the fall in admission rates. Clashes with senior staff prevented nurses from being fully integrated into the crisis intervention team. Like Foudraine's staff, many of them found it very hard to cope with the de-medicalising of their role and the handing over of more responsibility to the patients: 'Nurses who were trained to regard mental patients as sick people, and who were accustomed to helping, caring for, and comforting them in rather the same way as the physically ill, found it hard to adjust to a system whereby the patients were treated as responsible for their actions and capable of looking after their own physical needs',[30] as an investigation into the services put it. As on Foudraine's ward, there were threats to the very existence of the team during the intermediate stage of anxiety, chaos and squalor. But because the reforms challenged not only the way the psychiatric service was run but also the whole way in which GPs, the police, relatives and ordinary members of the public view mental illness, they came up against powerful resistance from outside the hospital as well. Lurid headlines appeared in the local and national press: 'Filth and brutality – treatment prescribed for mental patients';[31] 'Why we are brutal';[32] alongside shock-horror stories such as: 'Patients had to make their beds. The patients were expected to: MAKE their own beds; WASH their own crockery; SERVE their own meals; KEEP their ward clean. If they did not serve their own meals they did not eat, and if the ward became dirty the nurses were not allowed to clean it.'[33] The *Daily Mail* carried a report on 'The doctor who was too tough. He made patients face reality',[34] and even ran a leader entitled 'The arrogance of the psychiatrists'.[35] ('Patients living rough in the hospital grounds . . . a middle-aged schizophrenic who died of physical injuries which were never fully diagnosed . . . patients and their relatives living in terror of the doctors and nurses . . . filth and chaos in the wards – it all sounds like the worst Victorian snakepit. Yet the conditions . . . were not the result of poverty or neglect within the National Health Service. They were, it seems, directly and indirectly the results of treatment methods deliberately and passionately pursued by Dr Scott and his staff', and so on and so forth.)

Finally, the pressure of complaints led to intervention from the very highest level of the system when Sir Keith Joseph, the then Secretary of State for Health and Social Services, ordered a government inquiry into conditions at the hospital. The resulting document cleared the team of any professional negligence in the case of the patient whose death had triggered the investigation and found nothing to suggest deliberate ill-treatment or cruelty to any patient; in fact, they paid tribute to Dr Scott's work and believed that the crisis intervention team should be given a fair trial: 'Napsbury Hospital owes much to Dr Scott . . . He has functioned both as an innovator and an enabler.'[36] They did, however, criticise the conditions on some of the wards and felt that the new methods

> were pursued in an insistent and inflexible manner. The result was at times a seeming lack of compassion and of respect for the rights of patients, particularly from some of the more junior members of the team . . . It was not so much what was done, but the way in which it was done, that in our view left Dr Scott open to legitimate criticism.

They believed that a better programme of preparation and public relations would have reduced these difficulties. The verdict was summarised with something less than total impartiality in the *Daily Express* as 'Probe calls halt to "bizarre" doctor's toughline cure for patients',[37] while the local evening paper announced: 'The harsh facts of life at Napsbury Hospital – now it's official. How doctors doled out heartbreak and misery. "This method of treatment must not be allowed to spread".'[38]

Once again, the experiences of a reformer show how important it is for staff to be able to recognise their involvement with the system in which they work. For Scott and Foudraine, losing their own battles with the hospital and wider systems would have imposed crucial limitations on their ability to help their patients in their corresponding struggles towards autonomy in the smaller systems of their own families, friends and workplaces.

The second and even more important point highlighted by the passionate resistance of some sections of the press and the general public is the extent to which traditional medical-model psychiatry is identified with society as a whole. The values of the two systems are the same; and if the assumptions of psychiatry are challenged, then the substantial proportion of society which shares these assumptions can be expected to protest very strongly. We saw in Chapter 4 how the ritual of diagnosis, officially a function performed by the psychiatrist, is in fact very often only a rubber-stamping of a decision already made by lay people who have used their own criteria to select one person as the 'sick one' and who may become angry and abusive if the professionals refuse to go along with this. One critic illustrates the way in which we all demand that psychiatrists share and enforce our values with the story of an eccentric acquaintance who ended up being committed to hospital after breaching a number of social norms on an aeroplane: wearing strange clothes, raising his voice to a fellow-passenger, and so on:

> It was not some *law* that Noah broke but a social rule, something not written down in any code of justice anywhere in the United States. Thou shalt not raise thy voice in a Boeing 707. That is all Noah really did . . . No question about it – he'd flipped his lid . . . Yet who are these people who are making this judgement? There were no psychiatrists on the airplane. Not professionals, in other words, but everyday 'normal' people, police and passengers, decided he was crazy. Which is a way of saying that we – you and I, the public – made that diagnosis . . . Let the psychiatrist decide whether it's schizophrenia or involutional melancholia or some other arcana they suffer from. *That's* the psychiatrist's job. He confirms and refines what is fundamentally our diagnosis. He works for *us* . . . The mental hospital is essentially what we want it to be, and we want an institution which will take disturbing people off our hands . . . only a change in attitude on *our* part will eliminate the need for such custodial institutions.

The anger and abuse that a mental health professional may meet if he or she refuses to go along with this role in an individual case is even more apparent at a more general level when a whole psychiatric service refuses to go along with what the public is demanding, consciously or unconsciously, that it should supply, that is, the unquestioning removal of certain members of society who are thereafter to be labelled as not responsible.

This gives us additional insight into the dilemma that psychiatrists (and to a lesser extent, other mental health professionals) face, usually unconsciously. Working with the mentally distressed can be extremely fulfilling if you feel that you are able to offer real help to those in need. However, being caught both ways – required by society to uphold its values and sweep up its debris while being faced with an enormous amount of individual suffering – is highly uncomfortable and unsatisfying. By covertly demanding that psychiatrists act as police for our problems, we mystify them and make them, in some ways, as much victims of the psychiatric system as their patients. Perhaps it is not surprising if they turn to medical jargon, physical treatments and fifteen-minute appointments as ways of distancing themselves from this distasteful task. But more importantly, it gives a vital clue to the origin of the fundamental contradictions in medical-model psychiatry: the fact that it operates on the assumption that there is a physical basis for mental illness although none has ever been found; that its treatments lack a rationale for their effects and probably cause as much disability as they cure; that while calling for increased research and resources it resolutely turns its back on cheaper and more effective psychosocial approaches, and so on. In the case of an individual whose problems are handicapping and hard to understand and yet will not go away (a woman who cannot leave the house without panicking, for example), one has to look deeper to discover the underlying purpose that the difficulties may be serving – perhaps this enforced dependency is preserving her marriage. At the level of a whole system the same principle applies. Psychiatry suffers from numerous distressing 'symptoms': high readmission rates, low staff morale, public suspicion, inability to define basic terms like 'schizophrenia', low status among other doctors, and so on. The only way to make sense of the rigidity with which it resists reform despite all these problems is to expose its underlying purpose and the central paradox that leads to all the surface contradictions. In brief, *psychiatry is required to be the agent of society while purporting to be the agent of the individual; and its main function is not treatment but social control.* This theme will be explored in more detail in the next chapter.

Chapter 10

Psychiatry and wider society

In the previous chapter, a discussion of resistance to change in the psychiatric system led to the conclusion that this phenomenon could only be fully understood by seeing psychiatry as serving an important underlying purpose, and to the contention that *psychiatry is required to be the agent of society while purporting to be the agent of the individual; and its main function is not treatment but social control.*

This is not a new theory. As many readers will know, a number of arguments have been put forward in support of it. One is that to give someone a psychiatric diagnosis is in fact to make a social judgement rather than the objective scientific assessment that the medical model likes to pretend. As discussed in Chapter 4, there are no physical tests of temperature, blood pressure, X-rays and so on to help make the diagnosis (except in the minority of cases where, for example, a brain tumour or advanced senile dementia is involved). Despite the reams that have been written on the essential psychiatric skill of diagnosis, in the end decisions have to be made on descriptions (withdrawn manner, impulsive actions, aggressive outbursts, inappropriate affect, delusional remarks, pressure of speech and so on) that rely heavily on the psychiatrist's own assumptions about what is normal and acceptable behaviour. How quiet do you have to be before you can be called withdrawn? How angry is aggressive? How sudden is impulsive? How unusual is delusional? How excited is manic? How miserable is depressed? The answers to all these questions are to be found not in some special measuring skill imparted during psychiatric training, but in psychiatrists' and lay people's shared beliefs about how 'normal' people should behave (and, as we saw in Chapter 6, the selection and training of doctors mean that these beliefs are likely to be pretty conservative). Support for the social judgement theory comes from the writings of Emil Kraepelin, the founding father of medical-model psychiatry, who around the turn of the century was the first person to

DOI: 10.4324/9781003095958-10

attempt a definition of a new illness: dementia praecox, later renamed 'schizophrenia'. In the absence of physical markers he had to rely for his definition on descriptions of problematic behaviour, much of which consisted merely of breaking social rules and sex-role expectations:

> They do not suit their behaviour to the situation in which they are, they conduct themselves in a free and easy way, laugh on serious occasions, are rude and impertinent towards their superiors, challenge them to duels, lose their deportment and personal dignity; they go about in untidy and dirty clothes, unwashed, unkempt, go with a lighted cigar into church, speak familiarly to strangers, decorate themselves with gay ribbons . . . In their handiwork the loss of taste often makes itself felt in their choice of extraordinary combinations of color and peculiar forms . . . It was mentioned with very special frequency, particularly in the male sex, that children were mostly concerned who always exhibited a quiet, shy, retiring disposition, made no friendships, lived only for themselves. Of secondary importance, and more in girls, there is reported irritability, sensitiveness, excitability, nervousness, and along with these self-will and a tendency to bigotry.[1]

At a distance of a hundred years, it is glaringly obvious that Kraepelin was identifying, not illnesses, but ways of *behaving* that were disapproved of by him and by the society of the time. But how different are the supposedly scientific criteria of the twentieth century? The *Diagnostic and Statistical Manual of Mental Disorders* (DSM)*, which lists the criteria for diagnosing mental illnesses) makes little attempt to hide the fact that the crucial judgements are not medical but social ones; thus, someone suffering from 'schizophrenia' may display 'bizarre delusions, i.e. involving a phenomenon that the person's culture would regard as totally implausible . . . markedly peculiar behavior, e.g. collecting garbage, talking to self in public . . . odd beliefs or magical thinking, influencing behavior and inconsistent with cultural norms', and so on. The element of social judgement is even more obvious in less serious problems such as Histrionic Personality Disorder ('expresses emotion with inappropriate exaggeration, e.g. embraces casual acquaintances with excessive ardor . . . is inappropriately sexually seductive in appearance or behavior') or Antisocial Personality Disorder ('is unable to sustain consistent work behavior . . . abandonment of several jobs without realistic plans for others . . . fails to conform to social norms with respect to lawful behavior . . . traveling from place to place without a prearranged job or clear goal for the period of travel') or, in the case of children, Oppositional Defiant Disorder ('often actively defies or refuses adult requests or rules . . . often deliberately does things that annoy other people . . . often argues with adults').

A classic illustration is provided by perhaps the most spectacular instant cure achieved by modern psychiatry, when homosexuality was dropped as a category of mental illness from the *Diagnostic and Statistical Manual III* in 1973 and millions of people thus 'recovered' overnight. Here was a particularly clear example of a social judgement dressed up as a medical one.

There are a number of curious consequences to having a diagnostic system based on social judgements about behaviour and experiences. One is that you will automatically 'get well' by travelling to a country where your beliefs are widely shared. You can, in theory, get on a plane in the UK with a diagnosis of psychosis because you believe your ancestors are talking to you, and get off the plane in certain parts of the world 'cured'. This obviously does not happen with pneumonia or heart disease.

Another is that you can 'recover' by persuading a sufficient number of members of your culture to share your beliefs. For example, large numbers of Americans are apparently convinced that they have been visited by aliens. This (to British minds) bizarre idea cannot, nevertheless, be said to be a sign of mental illness because it is so common in the United States, although you would be very unwise to confide similar beliefs to a psychiatrist in the UK.

Another is that it becomes extraordinarily difficult to draw the line between 'normal' ideas and so-called 'mental illness'. Large parts of the population share beliefs – for example, in God, telepathy or ghosts – which are every bit as 'irrational' as those officially designated as crazy. Surveys of the extent of 'mental illness', both within and across cultures, have frequently foundered on this fact; for example, a Department of Health survey of 'mental illness' in the community found that mediums were being classified as 'psychotic' on the basis of their responses to questions about hearing voices.[2]

However, leaving these oddities aside for a moment, the important point is this: to give someone a psychiatric diagnosis is not to make an objective medical assessment, but to pass a concealed social judgement on their behaviour, at the request of lay members of their culture. A number of other critics have come to the same conclusion. Theodore Sarbin writes: 'Although masked as a medical diagnosis, schizophrenia is essentially a moral verdict. The conduct that leads persons into the diagnosis–treatment sequence is initially the target of value judgements by others

who have greater social power.'³ Thomas Szasz writes: 'Mental health
. . . has come to mean conformity to the demands of society. According
to the common sense definition, mental health is the ability to play the
game of social living, and to play it well. Conversely, mental illness is
the refusal to play, or the inability to play it well.'⁴ Richard Brothers,
an eighteenth-century religious leader, when asked why he had been
committed to Bedlam, replied: 'I and the world happened to have a slight
difference of opinion; the world said I was mad, and I said the world was
mad. I was outvoted, and here I am.'⁵

It is important to be clear about this point. All the people whose stories
have been recounted in this book had serious difficulties, caused great
and understandable concern to their friends, relatives and communities,
and were in urgent need of some kind of help. Their problems could not
simply be reduced to having breached some social norm. The argument
of this book is *not* that there is no such thing as severe mental distress, nor
that psychiatrists and other staff are wicked people who deliberately set out
to confuse and harm their patients, nor that psychiatric treatments are
universally unhelpful, nor that patients are suffering simply and solely
from labelling, scapegoating, political oppression, or whatever else. My
argument is, however, *that social and political factors are a crucial
component of mental distress; that through being identified with the wider
system of society, psychiatry shares its values and assumptions; that the
psychiatric system in its turn passes on these values and assumptions by a
process of identification on the part of its staff and mystification on the part
of its patients; that as a result the overall effect of psychiatry, if not the
conscious intent of its practitioners, is to reinforce social norms and political
interests; and that since none of this is made explicit, dissent can only emerge
in the form of continued symptoms on the part of the patients.* My further
contention is *that social control, the maintaining of society's status quo by
labelling dissent as illness, is actually the major function that wider society,
consciously or unconsciously, expects and demands that psychiatry should
fulfil; that while it is certainly not possible to explain all of an individual's
distress in these terms, psychiatry as a whole will be able to offer genuine help
to people struggling within their systems only to the extent that it is aware
of and successful in challenging its own role in the wider system of society;
and that where it fails most spectacularly (women's problems in general,
'schizophrenia', mental distress in ethnic minorities) is also where such factors
play the most important and ignored role in the problem.* My final point is
*that the principal mechanism by which psychiatry performs its function of
social control is the use of the medical model, that is, by propagating the myth
that psychiatry is engaged in an objective, scientific enterprise to which*

medical science will one day produce the solutions, which gives psychiatry powerful weapons for suppressing dissent (drugs, ECT) while enabling its true purpose to be concealed.

It is relatively easy to find evidence for the blatant use of psychiatry as social control if we look into the past, or at other countries, or at groups of people who are even more powerless and vulnerable than psychiatric patients. Perhaps the most horrifying example is the active involvement of psychiatry in the Holocaust, described in Chapter 7. We all know how Soviet dissidents were diagnosed with sinister syndromes such as 'paranoid delusions of reforming society' and 'hippieism', were incarcerated and forced to take medication that turned them into zombies (that is, major tranquillisers: exactly the same drugs that are described as miraculous cures in the West). Benjamin Rush, the founding father of American psychiatry, coined the diagnosis of 'anarchia' for people who were unhappy with the new political structure of the United States.[6] Slaves who bolted were said to be suffering from the mental illness of 'drapetomania', or the irrestistable urge to run away from plantations; in fact, slavery was said to be good for their mental health, since too much freedom and excitement would inevitably lead to insanity.[7] We saw how lobotomy was openly advocated as a means of suppressing society's 'misfits' such as communists and homosexuals, and how the pioneers of major tranquillisers and ECT were quite open about their potential for control,[8] and we read about the horrific 'treatment' inflicted on gay men in the 1960s and 1970s. Eighteenth-century novels frequently featured madwomen as victims of male/parental tyranny,[9] while arguments such as 'women become insane during pregnancy, after parturition, during lactation; at the age when the . . . menses first appear and when they disappear' were used to restrict women's access to higher education in the nineteenth century.[10] It is well known that women were institutionalised for having illegitimate babies in the recent past. In present-day Britain, major tranquillisers are widely and inappropriately used to sedate elderly people in nursing homes, people with learning disabilities, and prisoners. And, of course, psychiatry is sometimes used very overtly as social control if a person poses a grave risk to the safety of others due to his or her disturbed state of mind. Most people would agree that active intervention in these (rare) situations is sometimes necessary. Whether or not this is best achieved by labelling the person as 'mentally ill' and giving enforced major tranquillisers is another matter.

Many of these examples seem shocking to us, and yet they were widely accepted by ordinary, well-meaning lay people and professionals at the time. The challenge is to see how we are involved in such practices today.

While we have not seen, in the book so far, current examples of card-carrying communists or declared anarchists drugged into submission, what we have found is a number of people who are in conflict with the small systems (marriages, families, workplaces, sex roles) within which they live – systems which are cogwheels within the larger system of society and are microcosms of its values. In the words of Mary (Chapter 5), 'The whole system is that you've got to conform, but when you think about it, the ones in here are non-conformists.' There were, of course, other layers to their problems too, and the full personal meaning of each individual's dilemma could only be clarified by an understanding of the particular circumstances in which they found themselves and the lessons that they, as unique individuals, had drawn from them. But at another level, we saw in Chapter 5, for example, how in accepting unquestioningly society's assumptions about the role of women, psychiatry passes on these messages to its female patients, thus mystifying them about the origins of their distress ('I know I *shouldn't* be feeling like this'). One way of interpreting the depressed housewife's continued inability to cope with the chores is that she has, at an unconscious level, decided to go on strike in protest at the conditions under which she is expected to live. Her symptoms are the only way she can say 'no' to the role assigned to her by her family, at one level, and by society in general at another level (and also to that part of herself that identifies with these standards). It became apparent that in such cases the family's request to the hospital is not just 'make her happy again' but, covertly, 'make her happy to fit in with the role that we think women ought to have', and the covert response of the hospital is 'we'll try to do that; and if we can't, we'll at least make sure that she doesn't question it'. This is followed up with powerful sedative drugs which further reduce her ability to think and function autonomously while purporting to be the medical cure for the problem that has been diagnosed as an illness called depression. Once again, I emphasise that this is not the conscious intent of either party; the family are genuinely concerned and the hospital staff sincerely believe they are doing their best to help. However, it is by this kind of process of labelling dissent as an illness suffered by the individual that psychiatry can be said to be acting as an agent of social control.

We can see the same process at work in the stories of women whose problems take a different form. One of the women quoted in Chapter 5 had come, after many years of failed psychiatric treatment, to see her anorexia as a protest, a kind of hunger strike, at the conflicting demands placed on her as a woman. The 'hunger strike' analogy has been expanded by Susie Orbach in her book of the same name:[11]

> Like the hunger striker, she has taken as her weapon a refusal to eat. Like the suffragettes at the turn of the century in the United Kingdom or the political prisoners of the contemporary world, she is giving urgent voice to her protest . . . Her self denial is in effect a protest against the rules that circumscribe a woman's life.

Orbach also indicates the wider political processes that form the background to a culture where eating disorders are epidemic. She points out that with the growth of the consumer society over the last thirty years, where objects are valued not so much for their usefulness but as symbols of status, power, wealth or sexuality, women's bodies have increasingly been used to sell everything from cars to soft drinks:

> The sexuality of women's bodies becomes split off and reattached to a host of commodities reflective of a consumer culture . . . For women themselves, the body has become a commodity within the marketplace or, as I have suggested elsewhere, their own commodity, the object with which they negotiate the world . . . Women are encouraged to see their bodies from the outside, as if they were commodities.

She suggests that it is no coincidence that the obsession with slimness began

> just at that moment in history when women were demanding to be taken more seriously in the workplace and, in the language of the 1970s, 'demanding more space'. Body maintenance, body beautiful, exercise and the pursuit of thinness are offered as valued arenas for concern precisely at the moment when women are trying to break free of such imperatives.

Again we can see how psychiatric treatment which focuses solely on weight gain and imposes a strict feeding programme is, in effect, mystifying the young woman by conveying the message that the whole problem lies in her 'illness'. It is she who has the difficulty, and she who must adjust by following, in the words of one service user, 'the twin Gods of cure and normality'.[12] Denied the right to negotiate about conditions, continuing symptoms become her only means of protest. Yet, in the words of the same service user, 'eating distress is part of a struggle against socio-political oppresssion. A painful but sane response, particularly in Western culture. When we get together and change how we view ourselves and fight against injustice, then liberation is ours.'[13]

A woman who has experienced self-harm herself, and is now involved in supporting others who self-harm, also emphasises the need to see it in the wider context of sexual politics: 'Life experiences which underlie women's self-injury, such as sexual abuse and battering by partners, lack of recognition and response to their needs, lack of power and control and the imposition of caring roles, bear a direct relationship to women's social position and their socialisation towards this.'[14]

Similar themes were outlined in Chapter 5 in relation to men. We saw how identification with the belief that a man's most important role is to have a job and be a provider leads to such devastating psychological consequences for unemployed men, who find themselves in a particularly vicious trap. If they break down, the shame they already feel about being out of work will be augmented by the stigma of a psychiatric label, with its implication that their distress is an individual failing. In effect, men are punished for protesting about the conditions of their lives in the same way as women are. Again, by dispensing a form of treatment that sees the problem only in individual terms, psychiatry can be said to serve the function of disguising the results of political policy as illness and allowing it to be swept under the carpet, so that protest both on an individual and a wider level is neutralised, appearing only in the indirect form of psychological symptoms. Institutions that are more remote from public gaze and sympathy have to make correspondingly less effort to maintain the illusion of 'treatment' or 'rehabilitation': 'The abuse of institutionalised power in prisons and secure hospitals is one of the persistent scandals of modern times. Abuse is not something that happened only in old Soviet psychiatric hospitals. Drugs, isolation, electric shock treatment and mechanical restraints are each used without accountability.'[15]

The group of people who use the hospital mainly to meet social or economic needs and often the 'sick role' patients too (Chapter 3) are casualties of society who find a place for themselves in the mental-patient status offered by the psychiatric system. From an individual point of view this may be the best option available, but from a wider perspective it can be argued that this is one of the ways in which

> the sick role becomes a convenient tool to maintain the status quo
> . . . [It] permits temporary deviance from the usual role expectations.
> It also isolates the deviant and prevents the group formations which
> would be needed for fundamental social change. In this sense, the sick
> role cools out the opposition.[16]

Once again, I am not suggesting that social and political issues are the most important strand in every individual case, nor that it is always useful or possible to address them in treatment. Nevertheless, the argument of this book is that, if you go far back enough, a clash between the needs of the individual and the values of society can always be found. The behavioural treatment of agoraphobia, for example, always involves at some point a two-hour trip to the most feared situation of all, the local shopping mall, where the unfortunate sufferer learns the hard way that even the most extreme anxiety does eventually subside. But after the fiftieth woman has described how she cannot face these places without panicking, one starts to wonder who has the problem – the client or the planners who design these huge impersonal mausoleums.

A minority of other critics and mental health workers have also argued that individual distress can only be fully understood by placing it in a social/political context, and have pointed out the destructive consequences of a treatment approach that fails to take such factors into account. For example, there are no clear biological or hormonal causal factors in postnatal depression; the best predictors and interventions are to do with social support, quality of housing, financial stress and the woman's relationship with her partner.[17] Sheila Kitzinger, author of many books on pregnancy and childbirth, is sceptical of the way that

women are often told that postnatal depression is the result of a disturbed endocrine system and that it is all a matter of hormones . . . It is only too easy to explain away and dismiss women's understandable frustration, anger, and despair about what life is doing to them by labelling it as 'pre-menstrual tension', 'menopausal neurosis', or 'postnatal depression' . . . Many mothers feel some-how abandoned by society . . . Most of us are not prepared for the resentment, the sense of inadequacy, guilt, anger, and murderous feelings we have as mothers. There is delighted discovery and joy and sometimes sheer ecstasy too, and that makes it all worthwhile. But the trouble is that the image of motherhood is romanticised. We learn nothing about how we are going to feel when woken by a crying baby for the tenth time between 3 a.m. and 5 a.m., or what it is like to be alone in the house with complete responsibility for a child for 5 to 10 hours a day . . . Postnatal depression and despair is no accident, nor an act of God. It is the direct result of a society which puts motherhood on a pedestal while disparaging and degrading mothers in reality . . . When a new mother becomes depressed or constantly anxious she is the victim of a social system which fails to value women as mothers and does not consider housework or child care real 'work', and in which she is cut off from the sources of self-esteem that all of us usually depend on and from the support which in traditional societies comes from other women in the extended family and neighbourhood. It is a social system which, when she cracks under stress, labels her as 'sick', offers her tranquillizers to keep her going instead of changing anything, and implicitly blames her for her failure to adjust. Postnatal depression and the distress which women experience when they become mothers is not their own private problem. It is a political issue, something which can only be changed when there is social change, and therefore a challenge to us all.[18]

And another example: a psychiatrist working with the elderly writes:

although it is currently stated by practically all the textbooks that the aged are more prone to depression of an endogenous [that is, without external cause] nature . . . we believe that the unhappiness which is misdiagnosed and mistreated as an endogenous illness is a legitimate response to the plight that many of the aged find themselves in. A number of studies have established that the aged are an oppressed group, they are poorer than the rest of the population, with 50 per cent of them on society's breadline, supplementary benefit. They have some of the worst housing and are eight times more likely to be isolated and alienated. Add to this the burden of physical disease and social prejudice and we have a social situation in which stress symptoms are inevitable. The so-called depression, therefore, is not primarily due to a biochemical upset but an understandable reaction to the alienation, rejection, isolation, and social stress that the aged are subject to. The diagnosis of depression has three dangerous aspects. First, it tells a person who is lonely, isolated, and poor that on top of it all, he is mentally ill. This, we believe, merely worsens his morale. Second, the diagnosis is associated with the prescribing of potent neuroleptics and sedatives which impair cognitive function and cause serious side effects. Finally it mystifies and medicalizes a problem, preventing its rational resolution. We believe that the treatment of so-called depression is to treat the causes of it. Poverty by the fuller use of available benefits, alienation by establishing relationships, and isolation by the use of caring networks, social clubs and day centres. Such 'treatments' may involve non-medical activity but it is preferable to prescribing pills which worsen the patient's confusion and serve mainly to swell the profits of powerful drug companies . . . [Using this approach, the team found that] the need for acute provision has been slashed to a fifth of the minimum laid down by the DHSS, more than 1,200 beds have been closed . . . we have the lowest drug bill in the country and none of our patients has committed suicide in over a decade.[19]

Given the vulnerability and powerlessness of the elderly as a group, it is alarming to learn that elderly women are the most frequent recipients of ECT and of compulsory ECT.[20]

We have been looking at some of the social and political factors that form the background to individual distress and arguing that psychiatry, in so far as it ignores these factors and passes on the values and assumptions of the wider society with which it is identified, labelling dissent as illness, can be said to be performing the fundamental function of social control. If this is so, we should expect to find psychiatry reflecting and reinforcing other inbuilt prejudices of wider society as well. We have already discussed at some length how sexism in society is reflected in and reinforced by sexism in psychiatry at many different levels. The same is true of other forms of discrimination. Thus, although homosexuality is no longer officially categorised as a mental illness, gay men and women may still find that their sexual orientation is viewed as an abnormality and seen as the cause of whatever other problems they may have. However, it is the effects of racism and classism in psychiatry that have been most thoroughly documented.

RACISM

It is not hard to find historical examples of racist psychiatric theories being used as a means of exerting social control. Littlewood and Lipsedge, in their book *Aliens and Alienists*, describe how science and medicine have over the years been employed to 'prove' that members of ethnic minorities are different and inferior – that their brains are smaller (containing 'undifferentiated' and 'immature' nerve cells), that as childlike, happy savages in a state of nature they are incapable of experiencing depression, and more recently that blacks as a group have lower IQs than whites.[21] The conclusions drawn were clearly in the interests of the dominant white section of society; for example, the cure for the illness of dysaesthesia aethiopis, with its alarming symptoms of breaking tools and paying no attention to property, was plenty of hard work in fresh air, and a little light whipping.[22]

As usual, it is harder for us to recognise such practices in our own day and age. Nevertheless, there is abundant evidence for the existence of racism in contemporary psychiatry. A joint Department of Health and Home Office discussion document in 1992 noted that black people are more likely than whites to be detained in hospital compulsorily, to be diagnosed as suffering from 'schizophrenia', to be sent to locked wards and to receive high doses of medication. They are less likely than white people to receive appropriate treatment at an early stage or to be referred for psychotherapy or counselling.[23] Mainstream psychiatric services have generally failed to provide appropriate services for ethnic minorities or to consult them about what they need. And 'the dominant racialism in our society is reflected not just in the theories and practices of psychiatry but in its very structure: white consultants, Asian junior doctors, black nurses and domestics'.[24]

Currently, inner-city psychiatric services are operating under two opposing pressures: the requirement to take active measures (usually medication and admission) to avoid headline-grabbing homicides by psychiatric patients, and severe lack of space due to bed closures. Littlewood and Lipsedge describe the 'drama of mutual suspicion, lack of trust, resentment and fear' that is played out, they estimate, two or three times a week in such facilities:

> Almost invariably the patient, often black in an institution where senior staff are white, does not share the perspective of the mental health workers. Because of his (and it is usually *his*) lack of 'insight' (i.e. a reluctance to share the professionals' view of his emotions, thoughts and actions), he not only refuses to take his antipsychotic medication but, logically, refuses to come into hospital voluntarily where he knows that the medication will be administered forcibly. He does not attribute any aspect of his inner life to mental illness; he finds the side effects of medication intolerable (impotence, sluggishness, shakiness, restlessness and obesity) and he feels degraded by the fortnightly injection into his buttocks. When he refuses to open the door of his flat to the two doctors and the social worker who he knows are planning to force him to go back into hospital, the social worker applies . . . for a warrant which permits the police (often wearing riot gear) to break down his front door and convey him to hospital . . . Shortly after reaching the ward, the patient is given the 'choice' of oral or injected antipsychotic medication . . . The hard-pressed staff have

an increasingly custodial role, supervising those patients who are incarcerated in 'seclusion' or sitting at the door of the 'open' ward to prevent recalcitrant patients from running away. Given these siege-like conditions there is little time for staff to engage in therapeutic dialogue and to learn about the lives and intentions and meanings of their patients . . . While progressing along this 'pathway to care', the patient . . . his carers (if any) and the mental health professionals participate in a stereotyped *tableau vivant* which recapitulates the themes of power, of class, of colour and of Otherness.[25]

It is not surprising that, according to a recent report, young black people are highly suspicious of mental health services.[26]

A vivid example of this journey can be seen in 'John Baptist', an episode of the 1995 BBC2 fly-on-the-wall documentary series *Minders*. It is all the more powerful for its neutral stance; the series was intended as a record, not an exposé, of the work of a psychiatric team, who were happy for it to be shown. John Baptist is the adopted name of a black man who believes that he was born white, that he is descended from the royal family, and that his sister has been cannibalised, but he is apparently coping perfectly well with his life. He does not see himself as mentally ill and does not want medication, being extremely unhappy about his previous experiences of psychiatry. However, his beliefs are causing concern to the psychiatric team, who see him as 'very ill and need[ing] treatment', and they arrange a police escort to hospital. Articulate and assertive, John is not prepared to accept his (white, male, middle-class) consultant's view without challenge. He angrily describes how last time he 'came out of this hospital hardly able to brush my teeth, hardly able to eat, hardly able to stand . . . I was less than a baby. Now, what sort of medicine is that?' He demands to know what proof the consultant has that his beliefs are untrue, and forces the consultant to admit that this is in fact a matter of personal judgement: 'Well you're right in a way there . . . the only way I make that diagnosis is on people's thoughts and feelings.' However, in this unequal power battle there is little doubt whose delusion is going to carry the day, and we see the consultant telling the camera that 'I've no doubt this is a schizophrenic illness', while John is threatened with a locked ward if he tries to leave.

The rest of the programme charts John's determined but unsuccessful attempts to gain his freedom, while insisting on retaining his beliefs. His assertiveness and refusal to compromise about his ideas clearly count against him, for the chief evidence against him at a tribunal hearing is that he used to be 'angry, irritable, shouting at people, verbally aggressive'

and that he still has 'inappropriate beliefs'. Meanwhile, forcible administration of the medication he so hates gradually reduces him to a silent,
shambling wreck of his former self, with a heart-breaking expression of
sadness and hopelessness. This, to his consultant, is actually seen as
progress; by a deft shifting of the goalposts, he is able to claim that, though
John still retains his beliefs, his sadness indicates that he is 'more of
a whole person' and has therefore improved. In one of the final scenes,
we see a team member persuading John, in ultra-caring tones, to set the
seal on his degradation and defeat by signing a form to confirm that he is
'permanently and substantially disabled' by mental illness, in return for
a bus pass. John's mental illness is at last being properly treated; or, to put
it another way, he has now been permanently and substantially disabled
as a punishment for obstinately refusing to regulate his thoughts according
to white cultural norms.

Littlewood and Lipsedge discuss the various possible and not
necessarily mutually exclusive explanations for the apparently higher levels
of 'mental illness' in some ethnic minorities. For unknown reasons, Irish
immigrants to the UK have the poorest mental and physical health of
all minorities. However, the main focus of research has been on the fact
that Afro-Caribbeans in the UK receive a diagnosis of 'schizophrenia' up
to six times more often than whites,[27] and are more likely to be detained
against their will. Biological explanations include the suggestion that
breakdown is precipitated by malnutrition, viral infections, obstetric
complications or using cannabis. There is very little evidence to support
any of this. Environmental explanations focus on the stresses of immi-
gration and adjusting to a different culture, and the daily impact of racism
in all its forms (such as poorer access to housing, welfare and health care
facilities). Then there are theories that question the validity of the statistics;
white psychiatrists may be misdiagnosing cultural reactions or brief
atypical psychoses as 'schizophrenia'; the behaviour of black patients may
be more 'florid' when disturbed, increasing the likelihood that they will
be detained compulsorily; or statistics may be influenced in various ways
by the racism inherent in the whole psychiatric system. Some alarming
support for this last theory comes from a study by Loring and Powell in
America, who showed case histories, identical in every detail except for
gender and race, to 290 psychiatrists. Overall, both black and white
psychiatrists gave a diagnosis of 'schizophrenia' more frequently to black
clients, and were more likely to see them as violent, suspicious and
dangerous.[28]

Littlewood and Lipsedge see mental distress as having complex
roots both in biology and in culture, in the individual and in society.

However, they believe that it can be an intelligible response to racism and disadvantage. They found, for example, that 'the experiences of migration and of discrimination in housing, employment, and everyday life were frequently expressed by patients, not as conscious complaints, but symbolically in the actual structure of their illness'. They argue that 'the expression of mental illness, while it may not always be a valid communication to others, is still a meaningful reaction on the part of the individual to his situation', and a view of mental distress which ignores this aspect fits particularly badly in the case of ethnic minorities. Suman Fernando, in the programme about John Baptist, makes the point that unusual beliefs do not arrive from outer space but are rooted in people's lives and histories; similarly, Littlewood and Lipsedge discuss the many symbolic meanings that blackness and whiteness have come to carry, and that may be expressed through 'delusional' beliefs.[29] They also present evidence to support their suggestion that the greater incidence of paranoid reactions among immigrants (believing that one is being spied on, that witchcraft is being practised against one and so on) may be 'merely a strong reiteration of the experience of discrimination'. Immigrant housewives who 'often experience such bad bodily pains, insomnia and bad dreams that they are unable to provide a secure domestic base for an ambitious husband to launch a career' can be seen as

> protesting at their husbands' opportunities; he straddles two cultures, while for them life does not seem to have changed from that in their home country. While anger and frustration may occasionally be openly expressed, in the family they usually take the socially acceptable form of physical illness . . . the dominant political structure of the family can remain unthreatened.[30]

They conclude that 'considerations of normality and abnormality are not . . . "innocent" or value-free'. In fact, the reverse is true: 'every culture conceives of mental illness in relation to its dominant beliefs' and 'insane behaviour is generally expected to invert the basic rules of society'. Thus, 'the practice of psychiatry continually redefines and controls social reality for the community'.[31] In relation to ethnic minorities, the result has often been a medicalisation of difficulties that are intelligible in terms of personal and cultural factors and the power relationships within society.

This admirable book makes many important points. Where it falls down, in my view, is in its reluctance to take its arguments to their logical conclusion and challenge the whole concept of 'mental illness', and to admit that psychiatry's primary function is to regulate social norms not just for immigrants and ethnic minorities, but for all of us. Here, for example, is the intriguing case of a Hasidic couple who had asked for help with their 'insane' fourteen-year-old son, Chaim, who, according to his parents, 'was able to appear quite normal to outsiders and had concealed his illness from school friends and teachers'. On entering the house:

> The Weinberg household appeared very Orthodox – the men dressed in the traditional black clothes, their hair in ringlets with untrimmed beards; the women wore wigs. There was no radio, television or record player. The only books visible were various Talmudic texts. Along a table Chaim's brothers and brothers-in-law ignored us, bent over commentaries on the Torah. Chaim was naturally embarrassed at the arrival of two psychiatrists but, at his father's prompting, took us up to his bedroom to talk. To our astonishment the walls were convered with posters of football stars and the table was a litter of rosettes, scarves and exercise books full of the analyses of football results. Some months before while watching television with a friend . . . Chaim had seen a football match for the first time in his life. He was fascinated and surreptitiously started reading sports magazines and even by extreme cunning managed to see Saturday soccer matches. His parents had inevitably found out and the house for the last few months had been the scene of continual arguments . . . The family doctor was convinced the boy was developing schizophrenia . . . Compared with the acceptance by his brothers of the society in which they had been brought up, Chaim was certainly behaving strangely. On the other hand the Weinbergs refused to accept that they were also part of a wider society, a society which offered a variety of different lifestyles. They saw doctors as supporters of their authority – indeed, their first request to us was to make Chaim obey them![32]

To the majority of us who are not orthodox Jews, it is obvious that this is an example of social control disguised by medical terminology, with lay people requiring the psychiatrist to rubber-stamp their diagnosis of 'madness' and thus reinforce cultural norms and the family power relationships by which these are transmitted. But the stark contrast between the two cultures in this particular case is only a more dramatic example of the dynamics and issues that are in fact played out in nearly all cases of 'schizophrenia', as we saw in Chapter 4. The authors tie themselves in knots by insisting that there is such a thing as an illness called 'schizophrenia', and trying to distinguish it from meaningful reactions to personal and cultural conflicts and contexts. Not surprisingly, they are completely unable to work out how to draw this line.

A more radical critique comes from psychiatrist Suman Fernando, who argues that since all psychiatric diagnosis is inherently value-laden it inevitably reflects the myths and stereotypes of the culture from which it derives, including racist ones. Although the expression of overtly racist opinions has become less common, the psychiatric view of black people is still influenced by perceptions of alienness, craziness, inferiority, aggression and danger. He also points out that 'while the concept of "madness" is present in some form or other in most societies . . . the current concept of "schizophrenia" makes little sense outside Western culture'.[33] What we call psychiatric problems may, in other cultures, be seen in religious, spiritual, philosophical, psychological or ethical terms; where we emphasise control, personal autonomy, problem-solving and body–mind separation, Eastern values lean towards acceptance, harmony, contemplation and body–mind–spirit unity. To ignore the existence of non-Western world views because they are assumed to be inferior is racist; and to insist on the universal imposition of our own reductionist and mechanistic approach is, in his words, a form of 'psychiatric imperialism':

> With the spread of Western psychiatry into the non-Western world . . . personal distress, normally dealt with in religious modes or as problems within family and social systems, is being forced into illness modes to be treated by manufactured drugs or psychotherapies developed in an alien culture. This is the imperialism of psychiatry – an imperialism that is less obvious than the military domination by Europeans in the nineteenth century and its economic counterpart of the twentieth, but no less powerful and as destructive to the vast majority of people in the world.[34]

The remedies are not easy:

> Western psychiatry . . . must break out of its ethnocentrism, free itself from racism and reach out into the world it has so far ignored. In doing so it must recognise certain social realities concerned with power: the economic and military domination of the world by power blocks which identify with white superiority and with values that are largely to do with Western materialism . . . the blending of power with racism, both within nations and internationally; and the involvement of psychiatry with the exercise of power–state power working through psychiatry and personal power of professionals over patients.[35]

CLASSISM

It is well established that the working classes, like black and ethnic minority people, get a poorer deal than the middle classes in many areas. In 1980 the government tried to suppress the Black Report,[36] which attributed the greater risk of injury, sickness and early death lower down the social scale to glaring inequalities in income, education, nutrition, housing and working conditions. The 1987 report *The Health Divide*,[37] which updated these findings and confirmed that the gap between rich and poor had continued to widen, also met with attempts at suppression. In 1998, the Acheson Report found an even more critical state of affairs: inequalities have actually increased over the last twenty years, with a horrifying 25 per cent of the population living in poverty, and morbidity variations between rich and poor areas among the worst in Europe. As readers will have gathered from the stories presented in this book, working-class people are over-represented in the mental illness statistics as well: 'For nearly every kind of "mental" illness, disease or disability . . . poorer people are afflicted more than richer people, more often, more seriously and for longer.'[38] This applies to depression, dementia, self-harm, alcoholism, drug addiction, suicide, 'schizophrenia', and the neuroses in general.

There are various possible explanations for higher rates of psychiatric breakdown in lower social classes. One is that people with psychiatric problems may tend to drift down the social scale as their ability to cope with more highly skilled jobs diminishes and lower salaries force them to move to cheaper neighbourhoods. Research studies disagree about how much this does actually occur. Another possibility is that the greater stresses of a working-class environment actually contribute to the development of psychiatric problems in the first place. This is a difficult theory to test. As far as 'schizophrenia' is concerned, it is considered to be unproven, though it is rather perverse to acknowledge that increased life stresses in the lower classes can lead to higher rates of psychological symptoms, stress-related illness and death, and yet make an exception for 'schizophrenia'. (Two American psychiatrists suggest that the discounting of social class factors in schizophrenia 'may . . . reflect the fact that influential research and clinical writing and teaching most often come from persons and institutions with predominantly upper- and middle-class orientations, while a large number of schizophrenic patients are lower class and unemployed'.[39]) A well-known study in Camberwell, London,[40] found that depression was much more common among working-class than among middle-class women, and that the stressful events experienced by the former were more numerous and more severe, typically lasting longer and being harder to resolve. Some examples were: husband being sent to prison; being threatened with eviction; being forced to have an unwanted abortion because of housing difficulties, and so on. Class differences were also relevant to some of the factors that made the women more vulnerable to depression in the first place; for example, having three or more children under fourteen at home; losing one's mother before the age of eleven; and the lack of a confiding relationship with someone, all of which are more typically features of working-class than of middle-class mothers. A later study found that financial hardship doubled the risk of single mothers developing depression, probably via its direct and indirect influence on every other aspect of the women's lives.[41]

The whole issue is very complex and other factors are involved too. (Thus, for example, another study found that on the Isle of Wight as opposed to in London the association between social class and psychiatric disorder in women did not seem to hold,[42] and in small towns and rural areas the link between 'schizophrenia' and social class seems to be weaker.[43]) However, in general terms there is considerable evidence in support of a relationship between the particularly difficult social and economic circumstances of working-class life and consequently higher rates of psychiatric breakdown. Indeed, the links go further than that. It may be artificial to separate physical from mental illnesses in such analyses, for there is

a triangular relationship between social and economic conditions, physical illness and psychological stress . . . In this unholy triangle causality runs in all directions. Poorer people are more vulnerable to physical illnesses and physical disabilities; being physically ill or disabled is depressing and anxiety-provoking. Poorer people are more prone to "mental illnesses": "mental illness" lowers immunity . . . and is often associated with health-damaging behaviour such as excessive smoking and drinking, careless and risky activities, self-neglect, malnutrition and being roofless or without income. Once physically ill, psychological disturbance impedes recovery . . . And, to complete the triangle, ill health of whatever kind not only arises from social and material deprivation, but sometimes destines people to unemployment, low incomes and poor housing or no housing at all, all of which make a negative contribution to physical and mental health.[44]

What is especially relevant from the point of view of the political role of psychiatry is the kind of treatment working-class people tend to receive. The staff hierarchy, descending from well-paid, high-status, middle-class doctors down through the ranks to working-class, low-paid, low-status domestics, reflects the whole structure of wider society, as we also saw in the discussion on racism. A number of studies have found that severer diagnoses are given to working- than to middle-class patients, regardless of symptoms; that the former are seen as having a poorer prognosis; and that professionals are less interested in treating them. Working-class patients are, like black and ethnic minority patients, more likely to be prescribed physical treatments such as drugs and ECT, to spend longer periods in hospital regardless of diagnosis, and to be readmitted, and correspondingly less likely to be referred for the more 'attractive' treatments such as psychotherapy and group therapy.[45] These referral patterns have been justified by the assertion that working-class patients are less articulate and therefore less able to benefit from verbal therapies, although this may simply reflect the difficulty that predominantly middle-class doctors and therapists have in understanding and communicating with people from very different cultural backgrounds, and their inability to adapt their therapeutic approaches to take these differences into account. In any case, the end result is that those members of society who are least powerful and suffer most from social and economic hardship are most likely to receive the 'disabling' rather than the 'empowering' psychiatric treatments, which will tend to deprive them further of whatever degree of independence and autonomy they still retain. One woman gives a vivid description of this process:

> I had a working-class childhood, and grew up shy and lonely on a large council estate; a soulless concrete jungle. Shut up in my own world, I read books constantly and did well at school. I was one of the few from my school to pass the 11-plus, to my mother's great pride – I was to redeem the family's fortunes and win fame and money as a writer, as she had hoped my dad would do. However, I wasn't for a moment to be a 'hard, unfeminine career-woman' or to become 'big-headed' or 'obsessed' with my work, nor to change and put on airs and become a snob who would despise my family. The contradictions in my head became unbearable at teacher-training college . . . Depression was the diagnosis; ECT the treatment. A simple, straightforward case. Psychiatrists see dozens like me every day . . . Under ECT . . . my urge to question and rebel had been weakened, while my desire to conform, out of fear of society's power to punish,

had been reinforced . . . Many more years of depression followed . . . I married and had two children, and tried to block out both my own distress and my awareness of society's injustices. The silent explosions ECT had created were a warning against ever letting my feelings get out of control again.[46]

The importance of social factors is acknowledged to some extent by those who call themselves social psychiatrists – but, in accordance with a respectable medical approach, they can only be addressed by divesting them of their personal meaning. Social factors become just another variable to be added into the formula: dependent personality plus marital disharmony plus redundancy equals reactive depression, and so on. What it actually *means* to be unemployed after twenty years in work, what it actually *feels like* to bring up children on a low income in a high-rise flat – such matters cannot be discussed within a medical-model framework. The connection between life as subjectively experienced by the individual and the conditions of the wider society of which he or she is a part is disguised, and the individual is seen not so much as an active social agent as an object to be tuned and adjusted by experts. Once more we can see that the overall effect of psychiatry is to defuse legitimate protest, on an individual or a group level, by mystifying patients about the real origins of a substantial part of their difficulties.

The above illustrations of the social and political factors that form the background to individual distress have been little addressed in psychiatry, which is just what one would expect if its fundamental function of social control has to be concealed. It is not surprising then, to find that the relationship between the personal and the political has been most thoroughly explored *outside* psychiatry, although the book that links the whole field of mental health with a radical social critique in a thorough and convincing way has yet to be written. The failure to work out these theoretical issues contributed to the decline of the anti-psychiatry movement of the 1960s, personified by R.D. Laing, whose compelling books criticising the medical view of mental distress had far more impact outside than inside psychiatry:

> Its vague theories, its detachment from traditional politics, and its disregard to strategy all seem to have condemned it – like flower-power – to wilt when the good vibes faded away. A much more hard-headed approach, both intellectually and politically, is required if the message of that movement is not to be completely lost today.[47]

One recent and impressive contribution to this task, coming, unusually, from within psychiatry itself, is psychiatrist Dr Richard Warner's book *Recovery from Schizophrenia*.[48] The remarkable achievement of Dr Warner is to have presented his very challenging conclusions in such a well-documented and scholarly way that he has drawn praise from highly respected mainstream psychiatrists. The fact that Warner fundamentally adheres fairly closely to a medical model view of 'schizophrenia' has undoubtedly contributed to this acceptance. For example, he is quite clear that it fits the definition of an 'illness' and appears to see no role for psychotherapy, either individual or family, beyond the problem-solving approach developed by Leff and his colleagues (Chapter 4). In reading the following summary, we need to bear in mind Suman Fernando's point that though all societies recognise 'madness' as a category, the concept of 'schizophrenia' makes very little sense outside Western culture; it is a hypothesis, not an objective fact, and laden with cultural assumptions. It may be useful to substitute some such synonym as 'severe breakdown' or 'madness' over the next few pages.

The argument of the book is complex and a precis cannot do it full justice. In essence, though, Warner is demonstrating the links between recovery rates from 'schizophrenia' (madness/severe breakdown) in different societies and the political economy of those societies, or, as he puts it in the introduction:

> Does the way we make our living or the form of government under which we live affect whether or not we become insane? Does social class or the state of the economy influence whether schizophrenics recover from their illness? Has industrial development affected the number of schizophrenics who become permanently and severely disabled – lost to their families, costly to the country and leading lives of emptiness and degradation? These questions are at the heart of this book . . . It is not only biological, genetic, or psychological factors which determine the distribution and course of schizophrenia. We should be prepared to expand our concern with social factors, beyond family dynamics and socioeconomic status. It is in the relationship between all of these potential causes and the economic, technological and environmental facts of our existence that we may gain the broadest understanding of why some people become schizophrenic and why some of them never recover.

Reviewing the research, Warner establishes, among other things, that fluctuations in the economy are associated with increased symptoms of psychological distress, that the stresses of both working and unemployment can create significant hazards to mental and physical health, and that mental hospital admissions for people of working age increase during a slump – in other words, that there is a relationship between health, illness and the economy.

He then turns to recovery rates from 'schizophrenia' and demonstrates, with the help of eighty-five studies from Europe and North America, that the prognosis (outcome) of this disorder has not in fact improved significantly since the beginning of the century, despite the claims attached to various treatment methods in turn – insulin coma, ECT, psychosurgery, and more recently the major tranquillisers: 'Despite the popular view in psychiatry, the anti-psychotic drugs have proved to be a critical factor in neither emptying mental hospitals nor achieving modern recovery rates in schizophrenia.'[49] In fact, 'schizophrenia' seems to have had the best prognosis of all in America during the era of moral treatment, the non-medical approach that emphasised a compassionate, respectful and optimistic attitude to the mentally distressed (see Chapter 7), although American psychiatrists attempted to conceal this embarrassing fact by a dubious process of statistical juggling. Warner shows that what does correlate with recovery rates is the state of the economy, and more particularly the levels of unemployment: at times of high unemployment, prognosis is poorer, and vice versa. This sets the scene for him to argue that 'rather than psychiatric treatment having a big impact on schizophrenia, both the course of the illness and the development of psychiatry itself are governed by political economy'.[50]

High unemployment can influence 'schizophrenia' in various ways. Being unemployed is itself a stress, and Warner draws a telling comparison between the features of 'chronic schizophrenia':

> Patients may be abnormally tired, fatigue easily, and experience clinical depression. The chronic schizophrenic may sit blankly for long periods, unaware of the passage of time . . . He may remain in bed when he intended to look for a job, avoid or put off without reason any activity that is new, unfamiliar or outside of his routine . . . Life is routine, constricted, empty . . .

and of long-term unemployment:

> cannot be bothered to do nowt, just feel like stopping in bed all day; I go for a walk and try to do some reading if I can, but it's very hard

for me to get the brain functioning properly; I'm so *moody* you know; I think you start to lose your identity in yourself.[51]

He notes that anxiety, depression, apathy, irritability, negativity, emotional overdependence, social withdrawal, isolation, loneliness, and a loss of self-respect, identity and sense of time are all commonly found among the long-term unemployed.

Although 'in recent years . . . it has become so common for schizophrenics in the community to be out of work that mental health professionals rarely consider unemployment a significant stress for their patients', to label their deficits as biological rather than socially induced 'increases the pessimism regarding treatment and the stigma which attaches to the patient'. Warner also points out that:

> the similarity in the emotional reactions of the unemployed and of psychotic patients was highlighted by a study conducted in the Great Depression. The level of negativity and pessimism about the future in large samples of the Scottish and Lancashire unemployed was found to be greater than that of groups of psychotically depressed and schizophrenic patients. If the unemployed are as distressed as hospitalised psychotics, how can we hope that the unemployed psychotics will return to normal during hard times? In fact we may ask, as does the author of the study of the Scottish and Lancashire jobless, 'why the mentally distressed unemployed . . . do not become psychotic'. The answer is, of course, they may well do so. Brenner found that it was precisely that segment of the population which suffers the greatest relative economic loss during a depression – young and middle-aged males with moderate levels of education – which showed the greatest increase in rates of admission to New York mental hospitals for functional psychosis during an economic downturn.[52]

The other side of the picture is that periods of intense rehabilitation programmes and hence better prognosis – moral treatment, social psychiatry, and the 'Open Door' movement – were instituted in wartime or when there was a labour shortage. Moral treatment seems to have been particularly successful in America because there it was combined with a national demand for labour. Warner's argument – for which he advances a good deal of evidence – is that

> the treatment of the great majority of the mentally ill will always reflect the condition of the poorest classes of society . . . Despite the

fact that an improvement in conditions of living and employment for people with psychotic disorders may yield higher rates of recovery, this consideration will remain secondary . . . Efforts to rehabilitate and reintegrate the chronically mentally ill will only be seen at times of extreme shortage of labour – after the other battalions of the industrial reserve army have been mobilised. At other times, the primary emphasis will be one of social control.[53]

During the latter times, psychiatry will tend to turn from an interest in the social causes of mental distress to an emphasis on biological and hereditary factors, with the sufferers being seen as untreatable. In other words:

psychiatric ideology may be influenced by changes in the economy – a notion which implies a rejection of the conventional concept of scientific progress inherent in mainstream medical history . . . Ideological views which emerge counter to the mainstream of psychiatric thought make no headway in the face of a contrary political and social consensus . . . Ideology and practice in psychiatry, to a significant extent are at the mercy of material conditions.[54]

Warner then sets out to test various predictions that would follow from his argument. One is that the best outcome for 'schizophrenia' will be found in the sex and social class that is least affected by labour market forces, and also in industrial nations with continuous full employment. And there is evidence in support of this: among women and the middle and upper classes, and in Switzerland (unemployment below 1 per cent since the Second World War) and the USSR (continuous full employment from 1930 until the collapse of the communist regime, with jobs found for all workers even if they were barely productive) the prognosis is indeed better.

A further prediction is that outcome in 'schizophrenia' will be better in non-industrial societies where wage labour and unemployment are uncommon. Turning to the Third World, Warner finds startling evidence against the assumption of Western psychiatry that 'schizophrenia' is a serious disorder that frequently leads to long-term disability. On the contrary, the more typical picture in the developing countries is of a brief, acute episode with no lasting effects. Among various surveys pointing to this conclusion are two World Health Organization studies which used standardised methods of diagnosis and follow-up. Warner writes:

The general conclusion is unavoidable: schizophrenia in the Third World has a course and prognosis quite unlike the condition as we recognise it in the West. The progressive deterioration which Kraepelin considered central to his definition of the disease is a rare event in non-industrial societies, except perhaps under the dehumanising restrictions of a traditional asylum. The majority of Third World schizophrenics achieve a favourable outcome. The more urbanised and industrialised the setting, the more malignant becomes the illness.[55]

This is despite the fact that in the Third World psychiatric care is often virtually non-existent, while in America up to $4 billion a year is spent on the treatment of 'schizophrenia'.

Warner advances a number of reasons for these extraordinary differences. One is that 'in non-industrial societies that are not based upon a wage economy, the term "unemployment" is meaningless'. Although *under*employment is common, it will be far easier for the individual to find some productive task which will make a contribution to the community and match his or her level of functioning at any given time. One would expect that in such societies it would be the educated who suffer more acutely from labour-market stresses and hence, in a reversal of the pattern in the developed world, have a worse outcome for 'schizophrenia', and Warner shows that this is so. And while peasant life is in many ways very hard, there are some features of it that are particularly favourable to the social integration of the mentally distressed. For example, experiences such as hallucinations are far less likely to be labelled as madness, and the generally low level of stigma attached to mental disorder makes readjustment to family life much easier. Indeed, what we would call psychiatric symptoms can sometimes lead to an enhancement of social status. Moreover, the process of treatment in pre-industrial societies is vigorous and optimistic, with the disorder more likely to be seen as a problem for the community as a whole, not just for the individual. There is a strong emphasis on social reintegration, a factor that is closely related to outcome in all parts of the world. One especially interesting finding was that the High EE (high expressed emotion) which affects relapse in 'schizophrenia' (Chapter 4) is a much less prominent feature of relatives in Chandigarh, North India, where there is an extended family structure, leading Warner to speculate that

these Western responses to mentally disordered family members may be a product of emotional isolation engendered by nuclear-family life, or the result of high achievement expectations placed on the psychotic . . . The decline of extended-family living is largely a consequence of industrialisation, and educational and occcupational achievement standards are higher in our advanced technological society. Through such family dynamics as these, political economy may affect the course of schizophrenia.[56]

Warner also considers the question of whether political economy can actually affect the rate of occurrence of 'schizophrenia' in the first place, as opposed to affecting the course of the condition once it has already developed, and concludes that the Industrial Revolution in Britain may have caused a real increase in its occurrence, quite apart from the other factors which led to overcrowding in the Victorian asylums. Warner's depressing summary is this:

> Where pre-industrial cultures offer social integration with maintenance of social status and provision of a valued social role for many of those suffering from psychosis, Western society leaves schizophrenic people in a state of social disintegration with pariah status and a disabled role. In the non-industrial world, communal healing processes operate within a social consensus which predicts recovery and minimises blame, guilt, and stigma; whereas in Western society schizophrenia is treated through marginal institutions with a social expectation that all concerned are to blame to a high degree and that the condition is incurable . . . Political and economic factors influence the social status, social role and social integration of the psychotic – his or her sense of worth, meaning and belonging.[57]

He believes that the situation of the Western sufferer from 'schizophrenia' is best summed up by Marx's concept of alienation, which is 'illustrated in the popular imagination by the assembly-line worker who is so disgusted and bored that he wilfully damages the car on which he is working'. It is the most dehumanising and menial jobs that the psychotic patient is likely to find, but the fate of unemployment, which, according to Marx, is an unavoidable component of capitalist production, is even worse:

> To stand bored and idle, to be unable to provide for oneself, to fulfil no useful social function, to be of no value to oneself or others – these are the ultimate in alienation . . . The schizophrenic person, it

appears, is among the most alienated of industrial society, and it is in
this condition that one may perceive the causes of the malignancy
of the illness . . . The origins of the schizophrenic's alienation are to
be found in the political and economic structure of society – in the
division of labor and the development of wage work.[58]

One or two psychiatrists have come to similar conclusions starting
from the opposite end, that is, from the characteristic experiences of the
'schizophrenic' individual. For example, one writer has shown how
the 'symptoms' of being controlled and invaded by others violate a very
distinctive Western view of the self as autonomous, free and separate:
a view that is not shared by non-Western cultures.[59] Another writer links
these experiences to the central themes and paradoxes of modern
industrialised life; the separation of public and private selves, the turning
away from the external world towards self-awareness and self-reflection,
the emphasis on self-regulation and self-control within a highly regulated
environment, all of which find parallels in the 'schizophrenic' patient's
intense self-consciousness, withdrawal and tenuous connections with the
social world, and 'delusions' of being controlled.[60]

Following his lengthy analysis, Warner offers various suggestions for
treatment. He sees a limited role for medication in some but certainly not
all cases of 'schizophrenia' (see Chapter 8), but believes that the most
important ingredients will be 'stress reduction . . . close personal contact
with staff and other residents . . . making appropriate plans for his or her
life after discharge – finding a place to live and an occupation, neither of
which should be too stressful', and so on. 'In short, aside from a lessened
emphasis on stern paternalism and an increased emphasis on family
relations, these treatment approaches attempt to recreate the principles of
moral management as practised at the York Retreat.' He believes that only
a small number of patients are untreatable in the community, and that
measures such as providing guaranteed jobs and training for the mentally
disabled, a range of independent and supervised accommodation, support,
and education for relatives, and so on would cost little more than the
current vast social cost of treating (or not treating) 'schizophrenia' as we
do at present. His more general conclusion is less easy to implement: 'To
render schizophrenia benign we may, in essence, have to re-structure
Western society.' The conclusion of the second edition is slightly less
ambitious but has similar implications: 'we may have to re-structure our
provisions for all of the poor.'[61]

In summary, the argument of Warner's book supports the contention
that the primary function of psychiatry is not so much to treat (except

where this happens to suit the political climate) as to maintain the status quo by absorbing and suppressing society's casualties and misfits, and labelling all their problems as illness.

What, then, is our final understanding of the condition that in Western societies is often labelled 'schizophrenia': the 'prototypical psychiatric disease' or 'sacred symbol of psychiatry'[62] on whose existence the whole of biomedical psychiatry is predicated? In Chapter 4 we argued that although the concept itself has no validity, the experiences and reactions that tend to attract such a diagnosis can best be seen as meaningful responses to damaged and damaging relationships. We are now in a position to add in the sociopolitical dimension and argue that so-called 'schizophrenic' experiences may constitute *the most dramatic manifestation of the central contradictions of our modern Western industrialised way of life, filtered through family dynamics and appearing in disguised and symbolic form in the individual who is so labelled.*

Such an explanation would explain why the debate surrounding 'schizophrenia' has been so controversial, so heated and so inconclusive. To the vested interests in the medical model already enumerated in Chapter 9 (psychiatrists, drug companies and so on) we can add the following: our nuclear family structure; our work ethic and emphasis on individual achievement and personal responsibility; the destruction of community life; our view of the 'self' and its relation to others and to the world; indeed, our whole political economy and the complex consequences it has for every aspect of our daily lives including, as Mary Boyle has suggested, the 'rational, scientific and technologically sophisticated Western culture'[63] which supports it and which has so little space for non-rational experiences and beliefs. 'Schizophrenia' is an affront and a challenge to all of these; and psychiatry provides the smokescreen which prevents us from seeing these connections.

American psychiatrist and psychoanalyst Michael Robbins argues that current psychiatric theories about 'schizophrenia' are little more than pathological processes of denial, avoidance and repression dressed up in scientific language, reflecting and reinforcing the destructive family dynamics. A striking feature of such cases is the 'happy families' picture that is often presented by all parties – the child included. The child's breakdown threatens to blow apart the picture as it applies to a particular family, but also, perhaps, as it applies to wider society. In the inherent conflict between Western values of self-actualisation and the stability of society, it is psychiatry's role to suppress the individual in order to support, in Robbins's words, 'the myth of the happy family and the myth of treatment'.[64] He believes that:

because the recognition and validation of certain elements of genuine thought and feeling within the schizophrenic and his disturbed family have the potential to disrupt family structure . . . and hence pose threats to the stability of society, society appears to enact and support the totalitarian forces within the family designed to suppress and deny them.[65]

We can take the argument further. Suman Fernando warns against simply imposing the value-laden, Western medical concept of 'schizophrenia' on other cultures, although psychiatrists frequently claim that 'schizophrenia' is found at the same rates all over the world as a way of validating their view that it is a biological illness with a genetic basis, not simply a cultural construct. However, close inspection of the evidence does not support this statement.[66] In poorer countries, the condition typically starts suddenly, rather than slowly; the commonest 'symptoms' (such as visual hallucinations) are uncommon in the West; and, of course, the prognosis is much better. In the absence of biological markers to decide the case, it makes very little sense to assert that two conditions with different triggers, modes of onset, 'symptoms' and outcomes are in fact the same 'illness'. Craziness exists in various forms in all societies and cultures, but the particularly malignant manifestation that we call 'schizophrenia' does *not* appear to be universal. If we couple this with various pieces of evidence that suggest that what we call 'schizophrenia' was virtually unknown before the nineteenth century,[67] we may wish to extend our analysis beyond outcome studies and speculate that *the very existence of the condition labelled 'schizophrenia' is a product of industrialisation.* It is one of the highest of the high prices we pay for our modern way of life.

CONCLUSION: THE MEDICAL MODEL REVISITED

Psychiatry is unique in several respects. It is the only branch of medicine that treats people physically in the absence of any known physical pathology. It is the only branch of medicine that 'treats' conduct alone, in the absence of signs and symptoms of illness of the usual kind. It is the only branch of medicine that treats people against their will, in any way it likes, if it deems it necessary. It is the only branch of medicine that imprisons patients, if judged necessary.[68]

It is time to take another look at the medical model which is the vehicle for this process of social control, and in particular to return to the issue of psychiatric diagnosis. We have already discussed the bizarre theoretical and disastrous practical consequences of these concealed social judgements. However, the implications for psychiatry go beyond this, for 'Diagnosis is the Holy Grail of psychiatry and the key to its legitimation.'[69] To admit to the existence of the extra 'unscientific' factors that contribute to a diagnostic label (except by glossing over the problem with talk of the small amount of 'clinical judgement' that is involved) would be to give the whole game away, because if there is no agreement on basic classification, then the field of psychiatry can never be developed into a science. In fact, psychiatrists are engaged in a kind of parody of medical procedures:

> The crucial difference between medicine and psychiatry can perhaps best be summarised by saying that whereas medical scientists study bodily functioning and describe patterns in it, psychiatrists behave *as if* they were studying bodily functioning and *as if* they had described patterns there, when in fact they are studying behaviour and have assumed – but not proved – that certain types of pattern *will be* found there.[70]

We end up with a process that has no explanatory power whatsoever (although, of course, it does have *consequences*) because it is completely circular: 'Why does this person hold unusual beliefs? Because he has schizophrenia. How do you know he has schizophrenia? Because he holds unusual beliefs.'

The other standard explanations offered by psychiatry are equally vacuous. As one psychiatrist is brave enough to admit, telling people that they are suffering from a biochemical imbalance is about as enlightening 'as if you said to the patient, "You're alive"'.[71] Our bodies and biochemistry are in a constant state of reaction and change, otherwise we'd be dead. The only way in which such a theory is likely to prove relevant in psychiatry is in understanding the devastating effects of the chemicals introduced into the body in the form of medication.[72]

Another current favourite is the 'vulnerability–stress model' of mental distress. According to this, breakdown is caused by a combination of (unspecified) genetic predisposition and environmental stress. It would be hard to disagree with this, but then it would also be hard to find any example of human illness or behaviour that *doesn't* fit this model: 'By explaining everything, it explains nothing in particular.'[73] Similar criticisms could be made of another popular contender, the 'biopsychosocial model'. They do, however, allow psychiatrists to smuggle in the idea of genetic/ biological influences as being primary, under the guise of eclecticism and common sense.

It is not surprising to find that these unscientific and meaningless assertions are backed up by illogical and pointless investigations and research. We saw in Chapter 4 how psychiatric diagnoses fail to met the minimum scientific standards of reliability and validity. Herb Kutchins and Stuart Kirk have vividly described the process by which America's most prestigious psychiatrists draw up successive editions of DSM*. New mental disorders are brought into existence when 'a few influential insiders decide that a new category would be clinically meaningful and handy, and lobby for its inclusion'.[74] The process of acceptance depends not so much on scientific evidence as on 'negotiations among contending interest groups of theoreticians, researchers, clinicians, hospitals and drug companies . . . Since available scientific data seldom provide definitive answers to questions, most issues must be handled through complicated behind-the-scenes negotiation.' The enormous manual that is the end product of this deeply dubious process is best viewed as 'psychiatry's struggle to define its domain and expand its range', something that is happening at frightening speed as DSM swells from its original 106 categories to its current total of around 400. Everyday behaviour is increasingly pathologised as DSM 'oversteps its bounds by defining how we should think about ourselves; how we should respond to stress; how much anxiety or sadness we should feel; and when and how we should sleep, eat, and express ourselves sexually'. Thus, not sleeping, smoking, restlessness, worrying, bearing grudges, lack of sexual interest, feeling blue, getting into trouble at school, seeking approval, getting drunk, losing your temper, and even having bad handwriting can all, according to DSM IV**, be 'symptoms' of a mental disorder.

As Kirk and Kutchins observe, inventing new 'mental illnesses' can quickly turn into a parlour game. They suggest 'Excessive Motorised Speed Disorder' for people who drive too fast. However, it is a game that is played according to precise, although covert, rules. The controversial diagnosis of 'Masochistic Personality Disorder', described in Chapter 5, consists of criteria that can be summarised as: makes bad choices; isn't appropriately happy; rejects help; makes people angry; doesn't achieve own goals; and makes sacrifices for others. Kirk and Kutchins argue that this

> constitute[s] an ad hoc collection of behaviours that do not conform with late twentieth century notions of how to relate to others

to maximise one's self-interest. Apparently, to the proposers of the MPD diagnosis, it appeared self-evidently pathological for people to underachieve, to not use others for their own benefit, to feel or to be defeated, or to put the interests of others above their own . . . In this light, MPD is not just a dysfunction, it is anticapitalist.[75]

It will not, by this stage, be surprising to find that the vast, learned volumes of psychiatric journals and textbooks are so riddled with fundamental logical and conceptual errors as to be virtually worthless. In a devastating critique, two American professors of psychiatry, Colin Ross and Alvin Pam, conclude that 'biological psychiatry has not made a single discovery of clinical relevance in the past ten years, despite hundreds of millions of dollars of research funding'.[76] We outlined, in Chapter 4, some of the elementary methodological and logical errors that abound: failing to define basic terms; confusing causation with correlation; arguing from effect to cause; poor research design and dubious use of statistics; not controlling for the effects of medication; and so on. It is important to note that we are not talking about the occasional example of substandard practice; biological psychiatry is totally reliant for its credibility on these manoeuvres, which in Ross's words, are 'pervasive, tacit . . . ubiquitous in the profession and rarely challenged'. He adds his list of psychiatric fallacies, demolishing each proposition in turn:

If it runs in families it must be genetic; If it responds to medication it must have a biological cause; Laboratory tests can improve the accuracy of psychiatric diagnosis; The physician's role is to treat biological illnesses; The genetic nature of schizophrenia is established; The dopamine theory of schizophrenia deserves to be called a theory; Depression is based on a biological deficit; Biological psychiatrists treat chemical imbalances in their patients' brains; [and finally] 'The ascendance of biological psychiatry in the 1980s has resulted in a more scientific and effective psychiatry'[77]

He then demonstrates how these and other flaws contaminate 141 articles published between 1990 and 1993 in the most prestigious journal in the USA, the *American Journal of Psychiatry*, thus proving his thesis that 'pseudoscience is endemic in biological psychiatry'.[78]

Other critics have been equally scathing. A former lecturer in community health writes:

The present flood [of articles on the biochemistry of 'schizophrenia'] has one striking feature – the results are always contradictory and inconclusive; but whatever the result, the biochemical model is here to stay, and if it seems to be faltering, ad hoc hypotheses come to prop it up . . . They are random obsevations based on the likelihood that if something is measured often enough, sooner or later an abnormality will appear . . . [The belief that] the 'true' biochemistry of schizophrenia is complex and will not be quickly or easily discovered . . . is untestable: To say that an unknown number of biochemical substances may interact in an unknown way to produce schizophrenia is a tortuous way of admitting that we have no clue as to what the hell is going on.[79]

And another critic, this time from clinical psychology:

In reality, the consensus genetic beliefs are based upon illegitimate statistical and methodological manouevres, misreports of misreports, distortions of data, misrepresentations and selectivity, all of which signify a neglect of scientific thinking of such magnitude that it is clear that an analysis might best be provided in the context of the sociology of scientific knowledge.[80]

As David Ingleby has pointed out,[81] the medical model is itself only one example of positivism – the particular way of thinking that underlies nearly all scientific research and enquiry and is also deeply rooted in the minds of ordinary people. The scientist, according to this model, is someone who collects observations in an objective and detached manner, eliminating all traces of subjectivity and bias, testing and discarding theories in order to come to an ever more complete knowledge of the laws of nature. By adopting this approach from the natural sciences, psychiatry has tried to give itself an air of respectability and impartiality. (Psychology has tried to do the same by its claim to be rooted in the scientific and proven principles of behaviourism, largely based on experiments on laboratory animals, or as Ingleby caustically puts it, 'has sought to apply to human problems a theory which barely fits the albino rat'.)

The positivist approach has been enormously fruitful in the natural sciences and general medicine, but psychiatry has not been well served by the philosophy of 'studying people as if they were things'. Moreover, the psychiatric version of positivism is riddled with reductionist errors. Reductionism, the attempt to reduce complex phenomena to simple ones, or, in shorthand, 'nothing but' theories, is implied in statements such as 'depression is caused by an imbalance in brain biochemistry', or 'there is a gene for aggression/schizophrenia/alcoholism'. It assumes a hierarchy of sciences, from psychology to physiology to biochemistry, with explanations becoming somehow truer and more valuable the further down you go. Thus, the ultimate aim is to replace the statement 'She is depressed' with a detailed account of the brain chemistry of the woman in question; this, it is assumed, will fully explain the phenomenon of depression and give a complete account of its causes. Professor Steven Rose has unpicked the various strands of nonsense underlying such claims.[82] Any human behaviour can be described at various different levels (for example, social, psychological, physiological, biochemical) simultaneously. For example, we could seek to explain someone's speech in terms of the person who is asking them questions, their own memories and experiences, the physiology of their mouth and palate, and the brain state that undoubtedly correlates with all this. It makes no sense to say that any one of these levels *causes* the others; they are simply descriptions of the same activity from different viewpoints. Nor does it make sense to see the brain state description as somehow truer and more valid than the others; they are each valid in their own context. Nor, again, does any sensible person anticipate that one day we will be able to gain a full understanding of human conversation from study of the biochemical changes accompanying it; human beings are more than biological machines and it is impossible in principle to reduce their experiences to these terms. If this is acknowledged in biology, it ought to be even more obvious in psychiatry, the study of mental states. However, as Rose points out, we are dealing here not just with (bad) science but with ideology. The idea that there is a 'gene' for violence, for example, means that we no longer need to

> seek the causes . . . on the streets of the US in terms of poverty, racism
> or the ubiquity of handguns. Instead research programmes are
> directed towards locating abnormal biochemistry, itself presumed to
> be genetically caused, in the brains of inner-city infants that may
> 'predict' an individual to violence. Similarly the presence of vodka-
> sodden drunks on the streets of Moscow prompts a major Russian
> research effort into the molecular biology of alcoholism.[83]

Another distinguished geneticist, Richard Lewontin, commenting on suggestions in the prestigious journal *Science* that there may be genes for unemployment, domestic violence and even homelessness, writes: 'What we had imagined to be messy political and economic issues turn out, after all, to be simply a matter of occasional nucleotide substitution . . . the rage for genes is a manifestation of a serious ideology that is continuous with the eugenics of an earlier time.'[84] This is not an exaggeration. In the 1970s, the United States proposed to treat violence in the inner cities by performing lobotomies on known militants.[85]

Although this book has on the whole advocated psychotherapeutic approaches as an alternative to physical treatments, it is important to remember that the former can be just as powerful a way of enforcing social norms as the latter, as many have argued.[86] In fact, disaffected psychoanalyst Jeffrey Masson maintains that 'psychotherapy is merely an extension of the views of the dominant society . . . Every therapy I have examined displays a lack of interest in social justice. Each shows an implicit acceptance of the political status quo.'[87] It is not hard to find evidence for this argument. There are many examples of psychoanalysis reinforcing women's role problems.[88] Behaviour therapy, which again has made particular claims to be scientific and objective, has sometimes been for this very reason equally guilty of covertly promoting particular values and norms, as we saw in Chapter 5 in the case of gay men. The apparently more benign humanistic therapies from America have been accused of a naive individualism suitable for privileged clients with the time and opportunity for self-examination. It has been pointed out that the enormous growth of the counselling industry (literally hundreds of new therapists, therapies, training centres, self-help books and so on) can be said to be serving a very important political function at a time when, in the words of one critic, 'a special kind of mystification' is needed to conceal contradictions in the way the whole society is organised: 'It requires no feat of imagination to comprehend that capitalist society would come to reward the psychiatric profession for promoting a special type of psychological illusion', that is, the illusion that the path to happiness and the answer to all problems lies in individual psychological exploration: 'The rise of a purely psychological view of human difficulties is a handy way of mystifying social reality.'[89]

As we have said before, not everyone needs or wants formal counselling, and an acknowledgement of the individual can be delivered in many other ways as well; for example, self-help groups or simply someone to be there and listen with respect and compassion. Counselling has developed within a white, middle-class, Western culture and inevitably incorporates values such as individual autonomy, responsibility, self-development and achievement which are not universally shared. There is also a real danger of counselling being offered 'in lieu of or as a surrogate for practical help: advocacy, justice, competence, an apology or any one of a range of potential alternatives'.[90] Nevertheless, psychotherapy and counselling do provide a way of reintroducing the person and personal meaning and relationships into the understanding of mental distress, and of translating the language of individual illness into that of psychosocial conflicts, especially if accompanied by political awareness (see examples in the last chapter). Since there is no such thing as an objective, value-free approach to mental distress, therapies should aim at the very least to demystify the client about the values held by the therapist and implicit in the treatment. The aim of the therapist then becomes, in the words of one of them:

> to help reveal the meaning of experience, to 'demystify' it by liberating it from the normalising ideology of our time . . . One sides with the person rather than the social world, helping to drag out his or her *internalised* norms so that they can be seen for what they are: the *external* disciplinary apparatus of a fundamentally oppressive social organisation. At the very least, this gives people the freedom to think and feel what they like, to examine their experience for its significance rather than simply for its 'abnormality'.[91]

Such an approach can become part of a process of wider social change, not just an alternative to it or a disguise for the need for it.

Medical-model psychiatry is, of course, only the most recent in a long line of measures which various societies have employed to deal with their deviant members.[92] What is different is the way in which it fulfils this purpose:

> Psychiatry has . . . allied itself with the state as a covert agent of social control of the individual. This alliance . . . is a historical consequence of the limitations placed on the power of the state by the rule of law . . . [which has] motivated the invention of a covert, disguised means by which society can control the individual. Psychiatry has served this social function through its state sanctioned power to label certain forms of deviant or undesirable conduct as illness.[93]

Critiques of reductionism and positivism clearly have implications far beyond psychiatry itself, and lead into complex philosophical debates about the nature of knowledge and of human beings which are beyond the scope of this book. For the moment we can note that at the cutting edge of scientific enquiry, theoretical physicists are developing a much more holistic and indeterministic model of the universe and the systems within it: one which moves away from positivism and reductionism and values non-scientific understandings of the world, one which sees humans not as machines but as active agents in the world, and incorporates subjectivity and the reality of the inner life.[94] Such a model would be likely to meet Suman Fernando's demand for an appreciation of non-Western ways of thinking, and to allow for a psychosocial understanding of mental distress.

The time is long overdue for a new metaphor, a new way of understanding mental distress, and the overthrow of the whole medical-model tradition. This, according to a writer who has studied the evolution of scientific ideas, is:

> what scientists never do when confronted by even severe and prolonged anomalies. Though they may begin to lose faith and then to consider alternatives, they do not renounce the paradigm [that is, the whole pattern of thinking] that has led them into crisis. They do not, that is, treat anomalies as counter instances . . . They will devise numerous articulations and ad hoc modifications of their theory in order to eliminate any apparent conflict.[95]

The crucial hidden function of social control, under the guise of an objective, abstract, scientific, value-free approach, provides the impetus for this frantic shoring up of the model. However, as one critic has said: 'If history has any predictive validity at all, we can assume that our current ideas in this area are transitory and will eventually meet the same fate as their predecessors.'[96] Let us hope that this is so.

In the meantime, some optimistic signs are outlined in the last chapter.

Chapter 11

Pointers to the future

It has become increasingly apparent throughout this book that we must go far beyond psychiatry itself to understand both the problems inherent in the discipline and their possible solutions. Indeed, as we saw in the section on classism, it is to some extent artificial to separate out the social and political causes of mental from physical ill health. Recent analyses have pulled together a powerful range of evidence that the most pernicious effects of poverty, unemployment and poor housing are mediated, even in the case of physical disease, mainly through *psychosocial* processes. The crucial factor is not absolute material deprivation, harmful though that obviously is, but relative inequality within societies, which has increased dramatically in Britain over the last fifteen years, and which ultimately affects the security, social cohesion and life expectancy of the whole population:

> To feel depressed, cheated, bitter, desperate, vulnerable, frightened, angry, worried about debts or job and housing insecurity; to feel devalued, useless, helpless, uncared for, hopeless, isolated, anxious and a failure: these feelings can dominate people's whole experience of life, colouring their experience of everything else. It is the chronic stress arising from feelings like these which does the damage . . . The material environment is merely the indelible mark and constant reminder of the oppressive fact of one's failure, of the atrophy of any sense of having a place in a community, and of one's social exclusion and devaluation as a human being . . . The psychosocial processes round inequality, social cohesion and its effects on health, are overwhelmingly important . . . The deterioration of public life, the loss of a sense of community, and particularly the increase in crime and violence, are fundamentally important to the quality of life for everyone.[1]

DOI: 10.4324/9781003095958-11

Tackling social injustice and inequality is the key to ameliorating all types of dis-ease, not just mental distress, and to improving the lives of us all, not just those of us who are given a psychiatric label. The present Labour government has publicly committed itself to this task: 'This government recognises that poverty, poor housing, low wages, unemployment, air pollution, crime and disorder can make people ill in both mind and body.'[2] It remains to be seen how effective this crusade will be.

The downside of such an analysis is that it can leave us feeling helpless and powerless in the face of enormous problems and huge forces that are beyond our individual control. However, I believe we can interpret such findings more positively. If the roots of mental distress are intimately interwoven into every aspect of our daily lives, then we can all contribute in some meaningful way, at a number of different levels, to the myriad possible and necessary steps towards preventing and relieving it. It is beyond the scope of this book to describe how this might happen outside psychiatry, but we can at least take a brief look at some of the many innovative projects within the mental health system which are on the side of personal and social change, not control. These are based, by definition, within a largely non-medical, psychosocial model of mental distress. Between them they illustrate the key principles advocated in this book so far: looking at personal meaning and social contexts within a whole-person, whole-system understanding of distress; working in partnership with service users; placing less emphasis on physical treatments, and more emphasis on practical and social interventions; being aware of the different needs and values of minority sections of the community; and in general, shifting towards Loren Mosher's philosophy (Chapter 9) of de-medicalising, de-hospitalising, de-psychopharmacologising and de-professionalising. Examples from earlier chapters include the need-adapted treatment of 'schizophrenia' from Scandinavia, crisis intervention, the Hearing Voices movement, feminist approaches to psychotherapy, and Foudraine's work with psychosis. Here are some more.

The Soteria Project was founded in 1971 by American psychiatrist Loren Mosher.[3] At Soteria House, an ordinary building in San Jose, California, six people at a time with a diagnosis of 'schizophrenia' were cared for by a non-professional staff, mostly college graduates in their twenties. No formal counselling was offered, but staff tried to develop a shared understanding of breakdown in terms of the clients' particular personal and social histories, and by building close and supportive relationships with them. They saw themselves as providing a non-intrusive, non-controlling environment in which they could stand by their clients as they worked through their crises. The atmosphere was homely, protective and tolerant, with a focus on growth and learning. Expectations of recovery were high, unnecessary dependence was discouraged, and professional jargon, paperwork and bureaucracy were kept at a minimum. The parallels with moral treatment (Chapter 7) are clear. Major tranquillisers were rarely used. Two years later, Soteria clients were significantly more likely to be living independently and working at higher occupational levels, with less medication and fewer re-admissions, than a comparison group from the local hospital. Subsequent projects run along similar lines produced equally impressive results; overall, about two-thirds of people newly diagnosed as 'schizophrenic' recovered with little or no drug treatment within two to twelve weeks.[4] The original project closed in 1983 and, in Mosher's words, 'disappeared from the consciousness of American psychiatry'[5] because it presented such a challenge to its central tenets. However, the philosophy lives on at Soteria Berne in Switzerland, and has inspired a number of similar projects worldwide.

The Northern Birmingham Home Treatment Service has come up with a radical alternative to hospital admission and all its disadvantages by providing twenty-four hour a day, seven day a week intensive care at home to those in acute crisis.[6] The home treatment team, under the guidance of Dr Sashi Sashidharan, explicitly tries to avoid a medical model and believes that mental health difficulties cannot be understood or resolved in isolation from a person's social system. The team offers immediate access to a service which stands by people, helping them to make sense of their distress while respecting their views and experiences, gives support to carers, and at the same time deals with a range of practical matters such as childcare, benefits, housing problems and legal advice. There is also access to a service user-run respite house for short breaks. Longer-term clients may be offered help with daily living chores and activities, linking in with the local community, finding suitable work, and so on. Since the staff have small caseloads, they are able to visit as often and for as long as is required. All the available research shows that home treatment results in fewer and shorter admissions, is preferred by carers and clients, including those from ethnic minorities, and is cheaper overall.[7] A similar service, which is based on a social rather than medical model and does not use psychiatric diagnosis, has been set up in Bradford.

The Nafsiyat Inter-cultural Therapy Centre in North London is one of the very few organisations which offers psychotherapy specifically for black and ethnic minority clients, and which acknowledges the cultural and racial components in mental distress.[8] It offers therapy to individuals, families, children and adolescents, and also carries out training and consultation to other professionals. Short-term treatment is free, and fees are negotiable for longer work. Nafsiyat aims to redress the deficiencies of statutory mental health services where black and ethnic minority clients are often discriminated against in the provision of therapy, and to offer therapy which takes account of the cultural background and social realities of its clients' lives. The therapists themselves come from a diverse range of cultural backgrounds. Initial evaluation suggests that many of the clients have very severe difficulties, but that a majority gain substantial benefit from the service.[9]

Community psychology is a movement within clinical psychology which aims to develop an understanding of people within their social worlds and to use this to reduce mental distress through social action.[10] These psychologists draw a distinction between working *in* the community with the same models as before, as can happen in CMHTs, and working *with* the community, supporting people in gaining more control and influence over their own lives, often through encouraging social action at a local level. This empowering of communities is seen as the key to both ameliorating and preventing mental distress. Instead of seeing people's difficulties as a sign of their individual failure to adapt, community psychology focuses on the strengths they have developed in coping with a society which does not meet their needs. There is a particular emphasis on acknowledging discrimination related to class, race, gender and age.

A good example of this kind of work is the White City project developed by Sue Holland for women living in a large, multi-ethnic council estate in West London.[11] Women who are anxious or depressed are first offered weekly psychotherapy sessions in order to make sense of their distress in terms of present and past experiences, rather than as 'symptoms' of an illness. After this, they may be ready to make contact with a support network of neighbourhood counsellors, who are all ex-clients of the service; by talking together in groups, women have a chance to learn that their difficulties are not unique, that they share experiences and histories. They can support each other in building new strengths and relationships. This may, for some clients, lead on to a stage where they can use their collective voice to campaign for changes in their community. Over the years, this has included setting up a creche and a local suppport, advocacy and counselling service.

Sue Holland describes this model as 'social action psychotherapy', in which both professional and client move from private symptom to public action, as and when it is appropriate for the individual. Because it draws on a range of sociological and psychological sources and requires professionals to work alongside volunteers and clients, it makes very different demands on them. She describes:

> long nights at tenants' meetings or long hours lobbying councillors and committee meetings . . . getting out of bed at 2 am to advise a neighbourhood woman worker how to cope with a suicidal incest survivor . . . years of negotiating a therapeutic understanding with priests, teachers, community workers and neighbourhood police.[12]

The project was run on a shoestring, with only two therapists and an assistant. It has inspired the 'Shanti' project in West Lambeth, a counselling service for women in another multi-ethnic, working-class part of London.

Finally, we need to take a closer look at perhaps the most inspiring and greatest hope for real change, the service user movement. In Britain this is a loose coalition of national and local groups, rather than a single organisation. It took off in the mid-1980s, later than in countries such as America, where user-run drop-in centres and other community resources such as work projects have long been part of the scene, or the Netherlands, where service users are highly influential in shaping mental health policy. The movement has no set agenda, although it is safe to say that it gains its passion and conviction from shared experiences of having been profoundly damaged by psychiatry. Nor is there uniform agreement about language; preferred terms for those on the receiving end of psychiatric treatment range from consumer to recipient to survivor. However, there are broad principles which most service user activists would share: opposition to the medical model of mental distress and support for a more holistic view; a belief that service users can and should speak out and act for themselves (that is, self-advocacy); and a conviction that mental distress does not take away personhood and competence, but can give people special expertise to offer both to others in crisis and to society as a whole.[13] A number of demands follow from this. For example, the Mental Health Task Force User Group states that service users have a right to personal dignity and respect, information, accessible services, participation and involvement, choice, advocacy, confidentiality, complaints procedures, and the least restrictive, least harmful treatment available.[14] Service users have consistently called for crisis services and non-medical refuges, easier access to counselling, and less use of medication and ECT. Some have developed an interest in complementary therapies[15] and in the spiritual dimension to emotional breakdown and healing.[16] The key to resolving difficulties that stem from abuse, deprivation and powerlessness is not, service users argue, to impose further brutality and control through the psychiatric system, but to work towards genuine empowerment and change in one's life.

We discussed the work of the Hearing Voices Network in Chapter 4. Some other key organisations are:

Survivors Speak Out This was the first national user-run campaigning network, and it now has over fifty local groups as members. It provides information, supplies speakers and trainers for courses and conferences and supports new user groups. Its resolutions call for, among other things, the phasing out of ECT and psychosurgery, independent monitoring of drug use and an end to discrimination against people who receive psychiatric treatment.[17]

United Kingdom Advocacy Network (UKAN) This is a national federation of service user-led advocacy projects of various kinds. The role of an advocate is to assist a person or a group of people to put their viewpoint to other people in a more powerful position. As an example, a service user in hospital might ask an advocate to accompany him or her to a review of their treatment and for support in putting his or her views across to the professionals. Although this role could be taken by a friend, relative or mental health worker, there may be times when it is useful to call on a trained independent advocate if one is available. UKAN offers information, support and training as part of its overall aim of promoting user/survivor empowerment.[18]

ECT Anonymous[19] This relatively recent but increasingly high-profile organisation offers sympathetic support for survivors of ECT and their families and friends. They publish factsheets and a newsletter and have collected a large literature on the subject. Their position is that ECT 'is an outdated and barbaric practice that has no place in modern medicine', a view that they have expressed forcefully in the media and many other forums, and their ultimate aim is to have it banned.

National Self-harm Network[20] This organisation of people who self-harm campaigns for the rights, understanding and better treatment of self-harm. It supplies information, trainers and speakers, and is particularly concerned to change attitudes in accident and emergency departments. Its members have published a number of books and articles calling for a non-medical and empathic understanding of the reasons behind self-injury.

As well as general advice, information, training and support, service users are involved in an enormous range of other activities and initiatives,[21] such as:

- representing service user views on NHS and Social Services planning and management committees. Consumer feedback, satisfaction and choice have been key principles in health policy since the 1980s, although there have inevitably been struggles to ensure that service users are not just a token presence;
- training and consultancy to mental health professionals. The official bodies for social workers and nurses both actively encourage the involvement of service users in training. Consultancy is offered by various groups and self-employed individuals;
- service user-run resources: there are a number of user-run drop-in centres, clubs, day centres and telephone advice lines. Examples include a day centre run by Oxford Survivors, and a drop-in run by York Survivors. Non-medical crisis houses are, at least in this country, much rarer. An exception is Skallagrigg, the user-run crisis house that is available to the Birmingham Home Treatment Team described on p. 259. Here, workers who have all had their own experiences of recovery from severe psychological crisis offer practical and emotional support to up to four people at a time. The workers describe their role as supporting and standing by, rather than treating people, although some complementary therapies are available, as is work based on the Hearing Voices approach. They have a strong expectation that people can recover, take responsibility for themselves and rediscover their power and abilities. They see themselves as 'recovery guides', and in common with the Soteria staff, believe that simple human qualities of compassion and empathy are a powerful force for healing. The medical model of mental distress is explicitly rejected, with breakdown being seen instead in psychological, social and spiritual terms. In the two years that Skallagrigg has been open, there have been no incidents of aggression towards staff, although many of their clients are very disturbed; the cost is only a quarter of admitting someone to hospital;
- patients' councils: The first one was set up in Nottingham in 1986, inspired by the system in Holland where they are an established part of every psychiatric hospital. They provide a forum in which patient

representatives can meet with patients and staff to discuss any aspect of psychiatric care raised by the patients. About twenty such schemes have now been set up in this country, some run on a purely voluntary basis and some with funded workers. The scheme includes regular visits to the wards by 'patient visitors', and sometimes drop-in advice sessions. NHS trusts vary in their willingness to respond to problems raised, a common sticking point being (as we saw in Chapter 9) the issue of whether service users are permitted to have a say in what treatment they receive;[22]

- crisis cards: a crisis card is designed to be carried by people who are vulnerable to having mental health crises during which they may not be able to speak for themselves, and who want to state in advance the kind of treatment they would like to receive. For example, the card might specify the kind of medication that the person has found helpful or unhelpful in the past, and the kind of emotional or practical support that they would prefer. It also contains the name of someone whom they would like to be contacted in emergency, and who will accompany them and ensure their wishes are heard. Crisis cards have no legal force and do not override Mental Health Act stipulations, but they do encourage good practice. They were launched nationally by Survivors Speak Out;

- user-led research: an increasing number of research projects are designed and led by service users themselves, rather than simply keeping them in the role of subjects to be investigated. The advantages include a greater ability to relate to the situation that is being researched, and better rapport with the participants, who may be willing to express views that they would hesitate to share with a professional. The main disadvantage, as with patient visitors, may be the difficulty in dealing with the painful feelings that are stirred up in the reseacher. In both situations, support networks are vital.

None of these developments has emerged without struggle and conflict, and there is still a long way to go. An ongoing dilemma is whether to work with, or separately from, professionals and existing services. The separatist approach is very influential in America, but in this country both types of activity exist in parallel, and perhaps both are necessary. One leading activist, Peter Campbell, argues that:

> what is increasingly needed is a coherent, overall vision and sense of direction for the movement and a clearer exposition of the ideas and values that hold service user/survivor organisations together; a vision

that encompasses a social reconfiguration of 'mental illness' as well as the reform of mental health services.[23]

Such a vision might, it has been argued, learn from the ideas behind the social model of physical disability. It might also involve making alliances with other disadvantaged groups, such as black and ethnic minority people, and taking on a broader agenda of social change.

None of the reforms and innovations outlined above will happen overnight, nor should they, if the internal process of becoming aware of our values and assumptions and our identification with the present system is to keep pace with the external signs of change. With systems, as with individuals, change has to start from where people actually are and adapt itself to their pace, and it has to start not from a position of blame, but with everyone taking responsibility for his or her own contribution. If individuals can change – which they can – then systems can do so too. The necessary first step in any real change is creating awareness. I hope this book will be a contribution to that process.

Notes

Introduction to the Classic edition

1 L. Johnstone, *Users and Abusers of Psychiatry: A critical look at psychiatric practice*, London, New York: Routledge, 1989, p. 275.

2 J. Davies, *Cracked: Why psychiatry is doing more harm than good*, London: Icon Books, 2013.

3 For example, S. Timimi, *Insane Medicine*, 2020. Serialised on www.madintheuk.com.

4 A. Cooke (ed), *Understanding Psychosis and Schizophrenia: Why people sometimes hear voices, believe things that others find strange, or appear out of touch with reality, and what can help*, Leicester: British Psychological Society, 2017, available from www.bps.org.uk/what-psychology/understanding-psychosis-and-schizophrenia.

5 J. Cromby, D. Harper and P. Reavey (eds), *Psychology, Mental Health & Distress*, Basingstoke: Palgrave Macmillan, 2013.

6 A. Frances, 'One manual shouldn't dictate mental health research', *New Scientist*, 5 May, 2013, available from www.newscientist.com/article/dn23490-one-manual-shouldnt-dictate-us-mental-health-research.html#.U0_jR3JeF1s (accessed 12 December 2020).

7 Division of Clinical Psychology, *Classification of Behaviour and Experience in Relation to Functional Psychiatric Diagnosis: Time for a paradigm shift*, Leicester: British Psychological Society, 2013.

8 'Rebirth of psychiatry will be slow and painful', *New Scientist*, 7 May 2014, available from www.cientist.com/article/mg22229681-400-rebirth-of-psychiatry-will-be-slow-and-painful/ (accessed 18 January 2021).

9 L.Johnstone, *A Straight-Talking Introduction to Psychiatric Diagnosis*, Ross-on-Wye: PCCS Books, 2014.

10 L. Johnstone, *Users and Abusers of Psychiatry: A critical look at psychiatric practice*, 2nd edn, London, Philadelphia: Routledge, 2000, p. 76.

11 J. Barnes, 'Are critics of psychiatry stranded in a Jurassic world?' 27 October 2020, available from www.madintheuk.com/2020/10/critics-psychiatry-stranded-jurassic-world/ (accessed 18 January 2021).

12 A. Aftab, 'Moving beyond psychiatric diagnosis', *Psychiatric Times*, 14 August 2020, available from www.psychiatrictimes.com/view/moving-beyond-psychiatric-diagnosis-lucy-johnstone-psyd (accessed 18 January 2021).

13 See blog by Phil Hickey, 'Celebrating the antipsychiatry movement', 31 December 2020, available from www.madinamerica.com/2020/12/celebrating-the-anti-psychiatry-movement/.

14 Royal College of Psychiatrists, *Position Statement on Antidepressants and Depression*, 2019, available from www.rcpsych.ac.uk/docs/default-source/improving-care/better-mh-policy/position-statements/ps04_19---antidepressants-and-depression.pdf?sfvrsn=ddea9473_5, p. 7.

15 R. Pies, 'Nuances, narratives and the chemical imbalance theory in psychiatry', *Medscape*, 15 April 2014, available from www.medscape.com/viewarticle/823368 (accessed 24 June 2019); see also www.madinamerica.com/2019/07/chemical-imbalance-theory-dr-pies-returns-again/.

16 See this discussion between Richard Bentall and Lucy Johnstone on the genetics of 'psychosis': 'Genetic research into "schizophrenia": How much can it actually tell us?' available from https://blogs.canterbury.ac.uk/discursive/tag/richard-bentall-author/.

17 Quoted in G. Henriques, 'Twenty billion fails to "move the needle" on mental illness', *Psychology Today* (23 May 2017), available from www.psychologytoday.com/gb/blog/theoryknowledge/201705/twenty-billion-fails-move-the-needle-mental-illness.

18 J. Moncrieff, *A Straight-Talking Introduction to Psychiatric Drugs*, 2nd edn, Ross-on-Wye: PCCS Books, 2020.

19 C. Lane, '*The reckoning in psychiatry over protracted antidepressant withdrawal*', 28 November 2020, available from www.madinamerica.com/2020/10/reckoning-antidepressant-withdrawal/.

20 R. Whitaker, *Anatomy of an Epidemic*, New York, NY: Broadway Paperbacks, 2010.

21 Critical Psychiatry Network: see www.criticalpsychiatry.co.uk.

22 Critical Mental Health Nurses' Network: see https://criticalmhnursing.org/.

23 See www.adisorder4everyone.com.

24 See www.adisorder4everyone.com

25 See www.intervoiceonline.org.

26 Eleanor Longden 'The voices in my head', available from www.ted.com/talks/eleanor_longden_the_voices_in_my_head?language=en.

27 See for example J. Russo and A. Sweeney (eds), *Searching for a Rose Garden*, Monmouth: PCCS Books, 2016.

28 J. Hari, *Lost Connections: Uncovering the real causes of depression – and the unexpected solutions*, London, New York: Bloomsbury, 2018.

29 L. Johnstone and R. Dallos (eds), *Formulation in Psychology and Psychotherapy: Making sense of people's problems*, London: Routledge, 2013;

L. Johnstone, 'Psychological formulation as an alternative to psychiatric diagnosis', *Journal of Humanistic Psychology* 58 (1) (2018), 30–46.

30 'Team formulation' in Johnstone and Dallos, op. cit.

31 Johnstone 2018, op. cit.

32 J.L. Herman, *Trauma and Recovery: The aftermath of violence – from domestic abuse to political terror*, New York, NY: Basic Books, 1992/2001.

33 See for example B. Van der Kolk, *The Body Keeps the Score: Brain, mind, and body in the healing of trauma*, New York, NY: Viking, 2014; A. Sweeney, B. Filson, A. Kennedy, S. Collinson and S. Gillard, 'A paradigm shift: Relationships in trauma-informed mental health services', *British Journal of Psychiatry Advances* 24 (2018), 319–333.

34 Open Dialogue: see www.open-dialogue.net.

35 Leeds Survivor Led Crisis service: see www.lclcs.org.uk.

36 Psychologists for Social Change, www.psychchange.org/.

37 See resources and services here: www.bps.org.uk/power-threat-meaning-framework/anti-racism/resources; the Royal College of Psychiatrists' Equality Action Plan, www.rcpsych.ac.uk/about-us/equality-diversity-and-inclusion/equality-action-plan?searchTerms=equality; the British Psychological Society's Declaration on Equality, Diversity and Inclusion, www.bps.org.uk/sites/www.bps.org.uk/files/EDI/Declaration%20on%20equality%2C%20diversity%20and%20inclusion.pdf.

38 'Shining lights in dark corners of people's lives', pp. 4, 10, www.mind.org.uk/media-a/4408/consensus-statement-final.pdf.

39 UN General Assembly. *Report of the Special Rapporteur on the right of everyone to the enjoyment of the highest attainable standard of physical and mental health*, 2017. United Nations Human Rights Council, available from www.ohchr.org/EN/Issues/Health/Pages/SRRightHealthIndex.asp.

40 Johnstone, 2000, op. cit., p. 214.

41 D. Penney and L. Prescott, 2016, quoted in Russo and Sweeney, op. cit., p. 35.

42 P. Deegan, 'Recovery as a self-directed process of healing and transformation', in C. Brown (ed.), *Recovery and Wellness* (pp. 5–21), New York, NY: Haworth Press, 2001.

43 Division of Clinical Psychology. *Good Practice Guidelines on the Use of Psychological Formulation*, Leicester: British Psychological Society, 2011.

44 Royal College of Psychiatrists, *A Competency-based Curriculum for Specialist Core Training in Psychiatry*, 2013, p. 31, available from www.rcpsych.ac.uk/docs/default-source/training/curricula-and-guidance/core_psychiatry_curriculum_may_2019.pdf?sfvrsn=f8594b3e_6.

45 N. Craddock and L. Mynors-Wallis, 'Psychiatric diagnosis: Impersonal, imperfect and important', *British Journal of Psychiatry* 204 (2) (2014), 93–95.

46 American Psychiatric Association, *Diagnostic and Statistical Manual of Mental Disorders* (5th edn *DSM-5*), Washington, DC: Author, 2013.

47 Z. Woodbury, 'Climate trauma: Toward a new taxonomy of trauma', *Ecopsychology* 11 (1) (2019), 1–9.

48 Johnstone, 1989, op. cit., pp. 198–199; and 2000, pp. 174–175.

49 M. Horowitz and M. Moncrieff, 'Are we repeating mistakes of the past? A review of the evidence for esketamine', *British Journal of Psychiatry*, May 2020, available from www.cambridge.org/core/journals/the-british-journal-of-psychiatry/article/abs/are-we-repeating-mistakes-of-the-past-a-review-of-the-evidence-for-esketamine/C4BDC70050164FD9D88DF40967C2853A#.

50 Johnstone, 1989, op. cit., pp. 267–688.

51 See for example D. Leader, 'A quick fix for the soul', *The Guardian*, 9 September 2008, available from www.theguardian.com/science/2008/sep/09/psychology.humanbehaviour?fbclid=IwAR3HYwHaTvC7-Lx4FCp4Z12Zh9FdCS-yNjXqQXhnUsMlbn1l7wZfajfSLHw.

52 See https://thepsychologist.bps.org.uk/wellbeing-issues-facing-psychological-professionals.

53 www.globalmentalhealth.org.

54 Ingleby, 2014, quoted in Johnstone, 2000, op. cit., p. 203.

55 D. Summerfield, 'Afterword: Against "Global Mental Health"', *Transcultural Psychiatry* 49 (3) (2012), 1–12.

56 L. Johnstone, 'Does COVID-19 pose a challenge to the diagnoses of anxiety and depression? A psychologist's view'. *British Journal of Psychiatry Bulletin* (2020), available from www.cambridge.org/core/journals/bjpsych-bulletin/article/does-covid19-pose-a-challenge-to-the-diagnoses-of-anxiety-and-depression-a-psychologists-view/8DA1C1589B34DD753A50B803B33DCFA4.

57 A. Caspi, R.M. Houts, A. Ambler, A., Danese, M.L. Elliott, A. Hariri, . . . and T.E. Moffitt, 'Longitudinal assessment of mental health disorders and comorbidities across 4 decades among participants in the Dunedin birth cohort study', *JAMA Network Open* 3 (4) (2020), e203221.

58 Aftab, 2020, op. cit.

59 From Lucy Johnstone's Twitter account: https://twitter.com/ClinpsychLucy/status/1295066326051041280?s=20 https://twitter.com/ClinpsychLucy/status/1295066327468724225?s=20 https://twitter.com/ClinpsychLucy/status/1295066328743763971?s=20.

60 Johnstone, 1989, op. cit., p. 276; Johnstone, 2000, op. cit., p. 256.

61 Johnstone, 1989, op. cit., p. 275.

62 L. Johnstone, M. Boyle with J. Cromby, J. Dillon, D. Harper, P. Kinderman, E. Longden, D. Pilgrim and J. Read, *The Power Threat Meaning Framework: Towards the identification of patterns in emotional distress, unusual experiences and troubled or troubling behaviour, as an alternative to functional psychiatric diagnosis*, Leicester: British Psychological

Society, 2018a; L. Johnstone, M. Boyle with J. Cromby, J. Dillon, D. Harper, P. Kinderman, E. Longden, D. Pilgrim and J. Read, *The Power Threat Meaning Framework: Overview*, Leicester: British Psychological Society, 2018b.

63 Johnstone, 1989, op. cit., p. 272.
64 See blogs at www.madintheuk.com/2019/02/crossing-cultures-with-the-power-threat-meaning-framework/ and www.madintheuk.com/2019/03/crossing-cultures-with-the-power-threat-meaning-framework-australia/.

I The story of a depressed housewife

1 E.S. Paykel, 'Depression in women', *British Journal of Psychiatry* 158, suppl. 10 (1991), 22–9.
2 See Chapter 5 for more on this point.
3 Sainsbury Centre for Mental Health, *Acute Problems: A survey of the quality of care in acute psychiatric wards*, London: Sainsbury Centre for Mental Health, 1998.
4 *Guardian*, 10 October 1997. Figures prepared by health economists at the Institute of Psychiatry in London.

2 The Rescue Game

1 1994 Department of Health survey, quoted in J. Repper and C. Brooker, *A Review of Public Attitudes Towards Mental Health Facilities in the Community*, Sheffield: Sheffield Centre for Health and Related Research, Sheffield University, 1996; G. Wolff, S. Pathare and T. Craig, 'Community knowledge of mental illness and reaction to mentally ill people', *British Journal of Psychiatry* 168 (1996), 191–8.
2 T.W. Davies and A. Morris, 'A comparative quantification of stigma', *Social Work and Social Sciences Review* 1 (1989), 109–22.
3 *Guardian*, 6 July 1993; *Independent*, 17 July 1993.
4 Royal College of Psychiatrists, *Confidential Inquiry into Homicides and Suicides by Mentally Ill People*, London: Royal College of Psychiatrists, 1996.
5 G. Philo, J. Secker, S. Platt, L. Henderson, G. McLaughlin and J. Burnside, 'The impact of the mass media on public images of mental illness: media content and audience belief', *Health Education Journal* 53 (1994), 271–81.
6 Schizophrenia Media Agency, 23 New Mount Street, Manchester M4 4DE.
7 Parliamentary written answers, 14 October 1996, quoted in MIND Information Sheet *Mental Health Statistics*, undated.
8 *Mental Health Statistics*, ibid.
9 Ibid.
10 *National Confidential Inquiry into Suicide and Homicide by People with Mental Illness*, London: Department of Health, 1997.

11 P.J. Taylor and J. Gunn, Homicides by people with mental illness: myth and reality, *British Journal of Psychiatry* 174 (1999), 9–14.

12 L. Appleby, 'Suicide in psychiatric patients: risk and prevention', *British Journal of Psychiatry* 161 (1992), 749–58.

13 G. Williams and J. Watson, 'Mental health services that empower women', *Clinical Psychology Forum* 64 (1994), 6–12; A. Jacobson and B. Richardson, 'Assault experiences of 100 psychiatric inpatients', *American Journal of Psychiatry* 144 (1987), 908–18; M. King, A. Coxell, G. Mezey, D. Gordon, 'Lifetime prevalence, characteristics and association problems of non-consensual sex in men', *British Medical Journal* 318 (1999), 846–850.

14 J. Read and S. Baker, *Not Just Sticks and Stones: A survey of stigma, taboos and discrimination experienced by people with mental health problems*, London: MIND, 1996.

15 J. Handy, 'Stress and coping in mental health nursing: a sociopolitical analysis', in J. Carson, L. Fagin and S. Ritter (eds), *Stress in Mental Health Nursing*, London: Chapman and Hall, 1995.

16 Handy, op. cit.

17 L. Hart, *Phone at Nine Just to Say You're Alive*, London: Douglas Elliot Press, 1995.

18 H.G. Morgan and P. Priest, 'Assessment of suicide risk in psychiatric in-patients', *British Journal of Psychiatry* 145 (1984), 467–9.

19 Handy, op.cit.

20 L. Hart, 'Voice of my father', *Openmind* 87 (1997), 15.

21 Sainsbury Centre for Mental Health, *Acute Problems: A survey of the quality of care in acute psychiatric wards*, London: Sainsbury Centre for Mental Health, 1998.

22 C.A. Ross, 'Errors of logic in biological psychiatry', in C.R. Ross and A. Pam (eds), *Pseudoscience in Biological Psychiatry*, Chichester, W. Sussex: John Wiley, 1995.

23 A. Boulter and M. Campbell quoted in S.P. Penfold and G.A. Walker, *Women and the Psychiatric Paradox*, Montreal and London: Eden Press, 1983, p. 191.

24 A. Rogers, D. Pilgrim and R. Lacey, *Experiencing Psychiatry: Users' views of services*, London: Macmillan/MIND, 1993, pp. 26–7.

25 Quoted in L. Johnstone, 'Adverse psychological effects of ECT', *Journal of Mental Health* 8 (1) (1999) 69–85.

26 Ibid.

27 Rogers, Pilgrim and Lacey, op. cit., p. 176.

28 Ibid.

29 Ibid., p. 50.

30 Bristol Crisis Service for Women, *Women and Self-injury*, Bristol: Bristol Crisis Service for Women, 1995.

31 Mental Health Foundation, *Knowing Our Own Minds*, London: Mental Health Foundation, 1997, pp. 40 and 65.

32 P. Barham and R. Hayward, *Relocating Madness: From the mental patient to the person*, London: Free Association Books, 1995, pp. 61, 68–9.

33 D. Whitwell, 'The myth of recovery from mental illness', *Psychiatric Bulletin* 23 (1999), 621–2.

34 For example, A. Reeves, *Recovery: A holistic approach*, Gloucester: Handsell

Publishing; P. Deegan, 'Recovery', *Psychosocial Rehabilitation* 9 (4) (1988), 11–19; R. Coleman, *Recovery: an alien concept?*, Gloucester: Handsell Publishing, 1999; L. Spaniol and M. Kohler, *The Experience of Recovery*, Boston: Center for Psychiatric Rehabilitation, 1994.

35 V. Lindow, 'A service user's view', in H. Wright and M. Goddey (eds), *Mental Health Nursing: From first principles to professional practice*, London: Chapman and Hall, 1992.

36 Ibid.

37 Johnstone, op. cit.

3 The sick role

1 T. Parsons, 'Illness and the role of the physician: a sociological perspective', *American Journal of Orthopsychiatry* 21 (1951), 452–60.

2 P. Barham and R. Hayward, *Relocating Madness: From the mental patient to the person*, London, Free Association Press, 1995, p. 79.

3 Quoted in M. O'Hagan, *Stopovers on My Way Home from Mars*, Survivors Speak Out, 1993, p. 7.

4 Sainsbury Centre for Mental Health, *Acute Problems: A survey of the quality of care in acute psychiatric wards*, London: Sainsbury Centre for Mental Health, 1998.

5 Ibid., p. 41.

6 Barham and Hayward, op. cit., pp. 52, 57.

7 This description of treatment contracts is derived from C. Steiner, *Scripts People Live*, New York: Bantam Books, 1975, pp. 290–9.

8 Department of Health, *The Patient's Charter: Mental Health Services*, London: HMSO, 1996.

9 A. Rogers, D. Pilgrim and R. Lacey, *Experiencing Psychiatry: Users' views of services*, London: Macmillan/MIND, 1993.

10 Quoted in L. Johnstone, 'Adverse psychological reactions to ECT', *Journal of Mental Health* 8 (1) (1999), 69–85.

11 Rogers, Pilgrim and Lacey, op. cit, p.166.

12 Quoted in Johnstone, op. cit.

13 J. Handy, 'Stress in mental health nursing: a sociopolitical analysis', in J. Carson, L. Fagin and S. Ritter (eds), *Stress and Coping in Mental Health Nursing*, London: Chapman and Hall, 1995.

14 J. Read and S. Baker, *Not Just Sticks and Stones: A survey of the stigma, taboos and discrimination experienced by people with mental health problems*, London: MIND, 1996.

15 J. Repper and C. Brooker, *A Review of Public Attitudes Towards Mental Health Facilities in the Community*, Sheffield: Sheffield Centre for Health and Related Research, 1996.

16 L. Sayce, 'Stigma, discrimination and social exclusion: what's in a word?', *Journal of Mental Health* 7 (4) (1998), 331–43.

17 Barham and Hayward, op. cit.

4 The treatment barrier

1 L. Hart, *Phone at Nine Just to Say You're Alive*, London: Douglas Elliot Press, 1995, p. 11.
2 Haydn Smith, Letter to the *Guardian*, 26 October 1998.
3 I. Falloon, C. McGill and J. Boyd, *What is Schizophrenia?*, Education leaflet, Family Aftercare Programme, Los Angeles: University of Southern California, 1980.
4 P. White, Letter to the *Independent*, 13 January 1993.
5 L. Appleby, 'Pain and paranoia', *Observer Magazine*, 2 February 1992.
6 J. Miller, 'The doctor's dilemma: Miller on madness', *Openmind* 49 (1991), 12–13.
7 M. Wallace, Letter to the *Independent*, 13 January 1993.
8 S.E. Chua and P.J. McKenna, 'Schizophrenia: a brain disease?', *British Journal of Psychiatry* 166 (1995), 563–82.
9 A. Mortimer, 'Phenomenology: its place in schizophrenia research', *British Journal of Psychiatry* 161 (1992), 293–7.
10 *The Sunday Times*, 13 July 1997; *Daily Mail*, 12 May 1993.
11 *Independent*, 19 February 1998.
12 M. Boyle, *Schizophrenia: A scientific delusion?*, London, New York: Routledge, 1990.
13 P. Breggin, *Toxic Psychiatry*, London: Fontana, 1993, p. 505.
14 S. Kirk and H. Kutchins, 'The myth of the reliability of DSM', *Journal of Mind and Behaviour* 15 (1 and 2) (1994), 71–86.
15 See summaries in Boyle, op. cit.; R.P. Bentall, H.F. Jackson and D. Pilgrim, 'Abandoning the concept of "schizophrenia"', *British Journal of Clinical Psychology* 27 (1998), 303–24; P. Brown, 'The name game: towards a sociology of diagnosis', *Journal of Mind and Behaviour* 11 (3 and 4) (1990), 385–406.
16 Bentall, op. cit.
17 D. Hill, 'Psychiatry's lost cause', *Openmind* 61 (1993), 16–17.
18 See, for example, G.C. Davison and J.M. Neale, *Abnormal Psychology*, 6th edn, New York, Toronto: John Wiley, 1996, p. 401.
19 See summaries in Boyle, op. cit.; R. Marshall, 'The genetics of schizophrenia: axiom or hypothesis?', in *Reconstructing Schizophrenia*, ed. R. Bentall, London: Routledge, 1990; S. Rose, R.C. Lewontin and L.J. Kamin, *Not in Our Genes*, Harmondsworth, Middx: Penguin, 1990.
20 T. Sarbin, 'The social construction of schizophrenia', in W. Flack, D. Miller and M. Wiener, *What is Schizophrenia?*, New York: Springer-Verlag, 1991.
21 P. Tienari, L. Wynne, J. Moring, I. Lahti, M. Naarala, A. Sorri, K. Wahlberg, O. Saarento, M. Seitma, M., Kaleva and K. Laksy, 'The Finnish adoptive study of schizophrenia: implications for family research', *British Journal of Psychiatry* 164 (suppl. 23) (1994), 20–6.
22 J. Lehtonen, 'From dualism to psychobiological interaction', *British Journal of Psychiatry* 164 (suppl. 23) (1994), 27–8.
23 Quoted in L. Boley, 'Draining the gene pool?', *Openmind* 74 (1995), 16–17.
24 S. Rose, 'Disordered molecules and diseased minds', *Journal of Psychiatric Research* 18 (4) (1984), 351–66.

25 J.D. Bremmer, P. Rendall and T. Bronen 'MRI-based measurement of hippocampal volume in patients with combat-related post-traumatic stress disorder', *American Journal of Psychiatry* 152 (7) (1995), 973–81.

26 Sarbin, op. cit.

27 A. Rogers, D. Pilgrim and R. Lacey, 'Experiencing psychiatry', London: MacMillan/MIND, 1993.

28 Hill, op. cit.

29 J. Foudraine, *Not Made of Wood: A psychiatrist discovers his own profession*, London: Quartet Books, 1974, p. 365.

30 See the references listed at the end of the notes for this chapter.

31 G. Hogman, 'The experience of informal carers', *Clinician* 14 (6) (1996), 2–8; A. Borthwick, *Invisible Pain: The experience of being a relative of a person with schizophrenia*, Edinburgh: National Schizophrenia Fellowship, 1993, p. 4.

32 D. Rosenthal, *The Genain Quadruplets*, New York: Basic Books, 1963.

33 Ibid.

34 D. Holmes, *Abnormal Psychology*, 2nd edn, London: HarperCollins, 1994.

35 M. Robbins, *Experiences of Schizophrenia: An integration of the personal, scientific and therapeutic*, New York, London: Guilford Press, 1993, p. 3.

36 See the list of references at the end of the notes for this chapter.

37 Y. Alanen, K. Lehtinen and J. Aaltonen, 'Need-adapted treatment of new schizophrenic patients: experiences and results of the Turku Project', *Acta Psychiatrica Scandinavica* 83 (1991), 363–72. See also Y. Alanen, *Schizophrenia: Its origins and need-adapted treatment*, London: Karnac, 1997.

38 J.P. Leff and C.F. Vaughn, 'The role of maintenance therapy and relatives' expressed emotion in relapse of schizophrenia: a two year follow-up', *British Journal of Psychiatry* 139 (1981), 102–4; J. Leff, L. Kuipers, R. Berkowitz, R. Eberlein-Vries and D. Sturgeon, 'A controlled trial of social intervention in the families of schizophrenic patients', *British Journal of Psychiatry* 141 (1982), 121–34.

39 See, for example, L. Kuipers, M. Birchwood and R.D. McCreadie, 'Psychosocial family interventions in schizophrenia: a review of empirical studies', *British Journal of Psychiatry* 160 (1992), 272–5, G. Fadden, 'Research update: psychoeducational interventions', *Journal of Family Therapy* 20 (1998), 293–309.

40 R. Berkowitz, 'Therapeutic intervention with schizophrenic patients and their families: a description of a clinical research project', *Journal of Family Therapy* 6 (1984), 211–33.

41 L. Kuipers, J. Leff and D. Lam, *Family Work for Schizophrenia: A practical guide*, London: Gaskell.

42 Leff *et al.* (1982), op. cit.

43 Berkowitz, op. cit.

44 Leff *et al.*, (1982), op. cit.

45 K.G. Terkelson, 'Schizophrenia and the family: adverse effects of family therapy', *Family Process* 22 (1983), 191–200.

46 L. Johnstone, 'Family management in "schizophrenia": its assumptions and contradictions', *Journal of Mental Health* 2 (1993), 255–69.

47 Robbins, op. cit., p. 48.

48 G.E. Hogarty, C.M. Anderson, D.J. Reiss, D.P. Kornblith, R.F. Ulrich and M. Carter, 'Family psychoeducation, social skills training and maintenance chemotherapy in the aftercare treatment of schizophrenia', *Archives of General Psychiatry* 48 (1991), 340–7.

49 B. Davey, 'Upbringing and psychosis: an afterword', *Changes* 14 (1) (1996), 50–61.

50 L. Johnstone, 'Family therapy and adult mental illness', *Journal of Family Therapy* 15 (1993), 441–5.

51 Quoted in D. Kingdon and D. Turkington, 'Cognitive therapy of schizophrenia', in C. Mace and F. Margison (eds), *Psychotherapy of Psychosis*, London: Gaskell, 1997.

52 See, for example, G. Haddock and P. Slade (eds), *Cognitive-Behavioural Interventions with Psychotic Disorders*, London, New York: Routledge, 1996; D. Fowler, P. Garety and L. Kuipers, *Cognitive Behaviour Therapy for Psychosis: Theory and practice*, Chichester, Sussex: John Wiley, 1995; M. Birchwood and N. Tarrier (eds), *Innovations in the Psychological Management of Schizophrenia*, Chichester, Sussex: John Wiley, 1992.

53 P. Chadwick and M. Birchwood 'The omnipotence of voices', *British Journal of Psychiatry* 164 (1994), 190–201.

54 M. Boyle, 'Psychology and psychosis: new developments or a new conservatism?', *Psychotherapy Section Newsletter* 19 (1996), 34–41.

55 Ibid.

56 R.D. Scott, 'The treatment barrier. Part 1', *British Journal of Medical Psychology* 46 (1973a), 45–55.

57 R.D. Scott, '"Closure" in family relationships and the first official diagnosis', paper presented at the Fifth International Symposium on the Psychotherapy of Schizophrenia, Oslo, 1975.

58 Scott (1973a), op. cit.

59 Scott (1975), op. cit.

60 R.D. Scott, 'The treatment barrier. Part 2: The patient as an unrecognised agent', *British Journal of Medical Psychology* 46 (1973b), 57–67.

61 Scott (1973b), op. cit.

62 Scott (1973a), op. cit.

63 'Crisis in mind', *Nursing Times* (22 July 1976).

64 R.D. Scott and P. Seccombe, 'Community psychiatry: setting up a service on a shoe-string', *Mindout* 17 (July/August 1976), 5–7.

65 L. Ratna, 'Crisis intervention and community care, a comparative study', in *The Practice of Psychiatric Crisis Intervention*, Hertfordshire: League of Friends, Napsbury Hospital, 1978.

66 L. Sayce, Y. Christie, M. Slade and A. Cobb, 'Developing crisis services', in T. Heller, J. Reynolds, R. Gomm, R. Muston and S. Pattison (eds), *Mental Health Matters: A reader*, London: Macmillan/MIND, 1996; A. Cobb, 'Community crisis services cost less than hospital care', *Openmind* 73 (1995), p. 8.

67 P. Campbell, 'New paths to caring?', *Openmind* 63 (1993), 12–13.

68 Ibid.

69 See M. Romme, A. Honig, E.O. Noorthoorn and A.D.M.A.C. Escher, 'Coping with hearing voices: an emancipatory approach', *British Journal of Psychiatry* 161 (1992), 99–103; M. Romme and S. Escher (eds), *Accepting Voices*, London: MIND, 1993.

70 In P. Baker, *Can You Hear Me?*, Gloucester: Handsell Publishing, 1996.
71 M. Romme, 'Rehabilitating voice-hearers', in T. Heller, J. Reynolds, R. Gomm, R. Muston and S. Pattison (eds), *Mental Health Matters: A reader*, London: Macmillan/MIND, 1996.
72 *Independent*, 1 July 1997.
73 N. Rose, *Romme and Escher: The Dutch experience*, Manchester: Hearing Voices, 1992.
*American Psychiatric Association *Diagnostic and Statistical Manual of Mental Disorders 4th edition*, 1994, Washington DC: Author.
**International Classification of Diseases*, Tenth Revision, World Health Organization, 1987, Geneva.

Additional references on psychotherapeutic approaches to 'schizophrenia'

Bateson, G., Jackson, D., Haley, J., Weakland, J. (1956) 'Towards a theory of schizophrenia', *Behavioural Science* 1, 251–64.
Berke, J. (1979) *I Haven't Had to Go Mad Here*, Harmondsworth, Middx: Pelican.
Breggin, P.R. and Stern, E.M. (eds) (1996) *Psychosocial Approaches to Deeply Disturbed Persons*, New York: Haworth Press.
Esterson, A., Cooper, D.G. and Laing, R.D. (1965) 'Results of family-oriented therapy with hospitalised schizophrenics', *British Medical Journal*, 18 Dec, 1462–5.
Jackson, D.D. (ed.) (1960) *The Etiology of Schizophrenia*, New York: Basic Books.
Jung, C.G. (1939) 'On the psychogenesis of schizophrenia', in A. Storr (ed.), *Jung: Selected writings*, London, Fontana.
Karon, B.P. and Vandenbos, G.R. (1981) *Psychotherapy of Schizophrenia: The treatment of choice*, New York: Aronson.
Laing, R.D. (1960) *The Divided Self*, London: Tavistock Press.
Laing, R.D. and Esterson, A. (1964) *Sanity, Madness and the Family*, London: Tavistock Press.
Lidz, T., Fleck, S. and Cornelison, A.R. (1965) *Schizophrenia and the Family*, New York: International Universities Press.
Mace, C. and Margison, F. (eds) (1997) *Psychotherapy of Psychosis*, London: Gaskell.
McGlashan, T.H. (1984) 'The Chestnut Lodge follow-up study', *Archives of General Psychiatry* 41, 573–601.
Mosher, L. and Burti, L. (1994) *Community Mental Health: A practical guide*, New York: W.W. Norton.
Schiff, J.L. (1975) *Cathexis Reader: Transactional analysis treatment of psychosis*, New York: Harper and Row.
Sechehaye, M. (1951) *Autobiography of a Schizophrenic Girl*, New York: Grune and Stratton.
Selvini Palazzoli, M. (1989) *Family Games*, London: Karnac Books.
Steiner, C. (1974) *Scripts People Live*, London: Bantam Books.
Sullivan, H.S. (1953) *Schizophrenia as a Human Process*, New York: W.W. Norton.
Werbart, A. and Cullberg, J. (eds) (1992) *Psychotherapy of Schizophrenia*, Oslo: Scandinavian University Press.

278 Notes

Wynne, L.C., Cromwell, R.L. and Matthysse, S. (eds) (1978) *The Nature of Schizophrenia*, New York: John Wiley.

5 Women's and men's role problems and psychiatry

1 J. Busfield, *Men, women and madness: Understanding gender and mental disorder*, London: Macmillan.
2 Department of Health, *Mental Health in England*, London: HMSO, 1995.
3 P.B. Bart, 'Depression in middle-aged women', in V. Gornick and B.K. Moran (eds), *Women in Sexist Society: Studies in Power and Powerlessness*, New York: Basic Books, 1971.
4 P. Chesler, *Women and Madness*, New York: Doubleday, 1972.
5 I.K. Broverman, D.M. Broverman, F.F. Clarkson, P.S. Rosenkrantz and S.R. Vogel, 'Sex-role stereotypes and clinical judgements of mental health', *Journal of Consulting and Clinical Psychology* 34 (1970), 1–7.
6 For example, C.R. Brown and M. Hellinger, 'Therapists' attitudes towards women', *Social Work* 20 (1975), 266–70; L. Jones and R. Cochrane, 'Stereotypes of mental illness: a test of the labelling hypothesis', *Journal of Social Psychiatry* 27 (1981), 99–107.
7 P.A.C.E., *Diagnosis: Homophobic. The experiences of lesbians, gay men and bisexuals in mental health services*, London: PACE, 1998.
8 Ann Lloyd, 'Altered States' the *Guardian* 25 June 1991; MIND, *Stress on Women: Policy paper on women and mental health*, London: MIND, 1995.
9 B. Andrews and G. Brown, 'Stability and change in low self-esteem: the role of psychosocial factors', *Psychological Medicine* 25 (1995), 23–31.
10 British Household Panel Survey, reported in the *Independent*, 8 September 1997.
11 Mintel report summarised in the *Independent*, 21 December 1993.
12 Equal Opportunity Commission annual review, reported in the *Guardian*, 17 June 1999
13 J. Williams and G. Watson, 'Mental health services that empower women: the challenge to clinical psychology', *Clinical Psychology Forum* 64 (1994), 11–17.
14 G.W. Brown and T. Harris, *The Social Origins of Depression*, London: Tavistock Press, 1978.
15 S. Woodward and R. Lacey, *That's Life! Survey on Tranquillisers*, London: British Broadcasting Corporation in association with MIND, 1985, pp. 27–8.
16 E.S. Paykel, 'Depression in women', *British Journal of Psychiatry* 158 (suppl. 10) (1991), 22–9.
17 L. Eichenbaum and S. Orbach, *Outside In, Inside Out: Women's psychology. A feminist psychoanalytic approach*, Harmondsworth, Middx: Pelican, 1983.
18 Ibid., p. 35.
19 P. Dally and J. Gomez, *Anorexia and Obesity: A sense of proportion*, London: Faber and Faber, 1990.
20 M. Lawrence (ed.), *Fed Up and Hungry*, London: Women's Press, 1987.
21 J.E. Mitchell, R.L. Pyle and L. Fletcher, 'The topography of binge eating, vomiting and laxative abuse', *International Journal of Eating Disorders* 10(1) (1991), 43–8.

22 *Guardian*, 10 April 1992.
23 V.J. Lewis and A.J. Blair, 'Women, food and body image', in C. Niven and D. Carroll (eds), *The Health Psychology of Women*, London: Harwood, 1993.
24 Ibid.
25 D.E. Wilfley and J. Rodin, 'Cultural influences on eating disorders', in K.D. Brownell and C.G. Fairburn (eds), *Eating Disorders and Obesity: A comprehensive handbook*, New York, London: Guilford Press, 1995.
26 Susie Orbach, *Hunger Strike*, London: Penguin, 1993, p. xxiii.
27 'Eating disorders', *Health Which?*, April 1998, 24–7.
28 R. Caplin in L.R. Pembroke (ed.), *Eating Distress: Perspectives from personal experience*, London: Survivors Speak Out, 1992.
29 P. Calloway, P. Fonagy and A. Wakeling, 'Autonomic arousal in eating disorders: further evidence for the clinical subdivision of anorexia nervosa', *British Journal of Psychiatry* 142 (1983) 38–42; S. Bhanji and D. Mattingly, 'Anorexia nervosa: some observations on "dieters" and "vomiters", cholesterol and carotene', *British Journal of Psychiatry* 139 (1981), 238–41.
30 Caplin, in Pembroke, op. cit.
31 D. Tantam and J. Whittaker, 'Personality disorder and self wounding', *British Journal of Psychiatry* 161 (1992), 451–64.
32 G. Babiker and L. Arnold, *The Language of Injury: Comprehending self-mutilation*, Leicester: British Psychological Society, 1997; D. Harrison, *Openmind* 68 (1994), 20–1.
33 Quotes from L. Arnold, *Women and Self-injury*, Bristol: Bristol Crisis Service for Women, 1995.
34 Tantam and Whitaker, op. cit.; Arnold (1995), op. cit.
35 B.W. Walsh and P.M. Rosen, *Self-mutilation*, New York: Guilford Press, 1998.
36 Tantam and Whittaker, op. cit.
37 Arnold (1995), op. cit.
38 A. Baker and S. Duncan, 'Child sexual abuse: a study of prevalence in Great Britain', *Child Abuse and Neglect* 9 (1985), 457–67.
39 Williams and Watson, op. cit.
40 C. Sheldrick, 'Adult sequelae of child sexual abuse', *British Journal of Psychiatry* 158 (suppl. 10) (1991), 55–62.
41 J.L. Herman, J.C. Perry and B.A. van der Kolk, 'Childhood trauma in borderline personality disorder', *American Journal of Psychiatry* 146 (4) (1989), 490–5.
42 Lloyd, in the *Guardian*, op. cit.
43 R.L. Palmer, D.A. Chaloner and R. Oppenheimer, 'Childhood sexual experiences with adults reported by female psychiatric patients', *British Journal of Psychiatry* 160 (1992), 261–5.
44 Williams and Watson, op. cit.
45 Quoted in L. Johnstone, 'Adverse psychological effects of ECT', *Journal of Mental Health* 8 (1) (1999), 69–86.
46 J. Gorman, *'Stress on Women'*, London: MIND, 1992; *Independent on Sunday*, 28 March 1993.
47 J. Masson, *Against Therapy*, London: Fontana, 1990; J. Russell, *Out of Bounds: Sexual exploitation in counselling and therapy*, London: Sage, 1993; P. Rutter, *Sex in the Forbidden Zone*, London: Mandala, 1990.

48 Busfield, op. cit., ch. 7.

49 K. Pantony and P. Caplan, 'Delusional dominating personality disorder: a modest proposal for identifying some consequences of rigid masculine socialisation', *Canadian Psychology* 32 (2) (1991), 120–33.

50 Paykel, op. cit.

51 Quoted in Gorman, op. cit, p. 3.

52 G. Gifford, Audiotape accompanying Module 2 of *Mental Health and Distress: Perspectives and Practice*, Milton Keynes, Bucks.: Open University, 1997.

53 J. Read, ibid.

54 See, for example, N. Edley and M. Wetherell, 'Masculinity, Power and identity', in M. Mac an Ghaill (ed.), *Understanding Masculinities*, London: Oxford University Press, 1996; Susie Orbach in the *Guardian*, 28 November 1992; D. Gillette, *Wingspan* (summer 1990), 9–10.

55 *Guardian*, 26 May 1999.

56 *Observer Magazine*, 20 June 1999.

57 G.G. Maza, 'Men and mental health', *Openmind* 55 (1992), 12–13.

58 Quoted in ibid.

59 *Mental Health and Distress: Perspectives and Practices*, op. cit.

60 P.T. Salkeld, 'Psychiatry in prisons', *Asylum* 10 (3) (1997), 12–16.

61 G.C. Murphy and J.A. Athanason, 'The effect of unemployment on mental health', *Journal of Occupational and Organisational Psychology* 72 (1999), 83–100.

62 C. Pritchard, 'Is there a link between suicide in young men and unemployment?', *British Journal of Psychiatry* 160 (1992), 750–6.

63 P. Hodson, *Men: An investigation into the emotional male*, London: BBC Publications, 1984, p. 93.

64 P.M. Shahjahan and J.T.O. Cavanagh, 'Admissions for depression among men in Scotland 1980–95: a retrospective study', *British Medical Journal* 316 (1998), 1496–7.

65 Dr Pat Hartley quoted in the *Independent on Sunday*, 8 June 1997.

66 'Tomorrow's men', a study by Adrienne Katz, Ann Buchanan and Jo-Ann Brinke, reported in the *Observer*, 14 March 1999.

67 J. Boyd and N. Beail, 'Gender issues in male sexual abuse', *Clinical Psychology Forum* (February 1994), 35–8.

68 M. King, A. Coxell, G. Mezey and D. Gordon, 'Lifetime prevalence, characteristics and association problems of non-consensual sex in men' *British Medical Journal* 318 (1999), 846–50.

69 *Independent on Sunday*, 19 July 1998.

70 P. Hutchinson, in Pembroke, op. cit.

71 *Independent on Sunday*, 4 August 1996; M. King and A. Bartlett, 'British psychiatry and homosexuality', *British Journal of Psychiatry* 175 (1999), 106–13.

72 *Daily Express*, 6 November 1986.

73 Maza, op. cit.

*American Psychiatric Association *Diagnostic and Statistical Manual of Mental Disorders 3rd edition Revised*, 1987, Washington DC: Author.

6 The professionals and their training

1 *Who Puts Medical Students Off Psychiatry?*, proceedings of a meeting of the Association of Psychiatrists in Training held at the London Hospital Medical College, 6 February 1979, London: Smith, Kline, and French Laboratories Ltd, p. 7.
2 P. Bracken and P. Thomas, 'Putting patients first', *Openmind* 96 (1999), 14–15.
3 Dr. Nick Child, letter in the *Guardian*, 15 February 1992.
4 D. Double, 'Training in anti-psychiatry', *Clinical Psychology Forum* 46 (1992), 12–13.
5 *Observer*, 21 September 1997.
6 *Guardian*, 8 June 1999.
7 *Independent on Sunday*, 6 May 1998.
8 A. Clare, *Psychiatry in Dissent: Controversial issues in thought and practice*, 2nd edn, London: Tavistock Press, 1980, p. 402.
9 Perinpanayagam, quoted in Clare, ibid., p. 403.
10 Quoted in Bracken and Thomas, op. cit.
11 *Independent*, 6 May 1999.
12 *Guardian*, 4 August 1998.
13 J. Handy, 'Stress in mental health nursing: a sociopolitical analysis', in J. Carson, L. Fagin and S. Ritter (eds), *Stress and Coping in Mental Health Nursing*, London: Chapman and Hall, 1995.
14 H. Jones, 'All theory, no understanding?', *Openmind* 69 (1994), 6.
15 J. Hopton, 'The myth of client-centred nursing', *Openmind* 69 (1994), 4–5.
16 Mental Health Aftercare Association survey reported in the *Guardian*, 8 October 1999.
17 M. Shepherd, B. Cooper, A.C. Brown and G.W. Kalton, *Psychiatric Illness in General Practice*, London: Oxford University Press, 1966.
18 A. Rogers, D. Pilgrim and R. Lacey, *Experiencing Psychiatry*, London: Macmillan, 1993.
19 S. Onyett, T. Pillinger and M. Muijen, *Making Community Mental Health Teams Work*, London: Sainsbury Centre for Mental Health, 1995.
20 Ibid.
21 Sainsbury Centre for Mental Health, *Pulling Together: The future roles and training of mental health staff*, London: Sainsbury Centre for Mental Health, 1997.
22 K. Gournay, 'Reviewing the review', *Nursing Times* 91 (18) (1995), 55–7.
23 P. Barker, 'Psychiatry's human face', *Nursing Times* 91 (18) (1995), 58–9.
24 Department of Health, *Working in Partnership*, London: HMSO, 1994.
25 Sainsbury Centre for Mental Health (1997), op. cit.
26 Jones, op. cit.
27 Hopton, op. cit.

7 A brief history of psychiatry

1 I. Batchelor (ed.) *Henderson and Gillespie's Textbook of Psychiatry*, 10th edn, London: Oxford University Press, 1969, p. 1.
2 A.T. Scull, *Museums of Madness: The social organization of insanity*

in nineteenth-century England, Harmondsworth, Middx: Penguin, 1979, p. 15.

3 W. Clark, 'Remarks on the construction of public hospitals for the cure of mental derangement', quoted in ibid., p. 134.

4 G. Nesse Hill, 'An essay on the prevention and cure of insanity', quoted in ibid., p. 135.

5 W. Nisbet, 'Two letters to . . . George Rose MP on the Reports at present before the House of Commons on the State of Madhouses', quoted in ibid., p. 135.

6 G. Higgins, 'The evidence taken before a Committee of the House of Commons respecting the asylum at York; with observations and notes', quoted in ibid., p. 140.

7 W. Ellis, 'Letter to Thomas Thompson MP', quoted in ibid., p.140.

8 Higgins, op. cit.

9 S. Tuke, 'Description of the Retreat', quoted in Scull, op. cit., p.143.

10 *Journal of Mental Science*, quoted in ibid., p.165.

11 D.H. Tuke, *History of the Insane*, quoted in ibid., p.170.

12 E. Kraepelin, *One Hundred Years of Psychiatry*, London: Peter Owen, 1962.

13 J.M. Granville, *The Care and Cure of the Insane*, quoted in Scull, op. cit., p. 195.

14 B. Ackner, A. Harris and A.J. Oldham, 'Insulin treatment of schizophrenia: a controlled study', *Lancet* 2 (1957), 607–11.

15 R. Hunter and I. Macalpine (eds), *Three Hundred Years of Psychiatry*, Oxford: Oxford University Press, 1963.

16 L.C. Cook, 'Cardiazol convulsion therapy in schizophrenia', *Proceedings of the Royal Society of Medicine* 31 (1938), 567–77.

17 Quoted in W. Freeman, *The Psychiatrists*, New York: Grune and Stratton, 1968, pp. 47–8.

18 J. Shoot and F. Adams, 'The intensive electric shock therapy of chronic disturbed psychotic patients', *American Journal of Psychiatry* 107 (1950), 279–82.

19 G.C. Tooth and M.P. Newton, quoted in A. Clare, *Psychiatry in Dissent: Controversial issues in thought and practice*, 2nd edn, London: Tavistock Press, 1980, p. 283.

20 J. Miller, 'Psychiatry as a tool of repression', *Science for the People* (March/April 1983), 14–34.

21 'Adventures with an ice-pick', *Independent on Sunday*, 3 March 1996.

22 A. Cobb, *Safe and Effective? MIND's views on psychiatric drugs, ECT and psychosurgery*, London: MIND, 1993.

23 See M. Burleigh, *Death and Deliverance: 'Euthanasia' in Germany 1900–1945*, Cambridge: Cambridge University Press 1994; J.E. Meyer, 'The fate of the mentally ill in Germany during the Third Reich', *Psychological Medicine* 18 (1998), 575–81.

24 A. Scull, *Decarceration: Community treatment and the deviant: A radical view*, Cambridge: Polity Press, 1984, p. 80.

25 Ibid., p. 82; R. Warner, *Recovery from Schizophrenia: Psychiatry and political economy*, London: Routledge, 1985, p. 72; A. Treacher and G. Baruch, *Psychiatry Observed*, London: Routledge and Kegan Paul, 1978, p. 52.

26 D. Healy, 'Gloomy days and sunshine pills', *Openmind* 90 (1998), 8–9.

27 P.R. Breggin and G.R. Breggin, *Talking Back to Prozac*, New York: St Martin's Press, 1994.

28 C. Medawar, 'The antidepressant web', *International Journal of Risk and Safety in Medicine* 10 (1997), 75–126.

29 Cobb, op. cit.

30 J.F.J. Cade, (1949) 'Lithium salts in the treatment of psychotic excitement', *Medical Journal of Australia* (3 September 1949), 349–52.

31 Warner, op. cit., p. 19.

32 R. Hughes and R. Brewin, *The Tranquillizing of America: Pill-popping and the American way of life*, New York: Harcourt Brace Jovanovich, 1979, p. 36.

33 Ibid., p. 193.

34 R. Lacey and S. Woodward, *That's Life! Survey on Tranquillizers*, London: British Broadcasting Corporation in association with MIND, 1985.

35 R.D. Laing, *The Divided Self*, Harmondsworth, Middx: Pelican, 1965, p. 12.

36 T. Szasz, 'Schizophrenia: the sacred symbol of psychiatry', *British Journal of Psychiatry* 129 (1976), 308–16.

37 Hunt, quoted in Scull (1984), op. cit., p. 96.

38 J.E. Powell, (1961) Address to the National Association for Mental Health Annual Conference.

39 World Health Organization, *Expert Committee on Mental Health: Third Report*, quoted in Treacher and Baruch, op. cit., p. 81.

40 Team for the Assessment of Psychiatric Services, *Better Out Than In?*, London: North East Thames Regional Health Authority, 1990.

41 T. Craig, S. Hodgson, S. Woodward, S. Richardson, *Homelessness and Mental Health Initiative: Second report to the Mental Health Foundation* (unpublished).

42 G. Thornicroft, T. Wykes, F. Holloway, S. Johnson, and G. Szmukler 'From efficacy to effectiveness in community mental health services. The PRISM psychosis study 10', *British Journal of Psychiatry* 173 (1998), 423–7; M. Muijen, 'Home-based care and standard hospital care for patients with severe mental illness', *British Medical Journal*, 304 (1992), 749–54.

43 Clare, op. cit., p. 55.

8 Physical treatments and the role of the drug industry

1 J. Braithwaite, *Corporate Crime in the Pharmaceutical Industry*, London: Routledge, 1984, p. 159.

2 D. Rowe, *The Real Meaning of Money*, London: HarperCollins, 1997, p. 217.

3 A. Chetley, 'Pill pushers, drug dealers', *New Internationalist* 272 (1995), 22–3.

4 Dr John Brown, quoted in the *Guardian*, 8 August 1992.

5 *Guardian*, 8 August 1992.

6 *Guardian*, 18 November 1998.

7 R. Lacey and S. Woodward, *That's Life! Survey on Tranquillisers*, London: BBC in association with MIND, 1985, p. 25.

8 D. Hill, 'Tardive dyskinesia: a worldwide epidemic of irreversible brain

damage', in N. Eisenberg and D. Glasgow (eds), *Current Issues in Clinical Psychology*, Aldershot, Hants: Gower, 1986.

9 J. Greenwood, 'Producer interests in medicines policy', in G. Harding, S. Nettleton and K. Taylor (eds), *Social Pharmacy: Innovation and development*, London: Pharmaceutical Press, 1994.

10 *Guardian*, 21 August 1998.

11 D. Tiranti, 'A pill for every ill', *New Internationalist* 165 (November 1986), pp. 4–6.

12 Braithwaite, op. cit., pp. 172–6.

13 Ibid., p. 165.

14 *Guardian*, 8 August 1992.

15 A. Melville and C. Johnson, *Cured to Death: The effects of prescription drugs*, London: Secker and Warburg, 1982.

16 Braithwaite, op. cit., p. 215.

17 Ibid., p. 214.

18 S.P. Penfold and G.A. Walker, *Women and the Psychiatric Paradox*, Montreal and London: Eden Press, 1983, p. 199.

19 C. Medawar, *The Wrong Kind of Medicine?*, London: Consumers' Association and Hodder and Stoughton, 1984, p. 37.

20 'Miracle drugs or media drugs?', *Consumer Reports* (March 1992), 142–6.

21 D. Healy, *The Anti-depressant Era*, Cambridge, Mass. and London: Harvard University Press, 1997, ch. 6.

22 Ibid.

23 'Miracle drugs or media drugs?', op. cit.

24 Ibid.

25 D. Healy, 'Gloomy days and sunshine pills', *Openmind*, 90 (1998), 8–9.

26 *The Sunday Times*, 4 April 1999.

27 Melville and Johnson, op. cit., p. 51.

28 C. Medawar, *Power and Dependence: Social audit on the safety of medicines*, London: Social Audit, 1992, p. 234.

29 Tiranti, op. cit.

30 A. Hillman, quoted in 'Pushing drugs to doctors', *Consumer Reports* 57 (1992), 87–94.

31 Healy (1997), op. cit.

32 J. Braithwaite, 'The corrupt industry', *New Internationalist* 165 (November 1986), pp. 19–20.

33 Braithwaite (1984), op. cit., p. 259.

34 Ibid., p. 265.

35 Ibid., p. 34.

36 Medawar (1984), op. cit., p. 48.

37 Braithwaite (1984), op. cit., p. 310.

38 Ibid., p.20.

39 Association of the British Pharmaceutical Industry, quoted in Medawar (1984), op. cit., p. 62.

40 *Guardian*, 18 November 1998.

41 Medawar (1984), op. cit., p. 66.

42 P. Tyrer, 'The basis of drug treatment in psychiatry', in P. Hill, R. Murray and A. Thorley (eds), *Essentials of Postgraduate Psychiatry*, London: Academic Press, 1979, p. 628.

43 D.J. Greenblatt and R.I. Shader, 'Meprobamate: a study of irrational drug use', quoted in P. Schrag, *Mind Control*, London: Marion Boyars, 1980.

44 Ibid., p. 112.

45 Ibid., p.142.

46 R.E. Peck, 'The miracle of shock treatment', quoted in P.R. Breggin, *Electroshock: Its brain-disabling effects*, New York: Springer, 1979, p. 9.

47 M. Silverman and P.R. Lee, *Pills, Profits and Politics*, Berkeley Calif.: University of California Press, 1974, p. 82.

48 R.P. Fisher and S. Greenberg (eds), *From Placebo to Panacea: Putting psychiatric drugs to the test*, New York: John Wiley, 1997, p. 262.

49 Dr Thomas Stuttaford, quoted in *The Times*, 15 September 1998.

50 Ibid.

51 *Daily Mail*, 10 July 1995.

52 G. Jones-Edwards, 'An eye-opener', *Openmind* 93 (1998), 12–13.

53 Mental Health Foundation, *Knowing Our Own Minds*, London: Mental Health Foundation, 1997.

54 *Guardian*, 8 September 1998.

55 D. Taylor, 'Current usage of benzodiazepines in Britain', in H. Freeman and Y. Rue (eds), *Benzodiazepines in Current Clinical Practice*, London: Royal Society of Medicine Services, 1987.

56 Lacey and Woodward, op. cit., p. 60.

57 Ibid., p. 58.

58 *Independent*, 24 February 1987.

59 H. Ashton, 'Benzodiazepine withdrawal: an unfinished story?', *British Medical Journal*, 288 (14 April 1984), 1135–40.

60 W.G. Danton and D.O. Antonuccio, quoted in Fisher and Greenberg, op. cit., ch. 6.

61 *Guardian*, 22 October 1998.

62 P.R. Breggin, 'Adverse effects of benzodiazepines', *Journal of Mind and Behaviour* 19 (1) (1998), 21–50.

63 *Guardian*, 10 May 1994.

64 Breggin (1998), op. cit.

65 Committee on the Safety of Medicines, *Journal of the Medical Defence Union* (summer 1988).

66 *Observer*, 20 March 1988.

67 A. Chetley, 'Psychotropics: tales of dependence', in A. Chetley (ed.), *Problem Drugs*, Amsterdam: Health Action International, 1993.

68 W.C. Wirshing, S.R. Marder, T. Van Putten and D. Arnes quoted in Fisher and Greenberg, op. cit., ch. 5.

69 R. Warner, *Recovery from Schizophrenia: Psychiatry and political economy*, [2nd edn], London: Routledge, 1994, p. 215.

70 P.R. Breggin, *Psychiatric Drugs: Hazards to the brain*, New York: Springer, 1983, p. 35.

71 R.J. Baldessarini and J.F. Lipinski, 'Toxicity and side-effects of anti-psychotic, antimanic and antidepressant medication', quoted in Hill, op. cit., p. 95.

72 Hill, op. cit.

73 W.E. Fann, R.C. Smith, J.M. Davis and F.F. Domino, (eds), 'Tardive dyskinesia: research and treatment', quoted in Hill, op. cit., p. 95.

74 A. Cobb, *Safe and Effective? MIND's views on psychiatric drugs, ECT and psychosurgery*, London: MIND Publications, 1993, p. 17.

75 K.Z. Bezchlibnyk-Butler and J.J. Jeffries, quoted in Fisher and Greenberg, op. cit., p. 207.

76 Hill, op. cit.

77 D. Hill, 'Major tranquillisers: a good buy?', *Clinical Psychology Forum* 49 (1992), 20–22.

78 Breggin (1983), op. cit., p. 109.

79 Quoted in the *Independent*, 13 March 1993.

80 J. Waddington, H. Yousef and A. Kinsella, 'Mortality in schizophrenia: antipsychotic polypharmacy and absence of adjunctive anticholinergics over the course of a 10-year prospective study', *British Journal of Psychiatry* 173 (1998), 325–9.

81 Warner, op. cit., p. 235.

82 R. Warner, Recovery from Schizophrenia: Psychiatry and political economy [1st edn], London: Routledge, 1985, p. 143.

83 Warner (1994), op. cit., ch. 10.

84 Warner (1994), op. cit., p. 221.

85 L.M. Rappaport, H.K. Hopkins and K. Hall, quoted in Warner (1994), op. cit., p. 225.

86 D. Cohen, 'A critique of the use of neuroleptic drugs in psychiatry', in Fisher and Greenberg, op. cit.

87 See L. Johnstone, 'Family management in "schizophrenia": its assumptions and limitations', *Journal of Mental Health* 2 (3) (1993), 255–69.

88 D. Lam and L. Kuipers, 'Being critical is not a critical review', *Clinical Psychology Forum* 57 (1993), 14–16.

89 P. Breggin, *Toxic Psychiatry*, London: Fontana, 1993.

90 Heinz Lehmann, quoted in ibid., p. 68.

91 Breggin (1983), op. cit., pp. 126–40.

92 I. Grant, K.M. Adams, A.S. Carlin, P.M. Rennick, J.L. Lewis and K. Schoof quoted in ibid., p. 139.

93 Cohen, op. cit., p. 180.

94 Cohen, op. cit., p. 179.

95 Cohen, op. cit., p. 183.

96 P. Campbell, A. Cobb and K. Darton, *Psychiatric Drugs: Users' experiences and current policy and practice*, London: MIND, 1998.

97 A.M. McGrath and G.A. Jackson, 'Survey of neuroleptic prescribing in residents of nursing homes in Glasgow' *British Medical Journal* 312 (9 March 1996), 611–12.

98 P.T. Salkeld, 'Psychiatry in prisons', *Asylum* 10 (3) (1997), 12–16.

99 R. Gordon 'Prepsychotic treatment for schizophrenia', *Ethical Human Sciences and Services*, 1 (1999).

100 *Guardian*, 21 November 1998.

101 Cohen, op. cit.; K. Wahlbeck, M. Cheine, A. Essali and C. Adams 'Evidence of clozapine's effectiveness in schizophrenia', *American Journal of Psychiatry* 156 (1999), 990–9.

102 Ibid.

103 Royal College of Psychiatrists, 'Memorandum on the use of electroconvulsive therapy', *British Journal of Psychiatry* 131 (1977), 262–72, quoted in *The ECT Handbook*, London: Royal College of Psychiatrists, 1995.
104 Royal College of Psychiatrists, *ECT (Electroconvulsive therapy)*, Patient Information Factsheet no. 7, London: Royal College of Psychiatrists, 1997.
105 Ibid.
106 R.W. Kendell, 'The present status of electroconvulsive therapy', *British Journal of Psychiatry* 139 (1981), 265–83.
107 C.P.L. Freeman and R.E. Kendell, 'ECT: patients' experiences and attitudes', *British Journal of Psychiatry* 137 (1980), 8–16.
108 *The ECT Handbook*, op. cit.
109 R. Abrams, *Electroconvulsive Therapy*, Oxford and New York: Oxford University Press, 1988, p. 168.
110 Department of Health, 'Electro-convulsive therapy', 1992.
111 Department of Health, *Statistical Bulletin, 1999*, London: Department of Health, 1999.
112 J. Pippard and L. Ellam, 'Electroconvulsive treatment in Great Britain', *British Journal of Psychiatry* 139 (1981), 563–8.
113 Ibid.
114 P. Fennell, *Treatment Without Consent: Law, psychiatry and the treatment of mentally disordered people since 1845*, London: Routledge, 1995.
115 R.C. Hermann, M.D. Dorwart, C.W. Hoover and J. Brody, 'Variations in ECT use in the United States', *American Journal of Psychiatry* 152 (6) (1995), 869–75.
116 M. Haslam, *British Medical Journal* (13 August 1977), p. 455.
117 M. Lawson, the *Independent*, 17 December 1992.
118 D. Cauchon, Special Report in *USA Today*, 6 December 1995.
119 Breggin (1993), op. cit., p. 235.
120 Cauchon, op. cit.
121 S. Boodman, *Washington Post*, 24 September 1996.
122 Cauchon, op. cit.
123 Royal College of Psychiatrists Press, Release, February 1995.
124 Royal College of Psychiatrists, Factsheet, op. cit.
125 R. Abrams, *Electroconvulsive Therapy*, 2nd edn, Oxford and New York: Oxford Unversity Press, 1992.
126 R. Duffett and P. Lelliot, 'Auditing electroconvulsive therapy: the third cycle', *British Journal of Psychiatry* 172 (1998), 401–5.
127 R.E. Kendell, 'What are Royal Colleges for?', *Psychiatric Bulletin* 22 (1998), 721–3.
128 H. Buchan, E. Johnstone, K. McPherson, R.L. Palmer, T. Crow and S. Brandon, 'Who benefits from electroconvulsive therapy?', *British Journal of Psychiatry* 160 (1992), 355–9.
129 E.C. Johnstone, J.F.W. Deakin, P. Lawler, C.D. Frith, M. Stevens, K. McPherson and T.J. Crow, 'The Northwick Park ECT trial', *Lancet* 2 (8208–8209) (1980), 1317–20.
130 See, for example, D. Black and G. Winokur, 'Does treatment influence mortality in depressives?', *Annals of Clinical Psychology* 1 (1989), 165–73; V. Milstein, J. Small, I.F. Small and G.E. Green, 'Does ECT prevent suicide?',

Convulsive Therapy 2 (1986), 3–6; S. Fernando and V. Storm, 'Suicide among psychiatric patients of a district general hospital', *Psychological Medicine* 14 (1984), 661–72.

131 A. Rogers, D. Pilgrim and R. Lacey, *Experiencing Psychiatry: Users' views of services*, London: Macmillan/MIND, 1993; Mental Health Foundation, *Knowing Our Own Minds*, London: Mental Health Foundation, 1997.

132 Quotes from Rogers, Pilgrim and Lacey, op. cit.

133 J.E. Jones, 'Non-ECT', *World Medicine* (September 1974), 24.

134 Rogers, Pilgrim and Lacey, op. cit., p. 146.

135 C. Warren, 'Electroconvulsive therapy, the self and family relations', *Research in the Sociology of Health Care* 7 (1988), 283–300.

136 P. Breggin, *Brain-disabling Treatments in Psychiatry*, New York: Springer, 1997.

137 A. Kennedy, 'Critical review of the treatment of mental disorders by induced convulsions', quoted in Breggin (1979), op. cit., p. 141.

138 Group for the Advancement of Psychiatry, *Shock Therapy*, Report no. 1 quoted in ibid., p. 145.

139 Breggin (1979), (1983), (1993), (1997), op. cit.

140 C.P.L. Freeman and R.E. Kendall, 'ECT: Patients' attitudes and experiences', *British Journal of Psychiatry* 137 (1980), 8–16.

141 Breggin (1979), op. cit.

142 Ibid., p. 36.

143 *ECT Anonymous* Information Sheet EA 12, January 1997.

144 L. Johnstone, 'Adverse psychological effects of ECT', *Journal of Mental Health* 8 (1) (1999), 69–85.

145 Ibid.

146 L. Squire and P. Slater, 'Electroconvulsive therapy and complaints of memory dysfunction: a prospective three year follow-up study', *British Journal of Psychiatry* 142 (1983), 1–8; I.L. Janis and M. Astrachan, 'The effect of electroconvulsive treatment on memory efficiency', *Journal of Abnormal Psychology* 46 (1951), 501–11.

147 Breggin (1997), op. cit., p. 40.

148 Abrams (1997), op. cit.

149 See summary in Johnstone (1999), op. cit.

150 Ibid.

151 Cobb, op. cit.

152 Abrams (1992), op. cit.

153 D. O'Leary and A.S. Lee, 'Seven year prognosis in depression', *British Journal of Psychiatry* 169 (1996), 423–9; D. Kroessler and B.S. Fogel, 'Electroconvulsive therapy for depression in the old', *American Journal of Geriatric Psychiatry* 1 (1) (1993), 30–7; H. Babigian and L. Guttmacher, 'Epidemiologic considerations in ECT', *Archives of General Psychiatry* 41 (1984), 246–53.

154 D. Impastato, quoted in Cauchon, op. cit.

155 Cauchon, op. cit.

156 *ECT Anonymous* Information Sheet, EA 12, January 1997.

157 J.M. Friedberg, 'Shock treatment, brain damage and memory loss: a neurological perspective', *American Journal of Psychiatry* 134 (1977), 1010–14.

158 See M.S. George, E.M. Wassermann and R.M. Post, 'Transcranial

magnetic stimulation: a neuropsychiatric tool for the twenty-first century', *Journal of Neuropsychiatry and Clinical Neurosciences* 8 (1996), 373–82; M. Kirkcaldie, S. Pridmore and P. Reid, 'Bridging the skull: ECT and TMS in psychiatry', *Convulsive Therapy* 13 (2) (1997), 83–91.

159 MIND, *Anti-depressants: First choice or last resort?*, Special Report, London: MIND Publications.

160 See Greenberg and Fisher, op. cit., ch. 4.

161 T.J. Meredith and I.A. Vale 'Poisoning due to psychotropic agents', *Adverse Drug Reactions & Acute Poisoning Reviews* 4(2) (1985), 83–126.

162 MIND, op. cit.

163 *Guardian*, 4 September 1999.

164 P. Kramer, *Listening to Prozac*, New York: Viking, 1993.

165 Fisher and Greenberg, op. cit., ch. 4.

166 C. Medawar, 'The anti-depressant web', *International Journal of Risk and Safety in Medicine* 10 (1997), 75–126.

167 Ibid.

168 *Guardian*, 4 September 1999.

169 Fisher and Greenberg, op. cit., ch. 4.

170 J. Moncrieff, 'Lithium: Evidence reconsidered', *British Journal of Psychiatry* 171 (1997), 113–19.

171 National Institute of Mental Health booklet quoted in Breggin (1983), op. cit., p. 187.

172 R. Baldessarini and L. Tondo, 'Effects of lithium treatment and its discontinuation in bipolar disorders', *American Society of Clinical Psychopharmacology Progress Notes* 8 (2) (1997), 21–6.

173 A.F. Clark and N.L. Holden, 'The persistence of prescribing habits: a survey and follow-up of prescribing to chronic hospital inpatients', *British Journal of Psychiatry* 150 (1987) 88–91.

174 Jus *et al.*, quoted in Hill (1986), op. cit., p. 98.

175 A. Boulter and M. Campbell, 'An ethnography of minor tranquillizer use in selected women's groups in Vancouver', quoted in S.P. Penfold and G.A. Walker, *Women and the Psychiatric Paradox* Montreal: Eden Press, 1983, p. 191.

176 MIND, *Major Tranquillisers: The price of tranquillity*, Special Report, London: MIND.

177 Ibid.

178 Rogers, Pilgrim and Lacey, op. cit.

179 M. Wallace, 'Schizophrenia: a national emergency. Preliminary observations on SANELINE', *Acta Psychiatrica Scandinavica* 89 (suppl. 380) (1994), 33–5.

180 P. Barham and R. Hayward, *Relocating Madness: From the mental patient to the person*, London: Free Association Books, 1995, p. 67.

181 Campbell *et al.* (1998), op. cit., p. 20.

182 Braithwaite (1984), op. cit., p. 344.

183 Fisher and Greenberg, op. cit.

184 Tyrer, op. cit., p. 628.

185 Healy (1998), op. cit.

186 T.J. Moore, 'Hidden dangers of anti-depressants', *Washingtonian* 33 (3) (1997), 68–71 and 140–5.

187 T.A. Ban, quoted in Medawar (1997), op. cit.

188 D. Ingleby, 'Understanding "mental illness"', in D. Ingleby (ed.), *Critical Psychiatry: The politics of mental health*, Harmondsworth, Middx: Penguin, 1981, p. 37.
*American Psychiatric Association *Diagnostic and Statistical Manual of Mental Disorders 3rd edition*, 1980, Washington DC: Author.

9 Resistance in the system

1 Kurt Lewin, quoted in Introduction to J. Foudraine, *Not Made of Wood: A psychiatrist discovers his own profession*, London: Quartet Books, 1974.
2 Foudraine, op. cit.
3 Ibid., pp. 3–4.
4 Ibid., Introduction.
5 Ibid.
6 Ibid., p. 164.
7 Ibid., p. 195.
8 Ibid., p. 181.
9 Ibid., pp. 298–9.
10 Ibid., p. 199.
11 Ibid., Introduction.
12 Ibid., p. 170.
13 E.E. Evans-Pritchard, quoted in D. Ingleby, 'Understanding "Mental illness"', in D. Ingleby (ed.), *Critical Psychiatry: The Politics of Mental Health*, Harmondsworth, Middx: Penguin, 1981.
14 R.D. Scott, 'Support groups for hospital staff within the context of dynamic psychiatry', unpublished paper.
15 Foudraine, op. cit., p. 230.
16 L. Johnstone, 'Psychiatry: are we allowed to disagree?', *Clinical Psychology Forum* 56 (1993), 30–2.
17 D. Harper, 'Tablet talk and depot discourse', in C. Willig (ed.), *Applied Discourse Analysis: Social and psychological interventions*, Buckingham: Open University Press, 1999.
18 J. Marks, 'The re-emergence of anti-psychiatry: psychiatry under threat', *Hospital Update* (April 1994), 187–9.
19 R. Leifer, 'The psychiatric repression of Thomas Szasz: its social and political significance'. Available on: http://mentalhelp.net/pni/pniz24d.htm
20 Quoted in S. Jacobs, 'Loren Mosher discusses research on drug-free treatment of persons labelled as having schizophrenia', *ICSPP Newsletter* (Fall/Winter 1997), 6.
21 P.R. Casey, 'Book review of *Toxic Psychiatry* by Peter Breggin' *British Journal of Psychiatry* 164 (1994), 137.
22 A. Farmer, Letter, *British Journal of Clinical Psychology* 31 (1992), 375–6.
23 M. Wallace, Letter to the *Independent*, 13 January 1993.
24 D. Double, 'Training in "anti-psychiatry"', *Clinical Psychology Forum* 46 (1992), 12–14.
25 Ibid.
26 Ibid.
27 C. Newnes, 'Histories of "Clinical Psychology Forum"', *Clinical Psychology Forum* 84 (1995), 39–42.

28 P.R. Breggin, *Toxic Psychiatry*, London: Fontana, 1993, pp. 448–51.

29 Leifer, op. cit.

30 Department of Health and Social Security, *Report of the Professional Investigation into Medical and Nursing Practices on Certain Wards at Napsbury Hospital near St. Albans*, London: HMSO, 1972.

31 *Evening Echo*, 26 May 1972, St Albans, Hertfordshire.

32 *Evening Echo*, 27 May 1972, St Albans, Hertfordshire.

33 *Evening News*, 22 February 1973, St Albans, Hertfordshire.

34 *Daily Mail*, 22 February 1973, St Albans, Hertfordshire.

35 Ibid.

36 Department of Health and Social Security, op. cit.

37 *Daily Express*, 22 February 1973.

38 *Evening Echo*, 21 February 1973, St Albans, Hertfordshire.

10 Psychiatry and wider society

1 Kraepelin, quoted in D. Hill, *The Politics of Schizophrenia*, London: University Press of America, 1985.

2 Reported by J. Wallcraft, 'We're looking into it', *Openmind* 63 (1993), 5.

3 T. Sarbin, 'The social construction of schizophrenia', in W. Flack, D. Miller and M. Weiner (eds), *What is Schizophrenia?*, New York: Springer-Verlag, 1991.

4 T. Szasz, *Law, Liberty and Psychiatry*, New York: Macmillan, 1963, p. 205.

5 R. Brothers, quoted in 'When asked why he had been committed to Bedlam', in C.C. Colton, *Lacon; or, Many things in a few words*, 1823, p.130.

6 Quoted by P. Brown, 'The name game: towards a sociology of diagnosis', *Journal of Mind and Behaviour* 11 (1990), 385–406.

7 R. Littlewood and M. Lipsedge, *Aliens and Alienists: Ethnic minorities and psychiatry*, 3rd edn, New York and London: Routledge, 1997, p. 37.

8 See Chapter 7.

9 E. Showalter, *The Female Malady: Women, madness and English culture 1830–1980*, London: Virago, 1987, p. 10.

10 Quoted in V. Lewis, 'Women, food and body image', in C. Niven and D. Carroll (eds), *The Health Psychology of Women*, Reading: Harwood, 1993.

11 S. Orbach, *Hunger Strike*, London: Faber and Faber, 1986.

12 L.R. Pembroke, in L.R. Pembroke (ed.), *Eating Distress: Perspectives from personal experience*, London: Survivors Speak Out, 1992.

13 L.R. Pembroke in R. Caplin, 'Eating Distress', *Openmind* 54 (1991), 12–13.

14 L. Arnold, *Women and Self-injury*, Bristol: Bristol Crisis Service for Women, 1995.

15 P.T. Salkeld, 'Psychiatry in prisons', *Asylum* 10 (3) (1997), 12–16.

16 Parsons quoted in G. Baruch and A. Treacher, *Psychiatry Observed*, London: Routledge and Kegan Paul, 1978, p. 244.

17 C.A. Niven, *Psychological Care for Families, Before and After Birth*, Oxford: Butterworth-Heinemann, 1992; D. Riley, *Perinatal Mental Health*, Oxford: Radcliffe Medical Press, 1995.

18 *Independent*, 4 November 1986.

19 L. Ratna, 'Crisis intervention in psychogeriatrics: a two-year follow-up study', in L. Ratna (ed.), *The Practice of Psychiatric Crisis Intervention*, Hertfordshire: League of Friends, Napsbury Hospital, 1978.

20 See Chapter 9.

21 Littlewood and Lipsedge, op. cit.

22 H. Kutchins and S.A. Kirk, *Making Us Crazy*, New York: Free Press, 1997, p. 210.

23 Littlewood and Lipsedge, op cit, p. 259.

24 Ibid., p. 253.

25 Ibid., pp. 256–7.

26 *Guardian*, 8 September 1997.

27 H. Meltzer, B. Gill, M. Petticrew and K. Hinds, *Physical Complaints, Service Use and Treatment of Adults with Psychiatric Disorders*, Office of Population, Censuses and Surveys, Surveys of Psychiatric Morbidity in Great Britain, London: HMSO, 1995; J. Davies, G. Thornicroft, M. Leese, A. Higginbotham and M. Phelan, 'Ethnic differences in risk of compulsory psychiatric admission among representative cases of psychosis in London', *British Medical Journal* 312 (1996), 533–7.

28 M. Loring and B. Powell, 'Gender, race and DSM 111', *Journal of Health and Social Behaviour* 29 (1988), 1–22.

29 Littlewood and Lipsedge, op cit, pp. 230–7.

30 Ibid., p. 246.

31 Ibid., pp. 198, 200, 251.

32 Ibid., pp. 212–13.

33 S. Fernando, 'Confronting racism in mental health services', *Openmind* 61 (1993), 18–19.

34 S. Fernando, *Mental Health, Race and Culture*, London: Macmillan/ MIND, 1991, p. 137.

35 Ibid, pp. 144–5.

36 Department of Health and Social Security, *Inequalities in Health*, London: Department of Health and Social Security, 1980.

37 Health Education Council, *The Health Divide*, London: Health Education Council, 1987.

38 R. Gomm, 'Mental health and inequality', in T. Heller, J. Reynolds, R. Gomm, R. Muston and S. Pattison (eds), *Mental Health Matters: A reader*, London: Macmillan in association with the Open University, 1996.

39 R. Warner, Recovery from Schizophrenia: Psychiatry and political economy [2nd edn], London: Routledge, 1994, p. 34.

40 G. Brown, M. Ni Bhrolchain and T. Harris, 'Social class and psychiatric disturbance among women in an urban population', *Sociology* 9 (1975) 225–54.

41 G. Brown and P. Moran, 'Single mothers, poverty and depression', *Psychological Medicine* 27 (1997), 21–33.

42 M. Rutter, A. Cox, C. Tupling, M. Berger and W. Yule, 'Attainment and adjustment in two geographical areas. I: Prevalence of psychiatric disorder', *British Journal of Psychiatry* 126 (1975) 493–509.

43 Warner, op. cit., p. 35.

44 Gomm, op. cit., p. 113.

45 See summary in Warner, op. cit., p. 145; also R. Moodley, 'Psychotherapy with ethnic minorities: a critical review', *Changes* 17 (2) (1999), 109–25.

46 J. Wallcraft, 'Women and ECT', *Spare Rib* (October 1987).

47 D. Ingleby, 'Understanding "mental illness"', in D. Ingleby (ed.), *Critical Psychiatry: The politics of mental health*, Harmondsworth, Middx: Penguin, 1981.

48 Warner, op. cit.

49 Ibid., p. 74.

50 Ibid., p. 75.

51 Ibid., p. 133.

52 Ibid., p. 135.

53 Ibid., p. 137.

54 Ibid., pp. 139, 127.

55 Ibid., p. 157.

56 Ibid., p. 27.

57 Ibid., pp. 189, 26.

58 Ibid., p. 189.

59 H. Fabrega, 'The self and schizophrenia: a cultural perspective', in *Schizophrenia Bulletin* 15 (2) (1989), 277–89.

60 L. Sass, 'The consciousness machine: self and subjectivity in schizophrenia and modern culture', in U. Neisser and D. Jopling (eds), *The Conceptual Self in Context*, Cambridge: Cambridge University Press, 1997.

61 R. Warner, *Recovery from Schizophrenia: Psychiatry and political economy*, London: Routledge and Kegan Paul, 1985, p. 307; Warner (1994), op. cit., p. 289.

62 T. Szasz, 'Schizophrenia: the sacred symbol of psychiatry', *British Journal of Psychiatry* 129 (1976), 308–16.

63 M. Boyle, 'Form and content, function and meaning in the analysis of "schizophrenic" behaviour', *Clinical Psychology Forum* 47 (1992), 10–15.

64 M. Robbins, *Experiences of Schizophrenia: An integration of the personal, scientific and therapeutic*, New York, London: Guilford Press, 1993, p. 190.

65 Ibid, p. 470.

66 R. Marshall, Book cover review of 'Schizophrenia: Manifestations, incidence and course in different cultures. A World Health Organization 10-country study', *Clinical Psychology Forum* 95 (1996), 43–4.

67 See summaries in Sass, op. cit.; Warner (1994), op. cit.

68 R.D. Laing, *Wisdom, Madness and Folly: The making of a psychiatrist*, London: Macmillan, 1985.

69 J. Kovel, 'The American mental health industry', in Ingleby, op. cit., p. 86.

70 M. Boyle, *Schizophrenia: A scientific delusion?*, London and New York: Routledge, 1990, p. 179.

71 Z.J. Lipowski, 'Psychiatry: mindless, brainless, both or neither?', *Canadian Journal of Psychiatry* 34 (1989), 249–54.

72 I am indebted to Donnard White for clarifying this point for me.

73 P. Skrabanek, 'Biochemistry of schizophrenia: a pseudoscientific model', *Integrative Psychiatry* 2 (6) (1984), 224–8.

74 Kutchins and Kirk, op. cit., p. 126.

75 Ibid., p. 136.

76 C.A. Ross, 'Errors of logic in biological psychiatry', in C.A. Ross and A. Pam (eds), *Pseudoscience in Biological Psychiatry: Blaming the body*, New York: John Wiley, 1995, p. 116.

77 Ibid.
78 Ibid.
79 Skrabanek, op. cit.
80 R. Marshall, 'Science, "schizophrenia" and genetics: the creation of myths', *Clinical Psychology Forum* 95 (1996), 5–13.
81 Ingleby, op. cit.
82 S. Rose, 'Disordered molecules and diseased minds', *Journal of Psychiatric Research* 18 (4) (1984), 351–60.
83 S. Rose, 'When making things simple does not give the right explanation', *The Times Higher Educational Supplement*, 5 September 1997.
84 R. Lewontin, 'The dream of the human genome', *New York Review*, 28 May 1993.
85 V.H. Mark and F.R. Ervin, *Violence and the Brain*, London and New York: Harper and Row, 1970.
86 See, for example, C. Kitzinger and R. Perkins, *Changing our Minds*, London: Onlywomen Press, 1993; A. Howard, *Challenges to Counselling and Psychotherapy*, London: Macmillan, 1996; Maggie and Vron, 'Defying analysis: does therapy depoliticise us?', *From the Flames* 13 (1994), 3–11; W. Dryden and C. Feltham (eds) *Psychology and its Discontents*, Buckingham/ Philadelphia: Open University Press, 1992.
87 J. Masson, *Against Therapy*, London: Fontana, 1990.
88 See, for example, P. Chesler, 'Patient and patriarch', in V. Gornick and B.K. Moran (eds), *Women in Sexist Society: Studies in power and powerlessness*, New York: Basic Books, 1971.
89 Kovel, op. cit., p. 73.
90 J. Crichton, 'Wise counsel?', *Changes* 13 (1) (1995), 60–3.
91 D. Smail, 'Psychotherapy as subversion in a make-believe world', *Changes* 4(5) (1987), pp. 398–402.
92 See M. Foucault, *Madness and Civilisation*, London: Tavistock Press, 1971.
93 R. Leifer, 'The psychiatric repression of Thomas Szasz'. Available on: http://mentalhelp.net/pni/pni24d.htm
94 See, for example, P. Davies and J. Gribben, *The Matter Myth: Beyond chaos and complexity*, Harmondsworth, Middx: Penguin, 1992; D. Zohar, *The Quantum Self*, London: Flamingo, 1991.
95 T.S. Kuhn, *The Structure of Scientific Revolutions*, 2nd edn, Chicago: University of Chicago Press, 1970.
96 D. Hill, *The Politics of Schizophrenia*, London: University Press of America, 1985, p. 152.
*American Psychiatric Association *Diagnostic and Statistical Manual of Mental Disorders*, 1952, 1968, 1980, 1987, 1994, Washington DC: Author.
**American Psychiatric Association *Diagnostic and Statistical Manual of Mental Disorders 4th edition*, 1994, Washington DC: Author.

11 Pointers to the future

1 R. Wilkinson, *Unhealthy Societies: The afflictions of inequality*, London, New York: Routledge, 1996, p. 215.
2 Frank Dobson, quoted in the *Guardian*, 6 February 1998.
3 See L.R. Mosher and L. Burti, *Community Mental Health: Principles and*

practice, New York: W.W. Norton, 1989; L.R. Mosher, 'Soteria: a therapeutic community for psychotic persons', in P.R. Breggin and E.M. Stern (eds), *Psychosocial Approaches to Deeply Disturbed Persons*, New York: Haworth Press, 1996; L.R. Mosher and A. Menn, 'Scientific evidence and system change: the Soteria experience', in H. Stierlin, L. Wynne and M. Wirsching (eds), *Psychosocial Interventions in Schizophrenia*, Heidelberg: Springer-Verlag, 1983; L.R. Mosher and A. Menn, 'Community residential treatment for schizophrenia: two year follow-up', *Hospital and Community Psychiatry* 29 (1978), 715–23.

4   L. Ciompi, 'Affect logic: an integrative model of the psyche and its relations to schizophrenia', *British Journal of Psychiatry* 164 (1994), 51–5.

5   L.R. Mosher, 'Soteria and other alternatives to acute psychiatric hospitalisation: a personal and professional review', *Changes* 17 (1) (1999), 35–51.

6   Information from *Locality Services in Mental Health: Developing home treatment and assertive outreach*', London: Sainsbury Centre for Mental Health/Birmingham: Northern Birmingham Mental Health Trust, 1998.

7   M. Muijen, I. Marks, J. Connolly and B. Audini, 'Home based care and standard hospital care for patients with severe illness: a randomised controlled trial', *British Medical Journal* 304 (1992), 749–54.

8   Nafsiyat Inter-cultural Therapy Centre, 278 Seven Sisters Road, Finsbury Park, London N4 2HY.

9   S. Acharya, S. Moorhouse, J. Kareem and R. Littlewood, 'Nafsiyat: a psychotherapy centre for ethnic minorities', *Psychiatric Bulletin* 13 (1989), 358–60.

10   See S. Melluish, 'Community psychology: a social action approach to psychological distress', in P. Barker and B. Davidson (eds), *Psychiatric Nursing: Ethical strife*, London: Edward Arnold; *Clinical Psychology Forum*, special issue on community psychology (1998), 122.

11   See S. Holland, 'The development of an action and counselling service in a deprived urban area', in M. Meacher (ed.), *New Methods of Mental Health Care*, Oxford: Pergamon; S. Holland, 'From social abuse to social action: a neighbourhood psychotherapy and social action project for women', *Changes* 10 (2) (1992), 146–53.

12   S. Holland, 'Women and urban commuity mental health: 20 years on', *Clinical Psychology Forum* 100 (1997), 45–8.

13   See P. Campbell, 'The history of the service user movement in the United Kingdom', in T. Heller, J. Reynolds, R. Gomm, R. Muston and S. Pattison (eds), *Mental Health Matters: A reader*, London: Macmillan in association with the Open University, 1996; P. Campbell, 'The service user/survivor movement', in C. Newnes, G. Holmes and C. Dunn (eds), *This is Madness*, London: PCCS Books, 1999; A. Rogers and D. Pilgrim, 'Pulling down churches: accounting for the British Mental Health Users' Movement', *Sociology of Health and Illness* 13 (2) (1991), 129–48.

14   Mental Health Task Force User Group, *Guidelines for a Local Charter for Users of Mental Health Services*, London: HMSO, 1994.

15   For example, J. Wallcraft, *Healing Minds*, London: Mental Health Foundation, 1998.

16   Mental Health Foundation, *The Courage to Bare our Souls*, London: Mental

Health Foundation, 1999; P. Barker, P. Campbell and B. Davidson (eds), 'From the ashes of experience: reflections on madness, survival and growth', London: Whurr Publishers, 1999; V. Nicholls, 'Spiritual acceptance', *Openmind* 100 (1999), 12–13.

17 Survivors Speak Out, 34 Osnaburgh Street, London NW1 3ND.
18 UKAN, Volserve House, 14–18 West Bar Green, Sheffield S1 2DA.
19 ECT Anonymous, 14 Western Avenue, Riddlesden, Keighley, West Yorkshire BD20 5DJ.
20 The National Self-harm Network, c/o Survivors Speak Out, 34 Osnaburgh Street, London NW1 3ND.
21 V. Lindow, *Self-help Alternatives to Mental Health Services*, London: MIND, 1994. See P. Breggin, *Toxic Psychiatry*, London: Fontana, 1993, for a summary of similar facilities in the USA.
22 A. MacLachlan, 'A survey of Patients' Councils in Britain', *Clinical Psychology Forum* 98 (1996), 19–22.
23 Campbell (1999), op. cit.

Index

Abrams, R. 185–6, 190–1
admission, psychiatric admission,
  passim; cost of 16; and crisis
  intervention 93–6; different
  reasons for 19; inadequate
  explanations of 58; and lack of
  resources 163; re-admission rates
  16; and sick role 40–1, 51, 56–7;
  for 'time out' 53; and treatment
  barrier 90–3; women versus men
  100, 117, 125
advance directives 57
agoraphobia 18, 100, 227
alcoholism 17, 124–5, 158, 168, 174,
  236, 252–3
Alzheimer's disease 54, 168; *see also*
  dementia
American Psychiatric Association 214
amphetamines 175–6
anorexia nervosa 108–14, 119, 224
anti-depressants 34, 58, 120, 168,
  171, 175, 199, 200; development
  of 156–8; overview of 192–4
anti-psychiatry movement 76, 81,
  159, 211, 213, 239
art therapists, training of 140
asylums 42, 244–5; closure of
  159–61, 163, 182; history of
  146–51

barbiturates 175–6
Barham, P. 61
Barnet General Hospital 96
Bart, P. 100–1, 103, 107

Bedlam 145, 222
behaviour therapy, behavioural
  approaches 13, 55, 88, 119, 227,
  254; and anorexia 112–13; and
  self-harm 115; *see also* cognitive
  approaches, cognitive-behaviour
  therapy
benzodiazepines *see* minor
  tranquillisers
Bini, L. 152, 188
Boyle, M. 89, 213, 247
Braithwaite, J. 172–3
Breggin, P. 182, 187–90, 213–14
Broadmoor Special Hospital 103
Brothers, R. 22
Broverman, I.K. 102–3
bulimia nervosa 108–9, 113

Campbell, P. 264
Cerletti, U. 152–3, 188
Chesler, P. 102–3
clinical psychologists, psychologists
  55, 103, 126, 132, 142, 211; and
  cognitive approaches in
  'schizophrenia' 88, 139–40; and
  community psychology
  movement 260; training of
  138–9; *see also* counselling
  psychologists
cognitive approaches: in
  'schizophrenia' 88–9; *see also*
  behaviour therapy,
  cognitive-behaviour therapy
cognitive-behaviour therapy 88, 129,

Milton Keynes UK
Ingram Content Group UK Ltd.
UKHW020659110324
439251UK00013B/53